A Constructivist Approach to the National Educational Technology Standards for Teachers

V. N. Morphew

International Society for Technology in Education
EUGENE, OREGON • WASHINGTON, DC

A Constructivist Approach to the
National Educational Technology Standards for Teachers

V. N. Morphew

© 2012 International Society for Technology in Education

World rights reserved. No part of this book may be reproduced or transmitted in any form or by any means—electronic, mechanical, photocopying, recording, or by any information storage or retrieval system—without prior written permission from the publisher. Contact Permissions Editor: www.iste.org/learn/publications/permissions-and-reprints.aspx; permissions@iste.org; fax: 1.541.302.3780.

Director of Book Publishing: *Courtney Burkholder*
Acquisitions Editor: *Jeff V. Bolkan*
Production Editors: *Tina Wells, Lynda Gansel*
Production Coordinators: *Rachel Williams, Emily Reed*
Graphic Designer: *Signe Landin*
Copy Editor: *Cecelia Hagen*
Proofreader: *Kathy Hamman*
Indexer: *Stepping Stones Indexing*
Cover Design, Book Design, and Production: *Kim McGovern*

Library of Congress Cataloging-in-Publication Data

Morphew, V. N.
A constructivist approach to the national educational technology standards for teachers / V.N. Morphew. — First Edition.
  pages cm
 Includes bibliographical references and index.
 ISBN: 978-1-56484-313-5
 1. Educational technology—Standards—United States. I. Title.
 LB1028.3.M665 2012
 371.33—dc23

2012004819

First Edition
ISBN: 978-1-56484-313-5
Printed in the United States of America

Cover Art: © Fotosearch.com
Inside Art: page iv photograph, Erica Garrett © 2011
ISTE® is a registered trademark of the International Society for Technology in Education.

About ISTE

The International Society for Technology in Education (ISTE) is the trusted source for professional development, knowledge generation, advocacy, and leadership for innovation. ISTE is the premier membership association for educators and education leaders engaged in improving teaching and learning by advancing the effective use of technology in PK–12 and teacher education.

Home of the National Educational Technology Standards (NETS) and ISTE's annual conference and exposition, ISTE represents more than 100,000 professionals worldwide. We support our members with information, networking opportunities, and guidance as they face the challenge of transforming education. To find out more about these and other ISTE initiatives, visit our website at www.iste.org.

As part of our mission, ISTE Book Publishing works with experienced educators to develop and produce practical resources for classroom teachers, teacher educators, and technology leaders. Every manuscript we select for publication is carefully peer reviewed and professionally edited. We value your feedback on this book and other ISTE products. Email us at books@iste.org.

International Society for Technology in Education
Washington, DC, Office:
    1710 Rhode Island Ave. NW, Suite 900, Washington, DC 20036-3132
Eugene, Oregon, Office:
    180 West 8th Ave., Suite 300, Eugene, OR 97401-2916
Order Desk: 1.800.336.5191
Order Fax: 1.541.302.3778
Customer Service: orders@iste.org
Book Publishing: books@iste.org
Book Sales and Marketing: booksmarketing@iste.org
Web: www.iste.org

About the Author

V. N. Morphew joined the faculty of Fairmont State University, West Virginia, in August 2000. She has taught at the middle school, high school, undergraduate, and graduate levels. She holds a doctorate from West Virginia University and a master's degree from Virginia Tech. At Fairmont State, Morphew's responsibilities include teaching both undergraduate and graduate courses in the School of Education, Health and Human Performance. Her professional interests include technology integration and online learning.

Acknowledgments

I am fortunate to be surrounded by a large group of supporters on whom I leaned in writing this book. I thank Jeff Bolkan and Tina Wells from ISTE, who helped move my work from proposal to publication, and Megan Dolman from ISTE, who helped move it to its audience. Others who have been especially supportive include E. Warren Baker, Philip Berryhill, Allen Colebank, Erica Garrett, Cathy Holmes, Roxann Humbert, Donald Moroose, Melissa Nicholas, Tom Nicholas, Debbie Poling, Sharon Smith, and Janice Watts. I wish to thank my family for their untiring support, with special recognition given to my parents, Nicholas and Lorraine Gasparro, in-laws, Walter and Beth Shields, spouse and colleague, Kirk Morphew, and sons, Zachary and Joseph.

Contents

Chapter 1 nets•t1

Facilitate and Inspire Student Learning and Creativity

NETS•T1a

Promote, Support, and Model Creative and Innovative Thinking and Inventiveness

NETS•T1b

Engage Students in Exploring Real-World Issues and Solving Authentic Problems Using Digital Tools and Resources

NETS•T1c

Promote Student Reflection Using Collaborative Tools to Reveal and Clarify Students' Conceptual Understanding and Thinking, Planning, and Creative Processes

NETS•T1d

Model Collaborative Knowledge Construction by Engaging in Learning with Students, Colleagues, and Others in Face-to-Face and Virtual Environments

Chapter 2 nets•t2

Design and Develop Digital-Age Learning Experiences and Assessments

NETS•T2a

Design or Adapt Relevant Learning Experiences That Incorporate Digital Tools and Resources to Promote Student Learning and Creativity

NETS·T2b

Develop Technology-Enriched Learning Environments That Enable All Students to Pursue Their Individual Curiosities and Become Active Participants in Setting Their Own Educational Goals, Managing Their Own Learning, and Assessing Their Own Progress 86

NETS·T2c

Customize and Personalize Learning Activities to Address Students' Diverse Learning Styles, Working Strategies, and Abilities Using Digital Tools and Resources 103

Chapter 3 nets·t3

Model Digital-Age Work and Learning

NETS·T3a

Chapter 4 nets·t4

Promote and Model Digital Citizenship and Responsibility

Chapter 5 nets•t5

Engage in Professional Growth and Leadership

NETS•T5a

Participate in Local and Global Learning Communities to Explore Creative Applications of Technology to Improve Student Learning

NETS•T5b

Exhibit Leadership by Demonstrating a Vision of Technology Infusion, Participating in Shared Decision Making and Community Building, and Developing the Leadership and Technology Skills of Others

NETS•T5c

Evaluate and Reflect on Current Research and Professional Practice on a Regular Basis to Make Effective Use of Existing and Emerging Digital Tools and Resources in Support of Student Learning

Chapter 6

Concluding Remarks:
Facing the Challenge of Integrating Technology in the Classroom

Appendix

National Educational Technology Standards

Index

Preface

Few would question the rapid speed with which technology is advancing in all aspects of our lives, including education. Many veteran teachers, including me, remember a time when overhead and film projectors, along with video-cassette recorders, were the dominant classroom technologies. While these are still being used today, more and more technologies have become available to teachers to help students learn better and to increase teacher productivity.

This book was written to meet the challenge of helping prospective and practicing teachers integrate existing, new, and emerging technologies most effectively into the curriculum. It was written with a tone and style that I hope will appeal to the 21st-century learner. I aimed to provide an "easy read" without compromising content, scholarship, research, or pedagogical features, so that learning from this book will be an enjoyable educational experience rather than drudgery.

The exercises suggested in the Section Explorations toward the end of each section can easily be integrated into teaching. They address various learning styles, levels of learning, and multiple intelligences. By completing the exercises in the Section Explorations, prospective and practicing teachers will be exposed to a greater repertoire of assignment types for possible use in their own classrooms.

I have written this book primarily for undergraduate students preparing for entry into the profession, but it is also appropriate for graduate education students seeking initial teaching credentials, practicing teachers, and any others interested in integrating technology into the school curriculum to optimize student learning.

Comprehension of this book requires no specific prerequisite knowledge other than the essential skills and knowledge that most undergraduates bring with them to the college experience. Although success is not contingent on prerequisite knowledge, those with more advanced skills and knowledge will be challenged. More experienced readers should benefit from challenging, relevant, constructivist-based explorations that use their current understandings as a springboard to higher-order thinking and advanced applications of technology in teaching.

I used a constructivist perspective to write this book. Constructivist teaching and learning acknowledge that the teacher and the students are both important, contributing members in a teaching-learning relationship and that both bring prior knowledge and experiences with them into the learning environment. For this reason, constructivist teaching practices capitalize on concepts and experiences familiar to students to help them connect new knowledge with prior learning to construct new meaning.

Three key elements that contribute to a constructivist learning environment are (1) meaningful experiences, (2) interactions, and (3) prior knowledge (Morphew, 2002). These elements are repeatedly addressed throughout this book through explorations and boxed items (such as the "In Your Experience" boxes). In writing this book, I looked to the refreshed National Educational Technology Standards for Teachers (NETS•T) published by the International Society for Technology in Education (ISTE), considered by many to be the leading society in its field. The refreshed version was released in 2008 as an updated version of the first NETS•T, which was released in 2000.

The chapters are organized according to the NETS•T standards and are arranged in the order in which these standards appear. With the exception of the introductory and concluding chapters, each chapter is devoted to a refreshed NETS•T standard and its accompanying performance indicators.

Performance indicators are specific, measurable outcomes that assess what teachers should be able to do to show that they have achieved competency in the standard. An example of a NETS•T standard and its first performance indicator follow:

1. **Facilitate and Inspire Student Learning and Creativity**

    Teachers use their knowledge of subject matter, teaching and learning, and technology to facilitate experiences that advance student learning, creativity, and innovation in both face-to-face and virtual environments. Teachers:

    a. promote, support, and model creative and innovative thinking and inventiveness

Using this standard as an example, Chapter 1 collectively addresses Standard 1. The first performance indicator, 1a, is featured in the first section of Chapter 1. The other performance indicators associated with Standard 1 (1b, 1c, and 1d) follow. Arranging the chapters in this manner highlights the importance of each performance indicator and provides readers with opportunities to demonstrate competency of performance indicators through given explorations.

One distinct feature of this book is its emphasis on professional development. The refreshed NETS•T clearly acknowledge that teachers must be reflective, prepared practitioners and leaders who engage in continuing professional development. This book introduces readers to professional development and offers many different types of professional-development opportunities, such as formal and informal experiences, professional development through professional societies, collaboration with peers and the larger school community, networking in the virtual world, and other avenues for growth.

Another distinguishing feature of this book is its attention to reflectivity in the teaching process. Reflective practices—in lesson planning and journaling, through self- and peer-reflection, and in portfolio creation—are included to help develop a habit of reflection for a lifetime.

With the use of technology comes a sometimes unspoken element of responsibility. When technology is used safely and responsibly, it can have far-reaching, positive impacts on a teacher's professional and personal life. On the other hand, capricious use of technology without regard for safety, ethics, legal issues, and etiquette can bring untold pain, suffering, and destruction to a teacher's life. This book describes common human issues associated with the use of technology in teaching, such as ethics, legal issues, copyright and fair use, plagiarism, and exhibiting one's public persona in the virtual world.

Technology has evolved greatly since I first began my teaching practice in the mid-1980s. What has not changed in teaching is the need for well-prepared, caring, and competent educators who are willing to invest their time and talents in their students. In *Leaving Home*, Garrison Keillor (1987) wrote, "Nothing you do for children is ever wasted. They seem not to notice us, hovering, averting our eyes, and they seldom offer thanks, but what we do for them is never wasted" (p. 20). My hope is that this book helps prepare teachers to invest wisely and effectively in their students by providing meaningful learning experiences that integrate technology. Their efforts, and mine, will not be wasted.

Valerie N. Morphew, EdD
Professor
Fairmont State University

Introduction

You have probably heard countless times that teachers must be technologically savvy in order to meet the needs of today's generation of students. Like most prospective and practicing teachers, you are no doubt willing to expend the effort to attain this distinction, but you may not quite know what is expected of you or how to go about acquiring the necessary skills and competencies. That is the purpose of this chapter: to inform you of expectations and provide a roadmap for preparation.

LEARNER OUTCOMES

The reading presented should help you:

- Describe the International Society for Technology in Education (ISTE) and the ISTE National Educational Technology Standards (NETS) projects

- Recognize how the NETS•T were developed and how they are used in teaching

- Identify the relationship between the NETS•T and the accreditation process

- Recognize the performance profiles for teacher preparation

- Describe how a teacher candidate can prepare to meet the NETS•T

- Identify ways to use this book most effectively

Understanding ISTE and the NETS

When exploring a new area of interest, it is helpful to consult professional and amateur organizations associated with the area. These organizations, frequently called societies or associations, are often nonprofit entities comprised of individuals interested in research and dissemination of new knowledge in their fields. Although there are a number of organizations concerned with technology in education, ISTE is recognized as a leading professional society whose mission is to help prepare students, teachers, and administrators to use technology effectively. The work of ISTE has influenced teachers, students, and administrators worldwide. The mission of ISTE and the NETS projects is examined in preparation for the forthcoming chapters.

Examining the Mission of ISTE

The mission of a professional society is basically its purpose for existence. It is typically a brief, carefully framed statement, crafted by a group of its members to show what the society believes, what goals it hopes to accomplish, and how it hopes to accomplish those goals. A mission—or mission statement, as it is often called—helps a professional society remain focused on its purpose so that it does not stray from its intent with changes in leadership or other factors. It also provides those outside the society with a snapshot of the society and serves as a recruitment tool for those considering membership. It is worth noting that, from time to time, missions are revisited and modified to change with the times or reflect the changing nature of the profession itself. ISTE's mission is available to all prospective and current members and to all those interested in its purpose:

> ISTE is a nonprofit professional organization with a worldwide membership of leaders and potential leaders in educational technology. We are dedicated to providing leadership and service to improve teaching and learning by advancing the effective use of technology in PK–12 education and teacher education. We provide our members with information, networking opportunities, and guidance as they face the challenge of incorporating computers, the Internet, and other new technologies into their schools.

As part of ISTE's mission, sets of standards have been developed for PK–12 students (NETS•S), teachers (NETS•T), administrators (NETS•A), coaches (NETS•C), and computer science educators (NETS•CSE). Together, these standards are known as the National Educational Technology Standards, or NETS. The first four of these standards are located in the appendix.

Exploring the Early NETS•T Project

All professions have standards that professionals in the field are expected to meet or exceed. Standards help build integrity within and outside a profession by explicitly stating expected levels of competencies and skills. The original NETS•T (reproduced on page 3) were published in 2000 and consisted of the following six standards:

I. Technology Operations and Concepts: Teachers demonstrate a sound understanding of technology operations and concepts.

II. Planning and Designing Learning Environments and Experiences: Teachers plan and design effective learning environments and experiences supported by technology.

III. Teaching, Learning, and the Curriculum: Teachers implement curriculum plans that include methods and strategies for applying technology to maximize student learning.

IV. Assessment and Evaluation: Teachers apply technology to facilitate a variety of effective assessment and evaluation strategies.

V. Productivity and Professional Practice: Teachers use technology to enhance their productivity and professional practice.

VI. Social, Ethical, Legal, and Human Issues: Teachers understand the social, ethical, legal, and human issues surrounding the use of technology in PK–12 schools and apply those principles in practice.

ISTE NATIONAL EDUCATIONAL TECHNOLOGY STANDARDS (NETS) AND PERFORMANCE INDICATORS FOR TEACHERS

All classroom teachers should be prepared to meet the following standards and performance indicators.

I. TECHNOLOGY OPERATIONS AND CONCEPTS
Teachers demonstrate a sound understanding of technology operations and concepts. Teachers:

A. demonstrate introductory knowledge, skills, and understanding of concepts related to technology (as described in the ISTE *National Educational Technology Standards for Students*).

B. demonstrate continual growth in technology knowledge and skills to stay abreast of current and emerging technologies.

II. PLANNING AND DESIGNING LEARNING ENVIRONMENTS AND EXPERIENCES
Teachers plan and design effective learning environments and experiences supported by technology. Teachers:

A. design developmentally appropriate learning opportunities that apply technology-enhanced instructional strategies to support the diverse needs of learners.

B. apply current research on teaching and learning with technology when planning learning environments and experiences.

C. identify and locate technology resources and evaluate them for accuracy and suitability.

D. plan for the management of technology resources within the context of learning activities.

E. plan strategies to manage student learning in a technology-enhanced environment.

III. TEACHING, LEARNING, AND THE CURRICULUM
Teachers implement curriculum plans that include methods and strategies for applying technology to maximize student learning. Teachers:

A. facilitate technology-enhanced experiences that address content standards and student technology standards.

B. use technology to support learner-centered strategies that address the diverse needs of students.

C. apply technology to develop students' higher order skills and creativity.

D. manage student learning activities in a technology-enhanced environment.

IV. ASSESSMENT AND EVALUATION
Teachers apply technology to facilitate a variety of effective assessment and evaluation strategies. Teachers:

A. apply technology in assessing student learning of subject matter using a variety of assessment techniques.

B. use technology resources to collect and analyze data, interpret results, and communicate findings to improve instructional practice and maximize student learning.

C. apply multiple methods of evaluation to determine students' appropriate use of technology resources for learning, communication, and productivity.

V. PRODUCTIVITY AND PROFESSIONAL PRACTICE
Teachers use technology to enhance their productivity and professional practice. Teachers:

A. use technology resources to engage in ongoing professional development and lifelong learning.

B. continually evaluate and reflect on professional practice to make informed decisions regarding the use of technology in support of student learning.

C. apply technology to increase productivity.

D. use technology to communicate and collaborate with peers, parents, and the larger community in order to nurture student learning.

VI. SOCIAL, ETHICAL, LEGAL, AND HUMAN ISSUES
Teachers understand the social, ethical, legal, and human issues surrounding the use of technology in PK–12 schools and apply that understanding in practice. Teachers:

A. model and teach legal and ethical practice related to technology use.

B. apply technology resources to enable and empower learners with diverse backgrounds, characteristics, and abilities.

C. identify and use technology resources that affirm diversity.

D. promote safe and healthy use of technology resources.

E. facilitate equitable access to technology resources for all students.

Each standard was followed by performance indicators—specific measurable outcomes that assessed what teachers should have been able to do to show that they had achieved competency in the standard. For example, the first standard is numbered with the Roman numeral "I." The title, Technology Operations and Concepts, is followed by the description, "Teachers demonstrate a sound understanding of technology operations and concepts." The two performance indicators for Standard I (A and B) indicate what the teacher will be able to do to demonstrate competency.

I. TECHNOLOGY OPERATIONS AND CONCEPTS

Teachers demonstrate a sound understanding of technology operations and concepts. Teachers:

A. demonstrate introductory knowledge, skills, and understanding of concepts related to technology (as described in the ISTE *National Educational Technology Standards for Students*).

B. demonstrate continual growth in technology knowledge and skills to stay abreast of current and emerging technologies.

Although the 2000 standards were appropriate at the time they were published and for many years after, a need for updated standards arose to better reflect changes in technology, research, and the global community. As a result, the 2008 refreshed NETS•T were published. Like the 2000 version of the NETS•T, the newer version underwent scrutiny and revision from a wide array of educators and stakeholders. The current NETS•T (ISTE, 2008b) and their performance indicators appear below as well as in the appendix.

The Refreshed ISTE NETS and Performance Indicators for Teachers (NETS•T)

Effective teachers model and apply the National Educational Technology Standards for Students (NETS•S) as they design, implement, and assess learning experiences to engage students and improve learning; enrich professional practice; and provide positive models for students, colleagues, and the community. All teachers should meet the following standards and performance indicators. Teachers:

1. Facilitate and Inspire Student Learning and Creativity

Teachers use their knowledge of subject matter, teaching and learning, and technology to facilitate experiences that advance student learning, creativity, and innovation in both face-to-face and virtual environments. Teachers:

a. promote, support, and model creative and innovative thinking and inventiveness

b. engage students in exploring real-world issues and solving authentic problems using digital tools and resources

c. promote student reflection using collaborative tools to reveal and clarify students' conceptual understanding and thinking, planning, and creative processes

d. model collaborative knowledge construction by engaging in learning with students, colleagues, and others in face-to-face and virtual environments

2. **Design and Develop Digital-Age Learning Experiences and Assessments**

Teachers design, develop, and evaluate authentic learning experiences and assessments incorporating contemporary tools and resources to maximize content learning in context and to develop the knowledge, skills, and attitudes identified in the NETS•S. Teachers:

    a. design or adapt relevant learning experiences that incorporate digital tools and resources to promote student learning and creativity

    b. develop technology-enriched learning environments that enable all students to pursue their individual curiosities and become active participants in setting their own educational goals, managing their own learning, and assessing their own progress

    c. customize and personalize learning activities to address students' diverse learning styles, working strategies, and abilities using digital tools and resources

    d. provide students with multiple and varied formative and summative assessments aligned with content and technology standards and use resulting data to inform learning and teaching

3. **Model Digital-Age Work and Learning**

Teachers exhibit knowledge, skills, and work processes representative of an innovative professional in a global and digital society. Teachers:

    a. demonstrate fluency in technology systems and the transfer of current knowledge to new technologies and situations

    b. collaborate with students, peers, parents, and community members using digital tools and resources to support student success and innovation

    c. communicate relevant information and ideas effectively to students, parents, and peers using a variety of digital-age media and formats

    d. model and facilitate effective use of current and emerging digital tools to locate, analyze, evaluate, and use information resources to support research and learning

4. **Promote and Model Digital Citizenship and Responsibility**

Teachers understand local and global societal issues and responsibilities in an evolving digital culture and exhibit legal and ethical behavior in their professional practices. Teachers:

    a. advocate, model, and teach safe, legal, and ethical use of digital information and technology, including respect for copyright, intellectual property, and the appropriate documentation of sources

    b. address the diverse needs of all learners by using learner-centered strategies and providing equitable access to appropriate digital tools and resources

    c. promote and model digital etiquette and responsible social interactions related to the use of technology and information

    d. develop and model cultural understanding and global awareness by engaging with colleagues and students of other cultures using digital-age communication and collaboration tools

5. Engage in Professional Growth and Leadership

Teachers continuously improve their professional practice, model lifelong learning, and exhibit leadership in their school and professional community by promoting and demonstrating the effective use of digital tools and resources. Teachers:

a. participate in local and global learning communities to explore creative applications of technology to improve student learning

b. exhibit leadership by demonstrating a vision of technology infusion, participating in shared decision making and community building, and developing the leadership and technology skills of others

c. evaluate and reflect on current research and professional practice on a regular basis to make effective use of existing and emerging digital tools and resources in support of student learning

d. contribute to the effectiveness, vitality, and self-renewal of the teaching profession and of their school and community

© 2008 International Society for Technology in Education (ISTE), www.iste.org. All rights reserved.

The ISTE NETS performance indicators allow outcomes to be measured. Notice, for example, that in Standard 2, performance indicator a, the word "design" is used rather than "know" or "understand how to." To *design* is to do something, and that something can be observed. On the other hand, how can someone really be sure if someone else "knows" something? How many times, for example, have students nodded, looked interested, or uttered the proverbial "hmmm" when, in reality, they had no idea what you meant? Statements such as performance indicators that are written in a way that allows the outcome to be measured are known as *observable* or *measurable* performance statements. Someone can observe the behavior of another and measure to what extent the outcome was performed.

It is worth noting that the NETS for Students (NETS•S), originally published in 1998, were refreshed in 2007, and the NETS for Administrators (NETS•A), originally published in 2002, were refreshed in 2009. The NETS Refresh Project testifies to ISTE's commitment to staying relevant and up to date.

Global Reach of the NETS

"ISTE relied on the wisdom of educators to help us update the NETS during the three-year NETS Refresh effort. Educators from nearly 40 countries provided feedback to ISTE as the NETS were being refreshed, helping to strengthen them and to make them relevant to educators around the world. ICT skills are embedded in the NETS at all levels. … Schools in Norway, Costa Rica, Malaysia, Japan, Australia, Philippines, Micronesia, Korea, Turkey, are among many working to adapt the NETS as their information and communication technologies (ICT) framework."
(www.iste.org/standards/global-reach.aspx)

Examining the NETS•T in the Accreditation Process

ISTE's Accreditation and Professional Standards Committee is credited with developing the NETS Projects for students, teachers, and administrators. More than a decade of contributions by the committee has resulted in numerous standards, guidelines, and publications. The ISTE NETS•T Project has yielded the following with regard to teacher education:

- standards for accreditation of teacher preparation programs for specialization in educational computing and technology

- unit guidelines describing essential conditions needed to support technology use in teacher preparation programs

- general standards for providing a foundation in technology for all teachers

These standards and standard-related documents provide teacher educators with the wherewithal to prepare teachers to effectively use technology in education. Around the world the NETS are widely adopted, adapted, aligned, or referenced.

The National Council for Accreditation of Teacher Education (NCATE, www.ncate.org) is a coalition of 33 specialty professional associations (including ISTE) of teachers, teacher educators, content specialists, and local and state policy makers. NCATE uses a performance-based system in its accreditation process of schools, colleges, and departments of education.

NCATE is interested in teacher preparation as it relates to the knowledge, skills, and dispositions of teacher candidates. Being an NCATE-accredited school, college, or department of education testifies to the quality of teacher preparation the institution delivers. Of the 33 specialty professional associations involved with NCATE, some have submitted program standards that have been approved for use in teacher-education program review (NCATE, 2006). ISTE is one of these associations. It is worth noting that NCATE and the Teacher Education Accreditation Council (TEAC) are joining to form the Council for the Accreditation of Educator Preparation (CAEP). CAEP, which is scheduled "to become operational in 2013, will accredit over 900 teacher education institutions across the nation, producing approximately 175,000 graduates annually" (www.teac.org/category/caep).

ISTE's Essential Conditions

In order for students to be able to perform the competencies described in the NETS•S, ISTE asserts that certain essential conditions have to be in place from various stakeholders—such as university leaders, faculty, and school personnel—whose collective aim is to educate teacher candidates and beginning teachers at the various levels. These conditions underscore the importance of collaboration among university and school personnel and the larger educational community to help ensure the success of teachers and teacher candidates.

Essential Conditions

Necessary conditions to effectively leverage technology for learning

Shared Vision
Proactive leadership in developing a shared vision for educational technology among all education stakeholders including teachers and support staff, school and district administrators, teacher educators, students, parents, and the community

Empowered Leaders
Stakeholders at every level empowered to be leaders in effecting change

Implementation Planning
A systemic plan aligned with a shared vision for school effectiveness and student learning through the infusion of information and communication technologies (ICT) and digital learning resources

Consistent and Adequate Funding
Ongoing funding to support technology infrastructure, personnel, digital resources, and staff development

Equitable Access
Robust and reliable access to current and emerging technologies and digital resources, with connectivity for all students, teachers, staff, and school leaders

Skilled Personnel
Educators, support staff, and other leaders skilled in the selection and effective use of appropriate ICT resources

Ongoing Professional Learning
Technology-related professional learning plans and opportunities with dedicated time to practice and share ideas

Technical Support
Consistent and reliable assistance for maintaining, renewing, and using ICT and digital learning resources

Curriculum Framework
Content standards and related digital curriculum resources that are aligned with and support digital-age learning and work

Student-Centered Learning
Planning, teaching, and assessment center around the needs and abilities of students

Assessment and Evaluation
Continuous assessment, both of learning and for learning, and evaluation of the use of ICT and digital resources

Engaged Communities
Partnerships and collaboration within communities to support and fund the use of ICT and digital learning resources

Support Policies
Policies, financial plans, accountability measures, and incentive structures to support the use of ICT and other digital resources for learning and in district school operations

Supportive External Context
Policies and initiatives at the national, regional, and local levels to support schools and teacher preparation programs in the effective implementation of technology for achieving curriculum and learning technology (ICT) standards

Preparing Teacher Candidates to Meet the NETS•T

The ISTE standards and performance indicators provide a roadmap for attaining the competencies and skills needed to effectively use technology in education, as each student and indicator lends a piece to help teachers on their way.

NETS•T provide direction. The standard titles and descriptions provide a sense of direction. They show teachers where they are going and serve as the compass that sets them on the right path.

NETS•T show a destination. The performance indicators show teachers what they should be able to do once they have completed their journey of learning. These outcomes will be the destination.

Using This Book for Professional Preparation

Full comprehension of this book's contents relies on the relationship of the whole book to its parts. For example, teachers should understand the human issues and ethics related to technology use—primarily addressed in Chapter 4—before they integrate the technology addressed in other chapters. Taken as a whole, the book should help prospective and practicing teachers better understand expectations associated with NETS•T and how they can apply the NETS•T to their teaching practices.

Chapter Outline

This text was written so that prospective and practicing teachers can easily locate and comprehend the NETS•T and their respective performance indicators. The NETS•T are presented in sequential order, and each standard is assigned a chapter of its own. The structure of a typical chapter (in this case, Chapter 1) is outlined in the At-a-Glance Chapter Outline (next page). Chapters 1–5 follow this outline.

In Your Experience and Section Explorations

Each chapter's In Your Experience and Section Explorations are designed to help you develop reflective and effective practices in your teaching.

In Your Experience

How would you describe your current study skills? Do you typically progress through a text using some type of strategy, or do you skip straight to assignments? How can you improve your study skills?

Introduction Summary

In this Introduction you became familiar with the NETS•T, how the standards were developed, and their relationship to accreditation. You also learned about the performance profiles for teacher preparation and how a teacher candidate can prepare to meet the ISTE NETS for Teachers. Finally, you learned how to make best use of this book.

The remainder of this book is devoted to equipping you for your personal journey of learning. Each NETS•T standard and performance indicator will be addressed, and you will be given opportunities to practice new skills and competencies.

At-a-Glance Chapter Outline

Outline of Chapter 1 (as an example)

NETS•T1: Facilitate and Inspire Student Learning and Creativity

Standard in Brief
Indicators
Learner Outcomes

NETS•T1a: Promote, Support, and Model Creative and Innovative Thinking and Inventiveness

- [Content for performance indicator T1a]
  - *In Your Experience*
- Section T1a Explorations
- Section T1a Review

NETS•T1b: Engage Students in Exploring Real-World Issues and Solving Authentic Problems Using Digital Tools and Resources

- [Content for performance indicator T1b]
  - *In Your Experience*
- Section T1b Explorations
- Section T1b Review

NETS•T1c: Promote Student Reflection Using Collaborative Tools to Reveal and Clarify Students' Conceptual Understanding and Thinking, Planning, and Creative Processes

- [Content for performance indicator T1c]
  - *In Your Experience*
- Section T1c Explorations
- Section T1c Review

NETS•T1d: Model Collaborative Knowledge Construction by Engaging in Learning with Students, Colleagues, and Others in Face-to-Face and Virtual Environments

- [Content for performance indicator T1d]
  - *In Your Experience*
- Section T1d Explorations
- Section T1d Review

Chapter 1 Summary

References

International Society for Technology in Education (ISTE). (1998). *NETS and performance indicators for students.* Eugene, OR: Author.

International Society for Technology in Education. (2000). *NETS and performance indicators for teachers.* Eugene, OR: Author.

International Society for Technology in Education. (2002). *NETS and performance indicators for administrators.* Eugene, OR: Author.

International Society for Technology in Education. (2007). *NETS for students* (2nd ed.). Eugene, OR: Author. Retrieved from www.iste.org/standards/nets-for-students.aspx

International Society for Technology in Education. (2008a). *Essential conditions: Necessary conditions to effectively leverage technology for learning.* Eugene, OR: Author. Retrieved from www.iste.org/standards/nets-for-teachers.aspx

International Society for Technology in Education. (2008b). *NETS for teachers* (2nd ed.). Eugene, OR: Author. Retrieved from www.iste.org/standards/nets-for-teachers/nets-for-teachers-2008.aspx

International Society for Technology in Education. (2009). *NETS for administrators* (2nd ed.). Eugene, OR: Author. Retrieved from www.iste.org/standards/nets-for-administrators.aspx

International Society for Technology in Education. (2011). *NETS for coaches.* Eugene, OR: Author. Retrieved from www.iste.org/standards/nets-for-coaches.aspx

Morphew, V. N. (2002). Web-based learning and instruction: A constructivist approach. In M. Khosrow-Pour (Ed.), *Web-based instructional learning* (pp. 1–15). Hershey, PA: IRM Press. (Cited in Preface).

National Council for Accreditation of Teacher Education (NCATE). (2006). *Standards, procedures, and policies for accreditation of professional education units.* Washington, DC: Author.

nets·t1

Facilitate and Inspire Student Learning and Creativity

STANDARD IN BRIEF

Teachers use their knowledge of subject matter, teaching and learning, and technology to facilitate experiences that advance student learning, creativity, and innovation in both face-to-face and virtual environments.

PERFORMANCE INDICATORS

Teachers:

a. promote, support, and model creative and innovative thinking and inventiveness

b. engage students in exploring real-world issues and solving authentic problems using digital tools and resources

c. promote student reflection using collaborative tools to reveal and clarify students' conceptual understanding and thinking, planning, and creative processes

d. model collaborative knowledge construction by engaging in learning with students, colleagues, and others in face-to-face and virtual environments

FOSTERING INGENUITY

Endless possibilities for creativity, productivity, and ingenuity dwell within each and every student. Teachers can either invite students to explore their full potential, or they can stifle student exploration by withholding opportunities and support. In this chapter you will learn ways to advance the creative process, inspire ingenuity, and support knowledge construction through the use of technology.

LEARNER OUTCOMES

The reading and assignments presented in Chapter 1 should help you:

- Use technology to advance human creativity in the classroom

- Prepare and inspire students to use technology in problem solving

- Introduce students to collaborative tools that can promote critical and creative thinking

- Engage in the construction of knowledge in various learning environments

NETS·T1a

Promote, Support, and Model Creative and Innovative Thinking and Inventiveness

Creativity comes in many forms. It is evident in the performing and visual arts, in the innovation of inventions, and in the realm of deep and profound thinking. Who has not marveled at one time or another at the outcome of human creativity? Magnificent buildings, great literary works, beautiful melodies, and many other forms of creative expression have helped elevate the mundane to the magnificent, the ordinary to the remarkable, and the forgotten to the memorable. As the kernel of creativity takes seed in every student at every age, teachers must do all they can to foster its growth and support. Exploring creativity and the creative process is the focus of this section.

The concept of creativity has been explored and debated by scholars for centuries (Hausman, Jarvie, & Rothenberg, 2009), yet consensus on its meaning has yet to be reached. The creative process has been described by philosophers such as Aristotle and Plato (Hausman, et al., 2009); psychologists (Gardner, 1985, 1989, 1997); artists (Lehrer, 2009); scientists (Gross & Do, 2009); doctors (Heilman, 2005); educators (Hansen, 2005), and others who have used both quantitative and qualitative terms to describe this phenomenon. Regardless of the meaning attributed, creativity is consistently given high honor among all disciplines.

In education, "Create" is thought to be the most complex cognitive process for a learner, based on the revised work of Bloom's original taxonomy of educational objectives (Anderson & Krathwohl, 2001).[1] The ability to create generally relies on a learner's ability to remember, understand, apply, analyze, and evaluate. Figure 1.1 shows the hierarchical relationship of the revised structure.[2]

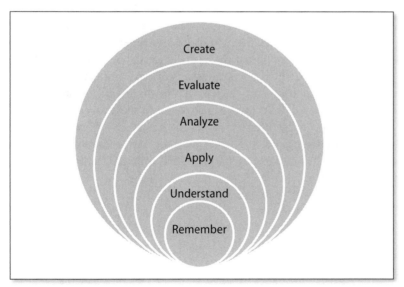

FIGURE 1.1 The cognitive process dimensions (based on *A Taxonomy for Learning, Teaching, and Assessing: A Revision of Bloom's Taxonomy of Educational Objectives*, Anderson & Krathwohl, 2001, p. 28).

The phenomenon of creativity can be thought of as involving both process and product. Anderson and Krathwohl describe creating as "putting elements together to form a novel, coherent whole or make an original product" (in Krathwohl, 2002, p. 215). The "putting together" implies process, and "to form or make" implies movement toward the creation of the resulting product.

According to Howard Gardner (1997) intellectual power plays a role in creativity, but it does not serve an exclusive role. Gardner believes, rather, that four dimensions are involved in the phenomenon of creativity: (1) intellectual power, (2) personality structures, (3) specific domains or disciplines, and (4) field. Figure 1.2 briefly illustrates each dimension as it relates to creativity.

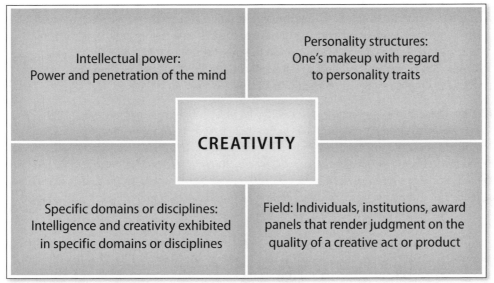

FIGURE 1.2 Dimensions of the phenomenon of creativity (based on the work of Howard Gardner).[3]

Gardner's theory of multiple intelligences (MI) has been widely embraced by educators as a way of understanding students' diverse talents and abilities. According to Gardner (1999), multiple intelligences exist, including the verbal/linguistic, logical/mathematical, visual/spatial, bodily/kinesthetic, musical/rhythmical, interpersonal, intrapersonal, and possibly naturalist, spiritual, and existential[4] (see Figure 1.3). These intelligences exist in all of us to varying degrees. Although an individual may excel in two or three intelligences and have, therefore, great intellectual power in these areas, he or she is thought to have some degree of intelligence in the other areas. Teachers may have a limited role in personality structure or in specific domains, disciplines, and fields, but they have great potential to promote intellectual power by providing rich and varied experiences, opportunities, and interactions to help students exercise their intellectual power.

Multiple Intelligences and Their Strengths

Bodily/Kinesthetic
Fine and gross motor skills

Existential
Aesthetics, philosophy, and religion and how these play into the big picture of life

Interpersonal
Social learning and connections

Intrapersonal
Understanding oneself

Logical/Mathematical
Mathematics, logic, reason, and problem-solving

Musical/Rhythmical
Perception of patterns (e.g., songs, poetry)

Naturalist
Categories and hierarchies

Verbal/Linguistic
Oral and written expression and mastery of foreign language

Visual/Spatial
Visualize ideas and solutions before expressing them orally, in writing, or through other means

FIGURE 1.3 Multiple intelligences and their strengths (based on Gardner, 1999).

Teacher as Facilitator of Creativity

Although it is still not clear precisely how nature and nurture impact learning and creativity, research suggests that both biological and environmental influences likely play a role in the outcome. Leaders in the field of brain research and creativity believe that creativity can be encouraged.

> Can creativity in individuals be encouraged regardless of the makeup of their brain, or are we limited by such factors as the number of glial cells and amount of white matter? "I believe creativity can be 'encouraged,'" Dr. Heilman responded. "We have known for decades that when young rodents are put in a stimulating environment, they have a much richer neural network than their sibs who were not raised in this environment. Thus, bringing up children in an enriched environment and making certain that they receive a good education is critical for their brain development.

> "The frontal lobes appear to be the part of the cortex that is most important for creativity, in that they are critical for divergent thinking and might modulate the coactivation of diverse cognitive networks so important in innovation. The means by which family and friends might be able to encourage the development of the frontal lobes is to encourage independent and divergent thinking." (Balzac, 2006, para. 17–18)

Fortunately, teachers have the opportunity to encourage all types of thinking—including independent and divergent—by providing a rich, stimulating classroom environment.[5]

The very act of teaching assumes that learners are teachable and that intelligence(s) can be developed. Constructivist teaching and learning acknowledge that both the teacher and the students are important and contributing members in a teaching-learning relationship, and that both bring prior knowledge and experiences with them into the learning environment. For this reason, constructivist teaching practices capitalize on concepts and experiences familiar to students so that students are able to connect new knowledge with prior knowledge and construct new meaning (Morphew, 2009).

Three key elements that contribute to a constructivist learning environment are (1) meaningful experiences, (2) interactions, and (3) prior knowledge (Morphew, 2002). Teachers can provide these elements in a variety of ways, such as through classroom experiences, interactions among peers, and collaborative and cooperative experiences.

> As a constant interaction among various biological and environmental factors, intelligences are educable; they change and grow. According to MI theory, the more time an individual spends using a particular intelligence and the better the instruction and resources, the smarter the individual becomes in that area. Translated into practice, this key feature reads: "All children can learn." It also works against pigeonholing or excluding individuals according to certain intelligences. (Baum, Viens, & Slatin, 2005, p. 22)

The experiences teachers introduce to students should be carefully planned, executed, and assessed for effectiveness. Walters and Gardner (1986) define "crystallizing experiences" as turning points in the development of a person's talents and abilities. These experiences often happen in childhood but can happen anytime in a person's life (Armstrong, 2009). Intelligences can be activated through crystallizing experiences, such as field trips, guest speakers, and hands-on open exploration that promote intellectual power and boost creativity.

In contrast, deactivators—described by Armstrong as paralyzing experiences—can squelch intelligences. Harsh criticism of a student's drawing, intentional withholding of resources, and anger and humiliation aimed at any educational attempt can thwart growth and development.

Armstrong (2009) identifies five environmental influences that can either promote or stunt intellectual growth:

1. Access to resources or mentors

2. Historical-cultural factors

3. Geographic factors

4. Familial factors

5. Situational factors

Access to resources or mentors includes both individuals and material items. Historical-cultural factors involve external factors related to the context of society and culture that may influence funding or promotion of creativity. Geographic factors entail the location and setting where a person is raised or lives, and familial factors include family associations that influence decisions and opportunities. Finally, situational factors involve the situation of one's life that influence development, such as socioeconomic status, responsibilities, and so forth. Figure 1.4 illustrates how each of these environmental influences impacts intellectual growth.

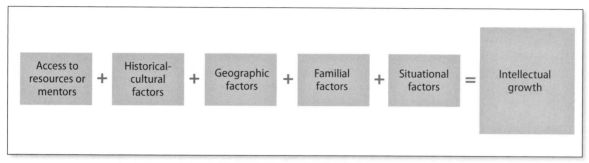

FIGURE 1.4 Environmental influences that impact intellectual growth (based on Armstrong, 2009).

Teachers can be especially instrumental with regard to Armstrong's first environmental influence because they serve as mentors and selectors/providers of resources. Even though teachers may have limited influence on the last four factors, they should be mindful of these influences as they pertain to their students' lives and histories in order to provide students with the most appropriate experiences. This requires higher-order thinking, creativity, and informed professional judgment on the part of teachers; they must understand the multiple factors that influence student development, be able to analyze and evaluate plans to meet students' needs, and engage in creativity to inspire student ingenuity.

Gardner acknowledges the important role teachers play in making education decisions when he speaks of their actions with regard to MI theory:

> There is no one right way or education approach to implement MI theory. The MI theory is not an educational prescription; [it is] best left up to educators to determine uses to which MI theory can and should be put to use. (Gardner, 1995, p. 206)

Although Gardner denies a one-size-fits-all approach to activating multiple intelligences, he does offer a preferable or optimum sequence to promote creativity and growth:

> I find it preferable to devote the early years of life—roughly speaking, up to the age of seven—to a relatively unstructured or "creative orientation" where students have ample opportunity to proceed as they wish and to explore media on their own. ... Thereafter, given the child's increasing inclination toward the learning of rules, it is both appropriate and advisable to inculcate basic skills. This is a time when children readily acquire skills and have some appreciation of the reasons for doing so.
>
> Even though the focus should ideally shift from creativity to basic skills and then back again, it is crucial that the other alternative be kept in mind during each developmental phase. The early years of life ought to feature at least some areas of skill acquisition, some development of useful working habits. By the same token, the years of middle childhood should incorporate some open-ended exercises, some free productions, as well as constant reminders that there is never a single best way to do something. So long as these alternative options—the accent on skills and the flair for creativity—are kept in mind at all times, the growing child is likely to be able to capture the best of both orientations. (Gardner, 1989/2006, p. 128)

Figure 1.5 illustrates the preferable sequence to promote creativity and growth according to Gardner.

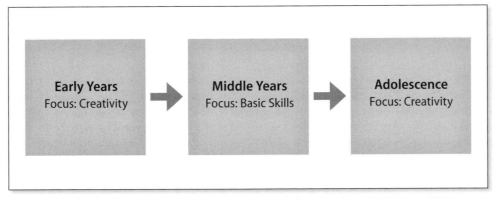

FIGURE 1.5 Preferable sequence to promote creativity and growth (based on the work of Gardner, 1989).

As noted earlier, teachers can provide a variety of crystallizing experiences, but they can also model creativity and innovation. Hansen (2005) argues that the creative teacher is the responsive teacher. He writes:

> Rather than issuing solely from what the teacher brings to the educational setting—consider again terms such as expertise and knowledge—creativity can point to what the teacher is capable of deriving or drawing from it. Creativity as responsiveness denotes a form of openness to the setting, which may or may not complement or fit harmoniously with what is preset, prefigured, or anticipated. Experienced teachers would be the first to say that there are times when it becomes educationally vital to shelve a preset plan. There are times when one form of creativity in teaching, embodied in a well-wrought lesson plan, must give way to another form, embodied in what I am calling responsiveness. The art of teaching consists, in part, of balancing these expressions of pedagogical creativity. (p. 58)

So what, then, can teachers do to promote both the process and product of creativity? In light of the section discussion, a few general suggestions are offered:

- Become familiar with students' multiple intelligences and aim to boost their intellectual power

- Provide meaningful experiences that help students develop abilities at various levels, moving toward the highest level—create—and ones that promote independent and divergent thinking

- Provide experiences that promote independent and divergent thinking

- Foster creativity by addressing both process and product

- Provide crystallizing experiences and avoid paralyzing experiences

- Consider experiences that represent Gardner's optimum or preferable sequence for promoting creativity

- Be a creative, responsive teacher who is open to multiple ways of inspiring creativity (see Figure 1.6)

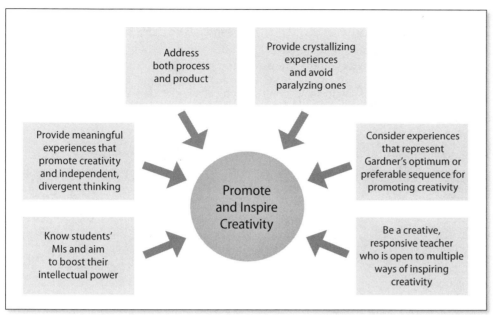

FIGURE 1.6 Suggestions for promoting and inspiring creativity.

Technology as a Creativity-Promoting Medium

Although some argue that computers can get in the way of design (Lawson, 2002), many (Armstrong, 2009; McKenzie, 2005; Moursund, 2003) view computers and technology as an adjunct to promoting creativity and intelligences. Multiple ways exist for technology to be used as a creativity-promoting medium. These ideas are not meant to be prescriptive but rather should serve as stimuli for teacher thought and creativity.

Identifying and Promoting Students' Multiple Intelligences

Everyone has all the intelligences. An intelligence can be strengthened. A number of inventories exist that can help teachers assess their students' multiple intelligences. Early on in the school year it might be worthwhile to administer an inventory and repeat the inventory at different times to determine growth and progress. Teachers may wish to use a spreadsheet or database (see Chapter 3) to help make sense of the collective and individual intelligences represented by their students. Keep in mind that these data should be used to help students and not to hinder their growth. This inventory is meant as a snapshot in time—it can change. MI is meant to empower people, not label them (McKenzie, 2005).[6]

In addition to multiple intelligences, students possess different ways of and preferences for learning. Some students learn best by seeing and hearing, and others by engaging in hands-on exploration. Furthermore, some students prefer quiet study, while others enjoy social learning. A number of print and online resources exist to help teachers identify learning preferences. Teachers may wish to explore learning preferences as a way to better serve students and promote intellectual power. Combining students' learning-preference data with their multiple-intelligence data should give teachers strong evidence for how they can plan effective, intellectual-power-boosting lessons.

Another way to help promote creativity and growth is to revisit and consider the different environmental influences affecting students mentioned earlier in this chapter. Being aware of these influences should help teachers make appropriate and informed education decisions and plans. Said succinctly, teachers should aim to know their students and plan to meet their needs.

In terms of resources, consider the many digital and nondigital technologies that are available to help address multiple intelligences (see Table 1.1).

TABLE 1.1 ▪ Digital and nondigital technologies that address multiple intelligences

Multiple Intelligences and Strengths	Digital and Nondigital Technologies
Bodily/Kinesthetic Fine and gross motor skills	Construction tools, kitchen utensils, screws, levers, wheels and axles, inclined planes, pulleys, wedges, physical education equipment, manipulative materials, mice, joysticks, simulations that require eye-hand coordination, assistive technologies, digital probes
Existential Aesthetics, philosophy, and religion and how these play into the big picture of life	Art replicas, planetariums, stage dramas, classic literature, classic philosophy, symbols of world religions, virtual communities, virtual art exhibits, virtual field trips, social media sites, blogs, wikis, virtual reality, simulations
Interpersonal Social learning and connections	Class discussion, sticky notes, greeting cards, laboratories, telephones, walkie-talkies, intercoms, board games, costumes, collaborative projects, social media sites, message boards, instant messengers, video chat (Skype)
Intrapersonal Understanding oneself	Journals, diaries, surveys, voting machines, learning centers, children's literature, class debates/discussions, real-time projects, online surveys, online forms, digital portfolios with self-assessments
Logical/Mathematical Mathematics, logic, reason, and problem-solving	Cuisenaire rods, unifix cubes, tangrams, measuring cups, measuring scales, slide rules, graphing calculators, spreadsheets, search engines, directories, file transfer protocol (FTP) clients, gophers, WebQuests, problem-solving tasks, programming languages
Musical/Rhythmical Perception of patterns (e.g., songs, poetry)	Pattern blocks, puzzles, musical instruments, phonographs, headphones/ear buds, tape players/recorders, digital sounds, online pattern games, multimedia presentations, online video sites (such as YouTube), speakers, CD/DVD discs and players, podcasting
Naturalist Categories and hierarchies	Magnifying glasses, microscopes, telescopes, bug boxes, scrapbooks, sandwich bags, plastic containers, databases, DVDs, USB portable storage devices, file managers, semantic mapping tools
Verbal/Linguistic Oral and written expression and mastery of foreign language	Textbooks, pencils, worksheets, newspapers, magazines, word processors, electronic mail, desktop publishing, web-based publishing tools, keyboard, speech recognition devices, text bridges

Multiple Intelligences and Strengths	Digital and Nondigital Technologies
Visual/Spatial Visualize ideas and solutions before expressing them orally, in writing, or through other means	Projectors, televisions, videos, picture books, art supplies, chalkboards, dry erase boards, slide shows, charting and graphing tools, monitors, digital cameras/camcorders, scanners, graphics editors, HTML editors, digital animation, digital movies

Sources: Adapted from McKenzie, 2005, p. 53; also based on Gardner, 1999.

If graphic organizers (such as concept maps or timelines) are developmentally and age-appropriate, consider using online tools or software applications to create visual representations of their multiple intelligences. Graphics may help students better grasp their strengths and the areas that need strengthening. Some of the available software applications and online tools to generate these kinds of graphic organizers are included in Resource List 1.1. TeAch-nology, for example, provides tools that generate graphic organizers for both registered and unregistered users.

RESOURCE LIST 1.1 ■ Tools and Software to Create Visual Representations of Multiple Intelligences

Inspiration: www.inspiration.com/kidspiration

Microsoft Visio: http://office.microsoft.com/visio

Scribus: www.scribus.net

TeAch-nology: www.teach-nology.com

If teachers decide to assign this activity, they should remember to promote it as a crystallizing experience. Promoting competition with regard to intelligences will likely be paralyzing for many students. Instead, teachers should aim to encourage and highlight intelligences at which students excel. In some cases, students who are not "high achievers" according to intelligences traditionally rewarded in schools (e.g., logical/mathematical), may find that they excel in several areas they were not even aware of.

Boosting Intellectual Power

Once familiar with students' multiple intelligences, teachers can consider opportunities—both experiences and resources—that can help boost students' intellectual power. The list should contain meaningful experiences that help students develop abilities at various levels, moving toward the highest level, create. Expect the list to change from year-to-year with each new group of students, and remember that expecting students to move straight from understand/remember to create is simply too great a conceptual leap for them to make without adequate preparation.

Teachers may want to revisit Table 1.1 to examine resources that address multiple intelligences and consider which level(s) of the revised Bloom's taxonomy they would best serve. For example, to promote remembering of business terminology, drill-and-practice software may be used. Simulation software, on the other hand, may best be used to help students create simulated businesses in the virtual world.

Encouraging Independent and Divergent Thinking

Helping students "think outside the box" requires practice and acceptance. If students provide creative answers that do not fit neatly with a teacher's preconceived expectation and are met with disapproval or disparagement, they may react by abandoning creative interpretation because it is simply easier to go with the flow and status quo. Conversely, providing open-ended experiences that allow for numerous "right" answers promotes creative thinking. One way to provide meaningful open-ended experiences is through project-based learning (PBL).

PBL allows students to work through a problem, either individually or in a cooperative group, to solve it. In PBL, technology-based tools can be used effectively to help solve problems. Moursund (2003) identifies three categories for uses of computer tools in education:

1. **Generic tools.** Software programs such as word processors, spreadsheets, database managers, graphics packages, email, and web browsers cut across many disciplines. A student who learns to use these tools can apply them in almost every area of intellectual work.

2. **Subject-specific tools.** There are tools designed for a particular academic discipline; for example, hardware and software that aid in musical composition and performance. Software for doing mechanical drawing (computer-assisted design) is another widely used subject-specific tool. Many different disciplines have developed hardware and software specifically to meet the needs of professionals within those disciplines.

3. **Learner-centered tools.** There are tools that require some programming skills but that also focus on learning to learn and on learning subjects besides programming. Most hypermedia and web-authoring systems serve as examples. Many of the generic tools include a built-in "macro" feature that adds learner-centered options. Both database managers and spreadsheets usually have such capabilities. (p. 90)

Moursund (2003) explains that by using computer-assisted learning, computer-assisted research, and distance learning students will experience first- or second-order effects, which will lead to creativity:

- "Computer-assisted learning (CAL) is the interaction between a student and a computer system designed to help the student learn. Computer-assisted research is the use of IT as an aid to doing library and empirical research. Distance learning is the use of telecommunications designed to facilitate student learning" (p. 91).

- Using these tools in one of these three ways can lead either to what Moursund describes as first- or second-order effects: A first-order effect essentially amplifies a task, and a second-order effect requires students to use higher-level thinking. Moursund writes, "The use of a computer to directly gather data from a scientific experiment is a first-order effect. Use of a computer to control the experiment is a second-order effect" (p. 96).

- Helping students to use both first- and second-order effects will help them move through the levels of learning needed to approach the creative process. Here again, teachers must use their own creativity to deliberately develop plans that provide first and second-order effects. "A major goal in PBL is to move students into routine use of the second-order levels of IT" (p. 96).

Promoting Independent and Divergent Thinking

Independent thinking does not preclude cooperative learning. Independent thinking, in the sense it is used here, implies thinking for oneself based on the meaning derived from an experience. Cooperative learning (which will be discussed in greater depth in Chapter 2) allows learning to happen in a social setting where the exchange of ideas stimulates growth of students independently and collectively. Students may share experiences and prior knowledge and engage in the construction of knowledge.

Addressing Both Process and Product

When planning experiences, teachers need to allow the opportunities and provide the resources needed to explore and produce an outcome. One way for teachers to help remind students and themselves that they value and expect both process and product is to include credit for both on rubrics and other assessment tools. (Chapter 2 deals with assessment in detail.)

Teachers can make technology work for themselves and their students by providing crystallizing experiences. Technology-related experiences should be positive ones. Providing a safe, comfortable computer environment with ample lighting and appropriate ergonomics is one way to provide a positive technology experience. (Chapter 4 covers how to set up an ergonomic and safe computer station.) Providing enough time to use technology is another way that can leave students feeling positive rather than frustrated when time is cut too short to complete learning that has begun. Virtual field trips, online chats with experts, and hands-on experiences used in conjunction with first-order and second-order experiences are examples of crystallizing experiences, as are user-friendly software applications that help students process ideas and produce creative outcomes.

Creating an Optimum Sequence to Promote Creativity

Teachers may do well to consider experiences that represent Gardner's (1989/2006, p. 128) optimum or preferable sequence for promoting creativity when planning learning experiences for their students. They should consider students' ages and developmental levels as they prepare opportunities for creative expression. In other words, creative explorations should be tailored to students and their characteristics, including age and developmental levels.

More specifically, Gardner's optimum sequence first involves exploration, then basic skills, and then exploration—again, to stimulate creativity. Keeping this sequence in mind may help teachers better tailor student opportunities for creativity based on age and developmental level.

Gardner notes that some level of basic skills instruction is advisable in the early years. Capitalizing on a young child's natural curiosity can actually help motivate students to learn the basic skills needed to explore further. For example, exclusive use of drill-and-practice software may be ill-advised for young students, but when it is used along with graphic-design software to create digital stories, the combination may inspire creativity and help students learn basic skills.

Being a Creative, Responsive Teacher

Creative teachers, as Armstrong noted, are flexible and willing to alter plans when the situation calls for it. They routinely hone their own skills, learn new ideas and concepts at various levels of learning, engage their multiple intelligences, seek out crystallizing experiences, collaborate with colleagues and students, engage in ongoing professional development (see Chapter 5), and inspire creativity through modeling. In other words, teachers, too, are students of creativity and can grow and develop as individuals and professionals by following many of the same strategies suggested in this section for student learners.

Inviting Multiple Ways of Inspiring Creativity

Once again, keep in mind that there is no one way to approach promoting creativity. Following a prescription would go against the very sentiment espoused here for approaching teaching and learning in novel ways. However, by being ready and open to new ways of practicing their profession, teachers can help their students blossom into the creative people they are capable of becoming. Approaching each teaching day with the expectation that something great can happen—that in class, at any given time, one or more students will make that one essential connection—may allow students to process ideas or produce something truly creative.

In Your Experience

Identify one crystallizing experience in your life.

- Did this experience impact your personal or private life?
- How so?

Section T1a Explorations

1. Create a graphic organizer that represents your understanding of creativity and the creative process. You may wish to use one of the graphic-organizer generators available online (e.g., www.teach-nology.com) or a software tool such as Microsoft Publisher, Open Office, or Inspiration.

2. List crystallizing experiences that you believe would help increase your creative potential at this point in your life. Explain how the items listed may achieve this. Create a table that depicts first-order and second-order effects you have experienced within the past 12 months. Analyze your table and explain how you may increase your second-order effects in the next 12 months.

3. Describe how your educational experience was either consistent or inconsistent with Gardner's optimum or preferable sequence for promoting creativity. How might your own experience impact your teaching? Create a timeline that shows your experiences of using instructional

technology, and extend it for the next 10 years. How do you project your use of technology in the next 10 years? You may wish to use timeline software (such as the free timeline at www.simile-widgets.org) to create your timeline.

4. Interview a person whom you consider to be creative. Is the content of this section consistent with the experiences of your interviewee? (For example, did the interviewee experience crystallizing experiences?)

5. Use your knowledge and experiences in your field to create a product that represents your understanding of this section. For example, if your field is music, write a song that summarizes the content of this section. If you are in the sciences, write an experiment that can test a hypothesis with regard to inspiring creativity. If your field is elementary education, create a bulletin board or a game for students that captures the creative process.

Section T1a Review

Creativity and the creative process can be fostered in your students and in yourself, but it will take a deliberate effort for this to happen. Expect to exert extra effort. Assessing students' multiple intelligences and meeting their needs and interests takes a great deal of thought and planning. Likewise, staying abreast of new technologies through collaboration and professional development takes energy and effort. Still, as a professional educator, your willingness to go the extra mile for your students can achieve much toward the greater good. Your classroom is full of potential Einsteins, Pasteurs, Mozarts, and Picassos. Think what the world would be like without human creativity. Now think of how much improved the world can be because you are willing to help your students become agents of creativity.

NETS·T1b

Engage Students in Exploring Real-World Issues and Solving Authentic Problems Using Digital Tools and Resources

A cursory review of world history reveals a wide variety of problems and issues that have challenged humans to take action for survival and prosperity. One does not have to look far or long to recognize that technology has played a role in many of these problem-solving efforts. Technology as it relates to agriculture and food production is one example. The field of medicine is another because of the ways technology has advanced the diagnoses and treatments of serious health issues and threats. Communication is yet another salient example, as telecommunications and other technologies have connected people worldwide. Education, too, has used technology to solve problems through distance education, instructional technology, and assistive technologies. This section explores how problems have been identified and solved through technology.

Technology's Role in Historical and Contemporary Issues

On a daily basis, the news media broadcasts endless catastrophes. Long ago, it took days, weeks, or even months to learn of a world calamity; now it takes minutes. Rather than wait for chariots to bring news of an impending war or distant disaster, one only needs to turn on a 24/7 television news program, connect to an online newspaper, or use some other technology to witness a visual and audio play-by-play report of late-breaking news across the globe.

Closer to home, the news is broadcast frequently enough to give the uninitiated a sense that their corner of the world is ridden with a steady stream of problems. Many television news stations have augmented their morning and evening broadcasts with online versions that provide frequent and sometimes immediate updates of newsworthy community problems such as crime, accidents, and natural disasters.

The immediacy of this reporting can be nearly overwhelming for adults who, through life experience, have learned to cope with a constant barrage of disturbing news. For the young, however, it can be even more unsettling. It is not difficult to see how advances in real-time communication and reporting can lead some to see the world's problems—both global and local—as too big and too plentiful for any human effort to solve effectively.

Although the constant supply of world problems and issues can weigh heavily on its citizens, it can also be viewed in a more positive light. Quickly knowing that a region of the world has experienced a disaster can give the worldwide community an opportunity to respond with offers of assistance. The devastating 2010 earthquake in Haiti is a recent example of a problem that triggered global efforts to help those affected. The response to the 2011 Japanese earthquake and tsunami disaster is another example of how human efforts came together to help a community in need.

The many human efforts that worked collectively to help those impacted by these two disasters no doubt involved a great deal of technology. The scientific community used advanced technology to determine the probability of further seismic danger. The medical community used life-saving equipment. The search-and-rescue teams used technology to help locate and assist victims, and other humanitarian efforts involved various forms of technology to provide food, clothing, and shelter.

Although some real-world problems are sudden, such as these two natural disasters, others are ongoing. Hunger, poverty, disease, deforestation, illiteracy, mental illness, economic declines, pollution, and crime are examples. Technology has a history of helping to solve problems by making the problems known and aiding solutions. Medical technology has helped practitioners better understand brain function and treat related illnesses, scientific instruments have helped scientists track existing environmental dangers and prevent others from occurring, and computer modeling has helped economists make informed economic decisions. to name a few. Whether the real-world issues are unexpected or ongoing in nature, technology clearly plays an important role in identifying and solving them.

ICT-Assisted PBL

An effective method that can be used in the classroom to explore and help solve problems of a sudden and ongoing nature is information (and communication) technology-assisted project-based learning. Project-based learning (PBL) was introduced in the previous section as an effective method for investigating topics. ICT-assisted PBL (which I sometimes refer to as PBL-IT and is also known as IT-assisted PBL) is a methodology that uses principles of PBL and information technology together to explore issues. According to Moursund (2003), the educational goals of an ICT-assisted PBL lesson plan are "authentic" and "closely aligned with what it takes to solve real-world problems and perform well on the job" (p. 58).

Moursund (2003) believes four goals should be a part of any ICT-assisted PBL lesson plan:

1. Students should get better at solving problems and carrying out complex tasks. … They should get better at working in a P/T Team [problem or task team] environment.

2. Students should improve their higher order and critical thinking skills and make use of their lower-order knowledge and skills.

3. Students should increase their knowledge and skill in undertaking a project and in using IT in a project environment.

4. Students should take increased responsibility for their own learning and work. They should make progress toward becoming independent, self-sufficient, lifelong learners and responsible workers. (p. 58)

Teachers can help students identify global and local problems and engage in Moursund's four components by following the steps shown in Figure 1.7. These planning steps may be used to help identify a contemporary world issue that needs to be addressed and solved and engage students in the creative exploration of solutions.

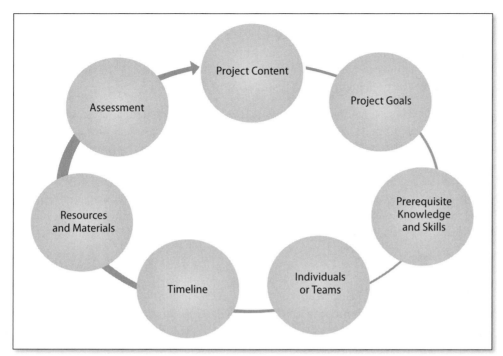

FIGURE 1.7 Factors to consider when planning for an ICT-assisted PBL lesson (based on the work of Moursund, 2006a).

According to Moursund, this seven-step process can be used to plan an ICT-assisted PBL lesson.[7] In brief, to begin, the project content must be decided, including a working title, mission statement, and brief summary of content area. Next, general and specific project goals are established. After defining goals, planners consider the prerequisite knowledge and skills students should have to successfully work through the project and any modifications they will need to foster student success. Teachers then need to decide whether individuals or teams will approach the project, the roles students will play, and the extent to which teams will be permitted to define their projects. A timeline for completion is established, including project completion and checkpoints along the way. Resources need to be selected based on availability and relevance, and finally, methods of assessment are chosen to determine the extent to which students meet or exceed expectations.

Boss and Krauss (2007) support a reinvented PBL that uses digital tools and resources as a boost to what we already know and use in the traditional classroom rather than a replacement:

> Reinventing the project approach doesn't mean discarding this venerable model. Rather, we advocate building on what we already know is good about project-based learning. By maximizing the use of digital tools to reach essential learning goals, teachers can overcome the boundaries and limitations of the traditional classroom. Some tools open new windows onto student thinking, setting the stage for more productive classroom conversations. Others facilitate the process of drafting and refining, removing obstacles to improvement. Still others allow for instant global connections, redefining the meaning of a learning community. When teachers thoughtfully integrate these tools, the result is like a "turbo boost" that can take project-based learning into a new orbit. (p. 12)

Boss and Krauss believe the hallmarks of a reinvigorated approach to projects include these characteristics:

- Projects form the centerpiece of the curriculum—they are not an add-on or extra at the end of a "real" unit.

- Students engage in real-world activities and practice the strategies of authentic disciplines.

- Students work collaboratively to solve problems that matter to them.

- Technology is integrated as a tool for discovery, collaboration, and communication, taking learners places they couldn't otherwise go and helping teachers achieve essential learning goals in new ways.

- Increasingly, teachers collaborate to design and implement projects that cross geographic boundaries or even jump time zones. (2007, p. 12)

Identifying Contemporary World Issues

The ICT-assisted PBL lesson plan, as described above, calls for identification of a problem. As demonstrated earlier in this section, technology plays an important role in awareness. Technology that makes online news programs possible is an obvious example of a means through which sudden and long-term real-world issues can be made known, but other less obvious communication tools exist, including email, blogs, social-networking sites, RSS feeds, news filters, and texting. In fact, any technology that connects two or more people can serve as an awareness-facilitating medium.

Many people are aware of how effective emailing can be for keeping up with news from friends and family, but they may not be as aware of how email can be used as a tool for identifying contemporary issues. Email users may sign up for any number of email alerts and updates offered by organizations associated with a cause. The alerts may contain information on current research efforts, ways to help with efforts, and emerging trends. Receiving these alerts is a time-saving way to stay abreast of self-selected contemporary issues in a timely fashion.

Email users can also sign up for email lists and email groups associated with a particular issue. Email users not only receive relevant and updated information, but they may also contribute to the conversation by posting information to the listserv or group.

Text message alerts are an extension of email and work in much the same way. Subscribers can receive text messages of an urgent or nonurgent nature based on their request. Text messages are especially helpful when an issue of immediate concern, such as a potentially volatile or dangerous situation, is at hand and readers are made aware of actions that need to be taken to avoid danger and remain safe. Another extension to email communication is the use of digital phone messages that play messages on phone speakers to alert listeners to important alerts.

Rather than using email, text, or phone alerts, some Internet users receive updates on important topics by using an RSS (Really Simple Syndication or Rich Site Summary) service that allows news on selected topics to be channeled to one website. This service is helpful for those who prefer to focus their Internet-viewing time on a few selected topics rather than on a broad range of issues.

Blogging and microblogging sites can also play a role in making individuals aware of potential, current, and emerging issues and can help focus readers on issues related to special interests. Blogs and micro-blogs are frequently topic specific. Some are strictly related to entertainment, others to politics, and others to education. Within these broad topics, some blogs and microblogs are narrower in focus. By regularly reading these blogs and microblogs, readers are able to pick up on contemporary issues that might not make it to larger news outlets. Readers can often post responses and comments related to blog and microblog content, making an exchange of ideas possible.

Social networking is a sometimes unrecognized source of news and information. Professional social-networking sites, for example, may serve as places to become aware of emerging issues in a field. A group of teachers communicating through a professional social-networking site may identify a delete-rious effect on the outcome of education following a change in education policy, thereby allowing them to work toward a course of action to help resolve the issue. (See Chapter 4 for an in-depth discussion of the ethical and confidential use of social networking with regard to teachers.)

As noted earlier, online news services are widely available to alert viewers and readers to global, local, ongoing, and unexpected issues through text, video, and podcasts. Some online news services allow viewers to filter what appears on their news page. If viewers prefer to read about health and politics but not about other available issues, they can opt out of the other issues and see only news on their selections.

As noted, any communication medium that allows two or more people to communicate can serve to bring issues to the forefront. Table 1.2 includes some of the many technologies that can help teachers and students identify contemporary world issues and define a project and project goals.

TABLE 1.2 ■ Technologies that can help identify contemporary world issues that may be used in ICT-assisted PBL

Technology	Example
Telephone	Land lines, mobile phones (including smart phones)
Internet	Online news, email, Really Simple Syndications (RSS feeds), blogs, micro-blogging, social-networking sites, email user groups, email lists, websites, podcasts, archived resources (e.g., news articles, primary documents)
Radio	News program broadcasts, two-way radio, Citizens' Band radio (CB radio), talk shows
Learning Management Systems	Blackboard, Moodle
Video	Documentaries
E-literature	E-books, e-journals, online databases
Television	News, talk shows, documentaries

Exploring World Issues

In ICT-assisted PBL, students explore an issue through research and examination. Technology plays an important role in the exploration of a topic, much like it does in the identification role. A number of software applications are available that can help students hone skills and acquire knowledge essential for exploring a topic.

Computer-based tutorials are interactive programs that allow users to gain mastery of a concept or skill. They exist for virtually every discipline and level. If students are exploring an environmental issue such as recycling, they may complete a tutorial that provides a thorough background on the recycling process and checks comprehension of content as they progress through the tutorial.

Teachers can use tutorials to spark student interest, refine skills, provide reteaching, or provide enrichment. Many free web-based tutorials are offered, and a multitude of commercially available tutorials are available at reasonable cost. Freeware and shareware tutorials are also relatively abundant.

Having easy and cost-effective access to quality tutorials allows students to learn about topics not included in their curriculum. "Taking the Mystery Out of Copyright," available through the Library of Congress website (www.loc.gov/teachers/copyrightmystery), is one example of a freely available tutorial that students and teachers can use to learn more about copyright and related issues.

The Multimedia Educational Resource for Learning and Online Teaching (MERLOT) website (www.merlot.org) provides a searchable collection of peer-reviewed and selected online learning materials including tutorials, simulations, case studies, and other learning objects. Although MERLOT is primarily a service to higher-education faculty, staff, and students, it is a gateway to a rich variety of online materials that may be appropriate for some elementary and secondary students.

Another tool that can help students acquire prerequisite skills or knowledge to explore a topic is an integrated learning system (ILS). An ILS typically utilizes networked hardware and subject-specific software, such as reading or math, that delivers programmed instruction to students and moves them through levels of mastery. Integrated learning systems may encompass the equivalent of several courses of a subject. Students progress at their own rates and appropriate levels. Practice is provided based on mastery, as is evaluation.

Many ILSs provide teachers with student data that help them use the ILS as a complement to traditional instruction. ILSs normally provide management tools to help oversee learning experiences. Compass Learning (www.compasslearning.com); Plato Learning (www.plato.com); and Pearson Education (www.pearson.com) are a few integrated learning systems available to the educational market.

In addition to tutorials and ILSs, informational websites can be used to make researching and exploring world issues easier. Reputable, quality websites, such as those included in Resource List 1.2, may provide a variety of resources, such as videos, podcasts, text, discussion forums, interactive maps, webcams, and other tools, to help students delve into topics in greater depth.

RESOURCE LIST 1.2 ■ Information sites for students to explore world issues

Government-sponsored sites

These sites provide a variety of resources, such as videos, podcasts, text, discussion forums, interactive maps, webcams, and other tools, to help students delve into a topic in greater depth.

NASA Kids' Club: www.nasa.gov/audience/forkids/kidsclub/flash

Kids.gov: www.kids.gov

Types of e-literature where students can locate information

Amazing Kids!: www.amazing-kids.org

Kid Outdoors: www.kidcrosswords.com/kidoutdoors

Scholastic News: www2.scholastic.com

E-zines that are adjuncts to printed material

Weekly Reader: www.weeklyreader.com

Highlights: www.highlights.com

Digital references

This links to many e-publications such as e-encyclopedias and e-books.

The Library of Congress's Virtual Reference Shelf: www.loc.gov/rr/askalib/virtualref.html

Sources of free text- and audio e-books

Thousands of free e-books and audio books can be accessed through these sites.

Project Gutenburg: www.gutenberg.us

Free Books: www.free-books.org

In addition to the sites in Resource List 1.2, other sources of e-publications, such as scholarly e-journals, may be available through school and community media and library services that often have paid subscriptions to these digital resources.

Online databases, such as those in Resource List 1.3, can be used by students to help locate research reported in journals and books. Field-specific databases are sometimes available through school and community library and media services.

RESOURCE LIST 1.3 ■ Online databases for students and teachers

Subscription-based searchable databases

EBSCOhost: www.ebscohost.com

H.W. Wilson: www.ebscohost.com/Wilson

LexisNexis: www.lexisnexis.com

Nonsubscription sites

Education Index: www.educationindex.com/education_resources.html

Lesson Planet: www.lessonplanet.com

Google Scholar: http://scholar.google.com

Before allowing students to explore topics through the aforementioned means, teachers should provide students with instruction (such as that described in Chapter 4) on how to distinguish between reputable and disreputable sites so that they can obtain reliable and updated information.

Solving World Issues

Identifying and exploring global and local issues are critical in ICT-assisted PBL, but alone they are not enough. In order to solve problems, action must be taken. Making informed decisions about possible courses of action comes about from considering all the factors involved and discovered in the exploration phase and deciding which action may have the most favorable outcome. A number of computer applications can help students in this phase.

One of the resources that may be helpful in the ICT-assisted PBL process is problem-solving courseware. Problem-solving software comes in a variety of forms, such as computer games and simulations that engage higher-level thinking. This type of courseware can help move students through the hierarchies described by Anderson and Krathwohl (2001), culminating in the use of higher-order thinking and creativity.

Problem-solving courseware may be web based, or it may be a stand-alone software product. Some problem-solving software provides informational feedback to help users master certain skills and grasp greater depth of understanding. Other products provide more specific feedback to users and are capable of adapting or changing the difficulty of content presentation and problem-solving exercises, based on the user's performance.

As students move through problem-solving courseware, they are required to make informed decisions based on their understanding of the problem. The outcomes—solutions—depend on student decisions and can, therefore, be very different for students or groups using the software. Engaging students in authentic problem solving that helps them experience both favorable and unfavorable outcomes based on their decisions makes this type of software especially useful in ICT-assisted PBL. Furthermore, because problem-solving courseware serves to move students through increasingly complex knowledge, it serves as an excellent means for fostering higher-order skills and creativity. Used in conjunction with traditional instruction, it has tremendous potential to maximize learning in the classroom. Problem-based courseware titles are available from such vendors as Plato.com.

Computer gaming is another type of computer application that allows students to influence outcomes based on their decisions. Computer games are an invention of relative recent history and serve to entertain and educate. Just about every traditional hands-on game now has a computer game counterpart. A matching card game traditionally played with physical, hand-held cards can be played on a computer. Similarly, a game of baseball can be played on a computer using Nintendo's Wii (www.nintendo.com/wii) game system. The natural allure of computer games has caught the attention of many manufacturers hoping to tap into the education market.

Computer games are interactive and typically use one or more types of graphics (such as text and video) and often sound (audio). Some games require players to input simple data, such as answers to questions, and provide feedback to players. More complex computer games, such as simulated real-world experiences, engage players in role playing, decision making, and action taking. Simulated games often require higher-order thinking skills and creativity to solve problems. Web-based brain games, such as those available at Luminosity (www.lumosity.com), are thought to help improve memory and attention.

Once selected, some games can be used as a whole class activity or multiplayer activity. Other games may be used by individual students for enrichment or as part of the regular curriculum. The nature of computer games naturally promotes higher-order thinking and creativity.

Moursund (2006b) supports the use of games in education:

> Games provide an excellent environment to explore ideas of computational thinking. The fact that many games are available both in a noncomputerized form and in a computerized form helps to create this excellent learning environment. A modern education prepares students to be productive and responsible adult citizens in a world in which mind/brain and computer working together is a common approach to solving problems and accomplishing tasks. (p. 8)

Moursund believes that games can be an effective educational tool because they are able to immerse the player in the environment (situation) of the game: "The attention grabbing and attention holding characteristics tend to shut out distractions" (2006b, p. 35).

One of the most recent developments in computer video gaming is massively multiplayer online games (MMO). These allow multiple users to play simultaneously across the Internet. For example, NASA has developed an MMO educational game (http://ipp.gsfc.nasa.gov/mmo).

Computer simulations are yet another type of interactive application that allows users to engage in authentic problem-solving activities. Many simulations create virtual worlds that mimic the real world but lack certain features that are not easily or reasonably available or accessible. For example, experiencing an ancient civilization is not normally feasible. Most students do not have the luxury of traveling long distances or even visiting relevant museums, and, of course, they are unable to travel back through time. However, a well-developed simulated game can make an ancient culture seem realistic and exciting to students in the classroom.

Discover Babylon (http://fas.org/babylon) is one such game that allows users to visit ancient Mesopotamia. It was developed jointly by the University of California at Los Angeles' Cuneiform Digital Library Initiative, the Federation of American Scientists, Escape Hatch Entertainment, and the Walters Art Museum.

The Education Arcade (TEA, http://educationarcade.org), a Massachusetts Institute of Technology and University of Wisconsin-Madison partnership, is working toward making the use of video games an integral, important, and effective part of education. Their mission reflects their focus:

> Our mission is to demonstrate the social, cultural, and educational potentials of video games by initiating new game development projects, coordinating interdisciplinary research efforts, and informing public conversations about the broader and sometimes unexpected uses of this emerging art form in education.

Revolution is TEA's role-playing game based in colonial Williamsburg during the American Revolution. It promotes problem solving and creative thinking by introducing students to ordinary experiences in history and setting high expectations for involvement and critical thinking. As it says on the site (www. educationarcade.org/node/357):

> Developed as a multiplayer 3-D game, *Revolution* is designed to be played in a 45-minute classroom session in a networked environment. Each participant navigates the space of the town, interacts with other players and townspeople, and is given the opportunity to act in and react to various events that in one way or another represent the coming of the war. *Revolution* includes a strong narrative component, an important aspect to drawing the player into a world of actual historical events. But players also improvise their own stories, based on the resources available to them as well as the choices they make in real-time as the game unfolds. Because the game is networked, players collaborate, debate, and compete, all within a simulation that maintains historical suspension of disbelief with graphical and behavioral accuracy. *Revolution* combines the best elements of live classroom role-playing exercises and period drama films to provide a new kind of teaching resource for understanding American history.

Note the higher-order expectations for student participants to improvise, make choices, collaborate, debate, and compete.

Another brainchild of TEA, developed in conjunction with the MIT Teacher Education Program, is the development of "augmented reality" games that use real-life experiences together with simulated computer experiences. Its first augmented reality game, Environmental Detectives (www. educationarcade.org/node/356), uses global positioning system (GPS) technology in an outdoor environment to discover the origin of toxic spills. Virtual characters are interviewed, and large-scale simulated environmental measurements and data analyses are conducted in the quest to unveil sources. Here again, note the expectations for players to discover, analyze, and problem solve.

Another simulation, RockSim—Model Rocket Design and Simulation Software (www.apogeerockets. com/Rocksim/Rocksim_information), allows users to create rocket designs and play with design parameters to alter rocket performance. The commercially available game by Viva Media, Crazy Machines: The Wacky Contraptions Game, allows students to build virtual machines according to objectives. All of these examples demonstrate how software can be used for creative expression and working out solutions to objectives or problems.

To locate quality programs that promote higher-order thinking and creativity, teachers may wish to consider the following suggestions: look to professional society recommendations and/or do a general search for games related to the content or topic to be taught. Read the literature written to promote the games and note student expectations for higher-order thinking skills and creativity. Search for reputable, reliable reviews of the game. If available, test drive game demos yourself. If you approve but still think further testing is in order, considering soliciting peer and/or student input. If demos are not available but you feel the game is worth a try, you may wish to order the game. Check for return policies in case the game doesn't suit your students' needs.

Presenting Solutions to World Issues

Once actions have been decided, it is important to provide students with the time and resources to present their findings and solutions to at least their peers, if not their community. Authoring software allows users to create interactive products for presentations, tutorials, movies, demonstrations, and more. Authoring software is used extensively in business and industry to promote products and services, for training, and for web-page development. Education uses authoring tools on many levels and for a variety of purposes, as well.

At the course level, authoring software allows users to create entire course systems for student use. Most course systems have various components, including content modules, assignment drop-boxes for student uploading of assignments, chat tools, and bulletin boards. Normally, teachers are not directly involved with the creation of courseware, although sometimes they serve as consultants to writers for courseware designers.

At the classroom level, teachers use authoring software to create multimedia presentations, tutorials, movies, and demonstrations. Some authoring tools that teachers and students may wish to use are listed in Resource List 1.4.

RESOURCE LIST 1.4 ■ Authoring tools

To create presentations

> **HyperStudio:** www.mackiev.com/hyperstudio
>
> **Microsoft PowerPoint:** http://office.microsoft.com/PowerPoint

For web-page designs

> **KompoZer:** http://kompozer.net
>
> **Adobe DreamWeaver:** www.adobe.com/products/dreamweaver

For animation and videos

> **Adobe Flash:** www.adobe.com/products/flash

For graphic-organizer designs

> **Inspiration:** http://store.inspiration.com
>
> **CMap Tools:** http://cmap.ihmc.us
>
> **Kid Pix:** www.mackiev.com/kid_pix.html

For computer-aided designs

> **Google SketchUp:** http://sketchup.google.com

Students can use various authoring software to exercise higher-order thinking, such as producing and composing, writing, imagining, and inventing. Students can use PowerPoint, for example, to create a presentation with text, audio, and video that summarizes the identification, exploration, and solving of a problem. They can use SketchUp to design a 3-D model of a solution, Inspiration to show relationships among contributing factors of a problem they explored, or Flash to animate a problem or solution.

Online collaboration tools make it relatively easy to create and share ICT-assisted PBL findings with others. Wiki tools and mind-mapping tools, such as MindMeister (www.mindmeister.com), Google Docs (http://docs.google.com), and SlideShare (www.slideshare.net), are but a few such collaborative tools.

Using digital tools as aids to learning has powerful implications, for as students leave the classroom and move on to the real world, they will already have experience in solving real problems that can impact their lives and the lives of others.

In Your Experience

- Identify one digital resource you have used in the past for helping to solve a real-world issue. Explain how you used the resource.

- If you are unable to identify one digital resource, explain how you used one nondigital resource to help solve a real-world issue. Consider how using a digital resource would have improved your exploration or problem solving.

Section T1b Explorations

1. Watch a 30-minute television news program and record the contemporary world issues identified. Note any contemporary issues that may be appropriate for student exploration and solving.

2. Connect to an online local news source and record the contemporary world issues presented. Note any local issues that may be appropriate for student exploration and solving.

3. Locate 10 blogs, websites, or other resources that you can use to receive regular updates on a topic of interest to you. Describe how you might use these resources in your teaching practice.

4. Create an ICT-assisted PBL lesson plan using a local, real-world problem as the topic. Explore the topic as if you were the student and offer possible solutions based on your research and use of resources.

5. Based on the contemporary issues you identified, identify resources appropriate for student exploration. For example, if a dip in the local economy was identified, locate computer simulations that might help students better understand how the economy works before trying to solve the real-world economic crisis.

6. Locate at least two online reviews that describe the effectiveness of the resources. Identify the source of the reviews (e.g., blogger review, competitor review) and how the source of the review may impact the review summary. Identify the first-order and second-order effects students might experience when using the resources. Identify which levels of the revised Bloom's Taxonomy might be engaged by students using the resources. (See Figure 1.1.)

Section T1b Review

Contemporary world issues dominate news programs both day and night and present many challenges for the world's citizens. With these issues, though, come an abundance of opportunities and resources for students to explore and help solve real-world issues. ICT-assisted PBL is an appropriate method for exploring these problems. Numerous digital tools are available to provide students with opportunities to engage in various levels of learning. Technology can be especially helpful in identifying issues, exploring issues, solving issues, and presenting solutions. Providing students with the tools and time to explore and help solve contemporary world issues will better prepare them as global citizens.

NETS•T1c

Promote Student Reflection Using Collaborative Tools to Reveal and Clarify Students' Conceptual Understanding and Thinking, Planning, and Creative Processes

Deliberate reflection can be a powerful tool to help students become aware of their own thinking, learning, and growth. Reflection can also be used as a springboard for deeper reflection, as new knowledge is learned and connected to prior knowledge. The reflective process involves students taking time to look back on an experience; identifying where they started, traveled, and ended up; and deciding where they want to go from there. Examining the learning journey using collaborative tools can enhance the reflective process. In this section you will learn how to promote student reflection using these tools.

Creating a Reflective Classroom Environment

As noted in the previous section, our world is full of problem-solving opportunities with options to consider and actions to be taken. Helping students become self-aware, thinking, and caring individuals who are capable of taking informed action is perhaps one of the most rewarding outcomes a teacher can promote, yet preparing reflective students to tackle these problems today and in preparation for tomorrow requires careful planning and effort. Not only must teachers create a classroom environment conducive to reflection, but they must also structure the curriculum so that reflection is possible, welcome, and fostered.

Forethought and planning can help establish a reflective classroom environment, one that allows deliberate thought, time, growth, and informed action. In her work with service-learning, Wade (1997) outlined 10 factors (see Figure 1.8) that should be present for an effective classroom environment that promotes reflection and can be regarded as a framework for other forms of learning.

Respect for students' ideas acknowledges that students bring experiences and knowledge to the learning experience; they are not simply empty slates, but rather important and vital members of the learning community (Morphew, 1994). Creating a classroom environment where students are expected and encouraged to be active participants rather than passive learners is consistent with constructivist learning and requires that students feel safe in offering ideas and suggestions about their own takes on a problem or project.

Student-to-student talk is an extension of this respect for student ideas. Teachers are viewed as facilitators and not as the proverbial sages on the stage. Within a brick-and-mortar classroom, the physical environment needs to be conducive for student-to-student collaboration. In the broader community of students, the virtual world should also be one that allows easy, safe, and reliable collaboration.

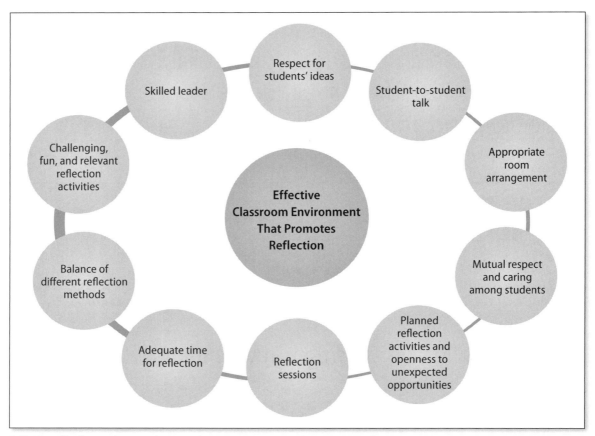

FIGURE 1.8 Ten factors that contribute to a classroom environment that promotes reflection (based on the work of Wade, 1997, p. 98).

Mutual respect among all in the learning community begins with teachers who model and foster respect. Planned, unexpected, ongoing, challenging, and enjoyable reflection opportunities require time and a facilitator capable of carrying out effective reflection. While it may seem time prohibitive to factor in time for reflection, it is essential if students are going to practice skills that can last a lifetime. In a complex world, it is imperative that citizens of all ages be able to work through options and consider benefits and consequences of their actions.

Wade (1997) describes core components of reflective thinking that lead to informed action:

> First, reflection is a deliberate thinking process that is applied to an experience, idea, or issue. Second, reflection takes time and the more time we can devote to reflecting on an experience, the greater potential for learning and insight. Third, reflection can lead to cognitive growth. Reflection should result in new understandings and appreciations. Finally, we reflect to inform our future actions. (p. 95)

Reflection itself can be thought of as a set of attitudes. Rodgers (2002a) distilled four criteria that characterize the concept of reflection and the purposes it serves:[8]

1. Reflection is a meaning-making process that moves a learner from one experience into the next with deeper understanding of its relationships with and connections to other experiences and ideas. It is the thread that makes continuity of learning possible, and ensures the progress of the individual and, ultimately, society. It is a means to essentially moral ends.

2. Reflection is a systematic, rigorous, disciplined way of thinking, with its roots in scientific inquiry.

3. Reflection needs to happen in community, in interaction with others.

4. Reflection requires attitudes that value the personal and intellectual growth of oneself and of others. (p. 845)

Rodgers (2002b) also identified four phases in the process of reflection:[9]

1. Presence in experience: Learning to see

2. Description: Learning to describe and differentiate

3. Analysis of experience: Learning to think critically and create theory

4. Experimentation: Learning to take intelligent action (pp. 234–249)

According to Rodgers, "one may move forward and backward through the process, especially between description and analysis" (p. 234).

Both Wade (1997) and Rodgers (2002b) acknowledge the role of community in the reflective experience, yet without a teacher's intervention, reflection may not happen at all. Hmelo-Silver (2004) writes, "… reflection rarely happens in groups without a facilitator and so alternative mechanisms, such as structured journals, are needed to ensure reflection" (p. 246). Hence, fostering collaboration in reflection plays a critical role in whether reflection takes place at all.

A number of digital tools are available to help teachers foster reflection in a collaborative environment. Keep in mind that this discussion is in no way exhaustive but may serve as a springboard for novel uses of existing and emerging technology.

Hard-bound journals. The traditional hard-bound journal served for years as a tool for reflection in English and other classes, when students were asked to think about where they have been, what they have done, where they wanted to go, or other such questions that triggered reflective thinking. This type of journal was read by a select number of recipients, such as teachers who assigned journal writing or close friends who were permitted to read the printed word. The nature of these journals limited the likelihood of reaching a wide audience and hence the active collaboration between the writer and a community of readers. Today, however, many technology tools exist that enhance journal writing further by promoting student-to-student interaction and collaboration. Some of these tools include blogs, microblogs, discussion boards, social-networking sites, wikis, digital stories, podcasting, videorecording, videoconferencing, and text-messaging systems, to name a few.

Blogging software has become simplified to the point that nearly anyone with basic computing skills can set up a blog in a matter of minutes, for free or at minimal cost. Students across the country are using a variety of different websites and software to blog, such as those in Resource List 1.5.

RESOURCE LIST 1.5 ■ Blogging software

Multiuser edublogging platforms

21Classes: www.21classes.com

ClassBlogmeister: www.classblogmeister.com

Gaggle.net: www.gaggle.net

Edublogs: http://edublogs.org

ePals: www.epals.com

Course management systems that allow students to blog within the systems

Blackboard: www.blackboard.com

Moodle: http://moodle.org

Most blogging software and sites allow users to post writings and allow readers to respond. Different levels of security and safety settings exist for control by administrators (e.g., teachers, technology coordinators), and teachers need to comply with district and school policies. In most cases, teachers should consider limiting access to blogs until students have learned safety guidelines and what is acceptable and appropriate material to post and respond to. For example, teachers want to protect students from "trolls" and "imposters" who post and pose as interested collaborators.

In some cases students may be permitted to blog freely on a project or problem, but it is advisable to provide structure for blogs so that they do not wander off on a tangent. While some degree of unexpected reflection is desirable and may lead to unexpected learning opportunities, students need enough structure to use their time to meet project goals.

Microblogs. When more frequent but shorter reflections are desired, microblogs (e.g., Edmodo) provide a good option. Microblogs are blogs that permit a limited amount of text to be posted at one time. Regular blogging software and sites may be used as a microblog if text limits are regulated and enforced. Microblogging allows users to learn to write succinctly and with more frequency than with regular blogs, which are typically posted only every few days.

Whether students use blogs or microblogs, they should be taught safety rules and policies (e.g., using screen names, not divulging personal information, using standard written English, and following guidelines for commenting on other students' blogs).

Teachers should provide rubrics or other assessment tools to students prior to student blogging so that students are aware of expectations. It might be worthwhile to allow students to have a trial run of blogging that will not count toward their class grade as a practice exercise.

To make blogs or microblogs more than reporting of events, students should be led to reflect critically on projects, problems, or class assignments. Guiding questions, for example, can be provided to students to focus their blog content. Another strategy can be for students to use a "KWL" blogging method: K represents what students know, W represents what students want to know or wonder, and L represents what students have learned.[10]

Wikis. As an adjunct or alternative to blogging software and sites, students can use wikis to record much of the same material. Wikis allow multiple users to edit content, thereby providing access and opportunities for collaboration. Wiki sites can be controlled for limited access.

Discussion boards can be used similarly and are often available within course management systems and through professional organizations and interest groups. In some cases, users must be registered members; in other cases, usage is open to anyone. At the time of this writing, most discussion boards used the written word, but some systems allow the use of recorded voice posts to create threaded discussions. It is critical that teachers are aware of district and school policies with regard to what discussion boards may be used by students for safety and security. The same types of precautions must be applied for students using discussion boards as for using blogs/microblogs, wikis, and other communication and collaboration tools.

Social-networking sites allow users to post pictures, content, videos, and other digital artifacts for limited or wide access, but security and settings vary from site to site and must be used with caution if students are permitted to use them. Much controversy surrounds the use of social networking in instruction, with some schools strictly forbidding its use, while others argue that its benefits outweigh the risks.

Digital storytelling is a way for students to think critically about themselves, their experiences, their classwork, and their projects by using multimedia tools to convey their reflections. VoiceThread (http://voicethread.com) and DigitalStoryteller (www.digitalstoryteller.org) are being used by educators to help their students think critically about themselves and others. Individuals or groups of students can collaborate on digital storytelling projects and grow individually and as communities of learners.

Podcasts. Podcasting can be used as a tool for reflection, as students reflect through recorded audio. Much like digital storytelling, students can record reflections of their journeys as they move through a PBL lesson, for example, or as they explore internship experiences. Vincent (2009) suggests using podcasts for weekly news broadcasts, documenting field trips, recording classroom discussions, and other such exercises that will naturally require student reflection to create and produce.

Podcasts can be sent to recipients through RSS feeds, listened to on mobile technologies such as iPods or Palms, or downloaded and reviewed on the computer. Students can create podcasts individually or in groups and may wish to create dialogue podcasts, in which students listen to other students' podcasts and create podcasts in response. This back-and-forth dialogue can show reflections over time and document student growth and learning.

Slidecasting, which use slides and podcasting together, is an additional tool that can be used to create and share reflections and invite collaboration and dialogue. SlideShare (www.slideshare.net) is being used by some educators to promote reflection in a collaborative environment. Webcasts, Internet radio shows, videoconferencing, webinars, and videocasts are additional tools.

Graphic organizing tools. Students may find graphic organizing tools helpful to visually lay out their reflections and collaborate on ideas and solutions. Collaborative digital tools, such MindMeister (www.mindmeister.com) and Mindomo (www.mindomo.com), are used by some educators to foster reflection in a collaborative environment. Brainstorming, expected and unexpected reflection, and connections with others are some of the possible outcomes of using such tools in this manner.

While the resources and possibilities are plentiful, some teachers may feel nearly paralyzed by the vast number of tools and applications available. Like anything else, if teachers have never used any or many of these tools, perhaps it is wise for them to take small steps and begin with only one or two tools or applications, rather than try to implement multiple resources and get discouraged by the inevitable setbacks.

Consider what makes sense for current students and what resources are available. Teachers should always investigate online privacy policies and terms of use for all online resources they may consider using to determine age restrictions, how personal information will be used, and other safety and security issues. Teachers can enlist the help of district and school technology coordinators who can help them implement ideas with safety and security in mind.

For instance, if teachers wish to encourage their students to reflect on their own experiences as they would have related to students in the 19th or 20th century, perhaps they can consider using digital storytelling in groups of two or three students. Podcasts, blogs, slidecasts, wikis, and other resources can also be used, but if digital storytelling will accomplish the lesson goals for reflection and collaboration, why not keep it simple? As teachers achieve success and see growth and development and as a collaborative environment develops, they can add additional tools and applications.

Teachers should remember to enlist the help of the district or site technology coordinator to help them set up the necessary software or locate appropriate safe and secure sites. As 21st-century educators, teachers should invite collaboration from their colleagues and from the community when appropriate. Teachers do not need to pursue these student-collaborative ventures alone; in fact, it would be counterproductive to do so. As teachers, we can learn so much from each other and community members and save hours of time by collaborating.

In Your Experience

Identify one collaborative tool you have used.

- Was it used for an educational purpose?
- Could it have been used for an educational purpose?

If you have never used a collaborative tool, what one tool would you like to investigate further for educational purposes (e.g., digital storytelling)?

Section T1c Explorations

1. Create a blog using one of the resources described in this section. Make a list of ways you can use blogging in your teaching practice. As you created your blog, what frustrations, if any, did you experience that might impact your students who use blogging software? What are some security precautions you must observe?

2. Create a podcast that reflects on your understanding of the section content. Exchange your podcast with a peer and comment on his or her podcast. Ask your peer partner to do the same.

3. Search the Internet and create a resource list for slidecasts, podcasts, or other collaborative tools your students may use. Exchange your list with peers and create a blog or other web-based resource that includes a compilation of lists.

4. In collaboration with one or more peers, create a digital story that records reflections on a concept or project.

5. With one or more peers, create a wiki that summarizes the concepts in this chapter.

6. Use collaborative graphic-organizer software to create a visual demonstration of your understanding of this chapter. Collaborate with one or more of your peers.

7. Visit one or more of the websites presented in this section. Bookmark any that you may want to use for future reference.

Section T1c Review

Many digital tools and technology resources can be used to help students reflect on experiences, learning, and growth. By providing a classroom environment conducive to exchanges of ideas as well as student-to-student and student-to-teacher interactions, you can help pave the way for enhanced collaborations.

NETS·T1d

Model Collaborative Knowledge Construction by Engaging in Learning with Students, Colleagues, and Others in Face-to-Face and Virtual Environments

Teachers are often referred to as role models. Every school day, they face a captive audience and project their attitudes and behaviors to impressionable students. Students look to teachers to better understand acceptable behaviors, appropriate communication, and a whole host of other actions. The emphasis on social modeling has largely been on behavior. In this section, however, modeling knowledge construction and creative thinking will take center stage.

Exploring Constructivist Learning

This book, as reflected in its title, has a constructivist perspective. Constructivist learning acknowledges that both teacher and students are important and contributing members in a teaching-learning relationship and that both bring prior knowledge and experiences with them into the learning environment. For this reason, the practices of constructivist teaching capitalize on concepts and experiences familiar to students so that they are able to connect new knowledge with prior knowledge and construct new meaning (Morphew, 1994).

Three key elements contribute to a constructivist learning environment:

- meaningful experiences

- prior knowledge

- interactions (Morphew, 2009)

Each of these elements should be present in a learning environment that supports the constructivist perspective.

Meaning here is defined as the co-created sense one makes of phenomena through the interaction of the subject and the subject's field (Morphew, 1994).[11] *Meaningful experiences*, therefore, are experiences from which meaning can be derived.

For experiences to be meaningful, they must make sense to the learner. An experience perceived by the student as meaningless, much like the expression "lw;jdlsk," renders the learning process impotent. Instructing students to wander aimlessly in a meadow without providing any contextual basis approximates the nonsensical expression, "lw;jdlsk." However, using the experience as a metaphor or analogy taps into students' *prior knowledge*, elevating the experience to one of meaning (Morphew, 2009).

Providing relevant curricula to students—curricula that help students connect what they already know to what they are now learning—helps deliver *meaningful experiences* to students. These are experiences that acknowledge student interests, abilities, and other characteristics and allow students to construct knowledge with others in the learning environment. Using examples that are foreign to students, such as actors and actresses from a bygone era, will not likely have the same appeal and relevance as using those who are easily recognizable. In this same way, presenting advanced concepts to students who have not yet grasped the fundamentals denies them the wherewithal to successfully make the conceptual leap expected.

Providing opportunities for *interactions* among students and between students and teacher is crucial to forming a constructive classroom environment. Contributions from all participating members of the learning community can trigger growth in all involved. Students with hobbies, interests, or talents help build a rich learning community and can help create greater awareness of connections that might otherwise go unnoticed. A student interested in baseball, for example, may be able to help her peers better understand statistics by presenting her baseball card collection to the class and explaining the content of the cards. A student interested in music may help students make the connection between music and patterns by sharing his sheet music with an explanation of refrains or patterns of notes.

Interacting in a Professional Learning Community

Teachers and students bring knowledge and experiences to the constructivist classroom, but by expanding the community of learners to include experts, community members, parents, and others, student learning can be further enhanced. An inclusive learning community, where stakeholders work together toward a common goal, is sometimes referred to as a professional learning community or PLC. Stoll and Louis (2007) suggest the following definition of PLC:

> In sum, the term "professional learning community" suggests that focus is not just on individual teachers' learning but on (1) professional learning; (2) within the context of a cohesive group; (3) that focuses on collective knowledge, and (4) occurs within an ethic of interpersonal caring that permeates the life of teachers, students and school leaders. (p. 3)

Stoll and Louis take an inclusive approach to PLC, extending membership to such examples as school district staff, higher education institutions, external consultants, and policy makers. They question whether teachers alone can be totally responsible for the success of their students:

> Teachers' knowledge base also traditionally encompasses subject knowledge, pedagogical knowledge, and that relating to child or adolescent development. Is this knowledge base truly broad enough to encompass all of the challenges that face children and young people in a diverse and changing society? There are other relevant and essential knowledge bases … that are likely to be critical in helping improve schools. (p. 4)

Although the question of who makes up the membership of a PLC is important. Stoll and Louis say the purpose of its existence remains unchanged: "to enhance student learning" (p. 5).

A constructivist classroom that is part of a larger PLC should include opportunities for interaction among all stakeholders, both immediate and extended. In terms of logistics, face-to-face interactions are easier within a school between student and teacher. Interactions between those housed within a school and those in a district may also find face-to-face interactions to be the first choice. In cases where it is impractical to have frequent face-to-face interactions with stakeholders, virtual interactions can be used to facilitate learning, communication, and collaboration.

Medley (2005), for example, uses computer-mediated discussion with experts to help facilitate student learning.

> Computer-mediated discussions with the experts have challenged and motivated my students. They have learned how to formulate insightful questions. They feel it is a privilege to discuss issues with the author of their textbook or other prominent experts. They not only appreciate new sources of information to which the experts refer them but also realize that they need a broader knowledge base to participate appropriately in a discussion. This realization motivates them to read their textbook or other material more carefully and purposefully. (p. 73)

Whether face-to-face or virtual, ample time and opportunities for interaction among all stakeholders in a professional learning community are well advised.

Modeling Knowledge Construction and Creativity

Opportunities for a richer and more expanded knowledge base increase when a variety of PLC members are invited to share experiences and prior knowledge within the learning community. When teachers, students, parents, experts, community members, and others contribute to the learning environment, they are helping to construct meaning socially for that community. An effective constructivist environment, where contributions are made and learning is experienced by all, invites active learning rather than passivity and construction of knowledge rather than transmission of it.

Lev Vygotsky, a 20th-century psychologist from the former Soviet Union, is known for his work on sociocultural theory. Sociocultural theory supports the social construction of knowledge in a community of learners. One of the principles associated with sociocultural theory is guided participation, a type of apprenticeship in which tutors work side-by-side with learners, guiding them in the construction of knowledge. Tutors not only guide but participate jointly in the learning activity with the learner (Berger, 2008). In this setting, tutors are both facilitators of learning and learners themselves.

Vygotsky formulated the term "zone of proximal development" or ZPD: "the distance between the actual developmental level as determined between independent problem solving and the level of potential development as determined through problem solving under adult guidance or in collaboration with more capable peers" (1978, p. 86).

A classroom or PLC environment where all are learners and, at least to some degree, all are teachers is one that is ripe for growth and development. This environment allows for the social construction of knowledge and skills and elevates students to more than mere vessels waiting to receive transmitted knowledge.

Face-to-Face Learning

The classroom provides an ideal venue for modeling knowledge construction and creativity as teachers engage in guided participation with their students, colleagues, and others in the professional learning community. This will not likely happen apart from deliberate efforts to make this type of learning a routine event.

To be consistent with an inclusive professional learning community and to maximize learning by students and teacher, both face-to-face and virtual learning should include students, colleagues, and other stakeholders. In such an environment, teachers become students and students become teachers; experts become novices and novices become experts.

Learning with students is something that often occurs naturally as teachers guide their students. Teacher-student dialogue helps students connect concepts as teachers provide meaningful experiences and interactions, while teachers make sense and meaning from student contributions and learn from student experiences. Figure 1.9 demonstrates how, in guided participation, students become teachers and teachers become students.

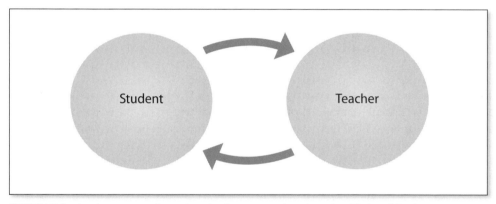

FIGURE 1.9 Student becomes teacher and teacher becomes student through guided participation.

Technology tools can help facilitate face-to-face learning where teachers can model knowledge construction and creativity through guided participation in a constructivist classroom environment. Although a multitude of practices can be used to help students become teachers and teachers become students, a few examples follow.

ICT-assisted project-based learning lessons can help teachers and students alike explore projects using digital and nondigital tools. Inviting students to explore topics of interest to them—topics that are relevant and meaningful—through ICT-assisted PBL allows teachers to capitalize on students' prior knowledge and skills. Teachers can participate in various phases of PBL and can demonstrate knowledge construction and creativity as they offer creative solutions and guided participation to students.

Teachers may get to know their students through interest inventories, learning-style inventories, and multiple-intelligence inventories (described previously in the NETS•T1a section). Teachers can help provide meaningful curricula that align with local and national standards based on student characteristics.[12]

Figure 1.10 demonstrates how teachers can use a variety of factors to help provide meaningful experiences for students.

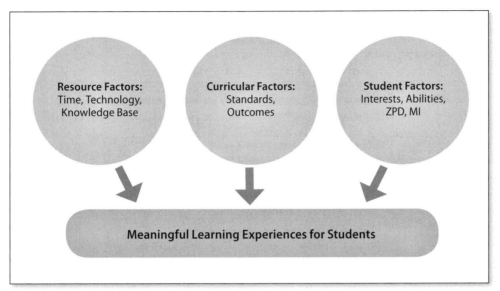

FIGURE 1.10 Factors that influence providing meaningful experiences to students.

Guided participation requires teachers to take an active role in guiding their students by participating in learning while leading students through their zones of proximal development. Teachers, too, have their own zones of proximal development (ZPDs) through which they can move and grow as professionals and individuals.

One way for students to grasp teachers' ZPDs is to observe teachers' movement through KWL charts. Teachers can create digital or printed KWL charts that both teacher and students can complete. Although teachers do not know everything, students are not always aware of this phenomenon. Teachers can share their KWL charts to show that, yes, they K (*know*) quite a bit about the topic at hand, but there is still much to learn. They can also discuss and share the processes that led them from the W (*what they wondered about or wanted to learn*) to the L (*what they learned*). This helps students witness the process of knowledge construction in which they, as active participants in the learning community, will likely have participated.

When assigning reflective blog assignments, teachers can create blogs themselves, and use their blogs as examples to students. They can allow and encourage comments from students with regard to teacher blogs. This can serve several purposes: from students' comments, teachers can assess whether students are grasping the blog content; teachers can learn from student feedback; and they can help students to reflect critically on teacher entries, giving students practice in critical reflection. Face-to-face discussions can follow to augment online dialogue.

Teachers can participate in many of the creative exercises they provide to their students. Simulations in which teachers participate will help students observe growth in their teachers and the process they use to learn and engage in creative solutions. Guided participation will allow teachers to model knowledge construction and creativity to their students.

As teachers plan lessons and select digital and nondigital resources for classroom use, they can share the process for how they selected these resources and why they decided against using other resources. They can demonstrate the selection process as a learning process and a reflective exercise.

Teachers can present some unexpected learning that took place as they conducted research for their lessons. They can demonstrate, for example, that they unexpectedly came upon excellent websites that clarified some misunderstandings they may have had or how they had an "aha" experience. Teachers can also share some newly learned skills that they acquired at a professional conference or workshop with other teachers to show that they are lifelong learners. Moreover, teachers may wish to share some creative works—such as paintings, writing, music—with students and explain the creative process as they know it and use it.

These examples clearly demonstrate that modeling knowledge construction and creativity is possible and can become routine practice in the classroom, allowing teachers opportunities to become students and students to become teachers.

Teachers can also model knowledge construction by fruitful face-to-face learning relationships with colleagues and others. For example, teachers are sometimes formally or informally assigned teacher mentors with whom they can learn through guided participation. Team teaching responsibilities also allow teaching colleagues to work together and learn from one another. In both of these cases, students are likely to see these collegial relationships played out in the classroom, hallways, lunchroom, and other areas of the school building.

Outside the classroom, teachers learn from other professionals through professional development workshops (see Chapter 5), seminars, and professional societies. Here again, teachers can share their own face-to-face learning with students upon their return to the classroom. Furthermore, local school district staff and local subject area experts can be invited to dialogue with students and teachers as they work through content and projects, opening up the knowledge base to teachers and students.

While face-to-face learning and knowledge construction can happen in the classroom, school, or school district with students and others, teacher learning can be expanded to the virtual environment to include those from different geographic regions, cultures, and professions.

Virtual Learning

Similar to face-to-face encounters, virtual interactions that lead to learning and growth both individually and collectively are abundant. Computer-mediated communication has the potential to bring together diverse populations that share a common goal and mission, but it is not without its challenges. Based on Trauth and Jessup's (2000) work, Stoll and Louis (2007) point out:

> Sustaining connections and community is made more complex by the explosion of technology, which permits the development of online groups that provide stimulating sources of information and safe, neutral arenas for support, but may also be unstable, more likely to involve imbalanced participation, and less amenable to the sustained, deep, reflective engagement that most of us associate with face-to-face relations that endure over time. (p. 8)

The study of computer-mediated learning communities has been explored with regard to social, political, and cultural factors, and in terms of the measurement of learning processes and interactions (Luppicini, 2002), but much is yet to be learned.[13] Yet, with careful attention to relationships and a focus on the mission of helping students learn, technology can play an important role in bringing together professional-learning-community members where all are capable of learning and growth.

Virtual learning communities (VLCs) or communities that exist in the virtual or blended environment generally use social learning as a means for growth and development. Networked learning involving VLCs emanates from two theoretical bases: (1) learning that involves cooperative or collaborative groups, based on the work of Vygotsky and the construction of knowledge, and (2) learning communities or communities based on sociocultural theory with a focus on the role that membership plays on the growth of an individual as a social being (Allan & Lewis, 2006).

Both orientations have something to offer teachers and, in the end, students. The more teachers learn from colleagues, parents, and others, and the more they share their knowledge with students, the more likely students will be able to witness modeling of knowledge construction and creativity.

Participation in social networks, such as Nings, professional societies, or special interest groups (SIGs), such as ISTE's mobile learning group, SIGML, or in managed communities of learners (see Allan & Lewis, 2006), allows teachers to learn from other professionals and contribute to the social community. Distance education (e.g., online learning) and e-learning (often associated with training rather than education) provide opportunities for virtual learning through webinars, course management systems, informational podcasts and other tools.

Most social networks allow users to post a blog or microblog. One way that teachers can learn in the virtual environment is to create dialogue-blogging opportunities. With dialogue blogging, teachers post blog entries and allow students from schools or districts different from their own to comment on blog content. In dialogue blogging, teachers learn from students who do not share their geographic boundaries or cultural heritage, and they can share what they have learned with their face-to-face students. In so doing, teachers are modeling their growth, awareness, and learning as citizens of the world.

Teachers can also connect with students in the virtual world by communicating with individual student e-pals. This relationship allows teachers to connect with students from other parts of their state, country, or world. As teachers communicate with these students, their own students will learn to appreciate how the teacher is growing in awareness, empathy, or some other sentiment.

Teachers who participate in virtual worlds, such as Second Life (http://secondlife.com), will likely learn much from other participants (known as "Second Lifers" in Second Life). They can invite their own students to observe their participation as a way of modeling their growth and learning as they socially construct content knowledge collectively with those outside their professional learning communities. In some cases, professional societies create virtual societies in which members can participate and learn. ISTE invites its members, for example, to participate in a virtual world and serve as volunteer docents who welcome new members and orient them to the virtual community.

Professional learning communities, too, might consider creating simulated professional learning communities in a virtual world where participants contribute to the growth and development of the community. In this way, they can see how virtual relationships play out and discover deficits that might need to be addressed in their real-world professional learning community. In such a virtual community, all members should be encouraged to contribute.

Learning about and contributing to a wiki is another way to show two-way learning. For example, helping to write an online text using wiki tools demonstrates a willingness to teach others in the global environment and to learn from others as they edit teacher entries and make helpful comments. The Wikimedia community Wikibooks (www.wikibooks.org) allows such collaboration. Here again, this process models knowledge construction and creativity to students.

Virtual learning with students, colleagues, and others provides teachers with opportunities for learning that, when freely shared with students, creates a classroom ripe for growth and development.

In Your Experience

As a student, have you ever engaged in guided participation with a teacher?

- If so, what did you learn, and what did you teach?

- If not, in what circumstances do you believe guided participation would have helped you learn a concept?

Section T1d Explorations

1. Create a blog using one of the resources described in this section. Request that your teacher and peers comment on your blog entries and, in turn, comment on their blog entries. What kinds of learning took place for you and those reading and commenting on your blog?

2. In narrative form, describe a classroom in which you would like to teach that welcomes exchanges of knowledge and experiences, where students can become teachers and teachers can become students. Create computer graphics to go along with your narrative.

3. Create a slidecast or podcast of the classroom you described in Exploration 2.

4. Suggest a wiki project in which your teacher, peers, and others can participate to share learning and experiences.

5. Make a list of digital and nondigital tools that you can use in your classroom to help facilitate face-to-face and virtual learning for students, teachers, and others in a professional learning community.

6. Explore Second Life to see how professional societies or professional learning communities are using the medium.

7. Make a list of individuals you think should be included in a professional learning community you would like to join. Describe how each might contribute to the community and how each person might learn, grow, and develop as a member.

Section T1d Review

Face-to-face and virtual learning can help teachers grow as individuals and as members of professional learning communities. While challenges exist to using digital tools to enhance learning with students, colleagues, parents, and others, the benefits of growth for teachers should be worth the effort exerted. Most important, when all members of the learning community are learning and teaching, the collective knowledge base grows and has the potential to improve and increase learning for students.

As teachers, when we allow ourselves to be learners alongside our students, we model what it is to be curious and open to learning. While revealing ourselves as fellow learners to students may at first seem a bit daunting, the benefits can be far-reaching and we can demonstrate in concrete ways how rewarding it is to be lifelong learners.

Chapter 1 Summary

In this chapter you became familiar with the processes and products related to creativity, you learned how digital and nondigital resources can be used to advance human creativity in the classroom, and you learned about ICT-assisted PBL as a way to prepare students to solve problems in the real world using collaborative tools. Finally, you learned how to model knowledge construction and creativity through face-to-face and virtual learning. Teachers need to deliberately create opportunities, select resources, and use strategies to promote a constructive classroom environment where these activities are possible. Though they may be daunted at first, teachers need to remember that they are not carrying the weight alone. Through collaboration and cooperation, they can share the responsibilities of educating students with all stakeholders in their professional learning community.

Chapter 1 Notes

1   For another alternative revision to Bloom's Taxonomy, see *The New Taxonomy of Educational Objectives* (2nd ed.) by Marzano & Kendall, 2006.

2   Unlike Bloom's original taxonomy, the hierarchical structure of the revised version contains less rigidity (Krathwohl, 2002).

3   Many of Howard Gardner's influential works can be found in *The Development and Education of the Mind: The Selected Works of Howard Gardner* (2006).

4   At the time of this writing, Gardner had not included existential or spiritual as intelligences. He has leaned toward including naturalist in the list of original seven intelligences and has considered including existential and spiritual intelligences (e.g., Gardner, 1999, p. 52). In Figure 1.3, the author has included naturalist and existential intelligences but not spiritual intelligence.

5   To learn more about brain research as it relates to learning, see Brown University's Brain Science website at www.brainscience.brown.edu/research/learning.html

6   To learn more about multiple intelligences and appropriate technologies to use with each, see McKenzie (2005). In this text you will learn to support intelligences through selections of media, software, the Internet, and various digital and nondigital resources.

7   **Problem-based learning vs. project-based learning.** *Problem-based learning,* which is also known as *PBL,* differs from *project-based learning.* According to Moursund (2007):

> A project in project-based learning need not be rooted in a specific problem that currently interests a lot of people. Thus, a project might be an exploration of food or medicine available to soldiers from the South and the North during the U.S. Civil War. Problem-based learning (also abbreviated as PBL) has students or teams of students working on specific problems. Quite often, the problems are quite specific to the course being taught or the discipline being studied. The goal is to develop a good solution to a specific problem. Problem-based learning has a number of the characteristics of project-based learning, but the goal is to produce a workable solution to a specific problem. (p. 33)

For more information on problem-based learning, see Moursund, 2007.

ICT-assisted PBL vs. IT-assisted PBL. Although *ICT-assisted PBL* and *IT-assisted PBL* (and *PBL-IT*) are similar, they differ in scope. The International ICT Literacy Panel (2002) described the difference and their use of the term *ICT* over *IT*:

> The panel has used ICT instead of IT (Information Technology). ICT is being used increasingly by global industry, international media, and academics to reflect the convergence between computer and communication technologies. Thus ICT can be viewed as a set of activities and technologies that fall into the union of IT and telecommunications. (p. 2)

8   Rodgers' (2002a) criteria were based on the work of 20th-century educator John Dewey.

9   Rodgers' (2002b) phases of reflection grew out of Dewey's conception of reflection.

10   Donna Ogle is credited with creating a K-W-L strategy sheet. For more information on the original model, see Ogle's 1986 *Reading Teacher* article, "K-W-L: A Teaching Model That Develops Active Reading of Expository Text."

11   Tiryakian (1973) writes of *meaningful entities*: "The subject's perceptions involve the transaction between the subject and the subject's field where things outside the subject are transformed into meaningful entities" (p. 195).

> Lowe describes *meaning* as "the sense given by our consciousness to lived experience" (1973, p. 129). To summarize this succinctly, when a subject experiences phenomena and perceives, meaning is possible. This transaction between the subject and the subject's field requires activity of the mind and body. In phenomenology, the mind and body are considered inseparable (Becker, 1992). (In Morphew, 1994, p. 9)

12   A word about standards is in order. Standards generally include outcomes or expectations, but they do not normally dictate how to facilitate the learning that will lead to the outcomes. Therefore, teachers generally have some degree of freedom about how they will teach to facilitate student outcomes. This is where teacher creativity—thinking outside the proverbial box—comes in.

13   See Luppicini's 2006 article for a review of computer-mediated communication research for education (available from www.springerlink.com/content/v023l4727u816016).

Chapter 1 References

Allan, B., & Lewis, D. (2006, November). The impact of membership of a virtual learning community on individual learning careers and professional identity. *British Journal of Educational Technology, 37*(6), 841–852. doi: 10.1111/j.1467-8535.2006.00661.x

Anderson, L. W., & Krathwohl, D. R. (Eds.). (2001). *A taxonomy for learning, teaching, and assessing: A revision of Bloom's Taxonomy of Educational Objectives.* (Abridged ed.). New York, NY: Addison Wesley Longman.

Armstrong T. (2009). *Multiple intelligences in the classroom* (3rd ed.). Alexandria, VA: Association for Supervision and Curriculum Development.

Balzac, F. (2006, May). Exploring the brain's role in creativity. *Neuropsychiatry Reviews, 7*(5), 19–20. Retrieved from www.creativitypost.com/science/creative_innovation_possible_brain_mechanisms1

Baum, S., Viens, J., & Slatin, B. (2005). *Multiple intelligences in the elementary classroom: A teacher's toolkit.* New York, NY: Teachers College Press.

Becker, C. S. (1992). *Living and relating: An introduction to phenomenology.* London, UK: Sage.

Berger, K. (2008). *The developing person through childhood and adolescence* (8th ed.). New York, NY: Worth Publishers.

Boss, S., & Krauss, J. (2007). *Reinventing project-based learning: Your field guide to real-world projects in the digital age.* Eugene, OR: International Society for Technology in Education.

Gardner, H. (1985). *The mind's new science: A history of the cognitive revolution.* New York, NY: Basic Books.

Gardner, H. (1989). *To open minds: Chinese clues to the dilemma of contemporary education.* New York, NY: Basic Books.

Gardner, H. (1989/2006). Chapter 15: The key in the key slot: Creativity in a Chinese key. In *The development and education of the mind: The selected works of Howard Gardner* (pp. 117–129). New York, NY: Routledge.

Gardner, H. (1995, November). Reflections on multiple intelligences: Myths and messages. *Phi Delta Kappan, 77*(3), 200–209.

Gardner, H. (1997). Norman Geschwind as a creative scientist. In S. Schacter & O. Devinsky (Eds.), *Behavioral neurology and the legacy of Norman Geschwind.* Philadelphia, PA: Lippincott Williams & Wilkins. Republished in 2006 in *The development and education of the mind: The selected works of Howard Gardner,* pp. 30–34. New York, NY: Routledge.

Gardner, H. (1999). *Intelligence reframed: Multiple intelligences for the 21st century.* New York, NY: Basic Books.

Gardner, H. (2006). *The development and education of the mind: The selected works of Howard Gardner.* New York, NY: Routledge.

Gross, M., & Do, E. (2009, June). Educating the new makers: Cross-disciplinary creativity. *Leonardo, 42*(3), 210–215. Cambridge, MA: MIT Press.

Hansen, D. (2005). Creativity in teaching and building a meaningful life as a teacher. *The Journal of Aesthetic Education, 39*(2), 57–68.

Hausman, C., Jarvie, I., & Rothenberg, A. (2009). Creativity. In Michael Kelly (Ed.), *Encyclopedia of aesthetics.* Retrieved May 26, 2009, from www.oxfordartonline.com.ezproxy.fairmontstate.edu/subscriber/article/opr/t234/e0136

Heilman, K. (2005). *Creativity and the brain.* New York, NY: Psychology Press.

Hmelo-Silver, C. (2004). Problem-based learning: What and how do students learn? *Educational Psychology Review, 16*(3), 246–266.

International ICT Literacy Panel. (2002). *Digital transformation: A framework for ICT literacy.* Princeton, NJ: Educational Testing Service. Retrieved January 23, 2012, from www.ets.org/research/policy_research_reports/ict-report

Krathwohl, D. (2002, September). A revision of Bloom's taxonomy: An overview. *Theory Into Practice, 41*(4), 212–218.

Lawson, B. (2002). CAD and creativity: Does the computer really help? *Leonardo, 35*(3), 327–331. doi:10.1162/002409402760105361

Lehrer, J. (2009). Unlocking the mysteries of the artistic mind. *Psychology Today, 42*(4), 72–77.

Lowe, D. M. (1973). Intentionality and the method of history. In M. Nathanson (Ed.), *Phenomenology and the social sciences, Vol. 2* (pp. 103–130). Evanston, IL: Northwestern University Press.

Luppicini, R. (2002). Toward a conversation system modeling research methodology for studying computer-mediated learning communities. *Journal of Distance Education, 17*(2), 87–101.

Luppicini, R. (2006). Review of computer mediated communication research for education. *Instructional Science, 35*(2), 141–185. DOI: 10.1007/s11251-006-9001-6; available from www.springerlink.com/content/v023l4727u816016

Marzano, R., & Kendall, J. (2006). *The new taxonomy of educational objectives* (2nd ed.). Thousand Oaks, CA: Corwin.

McKenzie, W. (2005). *Multiple intelligences and instructional technology* (2nd ed.). Eugene, OR: International Society for Technology in Education.

Medley, R. (2005). Inviting experts to class through computer-mediated discussions. *College Teaching, 53*(2), 71–74.

Morphew, V. N. (1994). *Change in meaning, change in action: A phenomenological study.* Unpublished doctoral dissertation. West Virginia University, Morgantown, WV.

Morphew, V. N. (2002). Web-based learning and instruction: A constructivist approach. In M. Khosrow-Pour (Ed.), *Web-based instructional learning* (pp. 1–15). Hershey, PA: IRM Press.

Morphew, V. N. (2009). Constructivist teaching and learning in a web-based environment. In P. Rogers, G. Berg, J. Boettecher, C. Howard, L. Justice, & K. Schenk (Eds.), *Encyclopedia of distance learning* (2nd ed.). pp. 418–424. Hershey, PA: Idea Group Publishing.

Moursund, D. (2003). *Project-based learning: Using information technology* (2nd ed.). Eugene, OR: International Society for Technology in Education.

Moursund, D. (2006a). ICT-assisted project-based learning: Planning a PBL lesson. Eugene, OR: University of Oregon. Retrieved from http://pages.uoregon.edu/~moursund/PBL/

Moursund, D. (2006b). *Introduction to using games in education: A guide for teachers and parents.* Eugene, OR: University of Oregon. Retrieved from http://pages.uoregon.edu/moursund/Books/Games/Games.pdf

Moursund, D. (2007). *Introduction to problem solving in the information age.* Eugene, OR: University of Oregon. Retrieved from http://pages.uoregon.edu/moursund/Books/IAE-PS/PS-in-IA.doc

Ogle, D. M. (1986). K-W-L: A teaching model that develops active reading of expository text. *Reading Teacher, 39,* 564–570.

Rodgers, C. (2002a). Defining reflection: Another look at John Dewey and reflective thinking. *Teachers College Record, 104*(4), 842–866.

Rodgers, C. (2002b). Seeing student learning: Teacher change and the role of reflection. *Harvard Educational Review, 72*(2), 230–253.

Stoll, L., & Louis, K., Eds. (2007). *Professional learning communities: Divergence, depth and dilemmas.* Berkshire, UK: McGraw-Hill.

Tiryakian, E. A. (1973). Sociology and existential phenomenology. In M. Natanson (Ed.), *Phenomenology and the social sciences, Vol. I* (pp. 187–222). Evanston, IL: Northwestern University Press.

Trauth, E., & Jessup, L. (2000) Understanding computer-mediated discussions: Positivist and interpretive analyses of group support system use. *MIS Quarterly, 24*(1), 43–79. Retrieved from www.eileentrauth.com/publications.html

Vincent, T. (2009). Podcasting for teachers & students. Retrieved from http://learninginhand.com/podcasting-booklet

Vygotsky, L. S. (1978). *Mind in society: The development of higher psychological processes.* M. Cole, V. John-Steiner, S. Scribner, & E. Souberman (Eds. & Trans). Cambridge, MA: Harvard University Press.

Wade, R. (1997). Reflection. In R.C. Wade (Ed.), *Community service-learning: A guide to including service in the public school curriculum* (p. 95). Albany, NY: SUNY Press.

Walters, J., & Gardner, H. (1986). The crystallizing experience: Discovery of an intellectual gift. In R. Sternberg & J. Davidson (Eds.), *Conceptions of giftedness* (pp. 306–331). New York, NY: Cambridge University Press.

nets·t2

Design and Develop Digital-Age Learning Experiences and Assessments

STANDARD IN BRIEF

Teachers design, develop, and evaluate authentic learning experiences and assessments incorporating contemporary tools and resources to maximize content learning in context and to develop the knowledge, skills, and attitudes identified in the NETS·S.

PERFORMANCE INDICATORS

Teachers:

a.   design or adapt relevant learning experiences that incorporate digital tools and resources to promote student learning and creativity

b.   develop technology-enriched learning environments that enable all students to pursue their individual curiosities and become active participants in setting their own educational goals, managing their own learning, and assessing their own progress

c.   customize and personalize learning activities to address students' diverse learning styles, working strategies, and abilities using digital tools and resources

d.   provide students with multiple and varied formative and summative assessments aligned with content and technology standards and use resulting data to inform learning and teaching

FACILITATING TECHNOLOGY-ENHANCED EXPERIENCES

In order to design or adapt meaningful learning experiences using digital and other resources, teachers must be reflective, well-informed practitioners. They must be aware of their students' and school's needs, cognizant of best practices, and willing to modify teaching strategies to best meet the needs of their students.

Every class and every school presents unique learning challenges. Some schools have plentiful technology resources while others have few. Some schools have great ethnic and cultural diversity; others have little. Some schools serve urban populations, and others serve suburban or rural students. While it may seem simpler to offer a prescription for the one right way to design or adapt meaningful learning experiences to promote student learning and creativity, this would be naïve and ill-informed. What works for one school may or may not work for another. To extrapolate further, what works for one school one year may not work exactly the same the next year. The fluid nature of the teaching context allows teachers ample opportunities to use their own higher-order thinking and planning skills to create optimum learning experiences.

This well-known adage attributed to Confucius clearly applies here: "Give a man a fish, and he will eat for a day. Teach a man to fish, and he will eat for a lifetime." Chapter 2 will not offer a one-size-fits-all prescription for promoting student learning and creativity. Rather, it will offer a process for coming to the best-informed decisions for designing and adapting meaningful learning experiences, based on the unique circumstances in which teachers find themselves.

This chapter helps inform teachers by introducing resources that lead to research on best practices. It also provides suggestions for using these resources to make informed decisions. Furthermore, action research is introduced as a way of addressing specific classroom issues that can lead to informed action for providing meaningful experiences to students.

Teachers will also learn strategies for managing student learning in classrooms with limited and extensive technology resources. Even with limited technology resources, teachers have many opportunities to present technology-enhanced lessons that maximize student learning. With greater resources and effective planning, they can offer their students plentiful learning experiences that should help them in and outside the classroom.

This chapter also presents strategies for planning and implementing technology-enhanced experiences that address technology standards. Teachers will learn about ways to support student-centered strategies that acknowledge diversity. They will also become familiar with ways to apply technology to encourage higher-order thinking skills and creativity, and to try strategies for managing learning activities in the context of technology-enhanced classrooms. By becoming familiar with specific strategies and creating plans for implementation, teachers' goals of maximizing student learning can be realized.

LEARNER OUTCOMES

The reading and assignments presented in Chapter 2 should help you:

- Design or modify meaningful learning experiences that promote learning and creativity

- Construct technology-enriched learning environments that help students become active and aware participants in their own growth and development

- Differentiate instruction using digital tools to meet the diverse needs of students using digital tools

- Provide a variety of assessments to students and use the results to inform teaching and learning

NETS·T2a

Design or Adapt Relevant Learning Experiences That Incorporate Digital Tools and Resources to Promote Student Learning and Creativity

Successful teachers know that it takes the work of many people to provide the best possible education to all students. They know that the contributions of teachers, students, parents, administrators, community leaders, lawmakers, and many others all make for safe and effective schools. In Chapter 1, professional learning communities (PLCs) and virtual learning communities (VLCs) were introduced as communities of learners that can expand the knowledge base available to students. As participants in PLCs and VLCs, researchers also serve an important role in the education of students because their work helps inform effective teaching practices. In this section you will learn how to become familiar with best practices for using technology-enhanced lessons in teaching and how to apply them to your own teaching practice. More specifically, you will learn how to construct meaningful learning experiences that promote student learning and creativity.

Using Research to Inform Teaching

Many successful people humbly credit others with helping them to achieve great things, affirming, as Isaac Newton once did, that, "If I have seen further it is by standing on the shoulders of giants." Many great teachers attribute their success to the giants in their own lives, such as former teachers, coaches, parents, and mentors. Some of the often-unsung giants in our day are those educators who sometimes work behind the scenes researching the most effective ways to maximize learning for all students. Their work helps the practices of teachers across the country and world, improving education for all students.

Using research findings to inform teaching practice begins with locating reputable, peer-reviewed and editorially reviewed research. Peer-reviewed research is research that has been scrutinized by peers familiar with research methods and the field in which the research is conducted. In the peer-review process, peers review the research methods and findings and critique the work with a critical eye. Normally, several peers from across the country or globe are involved in reviewing the work, and they are responsible for making recommendations to publish or not publish the research findings. Often peer-reviewed research is blind-reviewed, which helps eliminate bias by removing the identities of researchers in the review process. Using peer-reviewed research helps ensure that teachers are using reputable research findings to inform their teaching practices.

Studies, reflections, and other works that are reviewed by an editorial board rather than undergoing a peer-review process can also provide valuable insights for teaching. Work published in this manner may be of a more reflective nature and offer more in the way of "food for thought" than some of the work published in peer-reviewed journals. The work has typically undergone some type of editorial process and may be very well written, with improvements made to the original submission. There is a place for using this type of edited work to inform teaching. Just be aware that the review process, either peer or editorial, will yield different types of work.[1]

Locating Research

Peer-reviewed research is relatively easy to locate. Professional societies typically publish one or more publications that highlight peer-reviewed research in their field. They frequently host professional conferences that feature peer-reviewed presentations by researchers. This, once again, underscores the importance of membership in a professional society. Members are often eligible to receive one or more peer-reviewed journals and attend professional conferences sponsored by the society.

Some professional societies are using peer-reviewed websites to showcase findings. Members may be provided with a password for accessing the online publication; however, in some cases access may be granted to nonmembers. When professional societies publish online peer-reviewed publications, locating articles is often as straightforward as performing a simple search (e.g., for keyword or author) on the society's website.

Another web-based resource that can be used to locate peer-reviewed research, whether published through a society or not, is through the use of an online database. Using these databases allows teachers to easily locate numerous peer-reviewed and non-peer-reviewed research articles quickly through basic and advanced searches typically provided on the database website.

Many of these databases provide access to full-text articles from journals, magazines, newspapers, and other serial publications. Accessing the work typically requires a password and subscription. Libraries are excellent sources for these types of online databases, also known as indexes. Teachers should check with their school administrator and library media specialist to see what is available to them as teachers and consider the sites in Resource List 2.1.

RESOURCE LIST 2.1 ▪ Online databases

Subscription-based sites for articles in the education field

Academic Search Premier: www.ebscohost.com/academic/academic-search-premier

Education Full Text: www.ebscohost.com/wilson

General OneFile: www.gale.cengage.com/onefile

Nonsubscription databases

Education Index: www.educationindex.com

Education Planet: www.educationplanet.com

Google Scholar: http://scholar.google.com

Peer-reviewed and editorially reviewed publications are not the sole sources for locating best practices. Other sources include advanced coursework and professional development offered by school districts, which often bring to teachers' attention the best practices in teaching, based on reputable research findings. Textbooks and articles used in advanced coursework and professional-development opportunities often summarize research findings and present them in a well-written, palatable manner so that educators can quickly glean meaningful applications from them. For example, school- and district-based professional-development workshops are often provided to teachers before the start of a school year to help acquaint them with recent developments in brain research, emerging technologies, and so forth.

Commercially available publications that are field- or grade-specific often share the action research and reflections submitted by teachers in classrooms across the country. Although normally reviewed by an editorial board rather than by peers, the work is often well written and contains valuable insights for teachers. Magazines and journals of this type are located in bookstores and increasingly are being published as online magazines (also known as e-zines or zines) or journals. Figure 2.1 illustrates some of the sources for locating best practices.

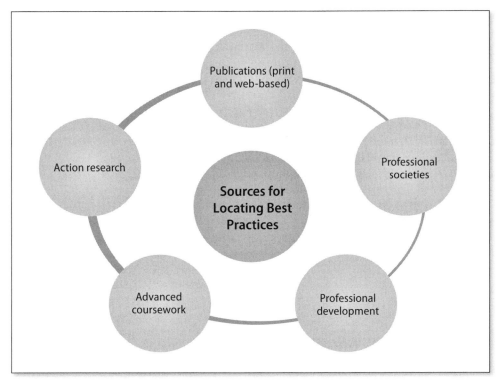

FIGURE 2.1 Sources for locating best practices.

More specific to this text, a number of sources are available that can lead to research findings related specifically to technology and teaching. Resource List 2.2 includes the addresses for some of the many professional societies, organizations, and offices that can help teachers locate best practices for integrating technology into their teaching practices. If several teachers are trying to locate the best ways to use MP3s in their instructional practices, for example, they can visit one or more of the listed websites and search for articles, resources, professional development opportunities and other helpful items related to the use of MP3 players in education. In this way, they can make informed decisions before investing time, money, and other resources that schools scarcely have in abundance.

Similarly, if a school is considering adopting a laptop policy for students, before doing so teachers can visit a number of societies and locate articles or references to research showing the pros, cons, implications, and best practices associated with laptop policies and usage. Here again, becoming aware of best practices helps teachers make the most of what is available to them.

RESOURCE LIST 2.2 ▪ Associations for locating technology in teaching best practices

Association for the Advancement of Computing in Education (AACE): www.aace.org

Association for Educational Communications and Technology (AECT): www.aect.org

Center for Applied Special Technology (CAST): www.cast.org

Center for Technology in Learning (CTL): http://ctl.sri.com

Computer-Using Educators (CUE): www.cue.org

EDUCAUSE: www.educause.edu

National School Boards Association (NSBA) Technology Leadership Network : www.nsba.org/tln

Institute for Learning Technologies (ILT): www.ilt.columbia.edu

International Society for Technology in Education (ISTE): www.iste.org

What Works Clearinghouse—U.S. Department of Education, Institute of Education Sciences (DOE-IES): http://ies.ed.gov/ncee/wwc

U.S. Department of Education, Office of Education Technology (DOE-OET): www.ed.gov/about/offices/list/os/technology

International Technology and Engineering Educators Association (ITEA): www.iteaconnect.org

The Sloan Consortium (Sloan-C): http://sloanconsortium.org

Society for Information Technology & Teacher Education (SITE): http://site.aace.org

Technology & Innovation in Education (TIE): www.tie.net

Resource List 2.3 shows specific print and electronic publications that teachers may find especially helpful in locating best practices for using technology in teaching. The list has been intentionally kept general, but be aware that subject- and grade-specific publications are also available with regard to integrating instructional technology.

RESOURCE LIST 2.3 ▪ Print and electronic publications for technology in teaching best practices

AACE Journal: www.editlib.org/j/AACEJ

Educational Technology: http://people.uis.edu/rschr1/et/blogger.html

Educational Technology Research and Development: www.aect.org/Intranet/Publications

Learning & Leading with Technology (L&L): www.iste.org
  (click on Learn and then Publications to locate)

Journal of Educational Multimedia and Hypermedia: www.editlib.org/j/JEMH

Journal of Educational Technology & Society: www.ifets.info/others

Journal of Information Technology Education: http://jite.org

Journal of Interactive Learning Research: www.editlib.org/j/JILR

Journal of Research on Technology in Education (JRTE): www.iste.org
  (click on Learn and then Publications to locate)

Journal of Special Education Technology: www.tamcec.org/jset

Journal of Technology Education: http://scholar.lib.vt.edu/ejournals/JTE/

Information Technology and Disabilities E-Journal: http://people.rit.edu/easi/itd.htm

Information Technology in Childhood Education: www.editlib.org/j/ITCE

International Journal of Educational Telecommunications: www.editlib.org/j/IJET

International Journal on e-Learning: www.editlib.org/j/IJEL

Meridian: A Kindergarten Through High School Information and Communication Technologies Journal: www.ncsu.edu/meridian

Tech & Learning: www.techlearning.com

Children's Technology & Engineering: www.iteaconnect.org/Publications/t&c.htm

TechTrends: www.aect.org/intranet/Publications/index.asp *(scroll down to the second heading)*

Technology and Engineering Teacher: www.iteaconnect.org/Publications/ttt.htm

WebNet Journal: Internet Technologies, Applications & Issues: www.editlib.org/j/WEBNETJ

Applying Best Practices

It is not enough to know what research says about teaching and learning; teachers need to be able to apply this knowledge if it is going to help their students. Research (Marzano, 2003) suggests that the impact of individual teachers on student achievement is potentially greater than even school-level factors.[2] More specifically, Marzano identifies three teacher-level factors—instructional strategies, classroom management, and classroom curriculum design—that contribute to student achievement.

Applying best practices to teachers' own teaching practices involves knowing their students and their students' needs. Starting from that point, teachers can enlist the help of research to see the best way of providing meaningful lessons so that students' needs are met.

Looking to peer-reviewed research is like looking to history to inform one's actions of today. Be aware, however, that history may not repeat itself under different circumstances. The same is true for the results determined through research: although research yields valuable insights into best practices for teaching and learning, it would generally be an error to consider the findings definitive for a specific research question. Researchers attempt to control as many factors as possible in investigations so that the independent and dependent variables are clearly identified and defined. In the real world, however, this is often not possible. When dealing with human subjects—namely students—any number of factors can cause the research findings to be skewed or misleading. It is important to keep this in mind when applying research findings to teaching practices.

In editorially reviewed publications, the work is sometimes the result of action research performed by teachers in their own classrooms or reflections and ideas based on their own experiences. Using their work to inform your teaching supports the constructivist perspective of construction of knowledge.[3] Here again, what works for one teacher in his or her classroom may or may not work with another teacher's unique circumstances. Furthermore, as should be expected, recommendations for best practices will be modified as new insights are discovered and shared with the education community. What locating best practice research can undoubtedly do, however, is provide a springboard for trying new instructional strategies, managing classrooms effectively, and designing classroom curricula to reach all students.

Action Research in the Classroom

The research of others serves an important role in informing teaching practices, but teachers' own research should not be neglected. Reflective teachers regularly perform research investigations when they use trial and error to see what strategies work for students and when they use assessment and evaluation data to make modifications to their teaching. Recording, analyzing, and making sense of the data teachers collect will help them make informed decisions in their teaching practices.[4]

Gillies (2009) describes three steps in action research. The first step involves identifying a topic or focus of inquiry. The second step is collecting and analyzing data, such as student records, test scores, and retention rates. The third step is action planning based on the findings in the second step. When teachers modify their teaching strategies based on analyses of data, they are following the process of action research.

Although some data are readily collectible, other data need to be generated. For example, teachers may track changes in student learning based on changes in their instructional approaches. Newly generated data (such as test scores, portfolio artifacts, perceptions) following these changes can help teachers select future action; they can continue, modify, or discard the instructional approach. Action research should ideally be a continuous one that helps teachers improve their teaching effectiveness.

Not only can classroom research help teachers become better, more-informed educators, but if they share their results with others through presentations, publications, or word-of-mouth, they can help other teachers do the same. This is where teachers' reciprocal roles in the educational community come full circle; the research they use from others informs their teaching practices, and their teaching practices inform research. Figure 2.2 shows this relationship.

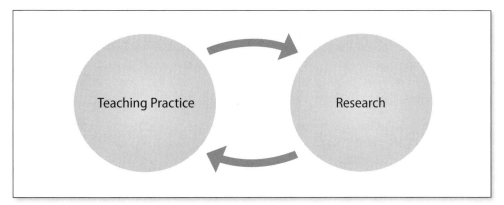

FIGURE 2.2 Research informs teaching, and teaching informs research.

In addition to informing instructional strategies, action research can inform teachers' classroom management and design of classroom curricula.

Working to improve these three teacher-level factors is challenging when resources are limited, but improvement is not impossible. For example, numerous challenges present themselves when technology resources are limited, and management of resources will need to be modified so that all students have access.

Managing Student Learning Experiences

As noted earlier, effectively managing classrooms is one of the teacher-level factors that contributes to student achievement (Marzano, 2003). Using technology effectively in classrooms to promote student learning and creativity presents its challenges. One of the more obvious challenges is that in some classrooms, technology is either lacking or outdated. Even with limited technology resources, however, many opportunities exist to present technology-enhanced lessons that maximize student learning. For those classrooms with extensive and up-to-date technology, effective management of resources can help teachers offer their students plentiful learning experiences that should help them in and outside the classroom.

Planning for Learning with Limited Technology Resources in the Classroom

Depending on many factors, teachers may find themselves in classrooms with limited, adequate, or extensive technology resources. With creativity and good planning, they can effectively use whatever technology resources are available to enhance student learning experiences.

In a classroom with limited technology resources, teachers will need to plan and manage student learning experiences carefully to ensure that all students have opportunities to benefit from the technology available.

One way to manage student learning is through the use of a well-planned learning station. A learning station is more than simply a computer located somewhere off to itself in a classroom. Learning stations should be designed to be interactive in nature, attractive to students, and situated so that students working at the station are not disturbed or disturbing to other students.

When deciding where to set up a learning station in a classroom, teachers should consider all the accessibility, assistive technology, and ergonomic issues (discussed in detail in Chapter 4). They will want to ensure that the station is accessible, usable, safe, and comfortable for all students. They should also consider what types of technology resources will be available at the station. If teachers have one computer, one tape recorder, and one computer game, for example, they will need to provide ample room so that one or more students can use the station effectively.

If possible and practical, teachers might consider moving the station close to a bulletin board that can be made into an interactive bulletin board. On the bulletin board, they can have handouts in folder pockets that contain directions for the activities students are supposed to complete at the station. These directions can also contain the grading scheme (e.g., rubrics, contracts) to be used to assess student learning. When appropriate, teachers can use separate folders of handouts explaining answers or detailed explanations for the work students perform that they may use after they complete their work. Furthermore, they may have some enrichment activities available for students in the event that they complete their work early.

Other items that can be included on the bulletin board might be the classroom technology use policy in an enlarged form. Perhaps teachers can leave a portion of the bulletin board to display exemplary student work. If this is done, teachers should be aware of their schools' and districts' policies regarding the use of student work. For example, some schools consider it a breach of confidentiality to display student work that identifies names and grades earned.[5]

To ensure that all students have access to the learning station, a rotation schedule should be established that allows students to use the station at regular, timed intervals. In some instances, depending on space and other conditions, cooperative groups of students can work together in the station and complete assignments during their scheduled time. By using cooperative groups in this manner, teachers can increase the frequency and amount of time students spend in the learning station. At the same time, students can benefit from effective cooperative-group practices.

At the station, the technology-enhanced assignments may be numerous and varied. One student-centered, effective strategy for creating technology-enhanced learning stations is to use WebQuests. According to the WebQuest homepage (www.webquest.org), the WebQuest model was first developed by Bernie Dodge with Tom March in 1995 and has grown into a widely used, technology-enhanced approach to constructivist learning. Dodge (1997, para. 2) describes a WebQuest as "an inquiry-oriented activity in which some or all of the information that learners interact with comes from resources on the Internet, optionally supplemented with videoconferencing."

Dodge writes there are six critical attributes of a WebQuest:

- an introduction

- a task

- a set of information sources

- a description of the process

- some guidance

- a conclusion (1997, para. 6)

WebQuests provide just enough structure to help students move progressively through an assignment, but they offer opportunities to explore the topic further in a more open-ended way. They can be completed alone or in cooperative groups and provide an excellent way of enhancing critical-thinking skills using a technology-enhanced approach.

Technology-enhanced lessons that utilize scavenger hunts are also appropriate for learning stations. Having an answer sheet that later is available to students helps them check their work and better understand any errors in their work or the processes they used to locate items. There are, of course, times when having easily accessible answers to student assignments is not an effective form of instruction. Once again, teachers must make informed decisions with regard to when this is and is not appropriate.

Having students help create assignments for the learning station can also be an effective strategy for creating student-centered, technology-enhanced learning experiences. Students can create WebQuests, scavenger hunts, crossword puzzles (generated using puzzle software), and other assignments for peers. Creation of peer assignments helps enhance and reinforce a number of student skills and higher-level thinking.

When using tutorials, problem-solving software, or integrated learning systems (ILSs) to promote creativity, a learning station may be a good venue for using these types of technology in a classroom with limited resources. Again, it is critical that teachers develop and use a rotation schedule that allows all students to experience learning in a technology-enhanced environment. Although a classroom with limited resources is not ideal and may require additional effort to manage so that all students benefit, students deserve this extra effort. If technology resources are less than desirable, remember that funding possibilities for acquiring additional, better, and more appropriate technology are available.

In addition to creating a learning station in a classroom with limited resources, teachers can use a computer-projecting device (e.g., computer projector, overhead LCD panel) in instruction to demonstrate technology use or to use interactively for whole-class instruction. For example, students can help the teacher develop a PowerPoint presentation on a given topic by taking turns at the computer while the teacher projects the image where all can see. If one MP3 player with speakers is available, the teacher can help students follow along collectively while listening to an audiobook. Likewise, a teacher can also use a projected image and have students interact with the class on traditional tools, such as a chalkboard or whiteboard, while the teacher operates the computer or other technology.

Teachers can use projecting devices with both first-order effects, such as those just described, or with second-order effects. As noted in Chapter 1, first-order effects amplify a task, and second-order effects require students to use higher-level thinking (Moursund, 2003). Students can collectively and collaboratively participate in simulations and computer games, for example. Moreover, students can use projecting devices with ICT-assisted PBL to project the various stages of project development as they unfold.

It may be apparent by now that having limited resources does not excuse teachers from using technology regularly in their classrooms to enhance instruction. If teachers become short on ideas, they should remember that they are part of a professional learning community (PLC), and they should consult other teachers, administrators, and technology specialists in their school or district. School library and media specialists are also excellent sources of ideas for using technology. Collaboration with all members in the PLC or virtual learning community (VLC) should yield plentiful ideas.

Planning for Learning with Adequate Technology Resources in the Classroom

The classroom with adequate technology resources has several advantages over the classroom with one computer and limited resources. One of the greatest advantages is that by increasing technology resources, greater frequency of use and increased amounts of time can be allocated for students to learn in a technology-enhanced learning environment.

In this setting, teachers may wish to apply some of the same strategies used with limited resources. For example, they can create several learning stations, with the same or different assignments, and set up a rotation schedule that allows all students to use the resources available. As with one computer in the classroom and limited resources, they may want to consider using both individual and cooperative group-rotation schedules. Furthermore, they can use projecting devices to lead technology-enhanced instruction and have cooperative groups follow along with instruction at their assigned learning stations.

If teachers are using tutorials, problem-solving software, or integrated learning systems in instruction, having several stations set up around the room may be a reasonable and effective way of providing access to all students to learn using these methods. WebQuests, scavenger hunts, peer-teaching, and other strategies described earlier can also work well with several computers and adequate technology resources.

Additional technology resources provide further opportunities to teach using technology-enhanced means. If interactive whiteboards or similar interactive technology tools are available, using technology to enhance instruction becomes easy and convenient. Many lessons can be enhanced when student interaction is introduced. Instead of the teacher being center stage, students can move front and center, participate in the teaching-learning experience by answering questions on the interactive whiteboard, or ask questions of peers. In some cases, students can lead instruction based on assigned research of a topic. Some may argue that the same can be done using the traditional chalkboard or whiteboard, but with an interactive whiteboard, such as SMART Boards (http://smarttech.com) or Mimio Boards (www.mimio-boards.com), students can toggle between work produced on computers or other technology, interjecting writing and computations as well.

If portable word-processing keyboards, such as NEO 2 (www.neo-direct.com), are available, students can take notes or make in-seat computations and later transfer work to a computer for more permanent storage. They can also share their work with others through projected images of their work.

When portable computer games are available, students can work independently and in cooperative groups to complete assignments and simulations. Having a schedule for rotation, once again, will help ensure that all students have an opportunity to use technology resources.

Some of the other technology resources that may be available in a classroom with several computers and adequate technology might be handheld calculators, tablets, personal digital assistants (PDAs), MP3 players, smartphones, book readers, and other portable technology. In this case, it would be wise not only to have a rotation schedule, but also a sign-out/sign-in sheet that students use to show they checked out and returned technology resources.

Whatever technology resources are available, they should be accessible and usable by all students, available on a rotation basis, used individually and cooperatively when appropriate, and accounted for through sign-out/sign-in sheets. The work accomplished and the learning gained by students through the technology resources should also help them meet the learning outcomes established in long-term and short-term plans and exemplify professionally defendable, evidence-based instruction.

Planning for Learning with Extensive Technology Resources in the Classroom

When extensive technology resources are available to students, teachers can use some of the same principles discussed above for creating learning stations, rotation schedules, sign-out/sign-in sheets, and the like. In a classroom where every student has continuous access to all technology resources, such as in a well-equipped technology-laboratory classroom, teachers can capitalize on this availability by individualizing instruction even more through differentiated instruction (DI). When using DI, teachers can use some of the ideas discussed in Chapter 4 to determine how each student will best be served. Based on teacher assessment and planning, some students may be using tutorials while others are using integrated learning systems or computer simulations. This is no doubt a challenge, but once teachers have established what technology resources would best help their students learn and begin their individual instruction, teachers will be able to realize their role as facilitator or oft-described "guide on the side" (rather than "sage on the stage"). After the initial set-up and planning, teachers will still need to monitor student learning to make sure students are progressing through the technology-enhanced assignments. Teachers need to review, update, and modify student-learning plans continuously, but the majority of teachers' efforts must be accomplished upfront.

In some cases in a classroom with many computers and extensive technology resources, all students will be working on the same assignment. This greatly simplifies teachers' work. Teachers should be sure to consider opportunities when students can work cooperatively even though they might ordinarily work independently. If computers are networked, cooperative group work can be used through networking. Even if computers are not networked, secure web-based networking sites can be used for student collaboration. Whether computers are networked or not, it is still a good idea to allow students to work cooperatively face-to-face on occasion to give them an additional way to interact.

Having extensive technology resources is only an advantage to students if teachers fully utilize resources and ensure fair and equitable access and use by all students. If technology resources are extensive but still not available for each student, it is important to set up a rotation schedule and sign-out/sign-in process so that teachers can keep track of all resources and so that students know that they are accountable. If all students have their own resources in the classroom, they should still be assigned resources and held accountable for what teachers assign them. This not only helps teachers keep track of resources, but it also helps enhance students' character development and provides teachers with data on what technologies are being used by students.

In a well-equipped classroom, there will be times when teachers want to lead whole-class instruction. By using a projector connected to technology resources and using interactive teaching techniques that allow students to participate and share in the teaching-learning experience, teachers can highlight what students are learning individually or cooperatively, in ICT-assisted PBL lessons, in collaboration with others in and outside the class, and so forth. This collective, whole-class experience, along with individual and cooperative learning experiences, will give students opportunities to learn in a number of different ways and through various interactions.

To help monitor what students are viewing in a class with multiple computers, teachers might consider using software such as SMART Sync (go to http://smarttech.com/us, select Education; then scroll through the products to find SMART Sync). This allows teachers to view thumbnail images of a student's computer screen to monitor student activity within a laboratory setting while teachers remain at their own computer stations. When possible and appropriate, they should also make regular and unexpected rounds throughout the room so that students know they are monitoring their work and actions.

While it is impossible to anticipate every combination of hardware and software available in a classroom that has many computers and is extensively equipped with technology-resources, the main idea is to use various grouping strategies (whole, cooperative groups, and individual) and apply the same criteria discussed earlier for an adequately equipped classroom to design or adapt learning experiences that promote student learning and creativity.

Individualizing Instruction through Differentiated Instruction

Individualizing instruction through differentiated instruction (DI) involves creating or modifying learning experiences that meet the specific needs of individual students. Hall (2002) introduces DI as a way to meet the diverse needs of students:

> Not all students are alike. Based on this knowledge, differentiated instruction applies an approach to teaching and learning so that students have multiple options for taking in information and making sense of ideas. The model of differentiated instruction requires teachers to be flexible in their approach to teaching and adjusting the curriculum and presentation of information to learners rather than expecting students to modify themselves for the curriculum. Classroom teaching is a blend of whole-class, group, and individual instruction. Differentiated instruction is a teaching theory based on the premise that instructional approaches should vary and be adapted in relation to individual and diverse students in classrooms. (p. 2)

One way to help promote individualized instruction is to create and use individual learning plans (ILPs) for each student.[6] Some states, districts, and schools are creating ILPs for identified students, such as at-risk students (Education Commission of the States, 2007a), and others for all students (Education Commission of the States, 2007b). Some are developed to better prepare students for the future (Kentucky Department of Education, n.d.), and others for any number of reasons, though primarily aimed at enhancing student learning through individualized instruction.

Cookson (2006) identifies some of the benefits of ILPs:

> I've worked closely with teachers who develop an individual learning plan for each student in their class and pursue that plan throughout the year. It's been my experience that those classrooms that emphasize individual instruction outperform other classes with amazing regularity. Many commentators treat education as though it were a wholesale business; education is intensely personal and, following the analogy, is best when it's retailed rather than mass-produced. As you work with your students, try to imagine their individual genius and remember there is research evidence that experts are made, not born. Very often a student who is acting out is seeking attention or crying for help. When we find something he or she is truly good at, many of the symptoms associated with his or her disruptive behavior are either minimized or disappear. (p. 16)

Teachers may initially discard this idea, thinking that creating ILPs for each student is simply not realistic and manageable, but this need not be the case. How extensive the ILP is depends on many factors, including purpose, student needs, parental involvement, administrative support, and resources (including time), to name a few.

Some specific ways for teachers to manage ILPs effectively is to create a computer-based or hardbound folder for each student. Each folder may contain such items as a plan for success, select student work that documents the objectives of the student's ILP (based on state or national standards, for example), and records of meetings/interactions with parents, guidance counselors, teachers, and others. Depending on teachers' and students' unique situations, teachers may wish to keep complete student portfolios created by each student and other significant artifacts, such as photos of students engaged in learning and anecdotal records of student progress.

It is easy to see how technology can significantly help teachers manage the paperwork involved with keeping these records. If teachers create databases of students prior to the opening of the school year, they can then export student names to an appropriate program and print off labels shortly after school begins. "No show" students' names can simply be deleted, and new names can be easily added to the database. It is important to have extra folders on hand so that teachers can create folders for new students as they arrive throughout the year.

Typically, secondary school teachers have greater numbers of students they teach throughout the day. Even with 100 or more students, recordkeeping can be managed effectively if teachers are organized and prepared. Hardbound file folders need to be conveniently stored for teacher (not student) access. A file cabinet or rolling crate that adequately holds folders or even a sturdy cardboard box can be used. Records must be securely stored and maintained so that confidentiality can be observed.

Teachers who do not wish to keep hard copies of files can create individual folders on their computer for each student. If they have a scanner or digital camera, they can scan or photograph artifacts that would normally be filed in hard folders. Having ILPs saved on their computer allows teachers to easily update records and make any necessary changes. As teachers become more experienced, they will learn what system works best for them and what helps facilitate individualized learning. Some school systems are using management systems, such as TaskStream (www.taskstream.com), to allow teachers and administrators to create folios of their students, maintain records, and document student achievement of standards and objectives. My-iPlan (www.my-iplan.com) describes itself as "a new, dynamic web-based individual learning plan (ILP) designed to support the 21st century learner."

Within the students' ILPs will likely be many of the technologies that have been described. The use of tutorials and integrated learning systems may be in one student's folder but, for another, simulation software may be the primary technology used. Keep in mind that whichever technology would best foster success for that student should be included in the student's ILPs.

Depending on the age and developmental level of the students, teachers should consider setting aside time to meet with individual students to discuss their progress. If this is not feasible, times should be scheduled for students to reflect and report on their progress through journal entries or other means. It is critical that teachers, students, and parents, when appropriate, participate in the process and realize their roles and responsibilities.[7]

Cooperative Learning Strategies

One of the purposes of education is to provide opportunities for students to experience and practice cooperation. According to the Framework for 21st Century Learning (Partnership for 21st Century Skills, 2009), 21st-century students must be able to communicate and collaborate with others and think critically about issues both locally and globally.

Cooperation involves respecting the roles and contributions of all involved in a collective pursuit. If students are expected to graduate from secondary or post-secondary education ready to work effectively in a global economy, it is imperative that their education provide them with opportunities and experiences to practice working effectively with others.

Cooperative learning models promote cooperation among members of a group toward a set of goals or outcomes. Teachers set clear expectations and assign students to small groups based on various factors. Cooperative learning groups give students opportunities to work with a wide variety of people. These heterogeneous groups work together cooperatively to achieve a common goal, such as those of ICT-assisted PBL lessons or expectations set by the teacher. Interactions among students, with appropriate and limited assistance from the teacher, help students rely more fully on the members of their group for success. In a typical cooperative group, each group member is assigned a particular role that is made known to all members of the group. Teachers may provide students with some type of role identification (e.g., stand-up signs) so that all students are made continuously aware of roles and responsibilities. Each role is critical to the success of the cooperative group.

Books, workshops, conferences, and research have been devoted to the implementation and study of cooperative learning. Resource List 2.4 highlights two websites where more can be learned about cooperative learning.[8]

RESOURCE LIST 2.4 ▪ Models of cooperative learning

The Cooperative Learning Center at the University of Minnesota: www.co-operation.org

> Robert T. Johnson and David W. Johnson, co-directors of the Center, are well-known for their work with cooperative learning. Links to content and resources on cooperative learning are located on their site.

Successes for All Foundation: www.successforall.org

> Robert Slavin is chairman and co-director, and Nancy A. Madden is president of the Successes for All Foundation. You will find resources on cooperative learning and on other means through which students achieve at their site.

Using technology in the process of cooperative learning involves effective management strategies. The numbers, quality, and types of resources available largely influence how technology will be used in cooperative groups. Although many classrooms use synchronous cooperative learning, this is not absolutely necessary. Students can operate within a cooperative learning group while other members of the class work on different assignments. Using learning centers, learning stations, or some other form of assignment-rotation strategy allows limited resources to be used by one group at a time. Abundant technology resources allow teachers to plan lessons where all cooperative learning groups can work at the same time.

Computer games and simulations that allow multiple players may be used in some cooperative learning groups. In this case, technology will typically serve as a supplement to the lesson, but this is not always the case. Discover Babylon (http://fas.org/babylon), described in Chapter 1, may be an ideal conduit to study ancient civilization in a cooperative group. Expectations, goals, or outcomes might come directly from the software itself and, at the same time, meet standards at local, state, national, or international levels.

Assessment in cooperative learning normally involves assigning credit based on individual contributions to the cooperative group and on the collective work of the group. Rubrics are useful in assessing progress.

Here are some of the questions teachers should ask before implementing cooperative learning strategies in the classroom:

- Who will make up the heterogeneous cooperative learning groups, and what factors will be used to make these groups?

- How many students will be in each group?

- What roles will be assigned, and how will assignments be identified (e.g., stand-up signs)?

- What expectations, goals, or outcomes will be assigned to the groups?

- What specific strategies will be used?

- What kinds of assessments will be used to monitor individual and group success?

- What types and numbers of technology resources are needed to maximize student learning?

Answering these questions will help teachers plan and manage cooperative learning that prepares students to work effectively with others by promoting individual and group responsibilities.

Whole-Class Learning Strategies

When planning whole-class learning strategies, teachers should keep in mind that constructivist learning should involve interactions and meaningful experiences that help students grow in understanding. Strategies should take into account the prior knowledge that students, teachers, and other significant individuals in the professional learning community (e.g., experts) bring to the learning environment. Beginning with these constructivist components and ending with the meeting or surpassing of objectives by students leaves teachers the middle part of the continuum: the experiences or strategies that would most effectively move students from beginning to end.

As with cooperative learning, it is important to consider the use of technology in the whole-group learning process. Technology should be used in instances and ways that enhance the strategy. For example, if discussion will be used as a strategy, teacher- or student-made presentations can help enhance the content discussed. Internet examples of content can similarly be projected to the entire class, or an interactive whiteboard can be used for teacher and student sharing.

Rather than prescribing certain strategies for certain content, teachers will serve their students well by making informed decisions when making choices for whole-class learning. After all, resources may be available one year but not the next. Prior knowledge of students will change from year to year. Current events and emerging research will impact the strategies and content. Even state and national content standards will change over time. Being flexible and recognizing that learning environments and external factors are ever changing will go a long way in planning effective whole-class instruction.

Classroom Organization and Management of Technology

Classroom organization and management of technology include strategies for creating and maintaining order in the classroom. Rather than stifling creativity, effective classroom organization and management strategies can actually help foster higher-order thinking and creativity by setting reasonable limits, expectations, and guidelines for students.

When organizing the physical classroom environment, teachers may wish to consider the three domains of learning classified by Bloom (1956): cognitive, affective, and psychomotor. How can the physical environment address each of these domains? For example, will desks be arranged in rows, circles, or some other configuration to better address the cognitive domain? Will the arrangement be changed if the lesson focus changes to the affective domain? How will physical movement be impacted by desk arrangement? These or similar questions to other components of the physical environment, such as placement of the teacher's desk, the arrangement of available technology, the location of supplemental books, and so on, should be asked.

Teachers may wish to create an ideal floor plan using graphic software to give them a bird's-eye view of their classroom. This view might allow teachers to better visualize teacher and student movement around the classroom. It might also help them become aware of access issues for wheelchairs and other devices. Teachers may wish to enlist the help of their students in refining the physical environment; students may have helpful suggestions that teachers did not consider.

The physical environment can help promote motivation for learning when some basic principles are observed. In a constructivist environment, interactions and experiences are critical to learning. Providing an environment that promotes interaction and meaningful experiences may make the difference between learning and not learning. When teaching a unit on photosynthesis, a concept typically hard to grasp for many students, teachers may set up space or learning stations to display student-grown plants around the room. For a lesson on aerodynamics, teachers may not have room to display all student-created paper airplane models, but room can likely be found for a display of photographs.

In terms of technology, the comfort and safety of students should be considered when arranging technology resources. For example, arrangements should be noted and adjusted for maximum use, such as lighting, monitor height, mouse and keyboard positions, seating height and tilt.

Ergonomics is the study of safety and productivity related to the use of equipment and technology. Many efforts have been made in recent years to improve the ergonomic qualities of technology. Computer mouse devices have undergone design refinements to better fit the human hand, monitor screens have improved, and computer chairs have improved for greater comfort, to name just a few. Teachers should make informed choices when selecting appropriate technology for student use and for arranging technology for student safety and productivity. For help on setting up ergonomically sound computer stations, see Chapter 4.

Classrooms vary in purpose and physical components. Computer labs have multiple computers and limited choices for computer arrangements. Still, much can be done to the exterior walls (e.g., bulletin boards) to improve the physical environment. Projection screens should be properly installed and arranged so that all students can view the screen well. Traffic patterns should be noted. Can teachers make swift, unobstructed movement around the classroom? If any type of group work is to be used, can this type of learning be accommodated? Temperature and overhead lighting should be adjusted, and glare and computer screens should be corrected. In summary, all ergonomic factors should be modified so that all students are kept comfortable and safe.

In a classroom with a few computers, teachers should consider how computers will be used for instructional purposes. Can the computers be easily rearranged to meet different strategies for use and learning? If not, careful thought should go into their arrangement at the beginning of the school year. Teachers should not be afraid to make changes later in the school year if action research or other findings reveal the room to be unaccommodating for comfort, safety, or instruction.

Another consideration involves how the computers will be used for instructional purposes. Consider the end instructional objectives and outcomes, and work backward to make appropriate arrangements. Starting with assessment first and working backward is known as "backward design."[9] With only a few computers in the classroom, teachers might want to establish computer learning stations where student rotation is used to ensure access and availability of computers to all students. This can work very well if students will be using the computers individually. They will probably want to consider a different arrangement if students will be using computers in cooperative groups, because generally more room will be needed for seating and viewing.

When only one computer is available in the classroom, teachers still need to consider the same ergonomic factors described for a few or for a classroom full of computers. In addition, they need to, once again, consider the instructional strategies used and the outcomes desired to optimize student achievement. With one computer in the classroom, teachers should use rotation strategies so that all students have access to the computer. For cooperative learning, a computer station can be established and used.

Regardless of computer numbers, strategies, or expected outcomes, teachers should make their expectations for computer use clear to students and parents/guardians. Many districts or schools require that both students and parents/guardians sign a contract before students are allowed to use computers and technology in the classroom. Teachers should check with their district or school administration for what is required in their district or school.

Consequences for inappropriate student use of technology resources or misbehavior should be communicated clearly to students and parents/guardians, and infractions should be enforced.

Posting the contract close to student computers or technology will remind students of their agreement to use technology appropriately.

Developing and Using a Technology Management Plan

Beginning teachers, as well as experienced ones, may feel overwhelmed with the expectations placed upon them. Lesson planning, teaching, and grading, alone, can consume large amounts of time and energy. Add classroom management, extra duty assignments, and other expectations, and teachers are prime candidates for early burnout. Ingersoll (2003) estimated a cumulative attrition of between 40% and 50% for all beginning teachers who have left teaching altogether. Mentoring programs have been set up between experienced teachers and new ones to ease beginning teachers into this demanding profession. This assistance may be helpful in retaining teachers, but there are other helpful actions teachers can take, whether or not such a mentoring program is available in their district.

Managing the Classroom Curriculum

A teacher-created technology management plan can assist teachers in staying organized and on top of teaching tasks. Such a plan is similar to a time management plan that uses calendars to prioritize long- and short-term commitments. Numerous tools, such as those listed in Resource List 2.5, are available to help teachers organize their work schedules.[10] These tools include graphic-organizer and mind-mapping software and web-based applications, which are useful in helping teachers see the overall picture of what they would like to accomplish over the course of the year.

RESOURCE LIST 2.5 ▪ Tools to help get organized

Google Calendar: www.google.com *(then navigate to Calendar)*

Microsoft Outlook: www.microsoft.com *(then navigate to Outlook)*

Inspiration: www.inspiration.com

MindMeister: www.mindmeister.com

A technology management plan should include curriculum outcomes, such as national, state, and local standards that must be addressed throughout the school year. This is part of the long-term plan that teachers must observe in order to ensure coverage of the material. Short-term plans may include monthly and weekly instructional goals and objectives, plans for action research, time for collaboration and reflection, and time for unexpected tasks, such as requests for parent/teacher conferences, meetings, and so forth. In many cases, the classroom curriculum is mandated by state and district policies. Still, the instructional strategies and classroom management used to ensure student attainment of these outcomes is often left up to teachers. In other words, long-term planning outcomes may already be mandated, but the sequence, instructional strategies, resources, and other decisions may be left up to individual teachers. (Curriculum planning and backward design are discussed later in this chapter.)

Ideally, management planning should be a collaborative process where school-based teachers work together to create long- and short-term plans and share resources and strategies for carrying out those plans. As noted in Chapter 1, numerous collaborative tools are available to help teachers plan, implement, and evaluate teaching practices and student outcomes. Some of these include course management systems, learning management systems, mind-mapping tools, and social-networking sites. Teachers who are willing and able to work together, either virtually or face-to-face, during nonteaching times (i.e., summer, professional-development days) may find that collaborating during these times actually saves time in the long run by planning ahead.

Figure 2.3 shows the process for using a management plan that can help teachers seize moments here and there to complete small and large tasks.

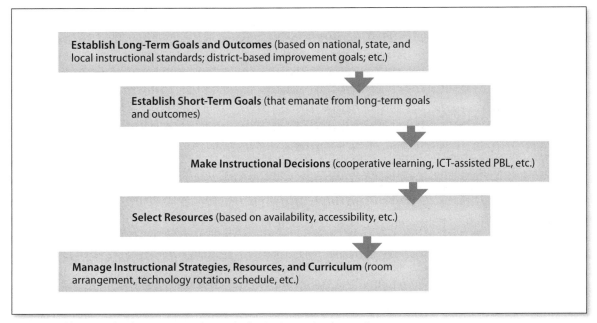

FIGURE 2.3 Managing the classroom curriculum and selecting instructional strategies.

Teacher-planning periods are admittedly short in relation to teaching time. However, if carefully used, planning periods can be managed wisely to account for most or all of teacher planning.

In Your Experience

- Describe management strategies, if any, that your former or present teachers use that you wish to adopt in your teaching practice.

- How did their management strategies contribute to their teaching success?

Section T2a Explorations

1. Select a tool that you would like to explore as a resource for student learning (e.g., MP3 player, web-based mind-mapping software). Search the literature for research related to best practices.

2. Using the tool that you identified above, write a proposal for an action research project that might help improve student learning. Include a focus question and a method for investigating the question.

3. Identify a national, state, or local instructional standard. Create a floor plan using a tool, such as Microsoft Visio (http://office.microsoft.com/visio) or Scribus (www.scribus.net), that demonstrates a room arrangement that can be used to effectively encourage attainment of the instructional standard.

4. Using a collaborative tool, such as a wiki, brainstorm ways with one or more peers to use cooperative learning with ICT-assisted PBL lessons of the group's choosing.

5. Locate a calendar or time management tool that you might use to help you in your teaching practice.

    ■   What are some of the advantages of using this tool?

    ■   What are some of the pitfalls?

6. Create a blog entry that expresses your understanding of how Marzano's three school-level factors impact student achievement. (See this chapter's endnote 2.)

7. Visit the Partnership for 21st Century Skills' website (www.p21.org). In a podcast, describe how classroom management, instructional strategies, and classroom curricula relate to the 21st-century skills included in the Framework for 21st Century Learning.

Section T2a Review

In this section you learned ways to locate and use peer-reviewed and editorially reviewed publications and research findings to promote learning and creativity. You learned about the limitations of research and how you can use your own research to inform your teaching practice and contribute to the knowledge base of the educational community.

In addition, you learned some of the ways to manage student learning activities to maximize learning in a technology-enhanced learning environment. Whether teaching with abundant, adequate, or scarce technology, you can use simple strategies that will help you stay on top of organizational tasks and manage the classroom and curriculum effectively. In the next section, NETS•T2b, we will cover ways to locate and evaluate technology resources that can help you design and plan your learning environments.

NETS·T2b

Develop Technology-Enriched Learning Environments That Enable All Students to Pursue Their Individual Curiosities and Become Active Participants in Setting Their Own Educational Goals, Managing Their Own Learning, and Assessing Their Own Progress

In the previous section, NETS·T2a, you learned how to locate and use research to help improve your teaching to maximize student learning. You also learned how action research can be used in your own classroom to inform your teaching. Moreover, you learned how individual teachers can impact student achievement by providing effective instruction, management, and curricula. In this section you will learn how to create technology-enriched classroom environments that help students become active and reflective learners.

Identifying Technology Needs

In order to develop technology-enriched learning environments that will help students become active and responsible learners, teachers must have resources that are developmentally and age-appropriate for their students and select the ones that will be most useful. Before investing a lot of time, energy, and resources purchasing and learning how to use newly acquired technology, teachers should consider the actual needs of their students. Each class likely represents a wide variety of learners and student needs. Identifying these needs is the first step in ensuring that the technology resources that are located and used are serving a useful purpose.

Developing and using a needs assessment can be helpful in the process of identifying needs. A needs assessment is an investigation teachers perform to determine the needs of their students, how they are currently being met, and what must take place to meet those that are not being met.

A simple needs assessment can be in the form of a table that contains columns for student needs, current resources, needed resources, and desired resources. The column provided for student needs will vary depending on the diverse needs of the learners in a class. The diverse learners described later in this chapter should be considered when completing this column. For example, if there are students who would benefit from assistive technology, this should be listed in the student needs column.

In a second column for current technology, available technology would be listed for each need, with the condition of the technology described. For the purposes of this section, technology resources should include both hardware, such as computer input and output devices, and software, such as software applications and interactive websites.

The next column should list any technology that is essential to meet the needs of students. Although some technology may be currently available that meets a need, the technology may be aging—also known as legacy technology— or inadequate in some way. For this reason, some items may be listed in both the current and needed columns next to a particular student need.

In a fourth column, nonessential (desirable) technology would be listed that would be beneficial to students, but that is not absolutely essential for student success. Figure 2.4 shows how one row might appear in a needs assessment.

Student Needs	Current Technology	Essential Technology Needed	Nonessential Technology
Screen reader	Screen reader without adequate functionality. Doesn't work with new computer system.	Screen reader with adequate functionality that works with new computer system. Must be installed on at least one computer.	Screen reader installed on every computer station. Can be helpful to all students, including those with and without visual challenges.

FIGURE 2.4 Needs assessment entry.

Completing a needs assessment helps give teachers an overall picture of the current state of technology resources and of what will be essential to help maximize student learning. Collaboration among teachers who will be sharing the technology is essential when completing a needs assessment to meet the needs of all students from all classes. Collaboration has the added benefit of accountability; all teachers must agree on what is truly necessary and what would be a nonessential technology.

Once the technology needs are determined, they should be prioritized. High-priority items should be listed at the top of a document, with the items below listed in descending order of need. For each technology item listed, there should be corresponding information related to vendors that sell the equipment and price quotes.

It is helpful to acquire at least three different price quotes to use monetary resources wisely. Teachers should always consider shipping and handling charges, warranties, return policies, and related items when comparing prices and services, to ensure they are receiving the best value for their money. In some cases, a district may already have a commitment to a particular vendor for purchasing equipment. Furthermore, in some schools and districts, teachers are asked to submit their requests to the school administrator or other personnel who will then find quotes and make purchases on their behalf. Even in these cases, it would still behoove teachers to be aware of costs and available equipment. As informed consumers, teachers may be better able to inform those charged with purchasing the technology about which products are preferable, based on teacher research.

Locating Technology Resources

The most convenient and efficient way of locating technology resources is via the Internet. Efficient searching will yield a number of manufacturers for the items sought. Normally, the websites provide details on the hardware or software under consideration and general pricing information. Discounts are often applied when technology is bought in bulk or when purchased for educational purposes. If a school has contracts with specific vendors to purchase technology resources, hard-copy and online catalogs from vendors will likely be available for teachers to review.

But searching for company and manufacturer websites assumes that teachers already know what they wish to acquire. If they have only a vague notion of what it will take to meet their students' needs, they may have to dig a little deeper. In this case, they may want to research into what kinds of technologies are available for specific needs. Since technology offerings change daily, it is important not to rely on past searches. There might be a new type of technology that may dramatically impact student learning, something that was not available even six months earlier. Through careful research, teachers can help make a significant difference in purchasing appropriate technology for their students. This is preferred to having someone else make decisions for teachers. In other words, it is better to be proactive with regard to technology acquisitions than to wait until someone else purchases technology and asks that it be used in your classroom.

A caution about using the Internet for purchasing or researching technology resources is in order: anyone, anywhere, can write anything, at any time, on the Internet; what is written could be true, false, or a combination of the two.

So how do teachers know if they are dealing with a reputable company and purchasing a worthwhile technology resource? One way is to read reviews from well-respected sources. Teachers will probably want to read more than one review to get an overall picture of the company and its products. Some trustworthy companies present links to reputable reviews right on their websites, so that potential buyers can easily access what is written about their services or products. Reviews are often published in hard copies of trustworthy journals and magazines as well, and reading them is one way to get a better picture of the company and products under consideration. If teachers wish to learn more about a specific company, they can also contact the Better Business Bureau (www.bbb.org) to see if any complaints have been lodged against it and how or if those disputes have been resolved. Futhermore, if teachers wish to purchase software, they can typically download a free demo to test drive the software and to learn a little about customer service and the company before buying.

The school or district technology coordinator is an excellent source of information. Teachers should check with coordinators early in their search. Other teachers and professional organizations associated with particular student needs are also helpful (see Tables 1.1 and 1.2).

For example, special education teachers will likely have insight regarding technology for students with special needs. They may receive catalogs and other mailings about new or emerging technologies. School library and media specialists are also quite knowledgeable and can provide assistance to teachers in searching for appropriate technology. In some cases, parents may be able to provide teachers with information regarding technology resources that would better serve their children in the classroom. All members in the professional learning community should be considered as potential consultants and, when appropriate, their input should be solicited.

Evaluating Technology Resources

In addition to reading the reviews of products and services, teachers may find other ways to help determine the accuracy and suitability of technology resources. Classroom resources may be ideally suited to students, or they may be completely inappropriate. In some instances resources that are too simple or complex can be modified so that they can be effectively used.

Website Suitability

Websites can be used effectively in teaching, but a number of factors should be considered before using websites in lessons. Some of the factors include readability, students' developmental levels and maturity, student interests, presentation of content, reputation, accuracy, and fair and varied representation of diverse populations.

Determining readability of websites is made much easier through the use of technology and the readability tools included in select word-processing software, available on some websites. By copying and pasting some of the written text into a Microsoft Word (http://office.microsoft.com/word) document, for example, and using the readability tool, teachers can easily determine the grade level for reading. If the readability level is close to what students need, this is one way to help ensure that the content will be well-received by students.[11]

Another factor to consider is whether your students' developmental levels, in terms of cognitive abilities, and their emotional maturity are well matched to the content of the website. Although the readability may be appropriate, if the photographs are too graphic for students, they may not use the website as intended. Some students are easily revolted by graphic images of medical procedures, for example. Although this factor alone may not determine the suitability of a website, it should be considered in the decision to use it or not.

Another consideration is student interests. Simple interest inventories can be used to determine student interests. Teachers can capitalize on their students' interests by using websites that are relevant and interesting to them. Teachers can teach the same math concepts using many different avenues. Students interested in sports can learn about statistics using sports-related websites. Students interested in animals can learn about statistics in relation to genetics and probabilities for offspring.

Presentation of content refers to how the website is presented in terms of number, types, and arrangements of graphics; amount and quality of text; ease of navigability; general eye appeal; and related characteristics. Although the content may be appropriate in terms of readability and graphics, a website that is difficult to navigate should not be used with students.

Determining the reputation of a website is no easy task. What at first glance may appear to be quality, trustworthy content can become questionable upon further investigation. Knowing who is hosting the website and the website's purpose can provide one hint of the website's trustworthiness, but this alone does not ensure credibility.

By noting the website's address, known as the uniform resource locator (URL), the website's purpose can be inferred. A website is made up of a protocol, a domain name (the Internet protocol address of a computer), and a pathway to a file. In the example shown in Figure 2.5, *http://www.firstgov.gov/ Citizen/Topics/Education_Training.shtml*, the protocol used is Hypertext Transfer Protocol (*http*), and the domain name is *www.firstgov.gov* with *Citizen/Topics/Education_Training.shtml* as the pathway to the file *Education_Training.shtml*. This file is located in a folder named *Topics*; *Topics* is located in a folder named *Citizen*. The *.gov* part of the domain name defines who owns the entity (United States federal government). The *firstgov* part identifies the entity.

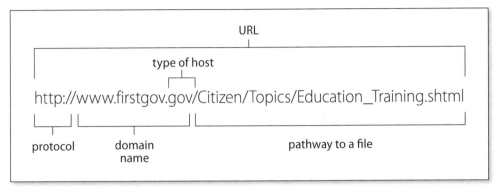

FIGURE 2.5 Sample uniform resource locator (URL).

In this example, by knowing the ending of the domain name, .gov, teachers can infer that the site is hosted by the U.S. federal government. Other common domain names end with .com (commercial), .net (networks), .org (organization), .mil (U.S. military), and .edu (educational institutions). These names help provide teachers with information about the website's purpose. Generally, domain names ending with .org, for example, are hosted by organizations whose primary purpose is not commercial.

Remember that knowing the domain name does not guarantee a reputation. For example, knowing that a website is hosted by a nonprofit organization rather than a commercial host helps teachers identify the purpose, perhaps, of the website, but it does not necessarily assure that the organization is trustworthy. Caution needs to be used when seeking out specific domains. Some hosts have used .org domains and website names similar to reputable sites to lure unsuspecting viewers to their websites.

The accuracy factor is related to reputation. Reputable websites generally contain accurate content and graphics, but, as with hard copy publications, errors sometimes occur. Using prior knowledge and experiences to determine the accuracy of websites is a first line of defense against using inaccurate websites in teaching. In addition, websites recommended by professional organizations have typically been reviewed by competent individuals and carry reasonable assurance for accuracy.

Chapter 4 will describe how teachers can check for fair and equitable representation of diversity in software. In websites, teachers need to consider these issues as well. How are cultural differences represented? How are special needs populations depicted? These are just a couple of questions teachers can ask.

Accessibility is a factor related to how accessible the website is to all populations, including the visually impaired. The Web Accessibility Initiative (WAI) of the World Wide Web Consortium (W3C) helps promote accessibility for all.

> The power of the Web is in its universality. Access by everyone regardless of disability is an essential aspect. (Tim Berners-Lee, director of the World Wide Web Foundation, on the WAI web page, www.w3.org/WAI, n.d.)

Websites that comply with the guidelines and techniques set forth by the WAI demonstrate their commitment to accessibility. Figure 2.6 shows the logos that may be present on websites that comply with accessibility guidelines and techniques as established by W3C.

FIGURE 2.6 W3C logos used to signify accessibility compliance.

Keeping all of these factors in mind when considering the use of websites in teaching will help ensure that the content received by students is what was intended. The usability of websites relates to these factors in that if one or more of these factors makes a website unsuitable, then the likelihood that it will be usable diminishes. Using a checklist or rating scale based on these factors (see Figure 2.7) may be useful when determining the suitability of websites.

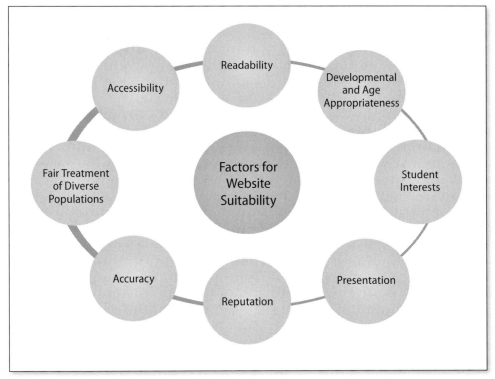

FIGURE 2.7 Factors for determining website suitability.

Hardware and Software Suitability

Some of the same factors that should be considered for website suitability can be considered when determining software suitability. Readability, developmental and age appropriateness, student interests, presentation, reputation, accuracy, fair treatment of diverse populations, and accessibility help determine how useful and appropriate a given software will be in the classroom. Teachers can often download demos of software to determine suitability before buying a software product to determine ease of use, customer-service availability, learner value, and so forth. Whether demos are available or not, teachers should check on return policies, consult with other teachers, read reviews, and fully investigate to ensure suitability. In some cases teachers will be asked to use a district-adopted software for which they had no input in the purchasing decision. In these cases, teachers should still determine software suitability to provide feedback to those who purchased the software, to administrators, and to colleagues.

Hardware suitability can be measured based on the same factors as those used for website and software suitability, with adjustments made accordingly. For example, readability would not apply to a computer mouse unless complex text were on the mouse itself and the text were needed for its operation. On the other hand, if a screen-reader hardware device uses screen-reader software, readability might come into play.

Particular attention should be paid to accessibility and usability by all. CAST, the Center for Applied Special Technology (www.cast.org), is working to promote and support universal design of technology (UDL) so that all may be served:

What is Universal Design for Learning?

Universal Design for Learning (UDL) is a research-based framework for designing curricula—that is, educational goals, methods, materials, and assessments—that enable all individuals to gain knowledge, skills, and enthusiasm for learning. This is accomplished by simultaneously providing rich supports for learning and reducing barriers to the curriculum, while maintaining high achievement standards for all students. (www.cast.org/udl/faq, para. 1)

On its website, CAST provides a number of resources that can help teachers ensure accessibility for all students. These tools and others are included in Resource List 2.6.

RESOURCE LIST 2.6 ■ Tools for accessibility and universal design

CAST UDL Curriculum Self-Check tool: http://udlselfcheck.cast.org

This tool helps teachers and others comply with the UDL framework.

CAST UDL Book Builder tool: http://bookbuilder.cast.org

The Book Builder site is designed to let users "create, share, publish, and read digital books that engage and support diverse learners according to their individual needs, interests, and skills" (para. 1).

CAST UDL Lesson Builder tool: http://lessonbuilder.cast.org

The Lesson Builder provides models and tools to users to "create and adapt lessons that increase access and participation in the general education curriculum for all students" (para. 1).

Closing the Gap: www.closingthegap.com

Closing the Gap helps make assistive technology available to everyone.

The Alliance for Technology Access: www.ataccess.org

ATA seeks to increase the use of technology by children and adults with disabilities and functional limitations.

Managing Technology Resources

Effective management of suitable resources will help classrooms run smoothly, allowing teachers to use these resources efficiently and effectively in the context of learning activities. More specifically, learning how to develop a technology management plan can help teachers maintain technology and acquire appropriate new technology.

Developing a Classroom Technology Management Plan

As with most things in life, having a plan helps make things run more smoothly. The same applies to managing technology resources. Developing a technology management plan can help teachers develop policies for technology use, establish a routine for maintaining and upgrading technology, and acquire new technology resources.

Policies for Student Use

Early in the school year, teachers should communicate technology policies with students, parents, and other interested parties. Their policies should consider a number of items that answer the following questions: Who is permitted to use technology resources, and what technology is available to these individuals? When, where, why, and how can technology be used? What are the consequences for failure to comply with policies?

When considering who is permitted to use technology resources, teachers should think about the variety of resources they have in their classrooms. Some technology should only be available for teachers to operate or use. For example, under most circumstances, the setup of an interactive whiteboard will be done by the teacher, but during classroom instruction, teachers may allow students to use this interactive technology. Teachers may or may not wish to allow students to use video cameras or certain software products that they use for planning purposes. Knowing to whom access is granted for which technology resources will help students identify and observe the boundaries teachers establish.

Establishing guidelines for when technology resources may be used can help prevent unnecessary disturbances. If computer stations are set up around a classroom, teachers may want to establish a particular time or rotation schedule for when students can use these stations. It may be that after students finish their regular class work they are permitted to use the stations. If this is done, teachers should be sure that they provide other opportunities for technology use so that all students have experiences with technology resources, as some students will never finish their work early.

Where students use technology is another factor to consider. If students have laptops, mobile computer games, smartphones, e-book readers, or MP3 players, for example, policies should be established and clearly communicated with regard to when and how students are permitted to use these technologies.

In many cases technology resources will be fixed in a particular location, but in those cases where they are not, teachers should have a plan for where technology resources may be used by students. If a technology is meant to be available only to teachers, the resources should be located in an area where teachers can easily keep an eye on resources and where resources are not easily accessible to curious students.

Students typically observe rules more readily when they know the reasoning behind them and are assured that the reasons are not arbitrary and capricious. Perhaps when writing technology policies, teachers should consider including brief statements that explain their policies. They can preface a policy statement with something such as, "In order to ensure safety and order," and then follow up with a policy statement. Description specificity depends on several factors, including students' developmental levels and ages. If students are not able to read, graphics can be used to illustrate teacher explanations.

How technology is used refers to the conditions under which technology resources will be used. Will students be permitted to use technology resources individually and/or in cooperative groups? Will students be permitted to use technology resources only after completing training or after demonstrating competency? Are students permitted to use technology resources strictly for educational purposes or for entertainment? Are there any other conditions under which students may use technology?

The policies developed need to be enforceable and should carry appropriate penalties if not followed. Students need to know up front what the consequences will be for noncompliance. It should go without saying that in order for policies to be effective, teachers need to follow through on consequences. When considering the consequences, teachers should remember that penalties for noncompliance and infractions should not preclude student learning where at all possible. For example, if teachers deny total and continued access to technology resources because a student committed a minor infraction of a technology policy, they are likely not going to maximize the student's learning. On the other hand, a temporary and appropriate hiatus from access might serve a useful purpose in emphasizing the importance of following policy. In summary, the consequences should be proportionate to the offense and should not deny students their long-term right to learn. At the same time, major offenses should be dealt with appropriately so that other students are not deprived of their right to learn.

Before allowing students to use technology resources, teachers should check with their district or school administration to determine what policies and procedures are in place for technology use. For example, most districts or schools require parents/guardians and students to sign contracts before students are permitted to use technology so that expectations, such as appropriate use and consequences for inappropriate use, are made clear to all.

Aptly, communicating a technology use policy can be made easier through the use of technology itself. Many software applications can help teachers create professional looking contracts, newsletters, brochures, and web pages that can inform parents and all in the professional learning community about teacher policies. It would be worthwhile for teachers to have one or more enlarged versions of their technology use policy prominently displayed in their classroom.

Technology Resource Maintenance Policy

Another component of an overall technology management plan is a hardware maintenance policy. Keeping track of what teachers have, what they need, and what they would like to have to maximize student learning is an important part of their technology resource maintenance policy. Elsewhere, this chapter addressed the policy of designing and using a needs assessment to determine student technology needs. The results of the needs assessment will go a long way toward helping teachers implement their hardware maintenance policy.

The current hardware teachers and students use should be recorded by teachers as inventory and routinely checked to make sure all technology is in safe, operating order. After doing some simple troubleshooting that teachers are qualified and permitted to perform (see Chapter 4), they should remove inoperable technology resources and contact the appropriate personnel to pick up and repair them. In some instances, the technology resources would serve students well if upgrades were made; in other cases, the technology may be so old or ill-equipped that it needs to be replaced. In any case, teachers should keep good and detailed records of the technology resources in their care and what has been sent out for repair or replacement. A simple inventory and resource maintenance log can be used to record routine checks, repairs, upgrades, and replacements.

Teachers should also keep good records of the software technology resources that they and their students use. They should periodically check software to make sure that it is operating properly and safely and is meeting the current and anticipated needs of their students. Here again, the results of a needs assessment will be an integral part of their technology resource maintenance policy. Teachers can keep track of their software inventory; deletions, upgrades, and additions of software; and other important information on the technology resource maintenance log. Database software is an excellent technology resource for creating, using, maintaining, and modifying a technology resource maintenance log.

Technology Resource Funding Plan

One additional component of an overall technology resource management plan is a plan for locating and requesting funds for technology resources. Teachers are often given a set budget for technology and other resources that are issued to them from their school or district. Before (or after) exhausting these funds or resources, teachers may wish to acquire additional resources to help maximize student learning. A number of funding sources are available to teachers if the need can be justified (see Figure 2.8).

Once again, the results of a needs assessment will help teachers identify new technology resources that they need or desire to benefit their students. By writing a grant proposal or other type of funding request application, teachers can provide details for what they need or desire, why they wish to acquire these items, and how their students will benefit from the items requested. Funding agencies often want to have a timetable for implementation of technology resource use and some type of evaluation to make sure the technology resources are being used effectively by teachers and students. Some types of funding sources teachers might wish to investigate when considering applying for funding are listed in Figure 2.8.

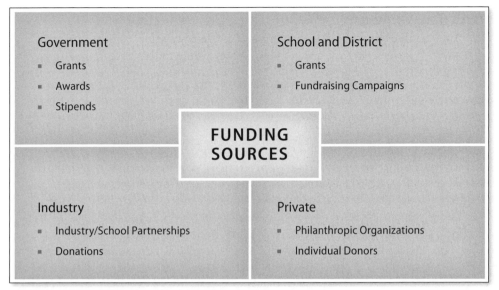

FIGURE 2.8 Funding sources for technology resources.

Evaluating and Modifying Your Technology Resource Management Plan

Action research was introduced earlier in this chapter as a way to investigate issues related to instructional strategies, management, and curricula. Technology resource management plans should be modified if action research reveals that any part of the plan is not working or could be improved. For example, if the plan proves to be too time consuming to use, too confusing, or deficient in some other way, it should be changed to be less time consuming, simpler, and more useful.

Encouraging Active and Reflective Learning in a Technology-Enriched Environment

The preceding discussion in this section dealt with creating an appropriate technology-enriched classroom environment. Strategies for identifying technology needs were addressed, as well as means for acquiring and maintaining technology. In a technology-enriched environment characterized by suitability, accessibility, and universal design for learning, students can be encouraged to be active and reflective learners.

In Chapter 1, a constructivist learning environment was described as one where students are respected, active, and reflective learners in a professional learning community. They are neither empty slates nor passive recipients of transmitted knowledge, but rather, contributors and receivers in a community of learners. When guided participation is used in the instructional process, students serve as both teachers and learners. In such an environment, it is appropriate that students contribute to their learning goals, manage their learning experiences, and assess their own progress.

In a technology-enriched environment that is designed to meet the needs of learners, students can avail themselves of student-appropriate technology resources to help them establish their educational parameters, including goal setting, managing learning experiences, and assessing their own progress. If teachers use individual learning plans or ILPs (described earlier in this chapter), students should be permitted to contribute to goals based on their interests and future plans. While all students will likely have some similarities in their ILPs (such as local or state standards that are assessed by the school and district), some flexibility in student learning goals may serve as a motivator for students.

If ICT-assisted PBL plans are used in instruction, teachers may wish to allow students some say in project selection or the process for carrying out the project. This allows students to have some control over their learning, with appropriate guidance to help them stay on course and schedule; hence, the teacher serves as facilitator and provider of resources and crystallizing experiences. (See Chapter 1.)

Teachers and students can collaborate to identify students' zones of proximal development (ZPD) (see Chapter 1) and to consider possible learning experiences that would motivate and move students from teacher-assisted action to independent development based on interests, learning preferences, and so forth. For instance, if a student is able to use first-order effects independently with regard to spreadsheet software but still needs assistance with second-order effects with the same software, the teacher and student can help identify projects that would help encourage growth and development in this area.

Marzano (2003) characterizes motivation as one of the student-level factors that impact student achievement. Allowing students to participate in the selection of learning experiences will likely help serve the purpose of motivating students more than assigning topics not even remotely interesting to students. For some students who may have a strong interest in science, using scientific simulation software along with ICT-assisted PBL may be motivating and appropriate and help students discover second-order effects using spreadsheet software. Other students with a similar goal may select a business-related project to achieve the same ends.

In many classrooms, students are encouraged to keep daily planners as a way to manage their learning experiences, including studying and meeting obligations. Assisting students to become organized, whether using hardbound tools or digital tools, can help students take more and better control of their learning. Teachers can help students set realistic and reasonable goals that are age and developmentally appropriate and select experiences that will help students achieve their goals. For instance, students can regularly record entries in their ILPs. They can reflect on their goals, attainment of goals, the process that led them to achieve their goals, and what they still would like to achieve. This reflective experience will help students assess their own progress and see where they fell short or exceeded their goals.

Teachers can also help students use their time wisely on projects by helping them set benchmarks for progress and due dates for project completion. A teacher who acts as the "guide on the side" will allow students to take better control of their own learning and to learn to become more accountable as they record their own progress.

Students can use a variety of technology tools made available to them in a technology-enriched environment that will help them plan, manage, and assess their learning, much like teachers use to plan, manage, and assess their technology plans. Database software, graphic-organizer and mind-mapping software, timeline-generating software, time management software, calendars, PDAs, and smartphones are a few of the many resources that students can use to help them plan, manage, and assess their learning.

Using Technology for Student Management

In Chapter 1, first-order effects were described as technology resources that help amplify a task. A variety of technology resources can be used to help increase productivity with regard to student goal setting, management, and assessment. The technology used for student management should be age and developmentally appropriate, and teachers will be better able to determine this appropriateness if they first assess student needs, as described earlier in this section. A few of the tools that may be helpful to students for managing learning experiences will be described here, but they should not be considered exhaustive.

Database software can help students create categories in which they would like to achieve. For example, learning goals and objectives can be one field (category), resources can be another, strategies for accomplishing goals another, and assessment or attainment another. With the teacher's guidance, students can identify fields and provide data, such as the goals they would like to achieve. They can use the sort and filter functions available in most database software to help analyze their learning goals and create reports for their own reflection and assessment.

Spreadsheet software can help students quantify their learning. They may wish to keep track of test scores, how many projects they complete, the number of blogs they post and respond to, and so forth. Students can create charts and graphs from spreadsheet data to get an overall picture of how they are progressing toward meeting their learning goals and calculate their grades based on teacher-provided weights.

Graphic-organizing and mind-mapping software can be used to help students visually represent their learning progress. They may use any number of graphics to show hierarchies (goal priorities), lists (what they would like to accomplish), and processes (in ICT-assisted PBL lessons), to name but a few.

Timeline-generating software and web-based applications are appropriate tools to use for setting benchmarks and goals for project completion. Students can create timelines prior to beginning the project and make modifications as they progress through project phases. Timelines provide a visual representation of the progress students are making, and they also provide teachers with an "at-a-glance" picture of how well the students are progressing through a project.

Teachers may wish to introduce students to software designed specifically to manage projects. Both proprietary (such as Microsoft Office Project Server, see www.microsoft.com/project) and open source (such as eGroupWare, see www.egroupware.org) project management software are available. Functionality varies, with some allowing collaboration, resource and document management, and tracking capabilities. Some of the programs are web based; others are intended for computer installation. All, however, provide users with functions for scheduling, managing project tasks, and generating reports for analysis. Figure 2.9 is a Gantt chart showing project progress, and Figure 2.10 shows a screenshot generated by the open source project management software, GanttProject 2.0.4 (www.ganttproject.biz).

Time management software programs that are specifically designed to be used as digital planners and digital calendars can help students see and reflect on how they are using their time and how they might use their time more wisely to achieve goals. Students may keep their planners or calendars on desktop or laptop computers, PDAs, smartphones, or other devices.

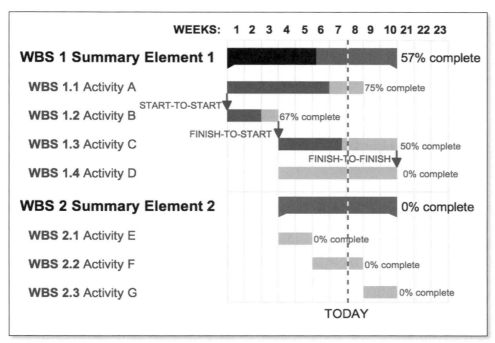

FIGURE 2.9 Gantt chart original (http://en.wikipedia.org/wiki/Gantt_chart).

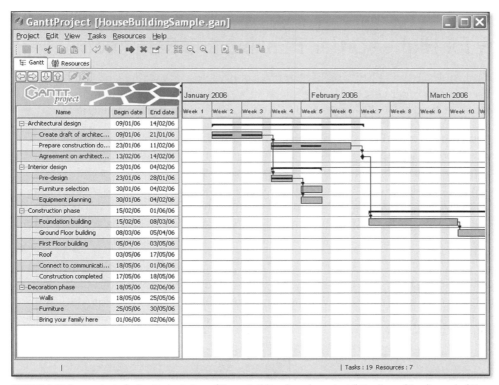

FIGURE 2.10 Screenshot of a Gantt chart view of HouseBuilding Sample project (http://en.wikipedia.org/wiki/File:Ganttproject-house-building-sample.png) by Masaqui, available under a Creative Commons Attribution-Share Alike license.

These are but a few of the many technologies available to students to plan, manage, and assess their learning goals and experiences. Being able to plan and manage learning experiences and goals as self-directed learners is consistent with the Framework for 21st Century Learning (as outlined by the Partnership for 21st Century Skills), especially in the area of life and career skills, such as flexibility, adaptability, productivity, and accountability:

> Today's life and work environments require far more than thinking skills and content knowledge. The ability to navigate the complex life and work environments in the globally competitive information age requires students to pay rigorous attention to developing adequate life and career skills, such as:
>
> - Flexibility and Adaptability
>
> - Initiative and Self-Direction
>
> - Social and Cross-Cultural Skills
>
> - Productivity and Accountability
>
> - Leadership and Responsibility (Partnership for 21st Century Skills, 2009, p. 2)

Providing students with opportunities to practice planning goals and experiences, monitoring their progress, and assessing attainment of their learning goals is one step toward helping to prepare students for what they will face in life and work.

Technology for Higher-Order Thinking and Reflection

The technology tools just described to help amplify the tasks of planning, managing, and assessing experiences were used as first-order effects. Many of the same tools can be used in higher-order thinking and reflection as students make informed decisions based on the data they generate.

Database software was described earlier as a tool for tracking the learning progress. Most database software allows users to create reports for analysis and reflection. Not only can students use the reports themselves for reflection and deliberation, but they can share these reports with teachers and peers to solicit their feedback. If students are not making the progress they wish, perhaps another peer will identify paralyzing experiences that appear to be impacting student progress or suggest crystallizing experiences that may motivate learning. (See Chapter 1 for a discussion on crystallizing and paralyzing experiences.) Students may wish to extrapolate the data and infer what might happen if they change their approach to learning.

In a similar way, students can analyze charts and graphs generated from spreadsheet software to assess their progress with tasks, time spent on tasks, or any other quantifiable variable. Here, too, they can extrapolate the data to see how changes in time or some other variable might impact learning outcomes. Students who find that they spend too much time up front in a project, for example, may wish to project how much time they would have with the final portion if they moved through the initial phases more quickly.

Students may wish to analyze a timeline that represents their actual progress and then compare an ideal timeline that represents what they would do differently if they could do the project all over again.

When these students prepare for the next project, they can use these comparisons to set more realistic goals the next time around. Figure 2.11 illustrates a comparison between an actual timeline and an ideal timeline.

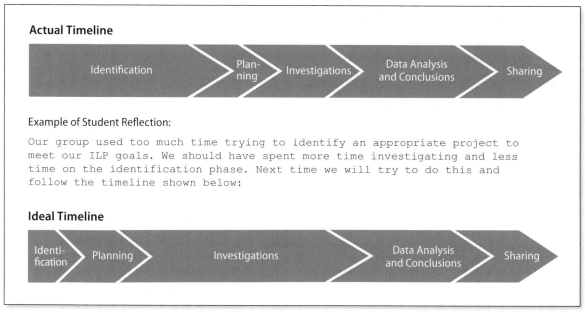

Actual Timeline

Identification Planning Investigations Data Analysis and Conclusions Sharing

Example of Student Reflection:

Our group used too much time trying to identify an appropriate project to meet our ILP goals. We should have spent more time investigating and less time on the identification phase. Next time we will try to do this and follow the timeline shown below:

Ideal Timeline

Identification Planning Investigations Data Analysis and Conclusions Sharing

FIGURE 2.11 Example of student comparison of actual to ideal timeline.

Analyzing Gantt charts and reports generated by project management software can help students follow and assess their project progress and completion. Time management tools and calendars can be used similarly to promote higher-order thinking, reflection, and extrapolation. For example, when students are faced with the realization that they have set unrealistic and unattainable goals and schedules, they can turn to peers and teachers to help them set more attainable goals and timetables. Helping students to honestly and concretely face their strengths and identify areas that need improvement in their formative years should help them make informed decisions for future goal setting and learning.

In Your Experience

Describe a time when planning helped make an effort go more smoothly.

- Was the time invested in planning commensurate with the outcome?
- Explain.

Section T2b Explorations

1. Select a technology resource that you anticipate using in your classroom. Locate three vendors that sell the resource. Compare price quotes, warranties, policies, and the like. How might this search apply to using a needs assessment?

2. Using Figure 2.7 as a guide for determining the suitability of a website, review a website of your choosing and share your review with your teacher and peers.

3. Visit the W3C website (www.w3.org). Visit a website that you regularly look at and evaluate whether it complies with accessibility guidelines. Explain your response.

4. Visit the CAST website (www.cast.org). Select one product that you have used as a learner and determine if it meets the criteria for universal design. Explain your response.

5. Locate a digital calendar, time management tool, or project management tool that students might use to help plan, manage, or assess their learning progress and goals.

   ■ What are some of the advantages of using a digital tool over a hardbound planner?

   ■ What are some of the disadvantages?

6. Create a timeline based on an actual project (personal or professional) that you completed. Now create a timeline based on what you would do differently if you could complete the project all over again.

   ■ How helpful was this exercise?

   ■ How do you think assigning a similar task to students would help them in their planning, management, or assessment of learning experiences or goals?

7. Visit the Partnership for 21st Century Skills' website (www.p21.org). Identify two or three technology tools not mentioned in this section that can be used to help students become 21st-century learners according to the framework provided.

Section T2b Review

In this section you learned how to identify, locate, manage, and evaluate appropriate technology for a technology-enriched classroom. You also learned how to enable students to use technology to help plan, manage, and assess their own learning progress and goals. In the next section you will learn to individualize student learning experiences to address various student needs.

NETS•T2c

Customize and Personalize Learning Activities to Address Students' Diverse Learning Styles, Working Strategies, and Abilities Using Digital Tools and Resources

Planning is an integral part of teaching. Planning serves many purposes: it helps teachers prepare students to meet long- and short-term goals and objectives, it allows teachers to gather materials and design learning environments appropriate for planned activities, and it provides a way to ensure that the needs of all learners are being met. In this section you will learn how to design developmentally appropriate learning opportunities that apply technology-enhanced instructional strategies to support the diverse needs of learners.

Defining Developmentally Appropriate Learning Opportunities

When planning lessons, it is important to keep in mind what is developmentally appropriate for the learners in a classroom. Some teachers look to the work of developmental psychologist Jean Piaget, who classified periods of cognitive development through which children mature. Piaget (1964) believed that while learners might progress at somewhat different rates, all children move through the following developmental stages:

- **Sensorimotor.** Children experience the world primarily through their senses.

- **Preoperational.** Children use symbols and intuitive thought to make sense of their world. Their logic is typically incomplete.

- **Concrete Operational.** Children exhibit accurate logic and an understanding of conservation and reversibility.

- **Formal Operational.** Children demonstrate abstract thought and reason.

Figure 2.12 illustrates the sequence of cognitive development based on Piaget's works. Note that at each stage, students are capable of different cognitive processes. This highlights the importance of planning activities appropriate to students' developmental stages. Asking students who are operating at the preoperational stage of cognitive development to hypothesize what may happen given a set of circumstances is not a developmentally appropriate expectation. On the other hand, asking students operating at the formal operational stage to do the same is recognizing the students' developmental level and asking an appropriate inquiry.

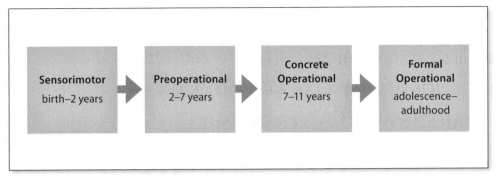

FIGURE 2.12 Piaget's periods of cognitive development.

Lesson planning should include addressing the abilities students currently have and moving them toward the next developmental stage. One of Piaget's contemporaries, psychologist Lev Vygotsky, described the region where students still need the assistance of a mentor to achieve a cognitive task as the zone of proximal development or ZPD (1986). In this zone, students are nearly capable of completing a cognitive task on their own, but they are not quite there. Teachers can help their students develop by providing experiences that help move them toward a higher stage of cognitive development and on to a new, more challenging ZPD.

If all students were at the same period of cognitive development or within the same ZPD, planning would be a great deal easier. But they are not, and it is not. In one class alone, teachers will not only note various types of diversity, such as cultural background, socioeconomic status, and student interests, but they will also see tremendous diversity in developmental levels. Within the same room, one student may be operating at the preoperational stage and another at the formal operational stage. Some students may be struggling with what teachers consider to be very basic concepts and understandings, while others are quickly becoming bored with what was just presented. Rather than become exasperated at this seemingly impossible situation, teachers can choose to see the glass as half full and embrace the challenge of meeting the diverse needs of all learners in their care. By using the concept of differentiated instruction, teachers can plan lessons appropriate for all.

Meeting the Diverse Needs of Learners through Differentiated Instruction

Differentiated instruction, also known as DI, is an approach to teaching that acknowledges the diverse needs of learners. Described as responsive teaching (Tomlinson & Eidson, 2003), DI not only acknowledges this diversity, it also supports the use of instructional strategies that meet each student's learning needs. Tomlinson and McTighe (2006) sum up the significance of effective instruction for all: "Simply put, quality classrooms evolve around powerful knowledge that works for each student" (p. 3).

Various types of diversities exist in today's classrooms, such as diversity related to culture, socioeconomic background, prior knowledge and experiences, student interests, multiple intelligences, and special needs, to name but a few.

In the planning process, teachers may wish to explicitly write out strategies to differentiate instruction so that all learners' needs are met. A lesson plan template can be quickly created to include sections for typical lesson content, such as goals and objectives met, standards addressed, modifications for special needs, materials needed, major concepts covered, and the like. However, a lesson plan that includes strategies for DI should also include a component entitled "strategies for differentiated instruction," which is not normally included. At first glance this section may seem unnecessary, given the presence of the modifications for special needs section, but the differentiated instruction section is meant to be more inclusive and encompassing.

For example, in a given lesson plan, an assistive technology may be employed to help a student with special needs complete an assignment. In the modifications for special needs section, the teacher can document the type of assistive technology used and its purpose. In the differentiated instruction section, specific instructional strategies, questions, and tasks can be documented that target different developmental levels, learning styles, and abilities. It is worth noting that the student who has benefited from the modification for special needs (in this case, the use of assistive technology) can also benefit from the attention given to diverse developmental levels and other characteristics. Typically, only a few students will be targeted in the modifications for special needs section, but all students should be targeted in the differentiated instruction section.

One way to document strategies for differentiated instruction is to list different strategies teachers plan to use, questions they plan to ask, or tasks that they plan to assign that collectively span all developmental levels, learning styles, and abilities present. If the majority of students are thinking at the preoperational and concrete operational levels, teachers should plan strategies, questions, and tasks that challenge students at both levels. Furthermore, it would be wise to consider strategies, questions, and tasks at the formal operational level for those who are quickly approaching that level. The main thrust is to apply developmentally appropriate strategies, questions, and tasks that can convey a concept in a way that permits all to learn.

To illustrate this idea, consider teaching the concept of supply and demand. Students can learn this concept by watching and reflecting on a digital video, participating in a WebQuest, word-processing an essay, completing a computer simulation, drawing an animated cartoon, participating in a cooperative group project, role playing, and so forth. Each strategy can have its own set of questions and tasks. Students at one level of learning might benefit more from one type of strategy, with its accompanying questions and tasks, than another. In many cases, one strategy can address several levels if various levels of questions and tasks are made available. Figure 2.13 shows that different approaches can reach the same goal of students learning the concept of supply and demand.

So how does a teacher fairly and efficiently assess what students accomplish when they are completing different strategies, questions, and tasks? This, again, is a challenge, but it is possible with a little know-how. One way to accomplish this task is to create a rubric with "either-or" statements that address the general terms used to assess students' grasp of goals and objectives. How students learn a concept is secondary to the students' goal of learning a concept. In other words, the means (strategy, questions, tasks) are simply ways to reach the ends (learner outcomes).

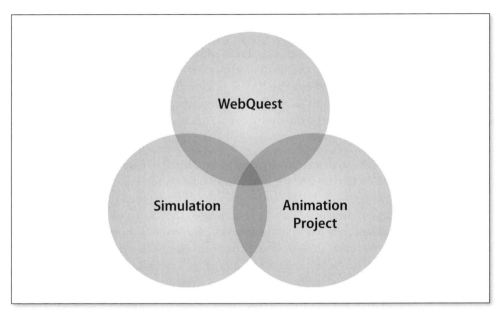

FIGURE 2.13 Different approaches to learning supply and demand and related concepts can lead to the same goal. The dark shaded areas represent concepts learned, and the lighter areas represent different approaches, including questions, resources, strategies, and tasks.

Teachers may wish to have general rubrics on hand that can easily be used (or modified) for different strategies, but there will be times when strategy-specific rubrics will be needed.

Before teaching a concept, teachers can distribute the lesson rubric to their students. Together, teachers and students can thoughtfully select the strategies, questions, and tasks that students should complete to maximize their learning. (With younger students, teachers may need to be the sole selector.)

Teachers will want to avoid obvious demarcations that unnecessarily draw attention to an individual student's or group of students' level. For example, it is unnecessary and potentially harmful to a student's self-esteem and learning to allude to strategy A as the bright students' strategy and strategies B and C as the strategies for the less-bright students. Doing this is not only inaccurate (levels and intelligences are not synonymous), but it also breeches the concept of "Do No Harm," a concept described more fully in Chapter 4. After all, no student wants to be assigned to what his or her peers consider the "dull" group. Teachers can avoid this negativity by having a variety of possible permutations from which they and their students can choose to maximize each child's learning. Having an assortment of permutations would naturally make it less likely that students could identify with one particular group. Furthermore when considering which strategies to use in differentiated instruction, it would be wise to consider more than simply the developmental levels of students. For example, if teachers factor in student interests, learning styles, and so on when choosing strategies, questions, and tasks for differentiated instruction, this further reduces the likelihood that any particular student will feel labeled as superior, dull, or any other such qualifier.

Another way to assess when multiple strategies are used to teach the same concept(s) is to make use of student contracts with "either-or" statements. Here again, depending on the age and developmental level of students, they can have some say in their learning goals and progress by participating in the selection process.

Some might argue that the use of differentiated instruction looks good in theory but that it is impractical in light of the many duties and tasks assigned to a typical teacher. If teachers needed to complete a separate DI plan for every instructional day of the year (typically 180–190 days), this, indeed, would be impractical. However, if they think about lesson planning in a broader sense, in which lessons can span a week or month to foster learner outcomes, the task of using differentiated instruction in this way is considerably less daunting.

Students at the Center of Learning

As discussed throughout this text, constructivist learning environments place students at the center of learning. Diversity creates opportunities to individualize instruction so that each student is at the center of his or her learning. A variety of ways to use technology to support learner-centered strategies based on the diverse needs of students will be presented in this section, yet many more are available to help all students learn.

Diversity is synonymous with different, dissimilar, unlike, and distinct. With this in mind, the diversity discussed below will include differences and distinctions among different types of learners. In this context, diversity takes on many forms, such as differences in learning, special needs, learning-style preferences, prior knowledge and experiences, interests, and culture. These differences will be discussed along with ways to use technology to support student learning.

Papert (1999), an innovative thinker in technology integration, has summed up the absurdity of the traditional education system's tendency to homogenize learners and learning and then fretting about diversity:[12]

> I think every baby comes into the world as a unique individual. If you've had several children, or, like me, recently gone through the experience of being a grandparent—it's wonderful how each one of them is different, does things in different ways, thinks differently. And then we're going to channel them into a school that homogenizes them? And then we're going to worry afterwards about how to free them from that homogenization and make them diverse again? It's backwards. It's the wrong approach. (Papert, 1999, para. 1)

Heeding Papert's call to acknowledge inborn differences in students capitalizes on the constructivist approach to learning. Acknowledging differences allows teachers to justify the individualization of instruction based on individual needs, multiple intelligences, learning-style preferences, prior knowledge and experiences, interests, and culture.

Special Needs

A comprehensive discussion on the special needs of students is far beyond the scope of this book. Instead, several different types of special needs are presented below, accompanied by ideas for using technology in student-centered ways.

Students with special needs are typically identified after being tested for learning difficulties or disorders. Parents and/or teachers can make referrals for testing, and the schools provide testing services. Reauthorization of the Individuals with Disabilities Education Act in 2004 (IDEA, 2004), brought attention to the practice of response to instruction (RtI). RtI is a data-driven approach whose purpose is to help all students, including those with disabilities, learn. The National Association of State Directors of Special Education (NASDSE) and the Council of Administrators of Special Education (CASE) give the following description of RtI:

> [T]he practice of (1) providing high-quality instruction/intervention matched to student needs and (2) using learning rates over time and level of performance to (3) make important educational decisions.
>
> … It is, first and foremost, a strategy to be used in the general education classroom. This paper [whitepaper by NASDSE and CASE] is a call from the special education community to the general education community to join together to commit to a uniform system of education, where RtI plays a key role in identifying and working with struggling learners in any setting and ultimately helps educators make better decisions about which children should be referred for additional targeted supports. (NASDSE & CASE, 2006, p. 2).

RtI strategies are used for math and reading instruction and are focused on early detection and prevention strategies in order to provide assistance before students fall behind (Gersten et al., 2008).

Although RtI has its critics (Fuchs, Mock, Morgan, & Young, 2003), it has experienced renewed interest among some educators and may be a topic of discussion in years to come.

Once students are identified as having special needs, they are eligible for special education services, which include providing education with the least restrictive environment and the development of an individualized education program (IEP).[13] Generally speaking, the law allows students with special needs the opportunity to learn in ways that best meet their needs.

IEPs outline goals and objectives for each student with special needs and include input from teachers, parents, administrators, and sometimes students, for how those goals and objectives should be met. Some types of special needs, as listed on the site for the National Dissemination Center for Children with Disabilities (http://nichcy.org/disability/specific), include:

- Attention Deficit/Hyperactivity Disorder

- Autism Spectrum Disorders

- Blindness/Visual Impairment

- Cerebral Palsy

- Deaf-Blindness

- Deafness and Hearing Loss

- Developmental Delay

- Down Syndrome

- Emotional Disturbance

- Epilepsy

- Intellectual Disability

- Learning Disabilities (includes dyslexia, discalcula, and disgraphia)

- Other Health Impairment

- Rare Disorders

- Severe and/or Multiple Disabilities

- Speech and Language Impairments

- Spina Bifida

- Traumatic Brain Injury

Resource List 2.7 lists a few web resources that teachers may peruse to learn more about how technology can be used to meet the needs of students with special needs.

RESOURCE LIST 2.7 ▪ Resources for special needs technology

The Alliance for Technology Access (ATA): www.ataccess.org

"The mission of ATA is to increase the use of technology by children and adults with disabilities and functional limitations. ATA encourages and facilitates the empowerment of people with disabilities to participate fully in their communities. Through public education, information and referral, capacity building in community organizations, and advocacy/policy efforts, the ATA enables millions of people to live, learn, work, define their futures, and achieve their dreams."

Center for Applied Special Technology (CAST): www.cast.org

"CAST's mission is to expand learning opportunities for all individuals, especially those with disabilities, through its universal design for learning."

Closing the Gap: www.closingthegap.com

"Closing the Gap answers the most common questions in special education and rehabilitation: What products are available? What do they cost, and where can I get them? How do I use them?"

AccessIT: www.washington.edu/accessit

"The National Center on Accessible Information Technology in Education (AccessIT) promotes the use of electronic and information technology (E&IT) for students and employees with disabilities in educational institutions at all academic levels. This website features the AccessIT Knowledge Base, a searchable database of questions and answers regarding accessible E&IT. It is designed for educators, policy makers, librarians, technical-support staff, students and employees with disabilities, and those who advocate for them."

NICHCY: www.nichcy.org

> "*The National Dissemination Center for Children with Disabilities (NICHCY) ... provides information to the nation on: disabilities in children and youth; programs and services for infants, children, and youth with disabilities; IDEA, the nation's special education law; No Child Left Behind, the nation's general education law; and research-based information on effective practices for children with disabilities.*"

OSERS: www.ed.gov/about/offices/list/osers/osep

> "*United States Department of Education, Office of Special Education and Rehabilitative Services (OSERS)) ... is dedicated to improving results for infants, toddlers, children, and youth with disabilities from birth through the age of 21 by providing leadership and financial support to assist states and local districts. The Individuals with Disabilities Education Act (IDEA) authorizes formula grants to states and discretionary grants to institutions of higher education and other nonprofit organizations to support research, demonstrations, technical assistance and dissemination, technology and personnel development, and parent-training and information centers.*"

The Center for Special Technology (CAST) strives to meet the needs of the diverse population of students and respond to individual differences with its universal design for learning or UDL. (Several CAST UDL resources are included in Resource List 2.6, p. 92.) As stated on the CAST website (www.cast.org/udl), "UDL provides a blueprint for creating instructional goals, methods, materials, and assessments that work for everyone." UDL promotes multiple means of representation to give learners various ways of acquiring information and knowledge; multiple means of action and expression to provide learners alternatives for demonstrating what they know; and multiple means of engagement to tap into learners' interests, offer appropriate challenges, and increase motivation. The UDL Guidelines are available at the CAST website.

Accessibility involves making technology available and usable to all students. Emphasis must be placed on both availability and usability; all the resources in the world will not promote learning if these resources cannot be used effectively by learners. There are a number of strategies that teachers can employ to ensure accessibility for all students.

Making Internet access available and usable includes having reliable technology and Internet access regularly available. Ideally, each student in a class is assigned his or her own personal computer with Internet access, but this is often not the case. Even with only one computer in the classroom, good management strategies can ensure availability for all students. Some of these strategies were addressed earlier in the chapter, but availability's complement, usability, follows.

Internet accessibility involves allowing the user to make full use of what technology has to offer. At the computer level, many options are available to modify settings to increase accessibility. Settings for reading and viewing, font and icon size, screen resolution, contrast, and magnification are a few choices that can be quickly altered to meet the needs of the visually impaired. Sound settings can be changed for volume, text-to-speech options, and other visual cues to indicate sounds. Changes to mouse or keyboard settings can help with dexterity issues. Furthermore, most computer systems have built-in accessibility options that will enable those who are hearing-, seeing-, physically-, or learning-impaired to use the computer effectively. Operating system and web browser manufacturers are working to make their software more accessible—Resource List 2.8 includes information about many of them.

RESOURCE LIST 2.8 ▪ Operating system and web browser manufacturers working toward greater accessibility

Apple: www.apple.com/education/special-education

Linux Accessibility Resource Site (LARS): http://larswiki.atrc.utoronto.ca/wiki/Software

>   The LARS wiki is hosted and supported by the Inclusive Design Research Centre (IDRC, idrc.ocad.ca) at Canada's OCAD University (www.utoronto.ca).

Microsoft: www.microsoft.com/enable

>   This site provides information on the Microsoft operating system.

Microsoft: www.microsoft.com/enable/products/ie6

>   This site links to accessibility tutorials for Microsoft products, including Internet Explorer.

Mozilla Firefox: www.accessfirefox.org

At the Internet level, several services are available that check web pages for accessibility for those with various disabilities. As discussed earlier in this chapter, the Web Accessibility Initiative (WAI), as part of World Wide Web Consortium (W3C), helps coordinate global efforts to ensure accessibility standards so that users of all abilities may operate computers effectively. Many web-accessibility evaluators exist that check conformance to these standards. Some evaluators or validators, as they are sometimes called, are more user-friendly than others and provide simpler means for correcting nonconformance problems. An extensive list of providers is available at www.w3.org/WAI/ER/tools on the W3C website.

Another tool available to teachers or anyone interested in determining the accessibility of websites for color-blind users is Vischeck (www.vischeck.com). Vischeck is a tool that simulates color-blind vision and may be used on web pages and image files. Daltonize (www.vischeck.com/daltonize) is a color-blind image correction tool available on Vischeck's website.

Accessibility issues relate to the availability and usability of technology by users. Assistive technologies can be used alone or in conjunction with a computer system to boost accessibility or assist usability. Some assistive technologies include touch screens, Braille embossers, screen readers, screen magnifiers, talking-book players, and eye-control input systems. Generally, for every disability, one or more assistive technologies are available. There are literally thousands of assistive technologies that not only benefit students with special needs, but also serve the general population by helping users make better and easier use of technology. AbleData (www.abledata.com) is a searchable database of thousands of assistive technologies that teachers may wish to consult to identify assistive technologies.

Multiple Intelligences

Before Howard Gardner's seminal work on multiple intelligences (1983), many educators associated intelligence strictly with success on standardized tests. Gardner proposed different types of intelligences that included far more than had been popularly recognized (see Chapter 1). Although some have been critical of Gardner's work (Schaler, 2006), teachers would be well advised to consider multiple intelligences as they plan learner-centered strategies that address the diverse needs of students. Recognizing students' inclinations in the various intelligences provides teachers with opportunities to modify their teaching strategies so that, as Armstrong (2009) notes, "There will always be a time during the period or day when a student has his or her own most highly developed intelligence(s) actively involved in learning" (p. 51).[14]

Learning Preferences

Research in learning-style preferences has resulted in rich resources for teachers to use as they create student-centered, technology-enhanced learning experiences. DeBello (1990) compared 11 major models of learning styles. A number of learning-style inventories exist, including those named in Resource List 2.9.

RESOURCE LIST 2.9 ■ Inventories of learning styles

The Learning Styles suite of online student assessments: www.learningstyles.net

Experience Based Learning Systems: http://learningfromexperience.com

The VARK guide to learning styles: www.vark-learn.com

Paragon Learning Style Inventory: www.oswego.edu/plsi

Paragon Learning Style Inventory

For brevity's sake, only the Paragon Learning Style Inventory, developed by John Shindler, will be discussed here. The Paragon Learning Style Inventory (www.oswego.edu/plsi) is a research-based survey for adults that helps users better understand their preferences for learning. A student version is available for children ages 8 and above. Both students and teachers can take the inventory to help them realize the way they best learn according to their natural preferences. The four learning-style Jungian dimensions are extrovert/introvert, sensate/intuitive, feeler/thinker, and judger/perceiver. Most individuals' preferences lead toward one side of each dimension. There are a total of 16 combinations of types (e.g., ESFJ, ISFJ, and so on) that help clarify preferences for learning and acting. Results from this inventory can help teachers prepare lessons that are individualized to learner preferences. Moreover, when results are available for both students and teachers, teachers can help teach effectively and maximize learning. For example, introvert teachers teaching extroverts are advised to use group work and cooperative learning, use wait time with questioning, provide time for movement, and value expression.

So how can teachers use these results in a technology-enhanced environment to maximize learning? Taking the example used above, introvert teachers can use cooperative learning with technology assignments, provide students with time to answer questions, provide ample time for movement away from computers, and value the expression of students. Most importantly, teachers can realize that each student and teacher brings different learning-style preferences to the learning environment, which creates an abundance of diversity in the classroom. Providing a wide variety of technology assignments—individual, cooperative, open-ended, close-ended, and so on—will eventually provide opportunities for success for all types of learner preferences. The jury is still out on whether or not learning preferences ever change. While researchers investigate this phenomenon, teachers should be mindful of diversity in learning styles and preferences to meet the needs of all learners.

Differences in Prior Knowledge, Skills, and Interests

Just as students bring different learning preferences with them into the classroom, they also bring diversity in prior knowledge, skills, experiences, and developmental levels. The constructivist approach to learning capitalizes on prior understanding and experiences by using familiar concepts to introduce new concepts. Using familiar examples, analogies, and metaphors to introduce new concepts will likely be more effective than using unfamiliar ones. Student-interest inventories, journal entries, and other tools described earlier in this chapter help teachers become aware of what concepts are familiar and which ones motivate and matter to students. Teachers who use only sports-related analogies, for example, are not serving those students who have little to no interest in or experience with sports. Rather, the teacher should deliberately vary examples, analogies, metaphors, and instruction to address a wider audience.

It is equally important to encourage student interactions and input by allowing them to share their prior knowledge and experiences. Students will often have better ways of helping peers understand a concept because they use terminology and experiences common and familiar in their explanations. Allowing students and the teacher to share and contribute to the learning environment multiplies the combinations of ways that concepts can be learned, maximizing the learning experiences of all.

In terms of technology, allowing students' interests, preferences, prior knowledge, skills, and experiences to guide technology assignments can improve the rate and depth of learning. Students who have experience playing music can complete Internet assignments that capitalize on this experience and their prior knowledge. The idea is that these students will naturally be more capable of learning new math concepts related to music than math concepts for math concepts' sake. Students experienced in sports can learn the same math concepts by exploring technology assignments related to sports. The end is the same, but the paths for getting there are different.

Vygotsky's zone of proximal development (ZPD) was discussed earlier in this chapter and in Chapter 1. If students are operating in different zones, it makes sense to provide them with different learning opportunities to move them through their unique learning sectors. Students who have extensive experience with technology should be given different assignments from students who have little or no experience. Similarly, students who have strong reading comprehension skills should not be forced to read very basic materials that could not only impede their learning but may turn them off to the process of learning.

In the same way that diversity in prior knowledge and experiences can help guide lessons for differentiated instruction, so, too, can student interests. Students bring diverse interests to the learning environment. Designing technology-enhanced lessons that at least partially revolve around student interests will be more motivating than those that are of little or no interest to students. Teachers need to be aware that their excitement with history or any other subject may not be the same for many of their students.

At-Risk Students

At-risk students are students who, for a variety of reasons, are at risk for either developing below their potential or for dropping out of school. These students are especially in need of learning that is centered on their particular needs, learning preferences, prior knowledge and experiences, and interests. It is infinitely sad to see a gifted student lose interest in learning due to boredom. Sad, too, is the plight of the struggling student who feels alienated from peers and teachers and who decides it is less painful to withdraw from learning than to face the daily struggle of fighting to learn in an uncaring, unfriendly environment.

Teachers can make a difference in the lives of at-risk students. Research shows that high expectations are critical in helping at-risk students succeed. Helping students develop thinking skills, providing them with meaningful experiences, promoting responsibility, and using cooperative learning and peer tutoring opportunities have been shown to encourage success in this population (Costello, 1996). These tools and strategies should seem familiar, for they are all a part of the constructivist approach to learning.

Gender Differences

Gender differences are apparent in many areas of technology, such as virtual-reality preferences (Space, 2001); online-learning experiences (Barrett & Lally, 1999); and software and computer game performances (Gorriz & Medina, 2000; Heeter, 2007). A University of Washington study concluded that the average woman has greater difficulty with spatial orientation in virtual environments than the average man. Researchers (Space, 2001) noted that this spatial difficulty is also present in the real environment for women but is exaggerated in the virtual environment. The results of this study have implications for the classroom, where more and more virtual environments are used as tools for instructional purposes.

Space (2001) reported the results from another study, conducted at the University of Michigan, that concluded that women in the study preferred passive virtual environments (e.g., preference for observing rather than participating), and men preferred interactive environments in which they could actively participate. If teachers use virtual environments as teaching tools, they should consider how the tool can best be used by males and females and whether any components of the virtual environment will hinder learning for either gender.

Researchers studying interactions in an online environment noted gender differences in the quantity and length of messages sent (Barrett & Lally, 1999). Men on average sent longer and more frequent messages, and they made more socioemotional contributions than women. Women, on the other hand, contributed more interactive messages. Here again, noting that gender differences may impact online learning implies that teachers should provide a variety of experiences when using online learning as a teaching tool.

Another study concluded that girls prefer computer games that are collaborative rather than competitive, that have nonclosure and exploration, and that are thought-provoking and require puzzle-solving (Gorriz & Medina, 2000). Once more, the implications of this study suggest that one size does not fit all when technology is used to maximize learning.

So how can a teacher stay abreast of these important differences and ways to modify teaching to meet the needs of all students? Becoming a member of a related professional society is one important way to stay aware and prepared. As a professional society member, teachers receive publications and attend conferences that reflect current research findings related to gender and other differences and will learn ways to apply this information to effectively teach students.

Another way to stay abreast is to become a voracious reader. Teachers can read publications—both printed and those that appear on reliable websites—that present findings related to differences in learning, such as those that suggest a digital divide between genders with regard to computers (Cooper & Weaver, 2003). Furthermore, teachers can take advantage of opportunities presented by school districts for professional development related to differences in learning. Perhaps most importantly, teachers should become aware of their own teaching practices and ask themselves if they are making accommodations related to gender differences.

Racial and Cultural Diversity

In nearly every classroom, there will be some degree of racial or cultural diversity. Students from diverse backgrounds typically reflect differences in one or more of the following: linguistic expression or language, norms for behavior, perceptions of one's place in society, religion and beliefs, clothing and attire, physical hygiene practices, and eating patterns and choices. Fortunately, much can be done in a technology-enhanced environment to celebrate differences and maximize learning for all.

One simple way of helping students who are English language learners (ELLs) to succeed is to use a translator program that is typically available on commonly used web browsers. If a teacher assigns a website as part of a WebQuest, for example, the teacher can allow the ELL student to view the web page in his or her own first language. Web translation programs are widely available, even outside web browsers, as freeware. One popular web-based translator is Yahoo! Babel Fish (http://babelfish.yahoo.com). Another web-based tool that can translate text or a web page is Google Translate (http://translate.google.com).

Teachers can also learn some of the words and phrases of their students' native languages. Many freeware programs and websites are available to teach users these words and phrases and typically have written words, graphics, and audio components to help users see and hear the words. Students will appreciate that their teachers took the time to learn their language in order to communicate with them more effectively. Teachers can even encourage students to learn the native languages of their classmates in this manner.

Using the Internet to study other cultures as a teacher and/or as a class is another way to embrace cultural awareness. Knowing students' cultural norms for behavior helps teachers interpret their classroom behaviors more accurately and allows them to relate to all students more effectively. Additional ways to address cultural and racial diversity are provided in Chapter 4.

Socioeconomic Differences

Students' socioeconomic experiences will invariably differ. Socioeconomic factors can relate to so many learning components that it is imperative for teachers to be aware they exist. It is even more important for teachers to have a repertoire of strategies that can ensure learning for all.

Socioeconomic differences surface in prior experiences and available resources. Typically, students with greater financial resources have greater access to outside experiences and resources, such as travel, extracurricular activities, learning tools, and technology.

Teachers can provide students with meaningful experiences and useful resources that promote student learning. Technology-enhanced lessons provide students with opportunities for virtual field trips and exposure to cultures and places unavailable to them in reality. Providing easy, safe, and ongoing access to technology resources in the classroom also helps make up for a lack of resources outside the classroom. If possible, teachers may be able to acquire resources that can be placed in a lending library for students to use at home. A number of government and private programs, such as GEAR UP (Gaining Early Awareness and Readiness for Undergraduate Programs, www.ed.gov/programs/gearup), recognize the importance of helping students acquire technology resources as a way of leveling the playing field.

It is worth noting that socioeconomic status also can affect student attire, hygiene, health, and other personal characteristics for which technology may play only a secondary or tertiary role. Still, educating students and providing rich experiences and resources is perhaps the best way to help them improve their socioeconomic status.

A word of caution is warranted when dealing with socioeconomic differences and, in fact, any student differences: students are often very sensitive with regard to their socioeconomic status. Even in schools with abundant resources, there are the haves and the have-mores. Teachers should be sensitive when planning ways to meet the needs of students from lower socioeconomic backgrounds so that teachers do not call attention to their status and risk alienating or embarrassing them.

Planning for Diverse Learners

A number of student-centered strategies have been introduced to address the diverse needs of students, but a few more specific strategies will be described that are applicable to all types of diversity. When planning lessons, it is important to note how each diverse need will be met.

As described earlier, differentiated instruction is an approach to teaching that acknowledges the individual and diverse needs of all learners. This approach supports various means of teaching in order to meet the wide variety of needs represented in a single class. Much has been written about differentiated instruction and how this approach can be used effectively in the classroom (Hall, 2002; Tomlinson & McTighe, 2006).

Varying instructional strategies to meet the needs of all students is student-centered and focuses on the needs of the students rather than on a prescribed, inflexible curriculum. Differentiated instruction (DI) does not preclude the use of a curriculum or standards; rather, it recognizes that delivery of that curriculum, and sometimes even the negotiable content, can be varied and tailored to better meet individual needs.

Developing individual learning plans (ILPs) to meet the needs of every student in a class may be an effective tool for ensuring the use of DI. For younger students, parents can help teachers complete ILPs for their child, helping to relieve the burden of additional paperwork for the teacher. In upper grades, either students and/or parents can help complete these plans.[15]

Helping students share in learning goals and providing them with opportunities to suggest strategies for meeting those goals fosters a sense of self-direction and responsibility for learning and helps teachers make informed instructional decisions. When parents have greater involvement in the learning of their children, they, too, have a greater awareness of what it takes to move students toward their goals. This system of setting and meeting individual learner outcomes for all students has the potential to bring teachers, students, and parents closer together in a common effort to maximize learning.

Using technology to facilitate ILP creation and maintenance is important in making this strategy manageable. Teachers can use secure, district- or school-approved Internet-based services to promote communication among teacher, students, and parents and to streamline tasks associated with ILPs. If teachers decide to try this approach, they should be sure to clear it with their school and other district administrators for their approval. Teachers should also check into any security and confidentiality issues associated with communicating in this way. Furthermore, they should not electronically convey any confidential, privileged, or protected information in such a way that is not expressly permitted by law and their school jurisdiction and that could reach an unintended audience.

In Your Experience

- In your educational experience, how well do you believe your individual learning needs have been met?

- If you could change anything, what would you change about your educational experiences?

Section T2c Explorations

1. Visit one of the websites in Resource List 2.8 (Operating system and web browser manufacturers working toward greater accessibility).

    - Summarize the types of accessibility issues addressed with regard to the operating system or web browser featured.

    - Share your findings with your peers.

2. Visit one of the websites in Resource List 2.9 (Inventories of learning styles).

    - Summarize what types of resources are available for teachers to help them better differentiate instruction.

    - Share your findings with your peers.

3. Use an accessibility validator (see www.w3.org) to check one of your favorite web pages. Is the page accessible based on guidelines?

4. Use Vischeck (www.vischeck.com) to simulate color blindness on one of your favorite websites. Share your reaction to the simulation with your peers.

5. Use Daltonize (www.vischeck/daltonize) to correct a photograph you have taken. Were you surprised by the correction? Share your reaction with your peers.

6. Select one of Gardner's multiple intelligences.

   ■ Identify a learner outcome, and create a list of differentiated instruction you could provide your students to address the intelligence.

   ■ What types of technology tools would help in the differentiated instruction?

7. Select one of Paragon's learning preferences (www.oswego.edu/plsi).

   ■ Create a list of differentiated instruction you could provide your students to address the preference.

   ■ What types of technology tools would help in the differentiated instruction?

8. Identify three technologies that could be used to help at-risk students.

   ■ Explain how the technologies would be helpful.

   ■ Share your list and explanations with your peers.

9. Locate an online game that students might use for learning.

   ■ How might gender differences account for success with the game?

   ■ If you expect success without regard to gender, explain characteristics of the game that contribute to this.

10. Visit an educational website of your choosing.

    ■ To what degree are various cultures and races represented?

    ■ Explain your answer.

11. Review a lesson plan you or someone else created.

    ■ Will students from all socioeconomic backgrounds be able to successfully meet the goals of the lesson?

    ■ If not, what modifications should be made?

Section T2c Review

In this section you learned to plan learning opportunities that help meet the diverse needs of learners. You learned that planning for diverse needs requires teachers to use multiple strategies and differentiated instruction to help students achieve the same learner outcomes. Teachers are challenged to find ways to reach each and every student each and every day. This is no small charge but one that brings great rewards to teachers, students, and the larger educational community. In the next section you will learn how to further maximize learning through assessment.

NETS•T2d

Provide Students with Multiple and Varied Formative and Summative Assessments Aligned with Content and Technology Standards and Use Resulting Data to Inform Learning and Teaching

Assessment and evaluation are a large part of teaching. In this section you will learn the differences between the two and various ways to use technology in the assessment and evaluation process. An assortment of assessment techniques is presented to help you become familiar with ways to maximize student attainment of content and technology standards. Finally, you will learn about different methods to evaluate student use of technology. Having a strong grasp of how assessment and evaluation fit into the overall teaching process can help teachers make more informed decisions regarding learning and teaching.

Technology Standards and the Curriculum

Keeping in mind all of the ways that students, teachers, and those from the larger professional learning community can contribute to the learning environment leads to the need for foci in teaching. Curriculum standards serve as these foci. Standards on many levels exist to channel teaching toward important goals in the learning environment of schools.

For every discipline and most subdisciplines, professional societies exist that support growth and understanding of that discipline. Professional societies that support subjects in the educational setting, such as ISTE, often develop and promote standards related to their discipline. In the case of ISTE, the standards are international in nature, yet various countries have their own sets of technology standards that they use in place of or as adjuncts to the ISTE standards. The same goes for standards for other disciplines. Therefore, both international and national technology standards should be reviewed as they relate to teaching. States and regions also have standards that they expect teachers to use to plan curricula or for program approval.

The majority of states use international and national standards as the backbone of their curricula. In some cases these standards are used as the guiding principles behind teaching, but in others, the standards have been modified to meet the specific needs of state citizens.

Resource List 2.10 shows just a few of the websites that address international, national, state, and regional standards related to technology either for student and teacher preparation or for program review.[16]

RESOURCE LIST 2.10 ■ Websites that address technology-related standards

International Society for Technology in Education: www.iste.org

National Educational Technology Standards (NETS) for Students, NETS for Teachers, NETS for Administrators, NETS for Coaches, NETS for Computer Science Educators

Partnership for 21st Century Skills: www.p21.org

Framework for 21st-century learning

International Technology and Engineering Educators Association (ITEEA): www.iteea.org/TAA/Publications/TAA_Publications.html

Technological literacy standards

Northwest Educational Technology Consortium (NETC): www.netc.org

Distance and online education standards of professional practice

Association for Educational Communications and Technology (AECT): www.aect.org

Standards for the accreditation of school media specialist and educational technology specialist programs

Minnesota Educational Media Organization (MEMO): http://memotech.ning.com/page/memo-information-and

Information and technology literacy standards

In addition to international, national, and state standards, district and school-wide standards are often introduced into the curriculum. These standards are more likely to reflect the specific learning needs of students within a geographic region. If, for example, a high percentage of state citizens are technology illiterate, district and school standards may place heavy emphasis on technology literacy. District and school standards typically reflect international, national, and state standards, but they are geared more toward specific regional needs.

Different districts emphasize different standards in instructional practices. Depending on accreditation and other requirements, some districts require teachers to follow international and national standards in addition to state and local standards. Since most of these standards parallel each other in content, it is important for teachers to know which standards their district uses as foci for learning.

Using standards as foci for learning allows teachers to select learning experiences that maximize learning in a technology-enhanced environment. Rather than start with experiences, teachers may begin their planning with a goal (such as a standard) in mind. From there they can consider student-centered experiences that might help students acquire the knowledge and skills related to the content based on student needs and characteristics.

In their book *Understanding by Design,* Wiggins and McTighe (2005) promote UbD (Understanding by Design) as a model for curriculum design. UbD uses backward design to promote and attain student understanding. They describe the process of backward design as first identifying the ends or understandings that are to be reached, followed by the second stage, determining acceptable evidence to know the students have achieved understanding, and then the third stage, planning appropriate learning experiences and activities that will help students achieve understanding. Note that the order of backward design begins with the end in mind; UbD is results driven.

Our lessons, units, and courses should be logically inferred from the results sought, not derived from the methods, books, and activities with which we are most comfortable. Curriculum should lay out the most effective ways of achieving specific results. It is analogous to travel planning. Our frameworks should provide a set of itineraries deliberately designed to meet cultural goals rather than a purposeless tour of all the major sites in a foreign country. In short, the best designs derive backward from the learnings sought. (Wiggins & McTighe, 2005, p. 14)

Tomlinson and McTighe (2006) see UbD as a way to address standards without compromising students' powers of mind and knowledge bases:

Beset by lists of content standards and accompanying "high-stakes" accountability tests, many educators sense that both teaching and learning have been redirected in ways that are potentially impoverishing for those who teach and those who learn. Educators need a model that acknowledges the centrality of standards but that also demonstrates how meaning and understanding can both emanate from and frame content standards so that young people develop powers of mind as well as accumulate an information base. For many educators, Understanding by Design addresses that need. (p. 1)

The constructivist idea of keeping students at the center of learning through the use of differentiated instruction was described earlier as an appropriate means to address the needs of all learners. Tomlinson and McTighe (2006) have coupled differentiated instruction with UbD as a means for addressing the unique needs of all learners:

Simultaneously, teachers find it increasingly difficult to ignore the diversity of learners who populate their classrooms. Culture, race, language, economics, gender, experience, motivation to achieve, disability, advanced ability, personal interests, learning preferences, and presence or absence of an adult support system are just some of the factors that students bring to school with them in almost stunning variety. Few teachers find their work effective or satisfying when they simply "serve up" a curriculum—even an elegant one—to their students with no regard for their varied learning needs. For many educators, Differentiated Instruction offers a framework for addressing learner variance as a critical component of instructional planning. (pp. 1–2)

Assessment in Student Learning

The second stage of backward design, according to Wiggins and McTighe (2005), addresses the need for thoughtful assessment practices to determine if and to what extent students have met or exceeded the goals set forth in stage one.

Before beginning a discussion on assessment, it is important to distinguish between assessment and evaluation. Russell and Airasian (2012) state that "assessment is a process of collecting, synthesizing and interpreting information in order to make a decision" (pp. 10–11). They go on to say, "*Evaluation* is the process of making judgments about what is good or desirable" (p. 11). Ward and Murray-Ward (1999) illustrate how assessment and evaluation can be used in education:

The term evaluation includes assessment but also refers to making judgments. In education, judgments may be made about the performance of a student, teacher, school, district, and so on. And judgments may be made about the quality or worth of an educational program or procedures." (pp. 70–71)

Looking first to assessment, it is clear that when assessment is used in this sense, it involves the rate or amount used to measure student learning. This is one place where the use of measurable (also known as instructional or behavioral) objectives is useful in assessment.[17] Having a criterion to measure an expected outcome gives teachers a benchmark to help measure learning. For example, if teachers expect students to be able to identify five different animals and if a student is only able to identify three different animals, he or she falls below the benchmark. On the other hand, if a student is able to identify 15 animals, he or she falls above the benchmark. Rather than automatically dismissing the one whose measure falls below the benchmark as "not getting it," perhaps teachers should consider the glass half-full rather than half-empty. After all, the student was able to identify some of the animals, so what caused him or her to not be able to identify others? In addition, was the student able to do things (identify, describe, relate, and so on) not stated in the objective either about animals or something else that was introduced in the lesson?

For the student who identified far more animals than expected, what prompted the student to be able to identify so many? Did prior knowledge play a part? Was the student exposed to experiences or opportunities such as books, movies, zoos, or computer games that played more of a part in his or her surpassing the benchmark than the actual experiences presented in class?

This example shows how something as simple as the measure used in an objective needs to be interpreted and critically analyzed rather than accepted at face value. In doing this, teachers are better able to improve learning experiences that may result in greater student learning. In this section several technology-enhanced techniques for assessing student learning are presented. Keep in mind that no technique is completely error proof and that the data should be analyzed within context.

Assessment Methods and Practices

Assessment involves the means and methods for measuring student learning. Over the years, educators and researchers have determined that some methods are superior to others in providing accurate data that can be reasonably analyzed and that can inform teaching.

Tomlinson and McTighe (2006) describe the components of teaching. In effective classrooms, teachers consistently attend to at least four elements: whom they teach (students); where they teach (learning environment); what they teach (content); and how they teach (instruction). They write, "If teachers lose sight of any one of the elements and cease investing effort in it, the whole fabric of their work is damaged and the quality of learning impaired" (p. 2).

They further assert the importance of the "what" and "how" of teaching in UbD:

Understanding by Design focuses on what we teach and what assessment evidence we need to collect. Its primary goal is delineating and guiding application of sound principles of curriculum design. It also emphasizes how we teach, particularly ways of teaching for student understanding. Certainly the model addresses the need to teach so that students succeed, but the model speaks most fully about "what" and "how." In other words, Understanding by Design is predominantly (although not solely) a curriculum design model. (2006, p. 2)

Brown and Wiggins (2004) assert that high-level users of backward design consistently note the value of its second stage:

High-level users consistently acknowledge the value of the backward design in Stage Two, particularly the way in which it reinforces the need to use the following four interrelated assessment processes to monitor students' growing understanding and support their achievement: Tests and quizzes with constructed-response items; Reflective assessments; Academic prompts; Culminating projects. (pp. 65–66)

Many factors should be addressed when considering which method of assessment should be used in a given learning situation to fulfill phase two of backward design. Some of the factors include time (when); under what conditions (where and how); who to assess (who); the purpose of assessment (why); and available resources (with what).

Formative and Summative Assessments

When looking at the time factor for when assessment should take place—the when of assessment—researchers typically divide assessment into two categories: formative and summative. Generally, formative assessment takes place as an ongoing process to provide data related to how learning is taking place throughout the learning process. Summative assessment follows the learning process. Using both formative and summative assessment data to make informed decisions about teaching is advisable.

Formative assessment might take the form of simple surveys distributed throughout a semester to collect feedback on student perceptions of learning. Based on feedback from students, changes in plans can be made to accommodate students. Another example might be the use of quizzes to collect data on student learning. In this instance, both teachers and students can gauge the learning that is taking place. Regardless of the methods or means for collecting data, analysis of the data serves to make learning better for students. Without formative assessment, teachers may falsely interpret verbal cues and assume students are learning when they are not. Data from formative assessment helps teachers gather concrete information from which to make informed decisions.

Similarly, summative assessment provides feedback to teachers and students on learning, yet it is of a cumulative nature. Summative data can help teachers understand if concepts were learned or need to be re-taught, or if concepts should be taught in a different manner. It can also improve future teaching for when the material is taught again. While not foolproof, using formative and summative assessments together can help teachers make appropriate decisions to maximize student learning.

Conditions for Assessment

In addition to the time, or *when*, factor, teachers should consider the conditions under which assessment should take place, or the *where* and *how* of assessment. Collecting data in a setting where students are also learning is using a naturalistic setting for assessment. In other words, if teachers want to assess student learning of laboratory skills, they should consider making those assessments in the laboratory setting rather than utilizing a regular classroom with a paper-and-pencil instrument. To use another, admittedly extreme, example of the importance of setting, teachers who normally teach their spelling lessons before lunch in a quiet, self-contained setting would do better to assess learning of spelling before lunch in a quiet, self-contained setting rather than on the playground or during recess.

Another condition to consider is *how* data will be collected. In some cases, anonymous feedback is preferred to feedback that can be attributed to particular students. If teachers want honest responses from students regarding perceptions of learning, it might be best to use anonymous surveys. There are times, however, when teachers may wish to be able to identify respondents, for instance, if they are trying to track individual student growth in learning.

Participants

The *who* of assessment relates to who will be asked to participate in the assessment process. In some cases, both student and parent feedback is appropriate to assess learning. There may be others who should be included in the assessment process if teachers are trying to pinpoint certain student data that requires the input of additional individuals. Distributing surveys to parents regarding how much time students spend on homework or how much time parents participate in their children's learning, for example, may provide clues as to why some students are learning while others are not. In some forms of research, the concept of triangulation is used for the sake of clarity. Triangulation refers to using several (more precisely three) angles to investigate a phenomenon so that a clearer, perhaps more accurate account of the phenomenon will be revealed. In this case, a type of triangulation is used if students, parents, and teachers provide feedback on learning. This is the proverbial case of two (or three) heads being better than one in helping to answer questions about student learning.

Purpose of Assessment

Before considering the when, where, how, and who of assessment, teachers must first ask themselves the purpose for which assessment will be conducted. Collecting data to interpret the best time to teach a subject during the day will involve different factors than assessing learning in relation to the physical environment. The former deals largely with time and related elements, such as when lunch is served or when recess occurs, and the latter involves all of those things that make up the physical environment, such as lighting, color, wall décor, seating arrangements, and the like. While both are concerned with assessing student learning, the methods used to collect data will likely vary.

Teachers may choose to start with the end in mind. They can select appropriate assessment by considering the end purpose for which they wish to collect data for interpretation and then decide on the other factors involved in assessment.

Technology-Enhanced Assessment Tools

With regard to technology, a number of the multiple types of assessments described by Brown and Wiggins (2004) can be enhanced by technology. For example, tests and quizzes can be computer generated, graded, and tracked; reflective assessments can be in digital journals, blogs, and microblogs;

academic prompts can be clearly articulated, word-processed documents that include expectations for performance-based assignments; and culminating projects can be ICT-assisted PBL (or PBL-IT) in nature, a digital creation, or involve a simulation. In summary, goals should drive assessment (stage one of backward design should drive stage two) and technology can be used to enhance or amplify tasks associated with administering, monitoring, and analyzing assessment data to inform decisions.

Looking back to the *what* of assessment involves what type of assessment to use and what resources are available to carry out the assessment.

Teachers can use a number of assessment tools to collect student data to see whether students are meeting or exceeding the goals set forth. Some of these tools include survey and quiz tools, editing and readability tools, demonstration-capturing tools (e.g., slidecasts, videocasts), group work and collaborative tools, digital journals, digital portfolios, digital stories, and recorded performances (e.g., video, audio, claymations, animations). Similar to the use of triangulation in who will participate in assessment, the use of many assessment tools may help teachers capture a more realistic and accurate picture of student learning. For example, using data collected from oral exams, demonstrations, and group work might provide better data than from any one tool alone.

Available resources will help teachers make decisions regarding which methods of assessment to use to measure student learning. Teachers may have lofty goals for collecting and analyzing daily assessments, but available time might prohibit this from occurring. They may desire to collect and interpret data from all students and parents through oral interviews, but again, this might be impossible due to scheduling conflicts and time. Other limiting factors might be the physical environment, the willingness of those asked to provide accurate and honest responses, the reliability and validity of testing instruments, and the tools themselves to distribute or use for collecting data. While the technology-enhanced tools are far too numerous to include here in their entirety, some examples will be provided to show how they may be used in the assessment process.

Determining Readability with Technology

At various developmental levels, teachers wish to assess learning in relation to reading. Various word-processing applications, such as Microsoft Word (http://office.microsoft.com/word) and Google Docs (www.docs.google.com), have readability tools built in. Some stand-alone programs, like Flesh (http://flesh.sourceforge.net), and several web-based readability applications, such as the one from Added Bytes (www.addedbytes.com/tools/readability-score), are also available. Some of the readability tools allow text to be entered and checked, while others check readability by entering URLs. Teachers can highlight passages of text to determine the readability of content they will use in class to ensure that the text is developmentally appropriate for students. Varying readability levels of text presented and then measuring student comprehension might help teachers more accurately pinpoint student reading levels.

Students' word-processed work can also be selected and the readability of their text easily determined. Measures of student writing samples can help provide teachers with data to analyze progress in reading and writing.

The Dynamic Indicators of Basic Early Literacy Skills (DIBELS) Data System (https://dibels.uoregon.edu) uses both hardware and software to assess students' reading: "The DIBELS measures assess the five Big Ideas in early literacy identified by the National Reading Panel: phonemic awareness, alphabetic principle, accuracy and fluency, vocabulary, comprehension" (University of Oregon, n.d., para. 3). The

DIBELS system provides tools to generate reports and track progress and includes many other features that can help students improve in reading.

Some tools, such as the Teacher Book Wizard (http://bookwizard.scholastic.com/tbw/homePage.do) available on the Scholastic website (www.scholastic.com/teachers), allow teachers to identify books based on interest level/grade, readability level, subject/topic, and genre/theme. Using this tool, developmentally appropriate books can be selected for each child to help determine his or her zones of proximal development and assess their reading levels, comprehension, and so forth.

Editing Tools

Other features commonly available in most word-processing software are the comment and editing tools. Teachers can provide specific and detailed feedback to students using comment and editing tools, and use corrections in the assessment process. A more unique way of using these tools for assessment purposes is to provide students with writing samples that contain correctly and incorrectly written text. Students can be asked to use the comment and editing tools to explain any incorrect text and make corrections. This can help teachers identify areas of difficulty that may not be easily identified using a traditional paper-and-pencil instrument.

Editing and commenting on work with word-processing programs that lack elaborate tools can still be accomplished, especially if teachers are engaging in minimal marking.[18] Minimal marking uses a system of marking that requires students to identify and correct their own errors. Check marks, brackets, and the like—available with nearly every word-processing application—can facilitate this process.

Online Communication

To collect survey data or feedback for assessment purposes that asks for comments from students, parents, teachers, or others, teachers can use a variety of online communication instruments. Some of the simple technology communications tools, such as email, can be used for feedback. Teachers can provide the option of having students, parents, teachers, or others provide feedback through secure electronic communication tools if district or school policy allows. For example, some Internet bulletin boards allow you to collect anonymous responses with options to release discussion entries (in this case survey responses) to whomever you choose.

Free survey-generating tools, such as Google Docs, and subscription-based ones, such as SurveyMonkey (http://surveymonkey.com), are provided on the Internet, but teachers must be sure to check with their school administration to find out any restrictions that may apply to the use of these tools. If teachers are permitted to use these survey-generating and data-collecting tools, they must ensure that they are using them from a reputable site. They should read the privacy policies and user agreements very carefully to see if they conflict with school, district, or professional codes of ethics.

Once teachers receive the data, they will still need to interpret what they have collected, but these technology-enhanced tools will make the collecting much more efficient, quick, and accessible to those with Internet access. Always be mindful that there may be some students, parents, and teachers who, for whatever reason, do not have or wish to use online-communication tools in this way. For them, be sure to provide alternative ways to receive feedback.

KWL Diagrams

KWL diagrams (K represents what one knows, W represents what one wants to know, and L represents what one has learned) were discussed in Chapter 1 as a means to monitor student or teacher growth and development.

Student-maintained KWL diagrams are also ways to collect data about student learning and growth. By using the form feature available in most word-processing software, teachers can create KWL diagram forms. If the forms are properly created, teachers can limit what students are able to modify on their forms by protecting the document and applying restrictions. In most cases, teachers will create text form fields, where students simply tab to all fields and type in their own text.

A wide assortment of assessment forms can be created (e.g., fill-in-the-blank assignments, interactive worksheets) that can also be used for assessment purposes.

Digital Portfolios

Digital portfolios, either web-based or created using presentation or portfolio-specific software, allow for a wide assortment of artifacts to be archived and organized for evidence of learning. Many books and resources exist to help teachers and students create digital portfolios, including those in Resource List 2.11.

RESOURCE LIST 2.11 ▪ Technology tools for organizing student work

edLine a Blackboard company: www.edline.com

DIGI[cation]: www.digication.com

TaskStream: www.taskstream.com

Portfolios can be created using blogs or web pages, and multimedia (such as videos and photos) can be used along with text.[19]

One advantage of having and reviewing digital portfolios over hardbound ones is their ease of transport and their compactness. Students can save portfolios on a computer, save to a CD, DVD, or other storage device, or save on a web-based server.

Another advantage is the ability to easily backup digital portfolios. If a hardbound portfolio is lost or destroyed, it may be difficult and time-consuming to replace it. On the other hand, a digital portfolio can be restored easily if properly backed up.

For ease of assessment, teachers may wish to create a rubric so that their assessment has more objectivity than it may have without the use of a rubric.

Interactive Quiz and Testing Software

Many textbook companies provide quiz and testing software to accompany their texts. Some of the software only allows teachers to create quizzes or tests from a large database of questions or from questions they add themselves. More sophisticated software allows teachers not only to create quizzes and tests, but also to create interactive tests that provide feedback to students, automatically grade tests, and calculate statistical data. Other kinds of interactive quiz and testing software not associated with textbook publishers are available to teachers as commercial products, shareware, and freeware.

Learning management systems provide teachers and administrators with quiz- and survey-generating tools to help assess student progress.

Interactive Puzzles and Assignment-Generating Software

Puzzles have proved to be great tools for enrichment and for exercising thinking skills (see Chapter 1 for more about using games in education). At one time, teachers had to create puzzles by hand, which was a lengthy and arduous process. Today, many interactive puzzle technology tools are available to teachers that allow them to easily create a wide variety of content-related puzzles—crosswords, word searches, Sudoku—for teaching and assessment. Generally, teachers can ask the same questions on a puzzle that can be asked on the traditional worksheet. One major difference is that students often like puzzles better and do not even realize they are engaged in learning or that teachers are engaged in assessment.

A number of web-based crossword puzzle-generating tools are available, such as those in Resource List 2.12.

RESOURCE LIST 2.12 ■ Web-based tools for making puzzles

Discovery Education's Puzzlemaker: www.discoveryeducation.com/puzzlemaker

Puzzle Maker from Lesson Corner: www.lessoncorner.com/puzzles

TeAch-nology Crossword Puzzle Maker: www.teach-nology.com/web_tools/crossword

Photograph Puzzle Maker: www.flash-gear.com/puzzle

   A photo puzzle maker that allows students to solve picture jigsaw puzzles using photos they upload

EclipseCrossword: www.eclipsecrossword.com

   A stand-alone program that allows teachers to create and use puzzles in assessment

Brothersoft's Crossword Puzzle: www.brothersoft.com/daily-crossword-widget-172398.html

   Another program for creating and using puzzles for assessment and other purposes

Note that some puzzle-making programs can be used on mobile technologies.

Digital Images in Assessment

Digital photographs can effectively capture still images for assessment purposes. (Check first with district or school policy to determine what types of permissions are needed to photograph or videotape students.) Some examples are photographs of students demonstrating psychomotor skills, such as a child balancing on one leg; a lab skill, such as the proper use of equipment; and a product created as evidence of learning, such as a tower built to specifications in a higher-order thinking exercise. These artifacts can be used as stand-alone assessments or as part of a larger method of assessment, such as in a portfolio. A series of digital photographs can be used to document and assess learning and growth. For example, a series of photographs can be taken of a student-created mural.

Digital video images can have a similar purpose in documenting and assessing learning and growth. Digital video is useful for capturing performances, demonstrations, oral reporting, cooperative group work, lab work, role-playing, and many other evidences of learning. Digital videos taken at different intervals throughout a given time or course can also provide evidence of growth in a skill, concept, or thought process. Using digital video with programs such as Camtasia, iMovie, and Movie Maker (see Resource List 2.13) can help teachers assess change over time. Some software programs, such as those manufactured by Dartfish (go to www.dartfish.com/en and navigate from Education to Teachers Training), are designed to be used for psychomotor skill analysis and improvement.

RESOURCE LIST 2.13 ■ Digital video programs

Camtasia: www.techsmith.com/camtasia.asp

Apple's iMovie: www.apple.com/ilife/imovie

Windows Movie Maker for Vista, Windows Live Movie Maker, and others:
http://windows.microsoft.com/en-US/windows/downloads

Microsoft products are available by going to the above link and selecting the platform of your choice.

Scanned images can also provide some of the same evidence of student learning for use in assessment. One of the advantages of using digital photography over scanning is that digital photographs can capture images of people, large documents, and documents that are not flat. Still, scanners can quickly "take pictures" of small, flat items, such as handwriting samples and student-created stories that can be easily, compactly, and digitally stored for assessment purposes.

Technology-Enhanced Rubrics

Rubrics are powerful tools to use in assessment. They can be used to assess learning for a great variety of methods and, if distributed early to students, provide them with concrete information about how they will be assessed for learning. Some methods for which rubrics can be effectively used are with essays, portfolios, writing samples, group work, performances, demonstrations, and oral reports.

Creating rubrics is easy if technology is used. Like some of the other tools mentioned above, commercial, shareware, and freeware rubric-creating software abound. In addition, some teaching websites provide these tools to users. Two examples of rubric-generating web resources include Rubistar (http://rubistar.4teachers.org) and the rubric-generating tool available from TeAch-nology (www.teach-nology.com).

Spreadsheets

Spreadsheets are software applications used to calculate, graph, and sort data. Microsoft Excel (http://office.microsoft.com/excel) is a widely used form of spreadsheet software today, but several other commercial, shareware, and freeware spreadsheet software applications, such as OpenOffice Calc (www.openoffice.org/product/calc.html), are available to teachers. In addition, spreadsheet software applications are specifically designed for use in grading, (such as EdLine's GradeQuick, available at www.edline.com) are widely available. Using spreadsheet software in your teaching practice is discussed in Chapter 3. Here, the discussion of spreadsheet software is limited to its use in assessment.

Spreadsheet software can be efficiently used with quantifiable data or data that use numbers. Recording student scores and noting changes for individual students over time can help teachers modify learning for individual students. Similarly, collective data can be analyzed and interpreted to help measure student learning. Most spreadsheet software can easily and quickly generate graphs, tables, and other graphic forms that can powerfully and clearly show comparative measurements and changes. Moreover, the ability to calculate grades and other numbers cannot be overlooked; this is typically what many users identify spreadsheet software with—the ability to calculate or "crunch numbers."

Using spreadsheet software in assessment is simply timesaving and labor efficient. It also contributes to accuracy and provides excellent graphic images to share with those vested in the education of students. For example, parents can easily see student learning and progress by viewing a graph, and likewise, principals can clearly see student assessment by providing such data neatly in a spreadsheet printout. In the following section, more specific ways to use spreadsheet software to collect, analyze, and interpret student data in the assessment process will be discussed.

Improving Student Learning through Technology-Enhanced Assessment

In the previous section, the tools that teachers can use to assess student learning were presented. To make meaning from the data collected, teachers need to analyze and interpret the data in order to improve instruction and share findings with others vested in their students' learning. A few ways will be presented in this section.

Assessment as a Means to an End

Teachers may keep the end goals and results in mind when considering the means through which they will assess student learning. They may wish to assess student learning both on an individual basis and on a collective, whole-class basis.

Perhaps the greatest broad-based outcome teachers wish to achieve as a result of assessment is to ultimately maximize student learning through improved instructional practices. All of the qualitative and quantitative student data in the world will have little value if they do not accomplish this goal. For this reason, teachers need to carefully consider all components in the assessment process and make informed decisions throughout.

To construct meaning from the data they collect, teachers may wish to design an assessment plan. More specifically, they may want to use a system for designing, implementing, and evaluating the assessments they carry out in their professional practice. Including the evaluation component in their assessment plan allows teachers to uncover methods and techniques that work better and to modify their plans accordingly. One approach to this is illustrated in Figure 2.14.

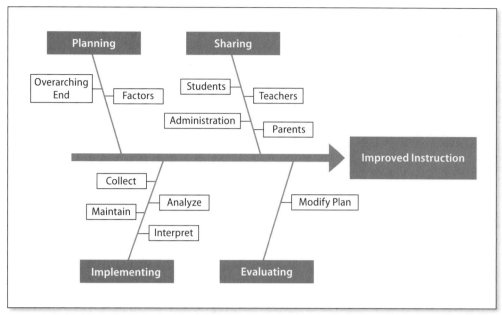

FIGURE 2.14 Outline for an assessment plan (shown on a Ishikawa diagram).

Planning

The planning phase can include many of the items discussed in the previous section. Teachers can begin with the ultimate end in mind, which will be improved instructional practices to maximize learning. Specific outcomes should be known from the beginning. If standards and performance indicators are the bases for outcomes, then they should be included as the end products. From there, everything else will follow.

The factors used to determine which method(s) teachers will select include those that address the who, what, where, when, how, and why of assessment, as described earlier in this chapter. Once these considerations have been addressed, some methods consistent with these factors and the overarching end can be selected. Here teachers can list the method(s) they intend to use to assess appropriately. Figure 2.15 illustrates a form on which teachers may record their thoughts in the planning process. Note that in this part of the assessment process, considerations for available resources will likely involve technology.

Implementing

When implementing the plan, teachers will carry out the collection, analysis, maintenance, and interpretation of data. Each one of these areas can be enhanced through the use of technology.

Data can be collected in a number of technology-enhanced ways. For quantitative data, spreadsheet software is ideal for recording measures of learning. Test scores, rubric totals, and the like can be easily entered into a spreadsheet, and formulas can be created to calculate averages. For times when teachers use spreadsheets specifically for grading, they can use spreadsheet software expressly designed for use as a digital gradebook. Rather than just view such software as a way to record and average grades, however, they can use this software as a type of data-collection repository.

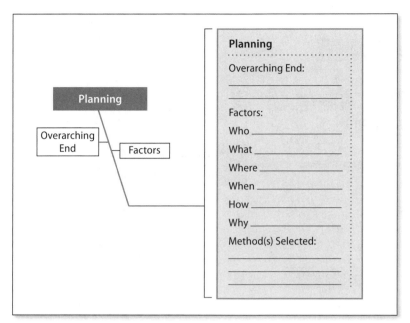

FIGURE 2.15 Planning in assessment.

For qualitative data, teachers can record measures of learning in a database using database software. Different kinds of database software are available as commercial, shareware, and freeware stand-alone products, such as Microsoft Access (http://office.microsoft.com/access) and OpenOffice Base (www.openoffice.org/product/base.html), and web-based applications. These database tools normally allow users to record, sort, and filter data.[20]

Many database software programs and applications also allow users to easily create reports. Journal entries, especially if completed by students in digital form, can be copied and pasted into database fields. Survey comments can be recorded in the same way. Some of the advantages of using database software include compactness for storage and the ease of sorting and filtering qualitative data. Later in this section, ways to use sorted data for analysis purposes will be presented. A number of software products, such as NVivo (www.qsrinternational.com), are specifically designed to record and help users analyze qualitative data.

Analysis involves breaking something apart into pieces in order to unveil patterns, changes, or other nuances that might help in the interpretation process of assessment. When using quantitative data, graphs, charts, and tables are very useful in analysis for showing patterns or changes. For qualitative data, sorting, filtering, and reporting tools typically included in database software may be used to help teachers identify patterns or changes.[21]

One of the advantages of maintaining an electronic spreadsheet or database of data is the efficiency of storage. When hard copies of data are used, large amounts of physical space are normally set aside in a classroom or storage closet for this purpose. Not only are teachers possibly infringing on instructional space when storing data in hard copy, but they also run the risk of physical damage of data from natural disasters and ethical violations from trespassers pilfering through records. This not only impacts data storage and safety, but also involves confidentiality, privacy, and security.

When data are stored electronically, much less physical space is required. Also, data can be protected more securely if appropriate measures are taken to safeguard files (e.g., password protection, file backups, appropriate physical storage). For these reasons alone, teachers may want to consider using electronic spreadsheets and databases in their assessment practices.

Interpretation involves deriving meaning from analysis of the data collected. In other words, what does the data say about student learning, and how is what it says related to instructional practices? For example, is there a pattern to learning (e.g., a cyclical pattern)? Is student learning improving, declining, or holding steady? Have any changes in instructional practices possibly influenced student learning? Does research support or contradict the interpretation? Learning to work through the implementation process of assessment takes some time and patience, but the rewards can be great if teachers identify instructional practices that truly maximize learning. And since that is the end purpose, all the effort will have been worth it. Figure 2.16 illustrates a form on which teachers can record some general notes on data collection, analysis, maintenance, and interpretation.

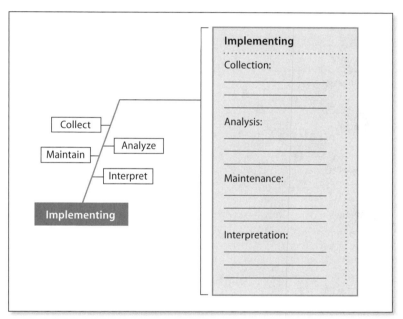

FIGURE 2.16 Implementation in assessment.

Sharing Findings

Communicating findings to vested members of the educational community can be efficiently done using technology-enhanced means. Some members of the educational community who share a vested interest in the education of students are the students themselves; other teachers in the school (when appropriate); administrators; and parents. Always observe confidentiality, privacy rights, and related concerns when sharing data so that individual students cannot be identified. Exceptions include sharing data with students and their legal guardians. In some cases, teachers and administrators should be privy to student identification, but often this is not the case when trends, patterns, or changes are being shared.

Communicating findings to others can be enhanced dramatically through the use of technology. Technology tools, such as email, web pages, reports (created easily from spreadsheet and database software), word-processed summaries, and so forth, can dramatically ease the speed and delivery of assessment findings. Again, always be mindful of confidentiality, privacy, and security when communicating face-to-face, in writing, or using technology. In the case of technology, teachers can utilize password protection when appropriate, although this, too, does not guarantee that the contents will not find its way into unscrupulous hands.

Another avenue for sharing findings might be at professional conferences where teachers present data on connections they have made between instructional practices and student learning (such as action-research findings). Here, too, be sure to observe confidentiality and other precautions. In this case, presentation tools, along with some of the tools already mentioned, might enhance communication of findings. There are so many ways to use technology communication tools to share assessment findings that they are limited only by imagination. Figure 2.17 illustrates how teachers might list various technology-enhanced tools to use for each category of individuals.

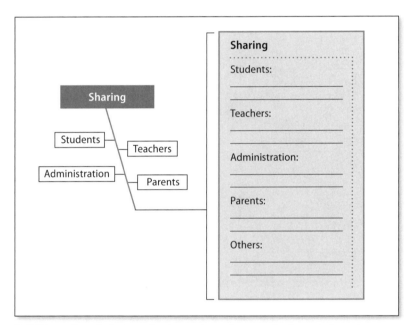

FIGURE 2.17 Form for listing technology-enhanced communication tools for each category of individuals.

Evaluation

Teachers might find a need to modify their original plan for assessment as they move through various components. If they find that one method for assessment is yielding what they suspect is contrived data, they may wish to replace or discard the method. This is another advantage for teachers who use multiple measures in assessment: if one is not working, they have another or others that will provide them with more accurate data. Figure 2.18 shows a form for making notes to evaluate the assessment process.

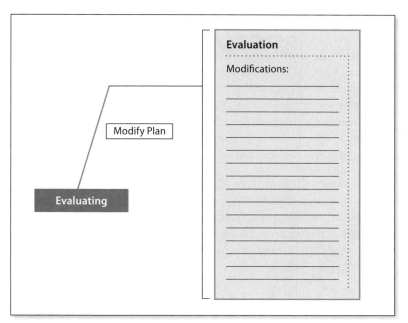

FIGURE 2.18 Evaluation form for recording modifications to the assessment plan.

Although in the original outline, Figure 2.14, evaluation is found near the end of the assessment process, it is really best to reflect on the plan throughout the assessment process and to make informed decisions regarding modification of the plan. If it helps, teachers can reevaluate their plan after every major data collection or analysis to see what is working and what is not. Using a technology-generated graphic organizer, such as the Ishikawa diagram that was used to create Figure 2.14, might also provide teachers with a visual way of keeping evaluation always in sight as they move through the process of assessment.[22]

Note that instructional programs encompass all the instructional practices used by the teacher, as well as the classroom environment; the curriculum and standards used; the interactions among teachers, students, and others in the educational community; the learning materials provided; and any other components that contribute to overall student learning. Therefore, program evaluation uses assessment data and other information to make important decisions for student learning.

As with assessment, answering questions related to who, what, where, when, how, and why can help guide evaluation.

Participatory Evaluation

Participatory evaluation (PE), has been discussed as a way to involve stakeholders in evaluation to improve programs and social conditions. Zukoski and Luluquisen (2002) define participatory evaluation as "a partnership approach to evaluation in which stakeholders actively engage in developing the evaluation and all phases of its implementation" (p. 1).

Specific to schools, Cousins and Earl (1995) assert, "In schools, we see participatory evaluation as a powerful learning system designed to foster local applied research and thereby enhance social discourse about relevant school-based issues" (p. 11). For the purpose of this text, PE will be greatly simplified to help teachers ease into an evaluation process that involves collaboration and improvement.

One element of PE is the idea that those impacted by change(s) as a result of evaluation—in this case, changes in educational programs—should play an important role in the evaluation process.[23] This involves more than just providing data, including considering stakeholders' ideas, concerns, and contributions for evaluating and proposing change. This participatory involvement and collaboration contrasts with an evaluation process designed and implemented by an individual or group of individuals who monopolize decisions and actions in the evaluation process. A second characteristic of PE is that the examined phenomenon (for example, the educational program) can be changed as a result of discoveries made in the evaluation process. A third feature recognizes the ongoing nature of the evaluation process; evaluation does not end when a single discovery is made or initial changes are made.[24]

Looking first to the *who* of evaluation, it is important to consider those who are a part of the phenomenon examined and will be impacted by any change initiated through evaluation findings. At times, those involved and those who will be impacted are the very same individuals, but they can also be different. For example, in an educational program, students are the primary players, but if changes are made to include changes in the home or community to improve the educational program, then members of these additional groups become important participants in the educational process.

The most obvious participants in an evaluation process that includes educational programs are students, for without students, an educational program is nonexistent. Others vested and involved in the educational program include teachers and others close to the program, such as administrative staff and counselors. Moving outward, parents and other community members, lawmakers, and many more individuals are involved, but they take secondary, tertiary, quaternary, or even more distant roles. When beginning the process of evaluation, teachers need to consider all of the other factors of evaluation, such as time and resources available. Teachers may wish to include every individual who remotely participates in the educational program, but it may not be feasible or realistic to do so. Here again, teachers should keep the end in mind when developing their plan for evaluation.

Once participants are identified, consideration should be given to what roles each will take. Keep in mind the developmental levels of students, their experiences, and their abilities to contribute. Older students may share a greater role in helping teachers decide on evaluation methods, whereas younger students may be less able to articulate ideas for methods but can still contribute by sharing, however simply, what they would like to receive from the educational program. Determining collaborative roles in the professional learning community (PLC) is key to creating a process that is truly participative.

Data collected and interpreted in the assessment process can inform evaluation practices. Some of the data collected may have been derived using standardized tests, criterion-referenced tests, surveys, and various forms of authentic assessment, including performances, demonstrations, and portfolios to measure student learning. Although these data allow teachers to make informed decisions regarding instructional practices, looking at the big picture requires using data from other sources to make programmatic changes.

Collecting data from survey instruments, questionnaires, and interviews from the larger population of students can also provide important clues that relate to the success of educational programs. Moreover, data from counselors, staff, parents, and other stakeholders can provide clues to the effectiveness of programs. Although standardized tests may indicate attainment of certain knowledge and skills, they are typically not as useful in providing data related to student dispositions. Parents, teachers, and student employers are often better sources of data for showing such attributes as discipline, work ethic, and the like. These individual attributes are normally a part of the intended outcomes of educational programs; thus they are important in the overall evaluation process.

Using multiple methods and sources of data in evaluation can help teachers determine learning, communication, and productivity of students, or, in other words, the effectiveness of the educational program being examined. In order to determine appropriate use of technology resources by students, an evaluation plan should be designed, implemented, and modified in relation to this focus.

Some of the obvious methods that can be used for collecting student data are those mentioned in previous sections of this chapter. Both quantitative and qualitative data should be used and should come from several different instruments or methods. Data that is collected throughout and just before a major analysis should also be a part of the ongoing process.

Some quantitative measures that can inform the evaluation process include records of student use (e.g., measured in time logged on the computer); information and means used for communication; how many different means of technology are used; and test scores that signify the presence of technology in learning. Home computer logs can document how often students use technology at home that was introduced in the educational program. The administration can provide student-tracking data to show when school-related technology is used most, as well as other important quantitative information.

Some of the qualitative measures that can yield insights into the effectiveness of student use of technology are student-questionnaire responses, parent responses to specific questions, and administrator feedback from interviews. Whether quantitative or qualitative, remember that spreadsheets, databases, and other technologies described in the previous sections are very helpful in recording, storing, maintaining, retrieving, and analyzing data.

Before planning tracking or collecting of data, teachers must be sure to check with their school administrator for prohibitions to these actions or for any necessary permissions they must acquire before implementing such actions.

How Assessment and Evaluation Can Improve Instructional Practices

Assessment and evaluation should lead to improved instructional practices to maximize student learning. In this section a variety of technology-enhanced tools were used throughout the assessment and evaluation processes to increase efficiency and productivity. Looking to research, it is well-known that certain instructional practices are more effective than others in given situations. Since no two teaching situations are alike, teachers' own classroom teaching experiences and the learning experiences of their students can reveal connections between instructional practices and student learning that may go unreported in the literature. Research can and should inform professional practice, but teachers' own research through assessment can be quite enlightening.

Documenting Standards Attainment

In this age of accountability, it is not enough for teachers to know that they are addressing the district, state, national, or international standards; they must also be able to professionally defend and document the learning experiences designed to help yield student achievement. Doing so is easier than one might think if teachers document standards directly in their lesson plans.

One way to accomplish this quickly and easily is to attach standards they are going to use to the lesson plans. Most standards use an alphanumeric system for identification. For every lesson objective written, the standard being addressed should be documented. Teachers can simply write the alphanumeric designation of the standard beside the objective in parentheses. If they are using more than one set of standards, they can use different colors to designate different standards. As long as they keep the printed standards with the lesson plan, it is not necessary to write out the standards they are documenting.

Another reason to keep these printouts with the lesson plans is because standards change in content and identification through the years. Maintaining easy access to the printouts provides evidence that teachers are addressing the standards required and serves as a reminder to them and administrators of how much they are accomplishing throughout the school year.

If lesson plans are kept in digital form, the same approach can be used, but the standards will be documented digitally. For example, lesson plans can include links to standards, or the standards can be word processed right into the lesson-plan template. For archival purposes, teachers may wish to save their lesson plans in a format that can be opened using a variety of computers and that may be usable in future years.[25] For example, saving documents as PDF files may prove helpful later if a word-processing software is discontinued. Furthermore, in some cases, files cannot be opened with later versions of the same software.

In Your Experience

What methods of assessment has a current or former teacher used to measure your learning?

- How effective do you think these methods were in assessing your learning?

- Explain.

Section T2d Explorations

1. Visit your local school board's website. Navigate the site to determine if the system is using a standards-based curriculum. If it is, what standards are being used?

2. Create a graphic organizer illustrating how this text uses backward design.

3. Use a readability tool to obtain readability statistics on a paper you have written.

   - Were you surprised by the statistics?

   - Explain and share with your peers.

4. Visit one of your favorite websites and use a readability tool to determine its readability.

   - Were you surprised by the statistics?

   - Explain and share this with your peers.

5. Using a peer's paper and word-processing software, use minimal marking or some other correction system to assess your peer's work. Exchange a paper you wrote with your peer and have him or her do the same.

6. Create a slidecast showing how a digital portfolio can be created using various technology resources. In the slidecast, explain the advantages and disadvantages of keeping a digital portfolio rather than a hardbound one.

7. Create a puzzle that assesses comprehension of the contents in this section. Exchange your puzzle with a peer. Provide feedback to each other.

8. Use digital images (still or video) to assess yourself on the performance of a skill. For example, you may photograph yourself at the beginning, middle, and end of the skill development. Make a list of how this tool can be used in assessment.

9. Use a rubric-generating tool to create a rubric that can be used in the assessment process.

10. Use spreadsheet software to record learning you are experiencing. For example, record your test grades in a spreadsheet program, and use the graphing tool to chart your progress.

    - How much, if at all, did the graph you generated help?

    - Will it help inform your learning?

    - Explain how much, if in any way, it will help inform your learning.

11. Use database software to record learning you are experiencing. For example, record the comments/feedback you received on essays you have written in a database program, and use the reporting function to show your progress.

    - How much, if at all, did the reporting data help?

    - Explain how much, if in any way, it will help inform your learning.

Section T2d Review

In this section you learned how to use standards as foci for learning and how to provide evidence that you are addressing these standards. You also learned ways to apply various technology-enhanced assessment techniques for assessing student learning and the distinction between assessment and evaluation. You learned factors that need to be considered when choosing which assessment methods to use and various ways to use technology in the assessment process. Designing, using, and modifying an assessment plan can be an effective way of informing your instructional practices to maximize student learning.

Chapter 2 Summary

In this chapter you were introduced to technology-enhanced instructional strategies that support the diverse needs of learners. You also learned how to use current research on teaching and learning to inform your teaching practice. You became aware of some ways to identify, locate, and evaluate technology resources, and you learned some strategies to manage technology resources and student learning in a technology-enhanced environment.

Creating learning environments that maximize student learning was also addressed in this chapter. More specifically, you learned how to provide technology-enhanced experiences that address technology standards at various levels. You became familiar with ways to use technology to support learner-centered strategies and that meet the diverse needs of students. You learned how to apply technology to foster higher-order thinking and creativity and how to develop strategies for managing learning activities in a technology-enhanced environment. To achieve most of these goals, you learned that it is important to keep the end outcomes in mind in order to make informed decisions about the best teaching strategies for specific lessons.

Furthermore, you learned ways to help students become self-regulated, self-directed learners who are capable of planning, implementing, monitoring, and assessing their learning progress, as well as methods to address the needs of the diverse learners in your class. Finally, you learned the roles that assessment and evaluation play in instructional and program improvement. Knowing how to effectively use assessment and evaluation in your teaching practice will help you make informed changes that may contribute to improved student learning. This should be every teacher's goal. In the next chapter you will learn additional uses for technology in a modern classroom.

Chapter 2 Notes

1   It is worth noting that there is sometimes overlap between the two review processes.

2   Marzano (2003) characterizes school-level factors as (1) guaranteed and viable curriculum, (2) challenging goals and effective feedback, (3) parent and community involvement, (4) safe and orderly environment, and (5) collegiality and professionalism. He characterizes (1) home atmosphere, (2) learned intelligence and background knowledge, and (3) motivation as student-level factors that impact student achievement (p. 10).

3   See Chapter 1 for a discussion of constructivist teaching and learning.

4   For more information about using assessment and evaluation data to modify teaching, refer to the NETS·T2d section of this chapter.

5   See www.ed.gov/policy/gen/guid/fpco/ferpa for information on the Family Educational Rights and Privacy Act (FERPA).

6   IEPs should not be confused with individual learning plans (ILPs). According to U.S. law, students with disabilities are entitled to a free and appropriate education and are provided with an individualized education program (IEP) (Individuals with Disabilities Improvement Act of 2004). Keep in mind that ILPs cannot and should not replace IEPs.

7 See section NETS•T2b for more on how students can monitor their own progress.

8 See Chapter 4 for a discussion of cooperative learning with regard to improving technology access for all.

9 See section NETS•T2d for more on backward design.

10 When using web-based calendars and management systems, observe ethical practices so that confidential information is not stored on servers that may be compromised.

11 See Lewin (2001) for how to use website content that is not at the desired readability level.

12 To learn more about Seymour Papert's work with technology in education, visit www.papert.org

13 A model IEP from ed.gov can be found at http://idea.ed.gov/download/modelform1_IEP.pdf. Answers to frequently asked questions with regard to IEPs can be seen by going to http://idea.ed.gov/explore/home and clicking on Individualized Education Program, then scrolling down to Q&A Documents.

14 See Chapter 1, Table 1.1, for specific digital and nondigital resources that address different intelligences.

15 As stated in Note 6 for this chapter, ILPs cannot replace IEPs.

16 For links to various state standards, visit Education World at www.education-world.com/standards.

17 For more information on instructional objectives, see R. F. Mager's (1997) work, *Preparing Instructional Objectives: A Critical Tool in the Development of Effective Instruction*.

18 For more information on Haswell's work on minimal marking, see Haswell (1983).

19 For more information and resources on e-portfolios, see Helen Barrett's website at http://helenbarrett.com.

20 See Chapter 4 to learn more about the importance of security and privacy when using student data.

21 It is worth noting that analysis naturally requires synthesis. Synthesis involves bringing back together the materials that were analyzed to make sense of the data. Teachers are using these higher-order thinking skills (see Chapter 1) when they analyze and synthesize in assessment.

22 Figure 2.14 is a cause and effect diagram. It is also known by several other names, such as fishbone diagram or Ishikawa diagram (after its creator, Kaoru Ishikawa). To learn more about Ishikawa, visit www.asq.org and search for his name.

23 For more on stakeholder involvement in evaluation, see Wallace and Alkin (2008).

24 For more on the related concept of participatory action research, see Hughes and Seymour-Rolls (2000), available from http://pandora.nla.gov.au/tep/13568.

25 Guarantees do not exist for which types of formats will be compatible with various user types many years from now.

Chapter 2 References

Armstrong T. (2009). *Multiple intelligences in the classroom* (3rd ed.). Alexandria, VA: Association for Supervision and Curriculum Development.

Barrett, E., & Lally, V. (1999). Gender differences in an on-line learning environment. *Journal of Computer Assisted Learning, 15*(1), 48–60.

Bloom, B. S. (Ed.). (1956). *Taxonomy of educational objectives.* Boston, MA: Allyn & Bacon.

Brown, J., & Wiggins, G. (2004). *Making the most of understanding by design.* Alexandria, VA: Association for Supervision and Curriculum Development.

Cookson, P. (2006, November). Creating the expert mind. *Teaching Pre K–8, 37*(3), 14–16.

Cooper, J., & Weaver, K. (2003). *Gender and computers: Understanding the digital divide.* Mahwah, NJ: Lawrence Erlbaum.

Costello, M. (1996). *Critical issue: Providing effective schooling for students at risk.* Oak Brook, IL: North Central Regional Educational Laboratory. Retrieved October 16, 2009, from www.ncrel.org/sdrs/areas/issues/students/atrisk/at600.htm

Cousins, J., & Earl, L. (1995). The case for participatory evaluation: Theory, research, practice. In J. B. Cousins & L. M. Earl (Eds.), *Participatory evaluation in education: Studies in evaluation use and organizational learning* (pp. 3–18). Bristol, PA: The Falmer Press.

DeBello, T. (1990). Comparison of eleven major learning styles models: Variables, appropriate populations, validity of instrumentation and the research behind them. *Journal of Reading, Writing, and Learning Disabilities International, 6*(3), 203–222.

Dodge, B. (1997). *Some thoughts about WebQuests.* Retrieved October 16, 2009, from http://webquest.sdsu.edu/about_webquests.html

Education Commission of the States. (2007a). *State notes: Additional high school graduation requirements and options.* Retrieved December 1, 2009, from http://mb2.ecs.org/reports/Report.aspx?id=740

Education Commission of the States. (2007b). *State notes: Student support and remediation: State requires individual learning plans for at-risk students.* Retrieved December 1, 2009, from http://mb2.ecs.org/reports/Report.aspx?id=1544

Fuchs, D., Mock, D., Morgan, P., & Young, C. (2003). Responsiveness-to-intervention: Definitions, evidence, and implications for the learning disabilities construct. *Learning Disabilities Research & Practice, 18*(3), 157–171. DOI: 10.1111/1540-5826.00072

Gardner, H. (1983). *Frames of mind: The theory of multiple intelligences.* New York, NY: Basic Books.

Gersten, R., Compton, D., Connor, C., Dimino, J., Santoro, L., Linan-Thompson, S., & Tilly, W. (2008). Assisting students struggling with reading: Response to intervention and multi-tier intervention for reading in the primary grades (NCEE 2009–4045). Washington, DC: National Center for Education Evaluation and Regional Assistance, Institute of Education Sciences, U.S. Department of Education. Retrieved November 24, 2009, from http://ies.ed.gov/ncee/wwc/pdf/practiceguides/rti_reading_pg_021809.pdf

Gillies, W. (2009). Leveraging action research. *Principal Leadership: High School Edition, 9*(7), 6–7.

Gorriz, C., & Medina, C. (2000). Engaging girls with computers through software games. *Communications of the ACM, 43*(1), 42–49.

Hall, T. (2002). *Differentiated instruction: Effective classroom practices report*. Wakefield, MA: National Center on Accessing the General Curriculum. Retrieved December 30, 2011, from www.cast.org/system/galleries/download/ncac/DifInstruc.pdf

Haswell, R. (1983). Minimal marking. *College English, 45*(6), 600–604.

Heeter, C. (2007). Changing girls, changing games. Section IV. In Y. Kafai, C. Heeter, J. Denner, & J. Sun (Eds.), *Beyond Barbie and Mortal Kombat: New perspectives on gender, games, and computing* (pp. 160–177). Cambridge, MA: MIT Press. Retrieved from gel.msu.edu/carrie/publications/bbmk-heeter-winn.pdf

Hughes, I., & Seymour-Rolls, K. (2000). Participatory action research: Getting the job done. *Action Research E-Reports*, 4. Retrieved from http://pandora.nla.gov.au/tep/13568

Individuals with Disabilities Education Act of 2004. (2004). Public Law 108–446. Stat. 2647, 118 (2004). Retrieved from http://frwebgate.access.gpo.gov/cgi-bin/getdoc.cgi?dbname=108_cong_public_laws&docid=f:publ446.108

Ingersoll, R. (2003). The teacher shortage: Myth or reality? *Educational Horizons, 81*(3), 146–152.

Kentucky Department of Education. (n.d.). *ILP*. Retrieved December 30, 2011, from www.education.ky.gov/KDE/Instructional+Resources/Secondary+and+Virtual+Learning/ILP

Lewin, L. (2001). *Using the Internet to strengthen curriculum*. Alexandria, VA: Association for Supervision and Curriculum Development.

Mager, R. F. (1997). *Preparing instructional objectives: A critical tool in the development of effective instruction* (3rd ed.). Atlanta, GA: Center for Effective Performance.

Marzano, R. (2003). *What works in schools: Translating research into action*. Alexandria, VA: Association for Supervision and Curriculum Development.

Moursund, D. (2003). *Project-based learning: Using information technology* (2nd ed.). Eugene, OR: International Society for Technology in Education.

National Association of State Directors of Special Education & the Council of Administrators of Special Education. (2006). *Response to intervention: NASDSE and CASE white paper on RtI.*

Papert, S. (1999). Diversity in learning: A vision for the new millennium, Part 2. Retrieved November 24, 2009, from www.papert.org/articles/diversity/DiversityinLearningPart2.html

Partnership for 21st Century Skills. (2009). *Framework for 21st century learning*. Retrieved October 16, 2009, from www.p21.org/documents/1.__p21_framework_2-pager.pdf

Piaget, J. (1964), Part I: Cognitive development in children: Piaget development and learning. *Journal of Research in Science Teaching, 2*(3), 176–186. DOI: 10.1002/tea.3660020306

Russell, M. K., & Airasian, P. W. (2012). *Classroom assessment: concepts and applications* (7th ed.). New York, NY: McGraw-Hill.

Schaler, J. (Ed.). (2006). *Howard Gardner under fire: The rebel psychologist faces his critics*. Chicago, IL: Open Court Publishers.

Space, S. (2001, July 4). Gender gap shows cyberspace bias. *Technology Research News*. Retrieved from www.trnmag.com/Stories/070401/Gender_gap_shows_cyberspace_bias_070401.html

Tomlinson, C., & Eidson, C. (2003). *Differentiation in practice, grades 5–9: A resource guide for differentiating curriculum*. Alexandria, VA: Association for Supervision and Curriculum Development.

Tomlinson, C., & McTighe, J. (2006). *Integrating differentiated instruction and understanding by design: Connecting content and kids.* Alexandria, VA: Association for Supervision and Curriculum Development.

University of Oregon. (n.d.). [Official DIBELS homepage]. Retrieved December 1, 2009, from https://dibels.uoregon.edu

Vygotsky, L. S. (1986). The genetic roots of thought and speech. In A. Kozulin (Ed. & Trans.), *Thought and language.* Cambridge, MA: MIT Press.

Wallace, T., & Alkin, M. (2008). The process of evaluation: Focus on stakeholders. *Studies in Educational Evaluation, 34*(4), 192–193.

Ward, A. W., & Murray-Ward, M. (1999). *Assessment in the classroom.* Belmont, CA: Wadsworth Publishing Company.

Wiggins, G., & McTighe, J. (2005). *Understanding by design* (Expanded 2nd ed.). Alexandria, VA: Association for Supervision and Curriculum Development.

Zukoski, A., & Luluquisen, M. (2002, April). Participatory evaluation: What is it? Why do it? What are the challenges? *Policy & Practice,* (5). Retrieved December 4, 2009, from http://depts.washington.edu/ccph/pdf_files/Evaluation.pdf

nets•t3

Model Digital-Age Work and Learning

STANDARD IN BRIEF

Teachers exhibit knowledge, skills, and work processes representative of an innovative professional in a global and digital society.

PERFORMANCE INDICATORS

Teachers:

a. demonstrate fluency in technology systems and the transfer of current knowledge to new technologies and situations

b. collaborate with students, peers, parents, and community members using digital tools and resources to support student success and innovation

c. communicate relevant information and ideas effectively to students, parents, and peers using a variety of digital-age media and formats

d. model and facilitate effective use of current and emerging digital tools to locate, analyze, evaluate, and use information resources to support research and learning

TEACHING IN THE DIGITAL-AGE CLASSROOM

Students are growing up with digital tools both at home and at school. It is not uncommon for today's students to awaken to digital clocks, prepare for school while listening to digital recordings, instant message greetings to friends around the world, text message their parents and friends, complete home-work using Internet resources, and so forth. Although students are familiar with a number of digital tools, they are not always aware of how to use them effectively to enhance their personal growth and development. Here teachers can be instrumental in helping students transfer their current knowledge to new technologies, gain new insights, and grow and develop as individuals and citizens of the world.

In this chapter you will become prepared to do this by becoming familiar with current and emerging digital technologies. You will explore hardware, software, operations of a basic computer, peripheral devices, storage, memory, assistive technologies, emerging technologies, and basic troubleshooting. You should also have a better understanding of how to use digital tools effectively to collaborate and commu-nicate with the professional learning community (PLC). Finally, you will become aware of how to locate, evaluate, and use digital technologies to enhance learning and research.

LEARNER OUTCOMES

The reading and assignments presented in Chapter 3 should help you:

- Use hardware and software efficiently

- Troubleshoot common technology errors

- Use technology terminology correctly

- Transfer current knowledge to new technologies

- Collaborate with students, parents, peers, and all members of the professional learning community using digital tools and resources

- Communicate effectively with students, parents, peers, and all members of the professional learning community using digital tools and resources

- Identify, locate, use, and evaluate digital tools in professional practice to promote student learning

NETS•T3a

Demonstrate Fluency in Technology Systems and the Transfer of Current Knowledge to New Technologies and Situations

Using digital tools effectively and efficiently requires a basic knowledge of computer applications and concepts. Having an understanding of how computer hardware and software operate will allow you to select appropriate resources to use in your teaching practice, recognize limitations of technology, and, most importantly, help your students make informed choices with regard to digital tools and resources.

Computer Hardware

Hardware comprises the physical components of technology—the tangible items such as monitors, keyboards, computer mice, and hard drives. Software refers to programs and the operating system, made up of computer languages, which are used to run a computer. Just as being aware of basic bodily functions allows people to make wise choices regarding their health, understanding hardware and software operations and concepts helps users to make informed choices regarding technology integration in their teaching practice.

Input and Output Devices

Hardware can be broken down into input devices and output devices. Input devices enable the computer to receive information from the user. Examples of input devices include computer mice, keyboards, joysticks, microphones, computerized drawing tablets, and scanners. All of these devices allow the user to tell the computer what the user wants from the computer. For example, when a user presses keys on a keyboard, the keyboard delivers characters to the software program running on the computer. The program, made up of computer code, interprets the information and performs the task requested by the user. In some cases, the user wants to type text for a letter or report. In other instances, the user wants the computer to open a software application. Either way, the information has to get to the computer for the computer to know what to do, and a keyboard is a basic input device that allows this. Table 3.1 highlights some common input devices.

Anyone who has ever used a digital telephone, video game, word processor, or typical children's digital-learning game has already had experience using hardware and software. For example, the phone dialed is hardware, and the computer code programmed to make the phone work is the software. Similarly, most children's digital-learning toys use simple computer programs (software) to run the toys (hardware).

Output devices include components that deliver information to the user. After users tell the computer what to do via an input device, the computer interprets and processes the request and provides some type of output to the user to let the user know the request was granted. Examples of common output devices include monitors, printers, and speakers. For example, a printer produces an output—a photograph—scanned into the computer by an input device. Table 3.2 illustrates common output devices.

TABLE 3.1 ■ Common input devices

Input Devices	Description
Drawing/Graphic Tablets	Drawing/graphic tablets allow precision drawing or writing on a flat surface. Artists are frequent users of drawing tablets. You may have used a tablet when signing for a credit card purchase.
Joysticks	Joysticks are often used with video games. In place of mice, laptop computers sometimes have miniature joysticks that can easily be manipulated with one finger.
Keyboards	Keyboards are common input devices for "typing" in text and commands. Laptop keyboards are generally smaller but usually carry the same functions as full-sized keyboards.
Microphones	Microphones allow you to record your voice, music, or other sounds as digital signals. Microphones are used in videoconferencing and Internet-based calling.
Mice	Mice use a small roller ball or optical sensor and "clicker" to select items on a monitor screen. Like keyboards and almost all input devices, mice can be attached to or detached from a computer.
Scanners	Scanners literally scan an image and transfer that image to the computer. Optical character recognition (OCR) scanners read text as text (rather than as a graphic) so that the user can edit the text once it is sent to the computer.

TABLE 3.2 ■ Common output devices

Output Devices	Description
Monitors	Monitors are screens that provide visual output to users. Most monitors used by home and school users are color, but some businesses use monochrome (one color) monitors. Flat-screen monitors are becoming more common among users. Touch-screen monitors are basically combination input and output devices (monitor and graphics tablet).
Printers	The three major printer types include dot matrix, ink jet, and laser printers. Businesses sometimes use dot matrix printers when carbon copies of printouts (such as receipts) are needed. Many home users purchase ink jet printers for their quality and price. Laser printers are often used by schools and businesses and are becoming more competitively priced for home users.
Speakers	Speakers provide sound output that can be important when viewing a digital video or communicating via Internet calling.

More and more technologies are both input and output devices in one. Much like the touch-screen monitors mentioned in Table 3.2, numerous devices can both send information to the computer and receive information.

Components of Basic Computer Systems

Basic computer systems generally contain a minimum of five components. In addition to at least one input and output device, basic computer systems also have a central processing unit (CPU), memory, and an operating system:

1. an input device

2. an output device

3. a central processing unit (CPU)

4. memory

5. an operating system

The CPU is made up of digital components, such as microcomputer chips, that process incoming and outgoing information (from input and output devices). The CPU's function is dependent on the computer code supplied by the operating system. The CPU is like a traffic controller: it allows certain information to pass while other information is directed to wait, stop, or be redirected.

In order for the CPU to remember input or output information, code must be held in memory to be quickly retrieved when needed. Memory refers to internal data storage that is housed on microcomputer chips. Different types of memory serve different important functions.

Consider how difficult or impossible it would be for people to process tasks without memory. Without retention, every effort would be like starting all over again. Little, if anything, would be accomplished. Similarly, memory serves a critical function in computer operation.

Memory that is stored on computer disks or other devices is referred to as "storage." Storage is the capacity to retain data on a medium and is often measured in megabytes (MBs) or gigabytes (GBs). Common forms of data storage for PK–12 teachers are CD disks (also known as discs), DVDs, and flash drives. CDs can hold around 650 MBs, DVDs around 9.4 GB (and more with some types), and flash-drive storage capacity measures in the megabytes and gigabytes. Each type of storage has its advantages and disadvantages. For example, CDs can be purchased for a reasonable price and can hold a relatively large amount of data, but if they are damaged, a relatively large amount of data can be destroyed.

Components that can be added onto computers are generally referred to as peripheral devices. Peripherals can be input devices, such as computer mice and scanners, and can also be output devices, such as printers and monitors. If peripherals are external to the computer system, they are called external peripherals. If they are internal—that is, contained within a computer tower, for example—they are said to be internal peripherals (also known as integrated peripherals). Peripherals can also be storage devices, such as CD/DVD drives. Many people purchase basic computer systems and later update or add on peripheral devices or memory as their needs increase or change. Minimum system requirements must be reviewed before using peripheral devices to ensure they will work properly on a computer system.

Some computer users choose to store portions or all of their data remotely, rather than locally on an internal or external device, using what is known as cloud computing. One can think of cloud computing as computing using an out-of-sight computer system that is accessible to the local user. Cloud-storage providers offer a variety of services, such as storage and security of data. Deciding whether to store data locally or remotely depends on many factors, including how much storage is needed, what level of security is desired, and so forth.

Computers and technology that are portable are known as mobile technologies. A variety of mobile technologies are available and becoming increasingly common in PK–12 classrooms. Some of the single-use devices that may be found in today's classrooms include e-readers, MP3 players, GPSs, tablets, and digital cameras. As technologies develop, availability increases, and costs decrease; thus more and more multifunction devices, such as smartphones, are making their way into classrooms.

Together, all these devices allow computers to perform valuable and timesaving tasks for users. These hardware devices, however, could not function without their necessary companions, software.

Software

Software provides the means through which computers can receive and interpret input and deliver output to users. Software is made up of computer language, also called code. Many different computer languages exist. For example, some languages are best suited for the business sector. Others are used primarily for graphics. Regardless of the language used, computer programmers write computer code to enable hardware to function. Three primary types of computer software are operating system software, driver software, and application software.

Operating System Software

Operating system software makes up the backbone of a computer system. One can think of an operating system as a resident caretaker. It allows a user to perform tasks (such as the start up or shut down of a computer), it monitors the computer system so that it runs smoothly and efficiently, and it performs other maintenance tasks that keep a computer system running. Although the operating system is responsible for many tasks, it largely depends on application and driver software, which "report" to the operating system software to perform specific tasks, such as word processing, calculating, and running peripheral devices on a computer system.

Different operating systems exist, but most PK–12 teachers use either a Microsoft operating system (such as Windows XP, Windows Vista, or Windows 7) or an Apple Mac-based operating system (such as OS9 or Mac OS X). Less common to educators is the Linux operating system (www.linux.org) as well as other lesser-known ones.[1, 2]

Specific application software is designed to work with specific operating systems. This makes sense. The code used in application software must be compatible with the code used in operating system software. If the codes are not compatible, the two different software programs will not be able to understand the code or language of the other and will not be able to communicate with the other. Before purchasing or using software applications, users must review the minimum system requirements that allow the software to run as it was designed. These requirements will specify the minimums needed with regard to operating system, processor, memory, and so forth.

Driver Software

Driver software allows hardware to run on computers. For example, if someone wishes to install a new scanner on a computer, the computer needs information on how to make the scanner work with the operating system and other hardware devices on the computer system. Without this code the operating system will not know what to do with the new hardware, and the hardware will not function at all or at least not as it was designed. Most operating systems come loaded with numerous drivers for different types of hardware devices; however, it is usually best to use the driver software that comes with the hardware when installing new devices.

Driver software, like all software, is usually updated as users and programmers find bugs, or glitches, in the software. Most updates to drivers are available for download at manufacturer websites. If a manufacturer no longer offers a driver on its website, users can sometimes download drivers from websites such as CNET (http://download.cnet.com/windows/drivers) and ZDNet (http://downloads.ZDnet.com).

Application Software

Teachers lead busy lives. In the course of one day, they carry out large numbers of teaching tasks, such as preparing, implementing, and evaluating lessons; grading papers; communicating with parents; ordering supplies; calculating (grades, lunch money, fundraising); organizing, decorating and arranging classrooms; performing lunch and other patrols; sponsoring clubs and teams; and guiding young, impressionable students to reach their utmost potential. These tasks can be daunting, especially for novice teachers. Seasoned teachers, however, still struggle to meet all the demands inherent in teaching. Technology is available to help streamline many teacher tasks, improve productivity, and help make the teaching-learning process more effective.

Application software is often described as productivity software. Productivity software enables a user to produce some type of product. Commonly used types of application software are word-processing and desktop-publishing software, spreadsheet software, database software, presentation software, web-development software, and photo/video editing software. Application software may be housed locally on a computer or mobile device or used remotely from service providers, e.g., Google Apps (www.google.com/apps); MS Cloud (www.microsoft.com/cloud); or iCloud (www.apple.com/icloud). Today's software applications are often capable of performing two or more applications, and therefore, overlap is common. Resource List 3.1 is not an exhaustive list. It provides examples of common applications and briefly describes how teachers and students may use them.

RESOURCE LIST 3.1 ■ Software applications for teaching and learning

Word-processing applications

Description and uses

These applications allow users to produce reports, letters, business cards, and other products with text and usually graphics.

Teacher uses: Create printable worksheets, puzzles, study guides, graphic organizers, certificates, WebQuests, rubrics, business cards, letterhead, flyers, newsletters, calendars, and brochures; determine readability; make corrections; track teacher and student editorial changes

Student uses: Complete teacher-created assignments (e.g., worksheets, puzzles, reports); create graphic organizers to demonstrate understanding; create books; word-process reports; design class newspapers, flyers, and brochures

Word-processing software

> **Microsoft Word:** http://office.microsoft.com/word
>
> **OpenOffice Writer:** www.openoffice.org/product/writer.html
>
> **AbiWord:** www.abisource.com
>
> **Corel WordPerfect:** www.corel.com
> *(click on WordPerfect)*

Remote word processing applications

> **Google Docs document application:** www.google.com/google-d-s/documents
>
> **Zoho Writer:** http://writer.zoho.com

Spreadsheet applications

Description and uses

> Spreadsheets allow users to calculate and record calculations using their own or pre-programmed formulas.
>
> **Teacher uses:** Create and maintain grade books and class records, calculate action research data
>
> **Student uses:** Complete assignments and projects that require calculations

Software spreadsheet applications

> **Microsoft Excel:** http://office.microsoft.com/excel
>
> **OpenOffice Calc:** www.openoffice.org/product/calc.html

Remote spreadsheet applications

> **Google Docs spreadsheet:** www.google.com/google-d-s/spreadsheets
>
> **Num Sum:** http://numsum.com
>
> **Zoho Sheet:** http://sheet.zoho.com

Database applications

Description and uses

> Database software allows users to digitally "file" useful information in a manner that is easy to retrieve, organize, and print out.
>
> **Teacher uses:** Create and maintain records of resources and contact information, create and maintain school-based reporting data, generate reports
>
> **Student uses:** Create databases of research, projects, and assignments

Software database applications

> **Microsoft Access:** http://office.microsoft.com/access
>
> **Oracle:** www.oracle.com/products/database
>
> **OpenOffice Base:** www.openoffice.org/product/base.html

Remote database applications

> **Intuit QuickBase:** http://quickbase.intuit.com
>
> **Zoho Creator:** http://creator.zoho.com

Presentation and multimedia applications

Description and uses

> Multimedia generally refer to media that simultaneously use multiple media forms—such as audio, images, and animation—to convey information. Presentation software is multimedia software that presents or conveys information to viewers.
>
> **Teacher uses:** Present concepts; create and present digital stories, present story starters; show change/growth, develop professional portfolio
>
> **Student uses:** Create and present digital stories, demonstrate grasp of objectives, develop portfolios; create multimedia shows to accompany live performances

Software presentation applications

> **Microsoft PowerPoint:** http://office.microsoft.com/powerpoint
>
> **Micromedia Flash:** www.adobe.com/products/flash
>
> **OpenOffice Impress:** www.openoffice.org/product/impress.html
>
> **Kid Pix:** www.mackiev.com/kid_pix.html
>
> **Camtasia:** www.techsmith.com/camtasia
>
> **Inspiration:** www.inspiration.com/kidspiration

Remote presentation applications

> **SlideShare:** www.slideshare.net
>
> **Animoto:** http://animoto.com
>
> **Glogster:** www.glogster.com
>
> **Prezi:** http://prezi.com

Web development applications

Description and uses

> Allows users to edit images and video to be used in a variety of applications (e.g., word-processing, presentation).
>
> **Teacher uses:** Document student and teacher progress, document events, show changes over time, create story starters, concretize concepts, collaborate with colleagues and students
>
> **Student uses:** Demonstrate comprehension, collaborate with peers and teachers, extrapolate change, morph images, create projects

Web editor and development software

> **Microsoft Expression Web:** www.microsoft.com/expression
>
> **Sharepoint Designer:** http://sharepoint.microsoft.com

Macromedia Dreamweaver: www.adobe.com/products/dreamweaver.html

W3C's Amaya: www.w3.org/Amaya

Bluefish Editor: http://bluefish.openoffice.nl

KompoZer: http://kompozer.net

Nvu: http://net2.com/nvu

Teacher-oriented sites that host teacher and classroom web pages (html knowledge not required)

TeacherWeb: www.teacherweb.com

SchoolWorld: www.schoolworld.com

Photo/video edition applications

Description and uses

These enable users to create documents that can be viewed on browsers for the World Wide Web.

Teacher uses: Develop web pages, create professional portfolio, share classroom work (with appropriate permissions), communicate with parents

Student uses: Develop portfolio, share research

Photos

GIMP: www.gimp.org

Microsoft Paint: www.microsoft.com
(search "Paint")

Adobe Photoshop: www.adobe.com/products/photoshopfamily.html

Videos

iMovie (for Macs): www.apple.com/ilife/imovie

Movie Maker (for Windows): http://explore.live.com/windows-live-movie-maker

Educational Software

Just as teacher- and student-created presentations can enrich the learning environment, so can professionally created educational software designed specifically to enhance teaching and learning. Educational software may include elements of various applications. For example, some programs may include spreadsheet, database, and multimedia software under one name.

Educational software is available to enhance basic and advanced skills and covers virtually any subject and grade level. JourneyEd (www.journeyed.com) offers educational discounts to qualified buyers and sells a wide variety of educational software to educators, students, schools, and nonprofits. To get a feel for the depth and breadth of software available, teachers can navigate the site based on grade level, subject, type, and so on.

Much of the software behind educational programs is web-based, using cloud computing. In other words, the software programs are housed on remote servers rather than on the users' desktops.

Some educational software products are available as freeware or shareware. Freeware is copyrighted software free to the public for an unlimited time, although some restrictions may apply. Although freeware programs do not require a monetary cost for download, developers sometimes request a donation. Shareware products are also copyrighted. They are normally available on a trial or limited basis for free, but after the trial period has ended, continued use requires a small fee for purchase.

A word of caution is due with regard to freeware and shareware. Many software developers write freeware software with the intention of disseminating knowledge to the public without strings attached; however, in some cases, there is a price to pay even if not measured in dollars.

Some freeware and shareware are bundled with adware, software that advertises a product or service through various means, including pop-ups. Some adware is spyware that tracks user activity and sells this information without user consent. Adware can also be malware, software that interferes with computer use in order to direct the user to some product or service. Before downloading and using any freeware or shareware, it is important to read reviews from reputable sources and to read licensing agreements carefully before agreeing to download software. Even then, there is some degree of risk involved. Although most experienced computer users have used freeware at one time or another, "user beware" is still good advice.

Learning How to Use Application Software

Using computer applications is normally a matter of learning the particular software. Nearly every software program available today has at least one tutorial for using it. Due to the sheer numbers, variety, and types of software programs, it would not be practical to list here tutorials for every possible program that a teacher may use. Software tutorials quickly become dated as newer software versions become available. Learning to find quality tutorials is a reasonable way for users to learn to use applications effectively.

Many software programs have a built-in tutorial available to users through a Help or similar menu. Some of the tutorials are very detailed and helpful, while others provide only cursory explanations. Some are mainly text based, and others include multimedia presentations.

Some programs provide an index so that directions for specific tasks (such as copying and pasting text) can be located quickly and easily. Programs are sometimes packaged with brief instructions for using the software, but here again, the instructions may be brief.

In some cases software programs have online tutorials as an adjunct or replacement for prepackaged printed or digital tutorials. Some of these online tutorials use a combination of media (e.g., audio, visuals, text) to convey information. Users can search software manufacturer websites to locate tutorials. When a tutorial cannot be located, the manufacturer can be contacted through email, live chat, phone, or through some other means.

Many book publishers offer printed books (and sometimes e-books) as tutorials for specific programs. Locating book titles is as easy as searching online bookstores for the program users want to learn. Many of the books come with digital accompaniments (e.g., CDs) to help users learn the software.

When using the program name as the search term in a keyword search, users will often find books on how to use the program at work or at home, in addition to tutorials for learning the software itself. Online bookstores often include reviews written by professional reviewers, as well as by people who purchased and read the books. Furthermore, users can digitally browse through portions of books to ensure they like the style of presentation, layout, and so on.

Brick-and-mortar bookstores have many of the same books in their inventories or, if copies are not on their shelves, can order the books. Potential buyers can also browse entire books to make sure they are pleased with what and how the content is presented.

Other ways to learn how to use software are given in Resource List 3.2.

RESOURCE LIST 3.2 ■ Places to look for software tutorials and help

Videos

TeacherTube: www.teachertube.com

Google Videos: http://video.google.com

eHow: www.ehow.com

Videojug: www.videojug.com

5min: www.5min.com

VideoPedia: www.videopedia.com

SchoolTube: www.schooltube.com

Podcasts for audio descriptions—with or without text and visuals

Podcast Alley: www.podcastalley.com

Apple iTunes Store: www.apple.com/itunes

Podcast.com: http://podcast.com

Learning objects

MERLOT: www.merlot.org

Wisc-Online Resource Center: www.wisc-online.com

Wikis

Wikibooks: http://en.wikibooks.org/wiki

Wikiversity: http://en.wikiversity.org/wiki/Wikiversity:Main_Page

Wikipedia: www.wikipedia.org

Social bookmarking sites

Delicious: http://delicious.com

Digg: http://digg.com

Diigo: www.diigo.com

Slidecasts

SlideShare: www.slideshare.net

User groups

Microsoft: www.microsoft.com/communities/usergroups/default.mspx

OOoForum.org (for OpenOffice): www.oooforum.org

Screencasts

ScreenCastsOnline: www.screencastsonline.com

Screencast.com: www.screencast.com

ShowMeDo: http://showmedo.com

TechScreencast: www.techscreencast.com

Webcasts

Microsoft TechNet: http://technet.microsoft.com

TechRepublic: http://techrepublic.com

ZDNet Community: www.zdnet.com/blog/community

Text-based articles

eHow: www.ehow.com

About.com: www.about.com

Ethorities: http://ethorities.com

Figure 3.1 illustrates some of the sources for locating software tutorials.

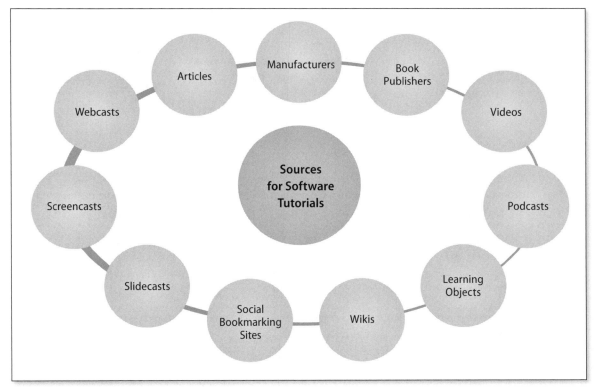

FIGURE 3.1 Sources for software tutorials.

Selecting a type of tutorial should be based on several factors, including how the user learns best according to learning style and other preferences. For example, those who have a strong preference for visual learning should consider screencasts, videos, slidecasts, or webcasts over podcasts without accompanying visuals. Those who like interactive learning experiences might consider joining a user group rather than reading a purely text-based article that offers only one-way communication.

Prior knowledge should also be considered. Teachers with a great deal of software experience may be able to transfer knowledge of previous software to new software relatively easily. Using the index provided in the software program's Help menu may be all experienced teachers need to begin using the new program effectively. Other less experienced teachers may need more detailed, step-by-step instructions.

When searching sites, users should read user agreements and privacy policies to be aware of how any information—such as search terms and tracking data—will be stored, used, and shared. Another consideration is the reputation of the company or organization hosting the web resource. In some cases, such as with MERLOT (www.merlot.org), the resources are peer evaluated, but on others, finding reviews of any type might take a little searching to ascertain the reputation and quality of resources.

Teachers who plan to use any of the resources for student use must be aware of several issues. Here again, teachers must read user agreements, privacy policies, and copyright permissions and restrictions, such as age restrictions, associated with the resources. In some cases, fair use will allow limited amounts of material to be used for a restricted time under certain situations. Each resource and situation should be considered on a case-by-case basis.[3]

If teachers are permitted to use the resources in teaching, they must ensure that the materials are safe, secure, and appropriate. For example, some web resources may contain offensive language or images. Teachers must make informed decisions and consult their administrators and technology specialists if they have any questions.

Assistive Technologies

Hardware and software that have been specially designed to assist individuals with temporary or permanent disabilities are known as assistive technologies (AT). Different technologies have been designed to accommodate a wide array of disabilities and challenges.

Individuals with some types of impaired vision, for example, may use glare protection screens, keyboard orientation aids (such as raised dots on home-row keys), and magnified displays of computer screens to assist their computer use. Blind users can use speech synthesizers (that convert screen text to speech), speech-recognition software, and Braille printers to assist them in performing computer tasks.

The hearing-impaired have numerous assistive technologies available to them. One such technology is the use of visual redundancy on a computer where important information that is auditory (such as speech) is also displayed visually. For the physically impaired, there are alternative keyboards, eye-scanning devices, Morse code input systems, and numerous other aids. The cognitively impaired can use grammar and spellchecker software. The availability and variety of assistive technologies continues to grow.[4]

Emerging Technologies

Emerging technologies are cutting-edge technologies that are becoming available in response to consumers' needs or demands. If history is in any way indicative of what to expect, today's emerging technologies will quickly become tomorrow's legacy (outdated) technologies. Not long ago, dedicated personal digital assistants (PDAs) and 3.5-inch floppy disks, for example, were considered cutting edge, but they have largely been replaced by newer technology such as smartphones and DVDs. Emerging technologies today—3-D display, software virtualization, 4G wireless, haptic devices—may soon become commonplace.[5]

Teachers often have limited classroom budgets and consider whether it is in the best interest of students to upgrade or replace technology. Individuals who use new technology shortly after it becomes available are known as early adopters. An advantage to being an early adopter is that newer technologies usually have greater functionality than older technologies, and using the newer technology may enhance the way technology is used in the classroom. A disadvantage is cost; early adopters will likely pay more than late adopters, who purchase technology after the product has been available for some time. Another disadvantage is that newer technology often has glitches that will work out in time but may cause frustration to early adopters. These and other relevant issues, such as available budget (upgrades often cost less than full replacement), teacher and student skill levels, and technology support should be factored into whether to purchase new technology or upgrade existing technology.

To learn about features associated with newer technology and upgrades, teachers may wish to visit some of the websites listed in Resource List 3.3.

RESOURCE LIST 3.3 ■ Places to find information about new technologies

For reviews and articles on new and emerging hardware and software

> **PC World:** www.pcworld.com
>
> **Macworld:** www.macworld.com
>
> **CNET:** www.cnet.com
>
> **Computerworld:** www.computerworld.com
>
> **ZDNet:** www.zdnet.com

For help in staying aware of new and emerging technologies through conferences and publications

> **International Society for Technology in Education (ISTE):** www.iste.org
>
> **EDUCAUSE:** www.educause.edu
>
> **emtech MIT (Emerging Technologies Conference at MIT):** www.technologyreview.com/emtech
>
> **Institute of Electrical and Electronic Engineers (IEEE):** www.ieee.org

Registered software users often receive notification of available software updates via email, popups, or other communications. Some software updates are free, while others require a fee. Updates normally have advanced functionality or improved usability. As noted earlier, it is important for users to review the minimum system requirements to make sure an update or upgrade will work well or at all with their computer system.

Basic Troubleshooting

Technology is great—when it works! As most have undoubtedly experienced, technology does not always work as or when desired. Cell phones do not make good connections, printers fail to print, and television images appear fuzzy. In the classroom, teachers find that from time to time technology fails. For this reason, it is important to know where to go if problems arise.

Most school systems have a protocol for how to report computer and technology problems. Some districts may provide on-call technical-support staff whose sole responsibility is to troubleshoot and repair problems.

Users can sometimes call the manufacturer free of charge and ask for troubleshooting tips if this is accepted protocol in the teacher's district. Be aware, however, that some manufacturers have fee-based help lines that will charge for troubleshooting advice. Chats may be available 24/7 on manufacturer websites as well. Users can contact manufacturers through email, but the response may not be immediate.

If assistance is sought from any source, users should be ready to tell the assistant what they have already done to troubleshoot. This will enable the help-line staff to identify the problem much more quickly.

In some cases a technology-savvy coworker might be able to identify an obvious problem, such as an unplugged computer or turned-off monitor, but it is important to follow district protocol. Teachers should never attempt any troubleshooting beyond their expertise.

Technology Terminology

Being able to understand technology content presented in tutorials, reviews, articles, and in conferences requires at least a basic understanding of terminology. Being fluent in a language infers that the speaker understands the common words and phrases associated with the language and is able to put the words and phrases together in a meaningful way to communicate with others. Technology has its own language and terminology.

Technology terminology changes rapidly. *Wiki*, *Ning*, and even *Facebook* would have meant nothing to a computer technician a couple of decades ago. Terms taken from nontechnical environments, such as "creepy treehouse," find their way into what might be termed tech-speak. (See endnote 9, p. 189.) Students are often quite familiar with newer terminology terms and lingo; this fact alone gives teachers an impetus to keep up with their students if they want to communicate effectively.

Resource List 3.4 includes a number of sites teachers can use to become acquainted with basic and advanced technology terminology.

Creepy Treehouse

"When professors create social networks for classes, some students see a 'creepy treehouse.'"

—Title of Jeffrey Young's *Chronicle of Higher Education* blog (2008)

RESOURCE LIST 3.4 ■ Places to learn about technology terminology

NetLingo: The Internet Dictionary: www.netlingo.com

TechDictionary: The Online Computer Dictionary: www.techdictionary.com

The Tech Terms Computer Dictionary: www.techterms.com

Webopedia: www.webopedia.com

WhatIs.com: http://whatis.techtarget.com

Reading technology-related content, whether in print or online, also is helpful for becoming more fluent in tech-speak. Some helpful websites are included in Resource List 3.5.

RESOURCE LIST 3.5 ■ Good sites for becoming fluent in tech-speak

Websites with many resources, such as articles and blogs

PC World: www.pcworld.com

Macworld301: www.macworld.com

CNET: www.cnet.com

ZDNet: www.zdnet.com

Technology section of the *New York Times*: www.nytimes.com/pages/technology

Additional technology blogs

Google blogs: http://blogsearch.google.com

BlogCatalog: www.blogcatalog.com

Blog Toplist: www.blogtoplist.com

In Your Experience

What terms, if any, were used in this section with which you were not familiar? Locate definitions for these terms. If you were familiar with all of the terminology, explain how you have become familiar with technology terms. For example, do you regularly read certain publications or blogs?

Section T3a Explorations

1. Create and share a multimedia presentation that explains the basic operation of a computer system.

2. Create a graphic organizer that illustrates the relationship between an operating system, application software, and driver software.

3. Locate educational software that is appropriate for the grade and subject you wish to teach. Create a table showing the name of the software, the software manufacturer's website, a description of the software, and website addresses where reviews of the software can be read.

4. Select a software application that you would like to learn to use. Locate at least three different types of tutorials (e.g., a book, a screencast, and a podcast with text). Report on the tutorials available and which one(s) you believe would be helpful to you based on your learning-style preference and other factors.

5. Search the Internet for three emerging technologies. Summarize the technologies using word-processing software and share this information with a peer.

6. Create a developmentally appropriate glossary of technology terms that includes terms with which your students should be familiar for technology literacy.

Section T3a Review

In this section you learned about computer hardware and software and about the basic operation of a computer system. Furthermore, you became aware of strategies for learning software applications, and you learned how to speak the language of technology better. Becoming fluent in technology helps ensure that you will be able to collaborate and communicate with students, peers, parents, and all members of the professional learning community (PLC). In the next section you will learn ways to collaborate effectively with PLC members.

NETS·T3b

Collaborate with Students, Peers, Parents, and Community Members Using Digital Tools and Resources to Support Student Success and Innovation

In Chapter 2 you learned how teachers are members of a professional learning community (PLC) and that all members of a PLC are important in helping students learn. Collaborating as a community of learners allows for all members' knowledge bases to be shared, explored, and built on so that a collective growth experience is possible for all members. In this section digital tools will be presented as a means to collaborate effectively with PLC members near and far.

Collaborating with Students

As noted in Chapter 1, constructivist teaching and learning acknowledge that both teacher and students are important, contributing members in a teaching-learning relationship and that both bring prior knowledge and experiences with them into the learning environment (Morphew, 2009).

In the constructivist classroom, the teacher helps to create a learning environment in which students are at the center of learning. Placing students at the center of learning requires teachers to step into the periphery and allows student interests, prior knowledge, and experiences to influence the teaching/learning context. For some teachers who were taught in schools in which the teacher dominated learning, this may be a bit of an adjustment. However, once mastered, student-centered learning can be a rewarding and enjoyable experience for teachers and students.

Recognizing and using student contributions, shared through collaboration in the learning process, is an essential component of constructivist learning. Recognizing and using teacher contributions is also essential. Student and teacher contributions are the prior knowledge, skills, and experiences they bring to the teaching/learning environment. This includes all of the formal and informal learning and experiences they have encountered and internalized in their lives. In a sense, because teachers are growing and developing on an ongoing basis, they will make different—more experienced—contributions as they progress through their careers. This is not to say that a first-year teacher will not have important contributions to offer; rather, veteran teachers have a greater repertoire of experiences from which to choose as they plan and implement lessons.

To summarize, in a constructivist learning environment, teachers acknowledge student and teacher contributions, recognizing that interactions, collaboration, and shared experiences among students and teachers combine to help make learning happen. Teachers do not dominate learning; rather they allow their role to be the often quoted "guide on the side" rather than the "sage on the stage."

Collaborating with Others

As noted in Chapter 2, the Framework for 21st Century Learning (Partnership for 21st Century Skills, www.p21.org) promotes the idea that students must be able to communicate and collaborate with others and think critically about issues locally and globally. Collaboration with others can be both taught and caught through formal instruction and modeling. One of the ways collaboration can be taught to students is by providing crystallizing experiences, such as cooperative learning opportunities and ICT-assisted PBL-based teaching, both of which promote student-to-teacher and student-to-student collaboration.[6] Modeling collaboration requires teachers to work cooperatively with all members of the PLC as partners in learning. With the advent of digital tools, sustained collaboration across geographic and other boundaries is possible.

Encouraging collaboration in a technology-enhanced learning environment is made easier when teachers have a repertoire of methods, strategies, and tools from which to choose. In the classroom, teachers can use cooperative learning strategies that require all students to contribute to the success of the group. Cooperative learning recognizes the contributions of all involved and helps focus contributions by assigning tasks to each member. Each member, then, is responsible for carrying out his or her own task. In this way, no one member feels the entire burden of responsibility, and all have a chance to share in the group's success. The various cooperative learning strategies are simply too numerous to include here, but it would be worthwhile for teachers to spend some time reading about these research-based and proven means of encouraging respect and interactions in the classroom. As noted in Chapter 2, much has been written on the implementation and study of cooperative learning.

Cooperative learning in a technology-enhanced environment follows the same general principle of allowing all individual members of a cooperative group to perform a task for the greater good of the group. Students can cooperate and collaborate with their peers and their teacher whether using limited or extensive technology.

In cooperative learning, teachers provide guidance, facilitate cooperation, provide cooperative goals and timelines as needed, lend expertise, encourage reflection, provide resources, and so forth. They engage in guided participation and are active learners, learning side-by-side with the students. Technology tools that allow sharing of documents, graphics, calculations, data, and the like help facilitate the cooperative learning experience and are described later in this section.

Project-based IT (see Chapter 1) is another excellent way for students to acquire collaboration skills. Boss and Krauss (2007) assert that collaboration is one of the hallmarks of a reinvigorated approach to projects. "Increasingly, teachers collaborate to design and implement projects that cross geographic boundaries or even jump time zones" (p. 12).

Collaboration with students in ICT-assisted PBL work should be ongoing. Teachers can facilitate brainstorming sessions for project ideas and planning, the acquisition of resources, questions to be addressed, and so forth. As the project proceeds, teachers can serve as guides and interject as needed to help students stay focused. For the evaluation and sharing phase, teachers can continue to work alongside students in the act of guided participation.[7]

Different platforms exist to help promote project-based learning. The Oracle Foundation sponsors ThinkQuest (www.thinkquest.org), an online learning platform that allows teachers to facilitate collaborative learning projects in order to promote 21st century learning skills. The platform provides the means by which students create projects; populate pages with text, images, multimedia, discussions, and more; communicate with project members; explore other projects from around the world; and learn in the global community. ProjectFoundry (www.projectfoundry.org) is an online PBL-management system that supports inquiry learning. These and a few additional online resources that may help teachers with PBL are shown in Resource List 3.6.

RESOURCE LIST 3.6 ▪ Where to learn more about project-based learning

ThinkQuest: www.thinkquest.org

Project Foundry: www.projectfoundry.org

Buck Institute for Education: www.bie.org

Edutopia: Project-Based Learning: www.edutopia.org/project-based-learning

Project-Based Learning: The Online Resource for PBL: http://pbl-online.org

Project Based Learning (checklists) from 4Teachers.org: http://pblchecklist.4teachers.org

Teachers will no doubt learn along with the students as they facilitate ICT-assisted PBL. One advantage of teaching is that teaching requires perpetual learning. Teachers should make it a point to share what they have learned as a result of their participation in the learning experience. Students who formerly saw teachers as fonts of knowledge may instead begin to see teachers as collaborative learners.

Teachers can serve as collaborators in a variety of other learning experiences as well. Collaborating with students on digital stories, the development of mind maps, and participation in simulations and games are a just a few of the types of additional learning experiences in which teachers can learn side-by-side with students, share prior knowledge, and help contribute to the collective knowledge base.

Digital Tools for Teacher and Student Collaboration

Any digital tool—including those in Resource List 3.7—that allows for sharing and strengthening of the collective knowledge base in a safe and secure manner is a candidate for use with collaboration. As always, be sure to read user agreements and privacy policies and obtain district or school approval before using sites with students.

RESOURCE LIST 3.7 ▪ Tools for teacher and student collaboration

For students and teacher to brainstorm

Bubbl.us: http://bubbl.us

MindMeister: www.mindmeister.com

Webspiration: www.mywebspiration.com

For collaborative writing projects (books, presentations, articles, documents)

Google Docs: docs.google.com

Zoho: www.zoho.com

NoodleTools: www.noodletools.com

TiddlyWiki: www.tiddlywiki.com

Writeboard: http://writeboard.com

For collaborative data collecting

Blog Analysis Toolkit: https://surveyweb2.ucsur.pitt.edu/qblog/page_login.php

EditGrid: www.editgrid.com

Survey Gizmo: www.surveygizmo.com

Virtual Lightbox for Museums and Archives (VLMA): http://lkws1.rdg.ac.uk/vlma/vlma.htm

For sharing research through social bookmarking resources

CiteULike: www.citeulike.org

WorldCat.org: www.worldcat.org

For collaborative creation of online presentations

SlideShare: www.slideshare.net

Glogster: www.glogster.com

VoiceThread: http://voicethread.com

SlideRoll: www.slideroll.com

For sharing video

Kids Vid: http://kidsvid.4teachers.org

KidsTube: www.kidstube.com

TestToob: www.testtoob.com

It takes a certain degree of humility for teachers to realize and acknowledge that they, alone, do not have all the answers. However, once they realize that two heads are better than one and that many heads are even better, they can develop the courage to learn from others, and the process will come more naturally. This applies to teachers and students and relates directly to the importance of creating student-centered classrooms. In classrooms that revolve around the teacher as the knowledge-filled director of learning, teachers fail to recognize that students are also filled with knowledge, skills, and experiences waiting to be contributed. Using technology in the ways described earlier helps maximize student learning by expanding the learning community of students and teacher alike.

Collaborating with Colleagues

Teacher-to-teacher collaboration can take many forms and be used for a variety of purposes. Teachers may exchange ideas and work related to successful teaching strategies; engage in collaborative action research; share useful teaching resources; and collaboratively author articles, books, and grants to name just a few. Here again, digital technology has provided ways for teachers to collaborate in these ways regardless of geography, language differences, and other limiting factors that would otherwise greatly hinder collaboration.

Teachers can share successful teaching strategies and solicit suggestions for improvement from colleagues by participating in social-networking sites, blogs, mind-mapping tools, wikis, social book-marking, and videosharing, such as those listed in Resource List 3.8.

RESOURCE LIST 3.8 ■ Tools for collaborating with colleagues

Social-networking sites

These sites provide a convenient way to share successful teaching strategies.

Ning: www.ning.com

H-Net: www.h-net.org

Blogs

The interactive nature of blogs, where readers can post comments and ask questions, makes blogs especially helpful in teacher collaboration. Note that some social-networking sites, like Ning, have both social-networking and blogging capabilities.

Edublog: http://edublogs.org

Blogger: www.blogger.com

Gaggle Blogs: www.gaggle.net
  (click on Gaggle Apps)

TeacherLingo: http://teacherlingo.com

Class Blogmeister: www.classblogmeister.com

Mind-mapping tools

These tools can be used for brainstorming ideas for teaching strategies and activities. They allow users to share ideas and "think out loud" in a collaborative environment, which may be especially helpful when teachers are considering new projects and teaching strategies.

Bubbl.us: http://bubbl.us

FreeMind: http://freemind.sourceforge.net

MindMeister: www.mindmeister.com

Vue: http://vue.tufts.edu

Wiki-creation tools

Creating and using wikis is an excellent way for a community of teachers to share best practices and experiences, edit work, and share resources.

PBworks: http://pbworks.com

WikiDot: www.wikidot.com

Wikispaces: www.wikispaces.com

Everything Wiki: http://wiki.wetpaint.com

Wiki services and searches

A vast number of wiki services exist, which can be somewhat confusing to beginning wiki users. Wiki services allow prospective wiki creators to search for comparable wikis based on factors important to them. Wiki search tools are helpful in locating content-, topic-, and user-specific wikis.

WikiMatrix: www.wikimatrix.org

Wiki.com: www.wiki.com

Google's wiki search engine: www.google.com/cse/home?cx=012986998404578862421%3Aevbsnkzvj30

Social-bookmarking sites

Some of the same social-bookmarking sites that allow teacher-to-student collaboration may also help teachers share resources with colleagues with regard to best practices and ideas for teaching.

Heurist: http://heuristscholar.org

Scholar (for Blackboard users): www.scholar.com/userHomepage.dobbb?op=view

Video-sharing services

Sharing videos is becoming easier and increasingly more popular. Video-sharing services can be used by teachers wishing to share teaching practices and ideas.

TeacherTube: www.teachertube.com

SchoolTube: www.schooltube.com

Google Video: http://video.google.com

Teachers who wish to exchange teaching materials (e.g., handouts, presentations) can use some of the same tools discussed in Resource List 3.8 for document and presentation sharing. Some additional resources include TeacherShare (http://teachershare.scholastic.com) and a variety of open educational resources, many of which are listed at wikiversity's page (http://en.wikiversity.org/wiki/Open_educational_resources#Where_to_find_OERs).

Other tools can facilitate collaborative action and other research projects, interpret data, and help with the authoring and editing of written works. Resource List 3.9 includes several sites teachers can use to collaborate.

RESOURCE LIST 3.9 ■ Tools for collaborating with colleagues: Research, data-based, and written projects

For database and spreadsheet tools

NumSum: http://numsum.com

Peepel: http://peepel.com

ThinkFree: http://thinkfree.com

EditGrid: www.editgrid.com

Freebase: www.freebase.com

Google Docs: https://docs.google.com

For displaying and interpreting data

    Chartle: www.chartle.net

    Exhibit: www.simile-widgets.org/exhibit

    GeoCommons: www.geocommons.com

    Many Eyes: http://manyeyes.alphaworks.ibm.com/manyeyes

    SIMILE Project: http://simile.mit.edu

    TagCrowd: http://tagcrowd.com

    Timeline Builder: http://chnm.gmu.edu/tools/timelines

For collaborative authoring and editing

    Writeboard: http://writeboard.com

    Zoho: www.zoho.com

    Socialtext: www.socialtext.com

    Gobby: http://gobby.0x539.de

    ACE: http://sourceforge.net/projects/ace

    Google Docs: https://docs.google.com

Because the tools in the resource lists are web-based, they cross geographic and other boundaries so that teachers can collaborate with colleagues from around the globe.

Collaborating with Parents and Community Members

Opportunities for collaboration are available not only in the classroom between students and teacher and between teachers and their colleagues, but also within the larger community of learners. In a professional learning community, all members—students, teachers, parents, experts, and all stakeholders—respect what members can share for the greater good and for increased student learning.

Parents, community members, and stakeholders are often eager to share the workload, their expertise, and responsibilities (such as fundraising) with teachers and schools. Many of the same tools that teachers use to collaborate with students and colleagues can be applied to collaboration with parents and community members. For example, many of the brainstorming and document-sharing tools already mentioned can help parents collaborate on projects, such as campus beautification projects, through the use of slidecasting, podcasting, and videosharing.

Some additional tools that may be used in teacher-stakeholder collaboration are listed in Resource List 3.10.

RESOURCE LIST 3.10 ■ Tools for collaborating with parents and community members

Calendars for collaboration

    Yahoo Calendar: www.calendar.yahoo.com

    Google Calendar: www.google.com/calendar

For sending and tracking invitations for volunteer opportunities

Evite: www.evite.com

VolunteerSpot: www.volunteerspot.com

For group projects, event management, scheduling, and assigning tasks

Remember the Milk: www.rememberthemilk.com

MangoTasks: www.mangospring.com/mango_tasks

TimeBridge: www.timebridge.com

Wiggio: www.wiggio.com

Zoho Planner: http://planner.zoho.com

ManyMoon: www.manymoon.com

Doodle: www.doodle.com

For soliciting suggestions, ideas, and criticisms through the use of polling tools

SurveyMonkey: www.surveymonkey.com

Easy-Poll: www.phppoll.net

KwikSurvey: www.kwiksurveys.com

It is worth mentioning that some parents and community members may not have Internet access or, for some other reason, may not avail themselves of the collaborative tools mentioned. It is important to make accommodations for these members so that they can fully participate in the professional learning community. For instance, printed invitations for volunteer opportunities should be used when teachers are reasonably sure that some parents may not receive electronic invitations.

Teachers often are in need of community and stakeholder support and collaboration. In addition to some of the tools already mentioned, teachers may wish to use videoconferencing, chats, instant messaging, discussions boards, VoIP, or some other means to meet and share in the virtual environment. Digital tools that offer these services are increasingly more abundant, including those in Resource List 3.11.

RESOURCE LIST 3.11 ■ Tools that facilitate collaborative meeting and sharing

Wetoku (broadcasting): www.wetoku.com

Vyew: http://vyew.com

Skype: www.skype.com

Adobe Connect: www.adobe.com/products/adobeconnect.html

Webex: www.webex.com

GoToMeeting: www.gotomeeting.com

Phuser: https://phuser.com

BabbleStream: www.babblestream.com

WizIQ: www.wiziq.com

Chatzy: www.chatzy.com

Tools should be selected based on the needs of collaborators, the willingness of community and stakeholders to collaborate this way, safety and security, and in response to other important factors. Again, nonvirtual opportunities for collaboration should be provided for those who will not or cannot participate virtually.

In Your Experience

In what types of collaborative efforts have you been a participant? If you could repeat the collaboration, what technology tools, if any, would be appropriate to use?

Section T3b Explorations

1. Create a table showing grade- or subject-specific learning outcomes (such as standards-based outcomes), learning experiences that can help facilitate outcomes, and collaborative tools that teachers may use to help facilitate student attainment of outcomes in the learning experiences shown. Share your list with your peers.

2. Collaborate with your peers and students through the use of a brainstorming/mind-mapping tool for ways to use collaborative tools with a cooperative learning experience.

3. Collaborate with peers through the use of a brainstorming/mind-mapping tool for ways to use collaborative tools with an ICT-assisted PBL learning experience.

4. Search for a wiki that provides collaboration opportunities for you based on your teaching area.

5. Author a paper with your peers using a collaborative tool.

6. Use a nondigital means to schedule another event with these same five peers (such as a face-to-face chat). Use a collaborative scheduling tool to schedule an event with five peers. Describe the differences in the experiences.

7. Create an online survey using a collaborative tool that you could use to solicit suggestions, comments, and criticism from parents and community members.

Section T3b Review

In this section you learned about the vast assortment of collaborative digital tools that teachers can use to help facilitate collaboration with students, colleagues, parents, and the larger professional learning community. These tools help remove some of the limiting factors that previously prevented collaboration across geographic and other boundaries. In the next section, you will learn how to use digital tools to communicate effectively with all members of the professional learning community.

NETS·T3c

Communicate Relevant Information and Ideas Effectively to Students, Parents, and Peers Using a Variety of Digital-Age Media and Formats

Teachers are expert communicators. They communicate daily with students, colleagues, staff, administrators, parents, and the larger school community. This section focuses on communication with all members of the professional learning community through digital media.

Communicating Using Digital Tools and Resources

Clarity is paramount in good communication. As the old saying goes, "Say what you mean, and mean what you say." Most of the time teachers heed this advice famously, but when they do not, it is helpful to have a backup system for communicating important information.

When verbal communication is rushed, what is spoken may not represent what teachers intend. In an effort to assign homework at the end of class, they may inadvertently omit important information, such as assignment page numbers or due dates. Even when teachers say what they mean, students often misinterpret or forget key information.

Most teachers use written communication along with verbal and nonverbal communication to ensure understanding by students. They often write homework assignments on the board, for example, in addition to verbally instructing students. Using technology as a communication tool is another way to improve clarity of communication and help assure more accurate interpretation.

Communicating with Students

A number of digital resources can be used to enhance and clarify teacher-to-student communication. Although these digital resources continue to grow in number and type, just a few of the common ones will be included here.

Using email to convey detailed instructions, to clarify misunderstandings and misconceptions, and to reinforce communication is time- and cost-effective. Most school systems have access to safe, secure email accounts for all students. Once email accounts have been established and students have been briefed on password usage and safety policies, teachers are able to communicate quickly and easily with all their students, either individually or as a group.

Teachers can send email messages to students to set up appointments, attach assignment documents, remind students of upcoming due dates or missed assignments, and so forth. When whole-class messages are warranted, teachers can set up email groups or usergroups, depending on email service features available. Whole-class messages might include changes to assignment instructions, attachments of additional instructional resources, links to websites, and any other helpful communication. Students can reply to the teacher, to selected members of the class, or to the entire class with additional requests for clarification or comments. WebMailPro (www.k12usa.com/webmailpro.asp) and Google's School Web mail (www.google.com/apps/intl/en/edu/gmail.html) are two available systems.

If teachers use email to enhance communication, they should ensure that all students have access to checking their accounts. Just because the school issues free, secure email accounts does not guarantee that students will be able to regularly check their email outside of school. For this reason, it is important to see to it that students have a few minutes every day to check their email accounts at school.

Teachers who use learning management systems (LMSs) as part of their regular instructional practice will have electronic mail available to them and their students within the system. In addition, they typically have tools for content, chats, assignments, grade management, and discussions available to help enhance communication between teacher and students.

If LMSs are used and updated regularly, they have great potential to reinforce classroom instruction and communication. For example, students who miss one or more days of school can quickly access resources and assignments and clarify questions with class members and the teacher through electronic mail, chat, or a discussion. Moodle (http://moodle.org); Blackboard (www.blackboard.com); and eChalk (www.echalk.com) are some of the many available LMSs.

Some LMSs include blog features that teachers and students can use to communicate. Teachers may want to discuss assignments in a blog and solicit comments or questions from students on the blog entries. Similarly, student blogs can be set up to receive comments or questions from the teacher or peers. Teachers can create blogs outside LMSs using resources such as those in Resource List 3.12.

RESOURCE LIST 3.12 ▪ Blogging services

Edublogs: http://edublogs.org

Blogger: www.blogger.com

Gaggle Blogs: www.gaggle.net

TeacherLingo: http://teacherlingo.com

Class Blogmeister: www.classblogmeister.com

Additional tools can be used within LMSs, including podcasting, slidecasting, and voice-threaded discussion to appeal to a greater variety of learning styles. Wimba (www.wimba.com/products/wimba_classroom) offers many such tools for the educational market. Outside LMSs, teachers may wish to use podcasting (e.g., to convey changes in classroom routine); screencasting (e.g., to enhance communication with regard to computer instruction); slidecasting (e.g., to explain an upcoming event); or video (e.g., to explain a concept) to further enhance communication.

In a very real sense, teachers can "magnify" teaching time by providing these adjuncts to face-to-face, real-time teaching. For example, a video of a teacher performing a demonstration can be replayed over and over again. A slidecast explaining an upcoming event, complete with audio and visual components, can also be replayed for those who need reminders or more time to process information.

Teachers may wish to create class web pages based on school policy. As described earlier in this chapter, a number of web page development tools exist that can help teachers build or modify pages rather easily. KompoZer (http://kompozer.net) and Adobe DreamWeaver (www.adobe.com/products/dreamweaver.

html) are web-page design resources. Or, as an alternative, teachers can use services such as Weebly for Education (http://education.weebly.com) and SchoolRack (www.schoolrack.com) to create web pages.

Web pages can contain a number of helpful widgets, such as calendars to show assignment due dates and events, or polls to solicit student feedback or suggestions. They can include information on classroom projects, supplemental readings, links to helpful resources, photos, videos, and so forth.[8]

Additional tools that teachers may wish to use include text messaging, instant messaging, voicemail, and videoconferencing, depending on the resources available to both teacher and students.

Teachers should be sensitive to students who resist using these or any social-networking resources as an invasion of their privacy or online space. For example, some students consider text messages from their teachers to be a "creepy treehouse" invasion of their personal life.[9]

Another caution is that some students receive so many school-related emails that they simply stop checking their school email accounts. It is better to send a few well-crafted, succinct email messages than bombard students with email messages that will never be read. As always, review district or school policy to see what is and is not permitted and investigate all sites for safety and security before communicating and collaborating with others.

Current Issues in Social Networking

Connecting with others via online social networking has become increasingly popular among computer users, including teachers. Using social-networking sites for professional networking has its advantages, such as connecting with teachers who share similar professional interests and for exchanging ideas for effective teaching. Many teachers use social networking for their personal connections as well. In recent years various ethical and legal issues have emerged with regard to the appropriate use of social networking by teachers. For example, Belch (2012) describes numerous cases where social network postings by teachers led to termination or suspension. Another issue is whether teachers should network with students (e.g., "friend" students in Facebook) or whether this is inadvisable. Some districts have banned teacher-student "friending" altogether (Kissell, 2011). Teachers are advised to check district policies to ensure that they are in compliance. Even when friending or connecting with students is permissible, teachers must consider ramifications and issues that might arise from teacher-student contact outside school. If a teacher witnesses cyberbullying off-campus via a social-networking site, what is his or her ethical and legal responsibility to intervene? As an alternative to using public social-networking sites, schools may choose to create their own school-based social networks that allow them to maintain control and establish policies for safe, legal, and ethical connections (see Winn, 2012).

Communicating with Parents

Teacher-to-parent communication can be enhanced with digital resources, much like teacher-to-student communication. A very effective means of communicating with a group of parents is through teacher-created and maintained web pages. On a web page, teachers can post homework assignments, course content, a class supply list (if permitted by district), classroom expectations, policies and procedures, teaching credentials, examples of exemplary work (with appropriate parent/guardian and student approval), a calendar of upcoming events (such as standardized tests), and so forth.

Parents can be better informed when assignments, content, and other important information are posted on a teacher-maintained web page. When homework assignments or other requirements are clearly and conveniently available on a web page, parents can play a more informed role in their children's learning.

If desired, teachers can apply password protection to their web pages so that only those with permission have access, but they can also make their web pages available to the larger school community. Notifying the public of all the exciting learning opportunities available to students not only informs parents about specific information, but also enlightens the community regarding the importance of teaching and the education system in general. It is easy to discredit the uninformed comment that "teachers do nothing all day" when tangible evidence is readily available to the contrary.

Parents are traditionally concerned about their children's grades and progress in the classroom. Many online systems, such as Edline (www.edline.net) and STI Education Data Management Solutions (www.sti-k12.com), are available to help keep parents informed of their children's grades, progress, and other important information.

Although some parents and guardians do not have home access to the Internet, many do. For those who do not, libraries and other public venues often allow patrons to browse the Internet. For those who do not have Internet access at all, teachers can provide parents with printed versions of what appears on their website.

Some of the tools mentioned earlier that can be used to enhance communication with students can also be used to enhance teacher-to-parent communication. Secure systems for communicating with parents—whether through email, chat, text messaging, voicemail, blogs, videoconferencing, slidecasts, or podcasts—can help promote communication and clarity.

At the beginning of the school year, teachers should consider asking parents their preferred means of communicating with teachers. It may be that some parents prefer face-to-face meetings or phone calls to any of the digital resources described in this section. Honoring parental wishes is perhaps the best action a teacher can take to promote open and effective communication with parents.

Communicating with Colleagues and the Larger Professional Learning Community

Communicating with colleagues within a school or district can also be enhanced using digital resources. Teacher-created open-access web pages, blogs, podcasts, and slidecasts can serve as means to communicate classroom projects, schedules, calendars, and so forth not only with students and parents, but also colleagues. Sharing teaching tips, practices, and strategies through these means can help promote collegiality, inspire creativity, and improve teacher effectiveness.

Teacher-created web pages are not only tools for informing parents and the larger school community, they are also helpful for peer collaboration. Teachers can quickly review the web pages of similar grade-level or subject teachers to get ideas and identify projects in which they would like to participate. In essence, a web page can be a virtual representation of a teacher's professional practice for others to explore. For instance, teachers can upload rubrics that they have created and solicit comments for peer review. They can also visit other teachers' websites and explore what their colleagues have shared.

Secure email, chats, text messaging, and voice mail also can be used to keep in touch with colleagues on a regular basis, such as maintaining professional connections between mentors and novice teachers. Email groups can be especially effective for keeping in touch with teachers who share similar interests and for exchanging effective practices. Having frequent, meaningful connections with peers may help improve job satisfaction and performance and build camaraderie among teachers.

Although communication among teachers in a school or school district is essential, communication with colleagues outside teachers' own geographic boundaries also has great potential for professional and personal growth and development. Professional societies often provide means of peer communication through printed material and through online chats and discussion boards. These are excellent ways to share with peers outside a teacher's immediate geographic region. Learning and sharing with those residing in geographically diverse areas may help teachers see issues and practices from a different perspective and may even lead to unexpected outcomes, such as opportunities for teacher exchanges or career advancement.

Subscribing to email groups devoted to a special interest or cause can be enriching. As members of an email group, you can receive messages from other members and have the ability to post messages as well. Teachers.Net (http://teachers.net/mailrings/) is one such free, subscription-based service. Teachers who subscribe are connected to thousands of other teachers, can specify one or several of more than 100 mailring topics, and share strategies and experiences with teacher colleagues around the world.

Within a professional society, teachers may have the opportunity to communicate in special interest groups (SIGs). Communication may be through user groups, discussion boards, email groups, video-conferences, webinars, blogs, and the like. SIGs can help teachers stay informed about new developments and research related to the special interest. They can also alert members to job openings, opportunities to contribute to publications, and avenues for professional development.

Email can be used in other ways to support peer communication across the miles. For example, teachers can build relationships with peers whom they previously met face-to-face at conferences. Teachers can also create their own email group and use it to meet and keep in touch with peers. These connections may lead to collaboration on projects, exchanges of ideas, and other forms of mutual support.

Videoconferencing tools and webinars allow long-distance opportunities for communication and collaboration. Videoconferencing typically uses video and audio for full two-way communication across the Internet. Connecting with peers, sharing ideas, and collaborating on projects are a few reasons why teachers may consider using videoconferencing tools as a part of their professional practice. Webinars typically are delivery oriented, with limited or no real-time interactive communication. Attending webinars is one way to stay aware of current trends and new research and to learn from leaders in the field. When participants are permitted to ask questions, teachers can benefit from presenter responses that specifically address their own professional interests or concerns. Webinars are also a means to learn about professional development opportunities.

Webinars are usually arranged around a special topic and can be either "live" or recorded. Typically they include audio- and often video-presentation tools. In a live webinar, text or even audio and video responses are sometimes solicited, much like a traditional Q and A session during a presentation or seminar. Depending on how the webinar is set up, participants "attend" conferences using their personal computers, through satellite technology at a specified geographic location (such as at a school district central office), or by some other means.

Teachers can initiate videoconferences and webinars, but textbook publishers, professional societies, and educational institutions sponsor and arrange them as well. Resource List 3.13 names a few of the many digital resources that allow varying degrees of video communication.

RESOURCE LIST 3.13 ■ Digital resources for video communication

Wetoku: www.wetoku.com

Vyew: http://vyew.com/site/index2

Adobe Acrobat Connect: www.acrobat.com/main/en

ooVoo: www.oovoo.com

Google talk: www.google.com/chat/video

Flash Meeting: http://flashmeeting.open.ac.uk

Skype: www.skype.com

Teachers can communicate their expertise and willingness to share by becoming a member of a professional social network, such as LinkedIn (www.linkedin.com) or Ning (www.ning.com), and they can communicate as avatars in simulated worlds, such as Second Life (http://secondlife.com). Furthermore, they can communicate their expertise by creating a professional online portfolio or vita. VisualCV (www.visualcv.com) allows users to upload video, audio, and a digital career portfolio for others to view. Similar services are offered by Dynamic Web Resume (www.dynamicwebresume.com) and LeadYou's E-Resume Portfolio (www.leadyou.com).

Communicating with others in the professional learning community, such as experts and community partners, can use many of the same tools mentioned for communicating with colleagues. Here again, teachers should ask professional learning community members to share their preferences with regard to communication and then do their best to honor these preferences. In this way, all members of a professional learning community will be heard, whether in a face-to-face chat or a virtual encounter.

In Your Experience

With whom would you like to communicate (for example, veteran teachers, professors, professional society members) as you grow and develop in the teaching profession? What form of digitally enhanced communication might best serve this communication?

Section T3c Explorations

1. Create a secure user group or email group that includes your teacher and peers. Select a topic from this section and construct an email message. Send the message to the group or to promote communication.

2. Create a blog that can be used to communicate information to parents and the larger professional learning community.

3. Create a web page that can be used to communicate with students, parents, and the larger professional learning community. Include at least one widget (such as a calendar).

4. Create a slidecast that might be provided to parents to explain your classroom routine. For example, for the elementary classroom the slidecast may contain the schedule of classes, how roll is taken, and the procedure for obtaining lunch tickets.

5. Create a podcast that might be used to explain a curriculum project in which your students are engaged.

6. Locate, list, and describe five email groups, user groups, or mailrings that you would consider subscribing to.

7. Conduct a videoconference with your teacher and peers. Describe some of the potential advantages to using videoconferencing to communicate with the professional learning community and some of the potential drawbacks.

8. Create a web-based resume or portfolio. Exchange your resume or portfolio with a peer for peer review.

Section T3c Review

In this section you learned about some ways to communicate with members of the professional learning community. Through effective use of technology tools, you can more clearly and easily communicate with peers, parents, and others in the educational community regardless of geography or other boundaries.

NETS·T3d

Model and Facilitate Effective Use of Current and Emerging Digital Tools to Locate, Analyze, Evaluate, and Use Information Resources to Support Research and Learning

In the previous section you learned how to enhance communication with students, parents, colleagues, and the larger professional learning community using digital tools. In this section you will learn ways to identify, locate, and evaluate technology for accuracy and suitability and for its potential to enhance research and learning.

Locating and Using Digital Tools

Chapter 2 presented ways for teachers to identify the technology needs of their students, based on many factors, including learning style, available resources, student preferences, and so forth.

Once needs are identified, resources can be located easily using the search tools available online. Online searches will yield a number of companies and manufacturers for the items students need for research and learning.

As noted earlier, some districts already have contracts in place that restrict purchases to specific vendors. If this is the case, teachers should have access to hard-copy or online catalogs. One advantage to having vendor restrictions is that selection of purchases is narrowed down considerably, potentially making the search less time-consuming. Another advantage is that the school has a history of working with the vendor and will likely have established rapport and a professional relationship to effectively handle disputes, returns, and so forth. Some of the disadvantages are that selections are limited to what the vendor offers and that comparison shopping is not possible. In some cases, districts allow purchases from outside vendors if purchases can be justified.[10]

In many cases technology resources will not need to be purchased because they are readily available for free to educators and, often, to the public at large through websites and services.

Chapter 2 described a wide assortment of software that teachers can use to enhance teaching, learning, and research. Many of the software products that were once only available through downloads or purchase are now available as web-based products whose data reside on company servers rather than customer desktops. A variety of web-based applications are listed in Resource List 3.14, but many more are available and will become available in the future.

RESOURCE LIST 3.14 ■ Web-based productivity applications

For word processing

> **Google Docs:** www.google.com *(navigate to Docs)*
>
> **Zoho Writer:** http://writer.zoho.com

For spreadsheet development

> **ThinkFree:** www.thinkfree.com

For collaborative spreadsheets

> **NumSum:** http://numsum.com

Social bookmarking sites

> **Delicious:** http://delicious.com
>
> **Digg:** http://digg.com

Social data networks sites

> **Socrata:** www.socrata.com
>
> **Thinkature:** http://thinkature.com

For photo sharing

> **Flickr:** www.flickr.com
>
> **Picasa:** http://picasa.google.com

The variety and number of web-based tools that teachers can use is both exciting and overwhelming. For this reason, teachers would be wise to visit sites that categorize online tools according to type, use, or some other qualifier.

Web Tools4U2Use (http://webtools4u2use.wikispaces.com) is one such site. This wikispace site was designed "for library media specialists to learn about cool web tools" (n.d.) and their uses. Teachers should find the resources at this site very helpful as they search for appropriate tools for particular tasks. Web Tools4U2Use allows users to search by category (such as productivity tools, quiz and polling tools, audio, and podcasting). It also provides brief, easy-to-comprehend introductions to categories of tools, ideas for using the tools, and the top five tools to test drive in each category. In addition, it provides a wealth of additional tools to explore beyond the recommended five.

One feature of this website is the Finding the Right Tool page, which helps users decide which tools will best meet their needs. This page directs users to the work of another wiki, Digital Research Tools DiRT (http://digitalresearchtools.pbworks.com). DiRT helps users decide which tools to use according to task or what the user wants to do (e.g., analyze statistics, collaborate, collect data). On the Web Tools4U2Use Finding the Right Tool page, users can also select tools based on cognitive level, learning style, and stage of inquiry. Furthermore, the site provides links to newly released tools and reviews.

Searching word clouds on technology integration sites is another way to locate appropriate tools without spending an inordinate amount of time searching the Internet. For example, by searching the word cloud available on Edutopia's (www. edutopia.org) Core Concept: Technology Integration page, users can find information related to specific tools or technology concepts.

Internet guides and web lists, such as those in Resource List 3.15, all provide a quick reference to tools that teachers use.

RESOURCE LIST 3.15 ■ Internet guides and web lists for teacher tools

Kathy Schrock's Guide for Educators: http://school.discoveryeducation.com/schrockguide/edtools.html

Top Tools for Learning: www.c4lpt.co.uk/recommended

Sites for Teachers: www.sitesforteachers.com

101 Web 2.0 Teaching Tools from the Online Education Database:
http://oedb.org/library/features/101-web-20-teaching-tools#agg

Wikis provide an invaluable service to viewers and collaborators and are an excellent resource to begin searching for and sorting through online teaching tools. The New Tools Workshop wikispace (http://newtoolsworkshop.wikispaces.com) provides an interactive homepage leading to a variety of tools. The wikispace Links for Teachers (http://linksforteachers.wikispaces.com) is another helpful resource. Cool Tools for Schools (http://cooltoolsforschools.wikispaces.com), another wikispace, provides an easy-to-use interface for searching tools by type (such as widgets, creativity, or writing).

Social bookmarking sites, such as Delicious (http://delicious.com), can help teachers quickly locate new and emerging technologies appropriate for classroom use. Users simply need to search according to need (such as collaboration or assistive technology), and they will locate sites that others have bookmarked.

Web pages, such as Inter4Classrooms (www.Internet4classrooms.com), can also serve as a starting point for locating appropriate tools.

Professional societies can point teachers in the right direction. By visiting the International Society for Technology in Education (ISTE) website (www.iste.org), teachers will find links to a variety of educator resources.

Brain games are widely available to help users strengthen basic and advanced skills. A few skills that brain games may strengthen include memory, problem solving, spatial awareness, reasoning, and logic. An assortment of games is available in Discovery Education's Brain Boost Library (http://school.discoveryeducation.com/brainboosters) and can be searched according to category. Thinkfinity (www.thinkfinity.org) has links to a multitude of interactive games and activities. Educators can search the site for resources based on keyword (try typing in "games"), type, grade level, subject, and partners.

Free online resources, such as those that generate tools and games, may also track user information, use popups, archive user input, or undergo some other activity. Again, teachers should carefully read the user agreements and privacy policies normally available as a link on web homepages to learn exactly how information will be used, stored, shared, and so forth. Also be aware that most agreements indicate that the terms of agreement can change at any time without notice. For this reason, it is important to read the user agreement and privacy policy each time the site is used for educational purposes to ensure safety and security for students, faculty, and staff. Always check district or school policies to make sure the resources you intend to use are compliant with district policies.

Selecting Software

As noted earlier in this chapter, various types of software exist for purchase, download or use in the Internet cloud. Software selection requires some forethought to achieve the best match between what the user wants and needs in software and what the software can deliver.

Software available for purchase on CDs is designed to be installed on a user's computer according to licensing requirements. Software purchased in this manner often comes with some type of user support in the event that the software malfunctions or the user needs assistance using the software. Some forms of support might include a help desk telephone service, an online chat service, or a website with answers to frequently asked questions (FAQs). Software purchased on CD will often be improved upon and upgraded; generally, the higher a version number, the more the software has undergone upgrades.

Some software is available for download. Instead of purchasing a CD, users download the software and install and use it on their computers according to the licensing agreement. Here, too, various forms of support exist, such as help desk assistance and website resources.

Other software may be obtained for download as freeware or shareware. Freeware is generally free, but developers sometimes request a donation. Shareware may be available on a trial or limited basis without cost, but after the trial period has ended, the user may be required to pay a small fee for continued use. Support for freeware and shareware may vary from no support to moderate or strong support. For example, one form of support may include a user forum where users can exchange questions, answers, and ideas for how to efficiently use the software.

Some software products are available as demoware. Demoware allows a user to try out a product before purchase to determine whether it suits the user's wants and needs. Demoware often carries restrictions for use. For example, it may only be available for a limited length of time, or it may have limited functionality, such as the inability to print or save. Demoware users should read licensing agreements to see precisely what they may and may not do with the software.

Some downloads are available as betaware. Betaware implies that the software product is still being tested, and, while it may be on the cutting edge in terms of design and functionality, it may also contain bugs that haven't yet been worked out.

Before downloading any software, read reviews from reputable sources and carefully read licensing agreements before agreeing to download. For example, a freeware product may not require a fee, but it may be bundled with adware, software that advertises a product or service by various means, including pop-ups. Some adware is spyware that tracks user activity and sells this information without user consent. Adware can also be malware, software designed to interfere with computer use to plant viruses, worms, and other malicious programs.

Another option for accessing and using software is cloud-based software. Some cloud-based software products are available for free based on licensing agreements, while others may charge a one-time or recurring fee. Other cloud-based software may be ad-supported. Here again, users should read and understand licensing agreements before using cloud-based software.

Before purchasing or using software available on CDs, through download, or via the cloud, users should do their homework:

- read software reviews from reputable sources

- determine the type and level of software support to be expected

- consider other salient factors that go into successful software selection

Locating and Using Information Resources

Many information resources are available to today's students in the form of hypermedia. Generally speaking, hypermedia refers to media of a nonlinear nature. The Internet is an example of a nonlinear medium, where users navigate from hyperlink to hyperlink as they access information. Users do not need to access information alphabetically from pages A–Z, in that order, or chronologically for the information to make sense or be helpful.

There is no denying that we live in an age of information. There is a certain pleasure in being able to find something about anything anywhere on the Internet; unfortunately, there is also a danger. Anyone can post something about anything anywhere on the Internet. In other words, information is widely available, but it may not be credible, and in fact, may be harmful or intentionally inaccurate.

For example, countless websites exist on the origin and treatment of various diseases. If users accept the information contained on the first site they locate, they may or may not reach scientifically sound content. They may, instead, find treatment information that lacks credibility and testing and that may prove harmful. For this reason, it is important to know how to judge which sites are credible, questionable, or outright incredible.

Uniform locator resources (URLs), commonly known as website addresses, can be helpful in sorting out fact from fiction. A website, for example, *http://www.firstgov.gov/Citizen/Topics/Education_Training. shtml*, is made up of a protocol, domain name (the Internet protocol address of a computer), and a pathway to a file.[11] The domain name can help users identify the website's purpose. If the domain name ends with .gov, for instance, the site is government sponsored; .edu indicates an educational institution; .org, an organization; and so forth.

Knowing the purpose of the website helps keep the content in perspective, but teachers need to keep in mind that some groups use website addresses similar to reputable sites to lure in unsuspecting viewers. This is especially important for students who mistype a URL and end up on an inappropriate website. Furthermore, just because a URL ends in .org does not necessarily make it viewable or appropriate for students.

If teachers are using a website as an information resource, they should take some time to run a readability check. This will help them determine how best to use the site in their teaching practice. It may be that a website's graphics are appropriate and worthwhile for teaching, even if the written text is above grade level.

Another way to sort through the copious amounts of information available is to use a search engine to limit or focus search results effectively. Some search engines can be subject-, profession- or other-specific, while others are used for more general purposes. Each search engine uses a system for simple and advanced searches. For example, by using "and" in certain search engines, teachers will locate sites that include the words preceding and following "and," greatly reducing the number of results.

Some search engines, such as Google, allow searches in specific areas, such as Google Scholar (http://scholar.google.com) and Google Image (http://images.google.com). Others yield results from several search engines combined. Large, complex, or heavily archived websites will often have a search engine on their pages that will search only that website. Resource List 3.16 names several search engines.

RESOURCE LIST 3.16 ▪ Some popular search engines

Single search engines

> **AltaVista:** www.altavista.com
>
> **Ask.com:** www.ask.com
>
> **Bing:** www.bing.com
>
> **GoodSearch:** www.goodsearch.com
>
> **Google:** www.google.com
>
> **Lycos:** www.lycos.com
>
> **Yahoo!:** www.yahoo.com

Engines yielding results from several search engines

> **Dogpile:** www.dogpile.com
>
> **WebCrawler:** www.webcrawler.com

Some websites help teachers and parents locate information and teaching resources using a searchable database. Some of the collections are peer reviewed, while others include non-peer-reviewed articles, worksheets, and resources in their collections. Many sites have links labeled "About Us" or something similar to describe the origin of their collections.

An additional tool for using websites effectively in teaching is to create and use WebQuests. WebQuests are Internet activity assignments that help students progress toward a certain goal or learning experience. WebQuests typically include web resources and questions that help students explore certain concepts or topics. Students are asked to gather, analyze, and synthesize information and report back on findings. WebQuests should help students stay focused but should also allow enough freedom to explore topics of interest discovered through exploration. At WebQuest.Org teachers can locate and share WebQuests. Additional resources to be found there include best practices in WebQuest design and resources (such as rubrics and checklists) to use WebQuests effectively in teaching.

Evaluating Websites for Teachers

As discussed, anyone can post anything at any time on the Internet. For this reason, it is important for teachers to use websites—from among the millions available—that are appropriate, credible, and accurate.

Teachers can start with known and trusted sites, such as government sites that serve as gateways to educator resources. Textbook provider sites are another place where teachers often turn for web-based resources. Technology coordinators at the district and state levels can also recommend sites that have been vetted for appropriateness, credibility, and educational value.

Accuracy is an important factor when judging sites and is related to reputation. Reputable websites generally contain accurate content and graphics, but as with hard-copy publications, errors sometimes occur. Using prior knowledge and experiences to determine the accuracy of websites is the first line of defense against using inaccurate websites in a teaching practice. Websites recommended by professional organizations have typically been carefully reviewed by competent individuals and carry reasonable assurances for accuracy.

One strategy to verify a site that has neither been recommended by a reputable group or party nor is familiar to the teacher is to explore the list of sites it links to. If none exist, that should put the teacher on alert. If links exist, but they seem to lead back to the same source, this, too, should give pause. Although it can be a bit time-consuming, teachers can also follow the links, then explore the new site's list of recommendations to see if the site being evaluated is among the links recommended. Essentially, anyone can link to a respected site, but it is not as easy for a disreputable site to earn a recommendation.

Some sites are supported by ads and/or commercials. Teachers can judge the appropriateness or credibility of ads and review the "About Us" links to learn more about the company behind the website. Websites that include links or ads that appear to have conflicts of interest with the site warrant further examination.

Evaluating and Using Information Resources and Digital Tools

Reading reviews from credible sources is one way to help determine the suitability, reliability, and accuracy of a technology resource. Professional societies often provide reviews, as do groups and publications.

In addition to reading the reviews of products and services, there are some other ways to help determine the validity, accuracy, and suitability of technology resources. The resources teachers wish to use in the classroom may be ideally suited to their students. On the other hand, they may be completely inappropriate. In some instances, resources that are too simple or complex can be modified so that they can be effectively used with students.

Websites can be used effectively in teaching, but a number of factors should be considered before including them. Some of the factors include readability, students' developmental levels and maturity, student interests and learning preferences, presentation of content, reputation, accuracy, and fair and varied representation of diverse populations.

Determining readability of websites is made much easier through the use of technology and through web-based applications. Chapter 2 describes the process for checking readability in more detail. If the readability is close to what students need, this is one way to ensure that the content will be received well by students.

As noted in Chapter 2, another factor to consider is whether students' developmental levels and their emotional maturity are well matched to the content of the website. Even if the readability is appropriate, if the photographs are too graphic for students, they may not use the website as intended. Some students are easily upset by graphic images of violence, for example.

Another consideration is student interests and learning preferences. Students can learn the same concepts using many different websites. Students who prefer more interactive websites can use games, simulations, or other interactive experiences while those who prefer less interaction can use other types of website resources.

Presentation of content refers to how the website is presented in terms of number, types, and arrangements of graphics; amount and quality of text; ease of navigability; general eye appeal; and related notions. In some cases, although the content may be appropriate in terms of readability and graphics, the difficulty of navigating the website precludes using it with students. In addition, are the websites compliant according to W3C (www.w3.org) guidelines for accessibility?

Determining the reputation of a website is no easy task. What at first glance may appear to be quality, trustworthy content can become questionable upon further investigation. Knowing who is hosting the website and the purpose of the website can provide one hint of its trustworthiness, but this alone cannot ensure credibility.

By noting the uniform resource locator (URL), the website address, teachers can infer the website's purpose, but, as noted earlier, this is not always reliable.

Accuracy is also an important factor and is related to reputation. Reputable websites generally contain accurate content and graphics, but as with hard-copy publications, errors sometimes occur. Using prior knowledge and experiences to determine the accuracy of websites is the first line of defense against using inaccurate websites in a teaching practice. In addition, websites recommended by professional organizations have typically been carefully reviewed by competent individuals and carry reasonable assurance for accuracy.

Chapter 4 describes ways for teachers to check for fair and equitable representation of diversity in technology resources. In websites, teachers need to consider these issues as well. How are cultural differences represented? How are special needs populations depicted?

Keeping all of these factors in mind when considering the use of websites in teaching will help ensure that the content received by students is what you intended. The usability of websites relates to these factors in that if one or more of these factors makes a website unsuitable, then the likelihood they will be useable diminishes.

A number of web-based tools are available to use for web-page suitability. To check for accessibility issues, visit the World Wide Web Consortium (W3C, at www.w3.org). To check web pages for colorblind barriers, visit Vischeck (www.vischeck.com). A website-evaluation wizard is available at Information Fluency (http://21cif.com/tools). On the site titled Kathy Schrock's Guide for Educators (http://school.discoveryeducation.com/schrockguide/eval.html), teachers will find a vast number of web-evaluation tools. These are just a few of the available online tools that can help teachers make informed decisions.

The same factors that teachers may use to consider website suitability can also be used when considering software suitability, such as fairness and equity. To determine hardware suitability, teachers must consider whether the items are accessible and usable so that all of their students' needs are met. Chapter 2 provides more considerations related to hardware selection.

Whether teachers wish to use digital tools and resources to create teaching documents or as adjuncts to their teaching or to enhance research, they should ask themselves a few questions before doing so:

- Will using this software ultimately enhance the learning experience for students, leading to the desired learning outcome? For example, creating a puzzle that is fun but lacks educational merit in terms of the learning experience cannot be justified.

- Second, what is the cost in time and other resources? For instance, is there a steep curve associated with learning the software?

- Can the cost of a commercial software program be justified when a comparable, free, online counterpart is available?

- How well does the resource serve diverse populations and meet the needs of current students?

- How well does the resource represent diverse populations?

- Have the resources been peer reviewed?

- Are the user agreements, privacy policies, and copyright policies consistent with district or school policies and professional ethics?

These questions will help guide informed decision making for acquiring and using digital tools and information resources.

In Your Experience

How do some of your favorite websites measure up to some of the criteria discussed in this section with regard to website suitability? Explain.

Section T3d Explorations

1. Select a task that you would like to accomplish (e.g., analyze, collaborate). Identify five digital tools that you can use to accomplish your task.

2. Select a learning style (e.g., visual). Identify five digital tools that you can use to address this learning style.

3. Create a table of 10 digital tools that you would like to explore. Your table should include a column for name of tool, website address, and description of the tool. Exchange your list with a peer.

4. Locate the homepage for a professional society associated with your field of expertise. Navigate the site and locate any digital resources available or referenced on the website.

5. Used the advanced search features of any two search engines to search for the same key terms. How similar were the results of the search?

6. Locate five information resources that you may be able to use in your teaching practice. For each resource, justify your selection in terms of appropriateness, credibility, and accuracy.

Section T3d Review

In this section you learned how to locate, evaluate, and use digital and information resources to promote learning and research. You learned that some technologies are better suited to different types of learners and that the decision to use technology should be based on outcomes sought.

Chapter 3 Summary

In Chapter 3, you explored hardware, software, operations of a basic computer, peripheral devices, storage, memory, assistive and emerging technologies, and basic troubleshooting. You also were introduced to digital tools and resources that can help you collaborate and communicate effectively with students, colleagues, parents, and others in the professional learning community. Finally, you learned how to locate, evaluate, and use digital tools and information resources in the classroom to promote learning and research. In the next chapter, you will learn more about addressing the diverse needs of learners and promoting digital citizenship.

Chapter 3 Notes

1 Computer users sometimes confuse operating systems with application software. For example, users may be using Windows XP for their operating system but using Microsoft Office 2007 for their application software. Furthermore, Internet Explorer, Netscape Navigator, Mozilla Firefox, and Google Chrome are Internet browsers that allow users to browse the Internet. Then there are Internet search engines, such as Google or Bing.

2 The source code for the Linux operating system is licensed under the GNU General Public License; its code is freely available to the public for use, modification, and redistribution. This contrasts with proprietary software, such as the Windows operating system, whose source code is not freely available.

3 See Chapter 4 for more information on copyright and fair use.

4 The use of assistive technologies is covered in greater detail in Chapter 2.

5 Chapter 6 covers emerging technologies in more detail.

6 Providing crystallizing experiences is discussed in Chapter 1. Project-based learning-IT/ICT-assisted PBL is discussed in detail in Chapter 1 and, to a lesser degree, in Chapter 2.

7 See Chapter 1 for more on guided participation.

8 See Chapter 4 for information on obtaining parental/guardian permission to use student photos, videos, work, and the like.

9 "Creepy treehouse" is described in Young's blog (2008) as "When professors create social networks for classes, some students see a 'creepy treehouse.'" Jared Stein has collected numerous definitions for "creepy treehouse" in his blog "Defining 'Creepy Treehouse'" (Flexknowlogy http://flexknowlogy.learningfield.org/2008/04/09/defining-creepy-tree-house).

10 See Chapter 2 for more information with regard to locating and purchasing technology.

11 A sample URL (http://www.firstgov.gov:Citizen:Topics:Education_Training.shtml) is detailed in Figure 2.5, Chapter 2.

Chapter 3 References

Belch, H. E. (December/January 2011–2012). Teachers beware! The dark side of social networking. *Learning & Leading with Technology, 39*(4), 15–19.

Boss, S., & Krauss, J. (2007). *Reinventing project-based learning: Your field guide to real-world projects in the digital age.* Eugene, OR: International Society for Technology in Education.

Kissell, M. R. (August 31, 2011). Local teachers banned from "friending" students on Facebook: Schools react to effect, growth of social media. *Dayton Daily News.* Retrieved January 23, 2012, from www.daytondailynews.com/news/dayton-news/local-teachers-banned-from-friending-students-on-facebook-1242934.html

Morphew, V. N. (2009). Constructivist teaching and learning in a web-based environment. In P. Rogers, G. Berg, J. Boettecher, C. Howard, L. Justice, & K. Schenk (Eds.), *Encyclopedia of distance learning* (2nd ed.), pp. 418–424. Hershey, PA: Idea Group Publishing.

Winn, M. (December/January 2011–2012). Promote digital citizenship through school-based social networking. *Learning & Leading with Technology, 39*(4), 10–13.

Young, J. (2008, August 18). When professors create social networks for classes, some students see a "creepy treehouse." [Blog post]. Retrieved from *The Chronicle of Higher Education*, Wired Campus, www.chronicle.com/blogPost/When-Professors-Create-Social/4176

nets•t4

Promote and Model Digital Citizenship and Responsibility

STANDARD IN BRIEF

Teachers understand local and global societal issues and responsibilities in an evolving digital culture and exhibit legal and ethical behavior in their professional practices.

PERFORMANCE **INDICATORS**

Teachers:

a. advocate, model, and teach safe, legal, and ethical use of digital information and technology, including respect for copyright, intellectual property, and the appropriate documentation of sources

b. address the diverse needs of all learners by using learner-centered strategies and providing equitable access to appropriate digital tools and resources

c. promote digital etiquette and responsible social interactions related to the use of technology and information

d. develop and model cultural understanding and global awareness by engaging with colleagues and students of other cultures using digital-age communication and collaboration tools

PRACTICING LEGAL AND ETHICAL BEHAVIORS

Teachers influence the lives of their young charges on a daily basis. Along with this privilege comes responsibility. Teachers not only affect those in their immediate care, but they also touch the lives of their students' families and others who will eventually benefit from the quality education they deliver each day. This can be a potentially daunting responsibility. As a teacher, students are always watching you, even when they look like they are not. For this reason, it is critical for teachers to model ethical, legal, safe, and healthy practices as they relate to technology. In this chapter you will learn ways to model these behaviors effectively. Always be mindful that the impressions you give and the lessons you live are potentially long lasting and far reaching. With this in mind, remember to act wisely.

LEARNER OUTCOMES

The reading and assignments presented in Chapter 4 should help you:

- Model ethical and legal technology practices

- Apply technology resources to enable and empower students with diverse backgrounds

- Use technology resources that affirm diversity

- Exhibit responsible behavior in social interactions involving technology

- Promote safety and health in relation to technology

- Provide equitable access to technology for all students

- Model culturally responsible behaviors involving technology-related communication and collaboration

NETS•T4a

Advocate, Model, and Teach Safe, Legal, and Ethical Use of Digital Information and Technology, Including Respect for Copyright, Intellectual Property, and the Appropriate Documentation of Sources

Any discussion of technology is not complete without including the human context. After all, not only have humans designed technology, but they also use—and sometimes abuse—it. In this section you will learn ways to teach and model appropriate behavior as it relates to technology. Some of the items with which you will become familiar are how to use copyrighted work, your students' work, and your own work. Knowing what is both acceptable and unacceptable will help you better teach and model appropriate behavior in the classroom.

As you have learned by now, providing effective technology-enriched experiences to all students involves more than setting up a computer in the corner of the classroom. It involves reflective thought and careful action to help maximize student learning. Another facet of promoting effective technology-enriched experiences is presented in this section. Here you will learn some strategies for promoting safe and healthy use of technology for all students.

Technology and Society

In this text the word "technology" is often used when referring to computer hardware and software. It makes sense in this day and age, when computers make up a large part of the technology used in every aspect of life. If this text were written even a decade earlier, the technology included would be very different from the technology that appears within these covers. It is expected that any useful text of the future will also include the new and emerging technologies of its time.

From their humble beginnings through to today, computers have fast become one of the most widely used technologies in the world, and they have the potential to increase significantly in presence and use in the future. Knowing how quickly computers have risen to the forefront of business, commerce, education, and communication helps teachers prepare themselves and their students for the dizzying speed at which future change is expected.

People design technology so that some aspect of life can improve in quality or efficiency. As noted in Chapter 6, the concept of supply and demand plays a huge role in the technology that is created and modified. A need (or want) arises in society that influences a response to meet the need or want. If society calls for more efficient and affordable communication technology, the technology industry usually responds to meet the demand with a supply of more efficient and affordable communication. The technology that has emerged in the educational setting is directly related to the need for better technology teaching tools.

In the same way that society impacts the kinds of technology that is designed and available for consumption, society is affected by the technology produced and supplied. A product that starts off with one use in mind, for example, may be used in other, more widespread, and unexpected ways. This wide-spread acceptance and demand may call for even better technology of its type and will impact demand. This constant relationship between supply and demand helps technology progress at a steady and supported pace. Moreover, as technology use spreads, the lives of technology users change. Technology influences it all, from the ways users transact business to the ways technology helps save lives and improve health. Technology is truly an integral part of life. Even in places where computer technology is limited, other forms of technology influence daily lives in untold ways.

Legal Issues in Technology

One way that technology has influenced society is in litigation and arbitration. Every day new legal issues arise that question the fair, safe, or ethical use of technology.

Very big questions arise when technology related to life issues is involved (Myers, Frieden, Bherwani, & Henning, 2008). In education, questions abound that involve such areas as fair use, copyright, piracy, privacy, confidentiality, danger, misuse, ethics, and etiquette (Colvin, 2007; Howard, 2007; Mason, 2008; Rife, 2007; Shariff & Johnny, 2007; Warnick, 2007). Because so much of technology is relatively new, in many cases, legal precedents have not been set. This leaves teachers in the unfortunate position of practicing their profession without definitive bounds. What is routinely acceptable today may be ruled unfair or illegal tomorrow, leaving teachers vulnerable to criticism or legal threats. There are some basic guidelines that may help guide teachers in their technology practices, but keep in mind that, like tech-nology, changes in the law progress rapidly. This is yet another reason to stay abreast of issues related to educational law.

Copyright, Fair Use, and Authors' Work

One of the most important concepts with which teachers should be familiar is copyright. Copyright refers to the legal protection given to creators of original works against unlawful copying and use of their work. Copyright recognizes literary works, visual arts, performing arts, sound recordings, and serial/publications as creative expressions and intellectual property. Just as it is unfair and illegal to take or use physical property without the owner's permission, it is unfair and illegal to use intellectual property without securing appropriate permission.

Teachers deal with issues of copyright every day. Some reproduced worksheets that teachers print for classroom use are protected by copyright law, as are many movies, photographs, paintings, and other material that might be used in their teaching practice. More specifically, the United States Copyright Office (2006a) describes work protected by copyright as follows:

> Copyright protects "original works of authorship" that are fixed in a tangible form of expression. The fixation need not be directly perceptible so long as it may be commu-nicated with the aid of a machine or device. Copyrightable works include the following categories:

1. literary works

2. musical works, including any accompanying words

3. dramatic works, including any accompanying music

4. pantomimes and choreographic works

5. pictorial, graphic, and sculptural works

6. motion pictures and other audiovisual works

7. sound recordings

8. architectural works

These categories should be viewed broadly. For example, computer programs and most "compilations" may be registered as "literary works"; maps and architectural plans may be registered as "pictorial, graphic, and sculptural works." (U.S. Copyright Office, 2006a, pp. 2–3)

Authors may allow limited copying of their work for a fee; at other times they may offer unlimited use without any strings attached. Knowing the permissions for every work used in teaching is critical if teachers wish to use and model ethical and legal practices.

Copyright protection provides limited protection for authors while also allowing fair use of the copyrighted work. Fair use refers to the use of copyrighted work that does not infringe on the creator's rights. The U.S. Copyright Office's factsheet on fair use presents the following:

Section 107 contains a list of the various purposes for which the reproduction of a particular work may be considered "fair," such as criticism, comment, news reporting, teaching, scholarship, and research. Section 107 also sets out four factors to be considered in determining whether or not a particular use is fair:

1. The purpose and character of the use, including whether such use is of commercial nature or is for nonprofit educational purposes

2. The nature of the copyrighted work

3. Amount and substantiality of the portion used in relation to the copyrighted work as a whole

4. The effect of the use upon the potential market for, or value of, the copyrighted work

The distinction between "fair use" and infringement may be unclear and not easily defined. There is no specific number of words, lines, or notes that may safely be taken without permission. Acknowledging the source of the copyrighted material does not substitute for obtaining permission. (U.S. Copyright Office, 2006b, para. 4–6)

So how can teachers know if, how, when, and how often they may use a work protected by copyright law? The easiest way is to check for reference to copyright on the work itself. Teaching materials often allow users to copy and distribute unlimited numbers of materials for teaching purposes as long as the work was legally obtained by the teacher and is being used by his or her students. The statement might read something like, "The original purchaser may make and use unlimited copies for teaching purposes." Variations in permissions exist, so copyright and permission statements should be followed carefully.

If a statement about copying is not present, teachers can check the copyright office for specific fair-use policies as they relate to the work under question. They can also contact the author and ask for written permission to use the work. Furthermore, they can ask their school library media specialists for assistance; these specialists are often quite knowledgeable about copyright laws. School administrators will likely have received a great deal of training related to fair use and copyright law as well. Table 4.1 summarizes some examples for applying copyright to specific situations.

Caution

Be aware that laws and interpretations of laws are subject to change. When in doubt, check with an attorney familiar with copyright law.

TABLE 4.1 ■ Help for understanding copyright and fair use

Question	Where to Look for an Answer
Can I copy and paste a photograph I found on a website onto my own website?	Look for a link entitled "user agreement" (or something similar) on the website. Here you should find information regarding use of content, including graphics, copyright, and so on. Contact information for permission to use work is normally included here. (Search for "user agreement" or "terms of use" in a search engine to see content of various agreements.) Review acceptable use policies (AUPs) for information as well.
Can I copy the contents of a blog and paste the content into an assignment I create for student use?	Review the definition of fair use on the U.S. Copyright Office website to see if what you plan to use falls under fair use. Review any copyright statements issued by the author and, if necessary, contact the author for written permission to use content. Furthermore, review the user agreement or terms of use and/or AUP of the host site to see if use of any content is prohibited or limited. Even if permission is granted, you must give proper credit.
Can I copy and distribute a booklet created by a U.S. government agency to students in all of my classes?	In most but not all cases, material available from U.S. government agencies is in the public domain, which allows you to copy and distribute material. Look for a copyright statement showing permissions to copy and distribute. When in doubt, contact the government agency in question. Make sure copyright permissions are included with the copies you reproduce.
Can I use a recording from a contemporary popular music group as background music in a class-produced video to be sold as a fundraiser?	Musical compositions and sound recordings fall under copyright law. Review copyright law (see phonograph records) and obtain necessary permissions. Enlist the help of your school library media specialist, administrator, or school district attorney to help you understand the law. You may be asked to pay to use the music, or you may be prohibited altogether.

Various online resources are helpful to determine copyright law as it applies to particular situations. Resource List 4.1 includes some of these websites.

RESOURCE LIST 4.1 ■ Online resources for copyright information

Copyright Clearance Center: www.copyright.com

The Digital Millennium Copyright Act (DMCA): www.copyright.gov/onlinesp

> The DMCA addresses a number of copyright-related issues, including the rights to intellectual property, downloading music, and the use of the Internet.

PBS SoCal Education, Copyright for Educators, Fair Use: http://video.pbssocal.org/video/2185959472

The Legal Information Institute of the Cornell University Law School: www.law.cornell.edu/bulletin

Library of Congress: Taking the Mystery Out of Copyright: www.loc.gov/teachers/copyrightmystery/#

SU LAIR: Copyright & Fair Use—Chapter 9: Fair Use:
http://fairuse.stanford.edu/Copyright_and_Fair_Use_Overview/chapter9

Technology, Education and Copyright Harmonization (TEACH) Act:
www.copyright.gov/docs/regstat031301.html

In addition to copyright law, a number of legislative actions govern the use of intellectual property, protection of children online, and the Internet, as shown in Resource List 4.2.

RESOURCE LIST 4.2 ■ Links to legislation about ethics and technology

Children's Online Privacy Protection Act (COPPA): www.ftc.gov/privacy/coppafaqs.shtm

The Digital Millennium Copyright Act (DMCA): www.copyright.gov/onlinesp

Family Educational Rights and Policy Act (FERPA): www.ed.gov/policy/gen/guid/fpco/ferpa

TEACH Act: www.copyright.gov/docs/regstat031301.html

Being informed is the first step in teaching legal and ethical practices related to technology use. Knowing what the law does and does not allow provides teachers with guidelines for fair use in the classroom. Pleading ignorance simply is not an option when confronted with using illegal practices in the classroom. Another unacceptable excuse is claiming that all of the other teachers are doing whatever unacceptable practice is under consideration. The U.S. Copyright Office publishes fact sheets and circulars related to copyright. For example, "Circular 21: Reproduction of Copyrighted Works by Educators and Librarians" can be found at www.copyright.gov/circs/circ21.pdf. Table 4.2 shows some practices that may or may not be legal.

TABLE 4.2 ■ Legal and illegal technology practices in the classroom

Practice	Where to Look for an Answer
Reproducing worksheets from a teacher's activity manual for individual student use	Legal if specific permission is granted to the purchaser to reproduce and distribute as described. Possibly illegal if specific permission is not explicitly granted; check with the copyright holder to obtain necessary written permission if you are unable to locate a copyright and permission statement in the manual.
Showing a commercial video rental as a reward for good student behavior	Normally illegal unless you are granted permission (in writing) from the copyright holder. Read the warnings that typically show at the beginning of a video about lawful and unlawful use and reproduction of the video.
Copying three chapters from a textbook and distributing chapters to students year after year until a new edition is published	This practice is illegal unless written permission to do so is obtained from the copyright holder. This practice does not fall under fair use in part because in essence it is hurting the copyright holder's opportunity to profit from his or her work.
Installing loaned proprietary software on your work computer	Illegal unless you received written permission from the copyright holder. Again, this does not fall under fair use in part because you are infringing on the copyright holder's ability to earn a profit from his or her work.
Using content copied from another web page on your own school web page	This depends on how much content was copied. For example, if a brief quote was used and properly cited, you may be practicing fair use. If you obtained proper written permission, you may use the content agreed upon by the copyright holder. Read the user agreements and copyright notices available for explicit permissions granted.

Software piracy is the unlawful use of software according to copyright law. Software piracy results in the loss of profits to businesses[1] and individuals by decreasing their chance to earn a profit from their work.

Teachers can avoid piracy by abiding by the license agreements that accompany every piece of software. In most cases, users are permitted to copy software onto one computer and make a copy of the software for backup or archival purposes. Certain other permissions may also be granted. If a single-user license is purchased and the software is installed in a networked lab where all students will simultaneously use the software, this violates copyright law unless such use is explicitly granted by the copyright holder. If one teacher borrows another teacher's copy of a single-user license software and installs it on his or her home computer for personal use, this is likewise software piracy unless the software license explicitly grants this permission.

Software piracy is a crime and carries penalties that no teacher wants to encounter. Even if software pirates never get caught or penalized, they are still practicing illegal and unethical behavior and setting a terrible example for students.

Many software distributors carry education discounts for the purchase of their software. Furthermore, using legal copies of software in lawful ways allows teachers to access certain services available from manufacturers, and legal software may be safer to a computer system than illegal copies. Among the many good reasons for using software lawfully is perhaps the simplest of all—it is the right thing to do.

For more information, teachers may visit the Software and Information Industry Association website at www.siia.net to review information on software piracy.

Open Source Software

Some software developers welcome the sharing, modification, and distribution of their program source code as open source software (OSS) or free software. The Open Source Initiative (OSI) calls itself the "stewards of the Open Source Definition (OSD) and the community-recognized body for reviewing and approving licenses as OSD-conformant" (www.opensource.org/about, para. 2). To locate OSS, users can visit the Open Source Software Directory (www.opensourcesoftwaredirectory.com).

The wiki Ohloh (www.ohloh.net) is a free public directory of open source software. In addition, open source alternatives to commercial products can be located at osalt.com (www.osalt.com). SourceForge (www.sourceforge.net) is another resource for finding (and developing) open source software.

The Free Software Foundation (FSF, at www.fsf.org) is also working to advance software freedom. The FSF's Free Software Directory (http://directory.fsf.org) helps users search for free software from a wide range of categories, such as education, text creation and manipulations, games, graphics, hobbies, and more.[2]

Copyright law can be conflicting and confusing for novice and even experienced teachers. They want to use the best available tools in their teaching practices, but they do not want to overstep the bounds of fair use. Interpretation of the law is not always easy, which gives some teachers pause in using any materials. These teachers may choose to use either work that is explicitly in the public domain or licensed for their use, or they may create their own work to use in teaching.

In an effort to make it easier for individuals to use, modify, and share their work, the nonprofit corporation Creative Commons (www.creativecommons.org) has worked to provide creative common licenses that allow copyright holders to specify how their work can be used.

> Creative Commons (CC) is a nonprofit corporation dedicated to making it easier for people to share and build upon the work of others, consistent with the rules of copyright. CC develops legal and technical tools used by individuals, cultural, educational, and research institutions, governments, and companies worldwide to overcome barriers to sharing and innovation. (Creative Commons, 2011, para. 1)

Wikimedia Commons (http://commons.wikimedia.org) is a media repository that uses creative commons licensing to share work with others. The nature of Wikimedia Commons makes it especially useful for educators.

> Wikimedia Commons is a media file repository making available public domain and freely-licensed educational media content (images, sound and video clips) to everyone, in their own language. It acts as a common repository for the various projects of the Wikimedia Foundation, but you do not need to belong to one of those projects to use media hosted here. The repository is created and maintained not by paid archivists, but by volunteers. The scope of Commons is set out on the project scope pages.
>
> … Unlike traditional media repositories, Wikimedia Commons is free. Everyone is allowed to copy, use and modify any files here freely as long as they follow the terms specified by the author; this often means crediting the source and author(s)

appropriately and releasing copies/improvements under the same freedom to others. The license conditions of each individual media file can be found on their description page. The Wikimedia Commons database itself and the texts in it are licensed under the Creative Commons Attribution/Share-Alike License. (http://commons.wikimedia. org/wiki/Commons:Welcome, para. 1 and 4)

Wikimedia Commons' sister project, Wikibooks (http://en.wikibooks.org), may be helpful to teachers in accessing content for professional purposes. Most work in Wikibooks is licensed under both the Creative Commons Attribution-ShareAlike 3.0 Unported License (CC-BY-SA) and the GNU Free Documentation License (GFDL).[3] Each work should be checked for specific permissions and requirements. With wiki projects, note that content may or may not be appropriate for minors to view because anyone can edit the work and the editing occurs spontaneously. Wikijunior (http://en.wikibooks.org/wiki/Wikijunior) aims to provide age-appropriate books to children ages birth–12. The books on Wikijunior have been reviewed before being listed, but even here teachers should note that inappropriate content may find its way into these books.

Work in the public domain is also helpful to educators. Public domain work, as it relates to copyright, refers to work that is not restricted by copyright law and is available to the public. Many U.S. government works are in the public domain, although some exceptions apply. Other works have been moved to the public domain because of copyright expiration. Searching for U.S. government documents can begin at the official web portal, USASearch.gov (http://usasearch.gov), with a search for trends, images, forms, or other resources. As always, teachers should check the copyright notice on resources before using them in their teaching practices.

Project Gutenberg (www.gutenberg.org) is a repository of free e-books that teachers may wish to explore. Most of the books are in the public domain in the United States, although some of the works are copyright protected.

Teachers who wish to create original artwork have many options, even if they do not consider themselves artists. Wordle (www.wordle.net) is a website that allows users to create word clouds that can be used for many different purposes. Figure 4.1 shows a word cloud created using Wordle.

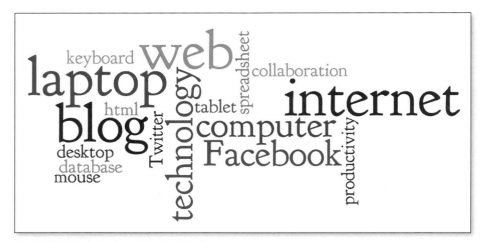

FIGURE 4.1 Word cloud created using Wordle.

The Internet Archive (www.archive.org) is an online library of digital materials, including text, audio, moving images, software, and archived web pages. Teachers can find many free downloads of materials, but they should check the copyright policies before using any works.

Teachers in need of clip art may wish to visit the Open Clip Art Library (www.openclipart.org), a repository for artwork that has been placed in the public domain by contributing artists. Site users may search the library, leave comments and reviews, contribute work, and make requests for art.

Flickr is a photo sharing site that allows users to share their work according to their preferences. You can search for photos in Flickr that have been placed under a creative commons license by visiting www.flickr.com/creativecommons.

Original art can be created using various software tools, as well as animations, comics, cartoons, worksheets, graphic organizers, rubrics, posters, and so forth, using the many software programs and online tools available. Resource List 4.3 includes software tools for creating original art.

RESOURCE LIST 4.3 ■ Software tools for creating original art

Adobe InDesign: www.adobe.com/products/indesign

GIMP: www.gimp.org

Gliffy: www.gliffy.com

Draw: www.openoffice.org/product/draw.html

In a very real sense, possibilities are limited only by a teacher's imagination.

Confidentiality, Parental Permissions, and Student Work

Another legal issue teachers should be aware of is use and misuse of student data. Teachers often have wide access to information of a confidential nature. Using this information in appropriate ways, for appropriate purposes, through appropriate means, and with appropriate parties will help keep teachers out of legal trouble and allow them to practice ethical behaviors.

Some of the confidential information teachers are privy to include parental rights, student health conditions, special education services, family circumstances, instances of abuse, and other sensitive issues. One of the reasons teachers are granted access to this information is to help them make learning the very best for students; knowing that a student has certain social issues may allow teachers to tailor their teaching to best meet the needs of that student.

Teachers are not granted access for gossip or to share information with anyone outside the profession. Even within the profession, it is important to become aware of what is permissible in terms of with whom information may be shared. In some cases, even parents are not permitted to be told certain information. One such case may be when a parent no longer has custodial rights.

When using student data, photographs, writing samples, or any other student work, teachers need to secure appropriate written permissions. Teachers should check with their school administration for what is specifically required. In some cases, teachers are asked to distribute permission forms at the beginning of a school year that allow teachers to use student work for professional purposes, for publicity, and so on. Even with written permission, teachers still need to use sound judgment when using these items so that students will not be jeopardized in privacy, safety, health, or education.

It is best to remove any identification from student work or data so that specific students cannot be connected to artifacts. With older students and for students of legal age, teachers should be sure also to receive written permission from them as well as from their parents/legal guardians.

When transmitting sensitive or confidential information via technology, also realize that the potential exists for someone to hack into the system and obtain the information. Although many consider email messages private transactions, email can be read and copied fairly easily by someone with access to the email server. Circumstances have arisen where individuals who used email to carry out unscrupulous behavior were later fired or exposed because someone read the email and/or shared it with others.

Privacy with regard to technology is a topic of discussion in the popular media (National Public Radio, n.d.; Kaste, 2009; Quenqua, 2009; Tartakoff, 2009). As new technology and associated issues emerge, so will additional questions as to how much and what type of information stored on Internet servers is private, how digital images can be used, and so forth. For example, what kinds of protections will be given to digital health records, and how are socially networked data archived and shared? If data are stored on any server outside district servers, how are the data protected?

Although it is impossible to anticipate every possible question and nuance associated with technology and privacy, teachers must always exercise caution and good judgment when using any type of technology—email, blogs, web pages, databases, spreadsheets, and the like—that contains student data. Teachers must protect students and student data. They should check with their school administration, obtain legal counsel, and use any necessary district- or school-approved legal forms and documents that will protect their students.

Plagiarism and Teacher Work

Much of what teachers use in their teaching practice will have been created using their own imaginations and expressed in their own ways. Their own work may have limited protection under copyright law, and they would do well to become familiar with their rights by visiting the U.S. Copyright Office website (www.copyright.gov). They may even wish to register their work with the Copyright Office. Details on how to do this are available on the Copyright Office's website. Teachers should be aware that under certain conditions, the copyright of their work may belong to another party, such as their school or district. Visit the U.S. Copyright Office website for the link to "Circular 9: Works Made for Hire under the 1976 Copyright Act" (www.copyright.gov/circs/circ09.pdf) for more information on works for hire.

When creating teaching materials and teaching-related work, teachers should provide appropriate credit when it is due. Most educators use citations according to the *Publication Manual of the American Psychological Association*, known as APA style, to cite references. Various citation services, such as those listed in Resource List 4.4, help writers construct proper citations.

RESOURCE LIST 4.4 ■ Sites for citation help

Citation Maker from Recipes4Success: www.recipes4success.com

Son of Citation Machine: http://citationmachine.net

EasyBib: www.easybib.com

mybibpro: www.easybib.com/products/mybibpro

By using proper citations, educators are not only keeping in step with ethical and legal practices, they also are modeling good practices for their students. Obtaining appropriate permission to use photographs, literary works, and the like and citing this permission will help teachers stay out of legal trouble and, again, demonstrate appropriate behavior. Remember, however, the caveat stated on the U.S. Copyright Office website: "Acknowledging the source of the copyrighted material does not substitute for obtaining permission" (U.S. Copyright Office, 2006b, para. 4).

Plagiarism is the practice of using someone else's work and claiming it as your own. In the teaching profession, teachers need to make their policies on plagiarism clear at the beginning of the school year and their penalties for practicing plagiarism known. Teachers who plagiarize in their own teaching practices run the risk of losing credibility among students—and even their teaching licenses. So, in a word about plagiarism: don't.

A number of websites and software programs exist that can help detect plagiarized material, often by allowing you to copy and paste content into the box provided to help determine the likelihood that a passage of content was plagiarized. The sites in the Resource List 4.5 can help you determine if work is the student's own.

RESOURCE LIST 4.5 ■ Tools to help detect plagiarism

The Plagiarism Checker: www.dustball.com/cs/plagiarism.checker

  A project of the University of Maryland

Article Checker: www.articlechecker.com

Plagiarism Checker: www.plagiarismchecker.com

WCopyfind: http://plagiarism.bloomfieldmedia.com/z-wordpress/software/wcopyfind

  Located on the Plagiarism Resource Site and available for download

Several plagiarism software programs have been designed primarily for teachers and education institutions for purchase, including Turnitin (http://turnitin.com) and EVE2 Plagiarism Detection System (www.canexus.com/eve). Search engines, such as Google (www.google.com), can also be used to detect plagiarized work by typing in phrases. Firefox (www.mozilla.com/firefox/), the open source web browser, has a plagiarism plugin to help combat plagiarism.

Teachers should be aware that some plagiarism services and programs archive in their databases the material checked for plagiarism. This material can later be used by the services or software companies themselves, or the material can be used by third parties. Teachers should always read policies before using plagiarism services or software to see if and how any material will be used. Furthermore, they should check with their school's policies for using plagiarism services or software. Lawsuits have already emerged over use of plagiarism software to detect plagiarism by students (Glod, 2007).

Teachers can help prevent plagiarism before it happens by taking several proactive steps:

- By taking class time to discuss issues of plagiarism, you will give students the message that plagiarism is a serious breach of academic integrity, that not tolerating it is important to you, and that rejecting it should be important to them.

- Teachers can provide instruction on guidelines for using information obtained over the Internet. Although laws that govern the Internet are changing and emerging daily, Table 4.3 lists some general principles that can be used as guidelines for ethical and legal practices in the classroom.

TABLE 4.3 ■ Guidelines for using the Internet appropriately

Practice	Guidelines
Use a quote from an e-article in your teacher-created worksheet	Be clear that the quote is not your own by using proper APA citation format and observe copyright law.
Paraphrase content from a website in a newsletter you send home to parents	Show proper APA citation, and do not use more content than fair use allows.
Present an idea you located in an e-resource in a paper you present at a teacher conference	Provide the URL and correct APA citation format and observe copyright law.

Internet Misuse and Other Dangerous Practices

The Internet literally opens up a world of possibilities for anyone able to access it. Responsibility comes with this privilege. Using the Internet for appropriate means should be a common-sense practice performed by ethical people, but unfortunately, this is not always the case. Less-than-honorable ways to use the Internet have emerged as use of the Internet has increased. Examples of unscrupulous practices include viewing child pornography, misrepresenting oneself in chat rooms, and ordering illegal items over the Internet.

The penalties for some of these inappropriate behaviors can be severe, resulting in prison, fines, and loss of teaching licensure. Doing what is right, just, and fair help ensure that teachers will be permitted to teach for the length of their desired careers.

Modeling Legal and Ethical Behaviors for Students

Generally, ethics refers to the practice of observing behaviors that rest on principles of right and wrong. Teachers are expected to adhere to high ethical standards, considering the especially influential nature of their work.

Honoring legal practices as they relate to technology is one way of behaving ethically. Observing copyright law, obtaining necessary written permissions for student work, eschewing plagiarism, and making appropriate use of technology are some of the ways teachers can practice and model ethical behaviors in the classroom. A number of professional societies and organizations have developed codes of ethics, such as the Association for Educational Communications and Technology's (AECT) Code of Professional Ethics (www.aect.org/About/Ethics.asp). All teachers should be familiar with the code of ethics associated with their work.

In order to model legal and ethical behaviors for students, teachers have to know what they are. This is the beginning of being informed and being capable of behaving legally and ethically. Some legal and ethical behaviors with regard to technology were noted previously in this chapter.

Teachers may have heard that knowledge is power. Perhaps knowledge is not only power but is also responsibility; in other words, teachers should act upon what they know is good, right, just, and fair. Their behavior inside and outside the classroom matters. What they do and say matters.

Throughout the previous discussion on legal and ethical behavior in technology were guidelines for classroom practices. Knowing and practicing good legal and ethical behaviors in and outside the classroom help teachers guide their students. Teachers may have heard that "some things can be caught by students rather than taught to students." In the realm of appropriate legal and ethical behaviors, learning what is right and wrong can be both caught and taught. If teachers want students to learn fair use of copyrighted material, they should practice it themselves. If they want students to eschew piracy, they must avoid it themselves. If they want students to credit sources appropriately on papers, they should do it themselves. Whether teachers know it or not, students are always watching in and outside the classroom. For this reason alone, it is important that teachers establish their public persona early in their career and be prepared to maintain and defend it.

Requiring students to practice legal and ethical behaviors in the classroom as they relate to technology, with appropriate and enforced penalties for not following policies, also sends a strong message to students about what is expected of them. Using a developmentally and age-appropriate student contract that outlines appropriate behaviors further affirms a teacher's commitment to teaching and modeling legal and ethical behaviors. As noted earlier, teachers should check with their school administration to determine district or school policies and procedures related to student use of technology.

An enlarged copy of a contract can be posted near the computer station or in some prominent place in the classroom for further emphasis.

Providing developmentally and age-appropriate instruction on appropriate use of technology and technology-related issues prior to allowing students to use technology is advisable. Teachers cannot assume that students' former teachers already conducted such instruction, and even if they did, technology issues change so rapidly from year to year that it is important to review them for new or emerging matters.

Creating assignments that require students to use higher-order thinking skills related to legal and ethical issues in technology is another way to teach appropriate behavior. For example, having students use role-play or case studies to investigate technology laws can be effective. Table 4.4 lists some strategies for teaching legal and ethical behaviors in the classroom.

TABLE 4.4 ■ Strategies for teaching legal and ethical behaviors

Strategy	Description
Case Study	Assign case studies where students determine the legality of using a copyrighted work based on law and the judicial process (court case precedents).
Role-Play	Role-play situations and allow students to discuss whether the behavior is legal and ethical. Allow students to devise role-play scenarios themselves that address legal and ethical issues.
Research	Assign research papers that highlight legal and ethical issues related to technology use and require proper citations.
WebQuest	Create a WebQuest related to laws that relate to legal and ethical practices.
Design of a Document	Ask students to design a web page, brochure, or poster that highlights principles of copyright and fair use.
Create a Video or Podcast	Ask students to create a video or podcast that highlights principles of copyright and fair use.
Interview	Conduct a class interview (via online chat, phone call with speaker phone, or face-to-face) with an authority on legal and ethical issues that impact the classroom.
Composition of Class Policies	Have students assist you in writing class policies of legal and ethical classroom behaviors. Post policies and send policies home to parents/guardians.

Promoting Safe and Healthy Use of Technology

Teachers are no doubt concerned with the safety of their students. "Volatile mismatch,"[4] broken homes, student addictions, and mental illness are a few potential threats to student safety in the classroom. At the beginning of every school year, it is common for school administrators to discuss emergency and safety procedures with teachers, staff, and students to ensure a safe working environment for all. Whether or not a plan for technology safety is included, teachers should still be aware that some dangers exist.

Teachers who include technology-rich teaching experiences in the classroom should have a plan for creating a safe technology learning environment. Two important safety issues include the use of blocking software and general Internet safety.

To Block or Not to Block: The Controversy

When students use technology in the classroom, they will be exposed to a wide variety of content. Teachers want to protect students from viewing content that can harm them in any way, but the way to do this is controversial. Censorship, or the filtering of dangerous material to prevent access to student viewing, has been controversial for a long time. Book burning is one example of how some communities dealt with material they deemed questionable and a way to keep these materials out of the hands of students. Today, blocking software is a form of protecting students from questionable material found on the Internet.

Proponents of censorship claim that students should be protected from viewing any material of a questionable nature. This includes such things as sexually explicit content, content that could cause danger to self or society, and the like. They argue that protecting children from these things is a necessary precaution, similar to installing cameras in schools to protect children from potentially threatening intruders. Typically, they promote censorship in books and other traditional teaching tools as well as technology resources. They argue that while some quality and wholesome material may be inadvertently blocked or prevented, this cost is justified because the risk of potential danger from unblocked material is great.

Opponents of censorship promote teaching critical thinking as a more reasonable measure toward student safety versus censorship of materials. They believe equipping students with skills to make informed, safe choices provides long-lasting, better assurances that students will choose wisely in technology and other avenues of life. They also argue that filtering software not only blocks questionable material, but blocks legitimate research content that might be interpreted by the software as questionable. They affirm that even with the best software and teacher supervision, students are likely to come across unanticipated websites, games, or other sources that contain questionable content. Other questions they raise are, "Who will determine what is questionable and what is acceptable?" and "Will these measures be consistent across the country or differ depending on community norms and mores?"

Regardless of teachers' positions on censorship, they should be aware that proponents on both sides strongly support their respective positions, and they should check with their school administration before installing or uninstalling blocking software on the technology used in the classroom.

Several popular blocking software programs are listed in Resource List 4.6. Although they differ in some ways, many features of these software programs overlap. To decide which blocking software programs best meet classroom needs, teachers would be wise to consult several independent reviews. A few places to look for such reviews are also provided in Resource List 4.6.

RESOURCE LIST 4.6 ■ Popular blocking software and sites to find reviews

Software

> **CyberPatrol:** www.cyberpatrol.com
>
> **Safe Eyes:** www.internetsafety.com
>
> **CYBERsitter:** www.cybersitter.com
>
> **Net Nanny:** www.netnanny.com

Reviews

> **PC World:** www.pcworld.com
>
> **Mac World:** www.macworld.com
>
> **CNET:** www.cnet.com
>
> **ZDNet:** www.zdnet.com

If teachers will not be using blocking software in their classrooms, they can still use the blocking software provided on most Internet browsers to block out sites other than the ones students will be using for a particular assignment, such as a WebQuest. With more open-ended assignments, it will be more difficult to effectively use the limited blocking tools provided, but teachers can still monitor students' work by walking around the classroom frequently.

Promoting Internet Safety

In addition to using blocking software, teachers can make their physical presence known by moving around the classroom and making their virtual presence known with monitoring software, such as SMART Sync (go to http://smarttech.com/us, select Education, then scroll through the products to find SMART Sync), which allows teachers to see what students are watching on their individual computers in a lab situation. Teachers can take other steps to help ensure student safety on the Internet as well. Students need to know the very real dangers that exist from using and communicating via the Internet. Some of the potential dangers include the following:

- **Communicating with individuals who misrepresent themselves.** Misrepresentation can include falsification in areas such as age, gender, occupation, visual appearance, incarceration, and location.

- **Being bullied or intimidated.** Any behavior that threatens the health, safety, or esteem of another (or is perceived to be of a threatening nature) falls into this category.

- **Establishing questionable relationships with virtual friends.** Minors who develop relationships with adults with ill intentions fall into this category. So do students becoming members of virtual groups that could threaten their own health or safety, or that of others.

- **Learning how to create dangerous materials that can harm self or others.** These may include bomb-making websites, websites that promote the use of dangerous combinations of drugs and alcohol, or ones that promote harmful sexual practices.

- **Being lured into meeting with individuals they meet on the Internet.** Students should never meet face-to-face with people they meet on the Internet.

- **Being taken advantage of in terms of sharing personal or family information.** Students may reveal their names, addresses, personal IDs, parents' credit card information, school name, etc. either voluntarily or by being tricked into sharing personal information. (Obtaining this information through technology and deception is known as "phishing.")

- **Using parents' or their own credit cards to order inappropriate items.** Students may intentionally or unintentionally order items that are neither age-appropriate nor legal.

- **Being self-disclosing in a way that may harm them now or in the future or in some way cause a loss of their privacy.** Students may not realize that what they write in a discussion forum, blog, chat room, email, or other virtual communication may come back to haunt them later when they look for employment. Search engines and other Internet tools make it very easy to locate anything anyone has ever written on the Internet.

- **Becoming victims of computer frauds.**[5] Students' computer systems may be hacked—used without authorization—and consequently infected with a virus or used in other fraudulent ways.

- **Becoming victims of hardware theft or vandalism.** Portable technology, such as laptop computers, smartphones, tablets, and flash drives, can be easily stolen or destroyed, contributing to the loss or sharing of sensitive content.

- **Participating in computer piracy.** Students may not realize the gravity of computer piracy or the unlawful use of computer software without a license and may find themselves in trouble with the law.

- **Downloading music illegally.** Students may not be aware of restrictions set forth by the U.S. Digital Millennium Copyright Act (www.copyright.gov/legislation/dmca.pdf) and may be penalized according to the law.

- **Knowingly or unknowingly failing to abide by an AUP.** Students may inadvertently share information from a website that is explicitly prohibited in an acceptable use policy (AUP) set forth by a computer network or website. For example, the student didn't read or fully understand the AUP before agreeing to use the website.

Resource List 4.7 includes more information regarding the laws, dangers, and prevention of computer fraud; the U.S. Digital Millennium Copyright Act; and Internet safety.

RESOURCE LIST 4.7 ■ Resources for computer and Internet safety

Connect Safely: www.connectsafely.org

CyberAngels: www.cyberangels.org

CyberSmart!: www.cybersmartcurriculum.org/safetysecurity

Family Online Safety Institute (FOSI): www.fosi.org/cms

FBI: A Parent's Guide to Internet Safety: www.fbi.gov/publications

FBI White-Collar Crime website: www.fbi.gov/about-us/investigate/white_collar

GetNetWise: http://kids.getnetwise.org/safetyguide

NetSmartz and NetSmartzKids: www.netsmartz.org; www.netsmartzkids.org

StaySafeOnline: www.staysafeonline.org

U.S. Digital Millennium Copyright Act: www.copyright.gov

Wired Kids: www.wiredkids.org

WiredSafety: www.wiredsafety.org

Table 4.5 summarizes some examples of potential dangers and some strategies for helping to prevent dangers. Even when the greatest care is taken to prevent dangers, teachers and students need to be aware that risks are always present when using the Internet.

TABLE 4.5 ■ Potential dangers associated with Internet use

Potential Dangers	Strategies for Prevention
Misrepresentation of Chat Partners	Do not give out personal identifying information, and don't agree to meet any chat partners face-to-face.
Bullying	Exit site immediately. Students should report bullying to adult (teacher or parent/guardian).
Questionable Virtual Friendships	Don't give out personal identifying information, and don't agree to meet any chat partners face-to-face.
Access to Dangerous Material	Blocking software can help prevent access to some sites that include dangerous practices (e.g., bomb making), but no software is 100% accurate. Students should exit any questionable sites immediately and inform an adult (teacher or parent/guardian) of the site.
Computer Fraud	Be aware of phishing, hacking, and other unlawful and unethical practices. Don't give out personal information. Ignore requests for personal information, and report such requests to an adult (teacher or parent/guardian).
Participating in a Crime	Be aware of copyright law and ethical practices, and don't participate in Internet crimes such as unlawful downloading of music, using Internet content unlawfully, and the like.

As noted earlier, one way teachers may help students and parents become explicitly aware of the potential dangers of Internet use is by distributing contracts to students and parents/guardians before students use any technology in the classroom. Teachers should check with their district and school administration to determine what policies and procedures are mandated before allowing students to use technology resources.

Promoting a Healthy Use of Technology

Promoting student safety while using technology is one important goal for providing an effective, technology-enriched classroom environment. Promoting the healthy use of technology is another. Creating a healthy environment includes such issues as ergonomics and the avoidance of physical wear and tear on the body. It also includes the mental and emotional health of students using technology.

Ergonomics is the study of design as it relates to human health, safety, and comfort. In recent years, consumers have increased their demand for ergonomically designed furniture, tools, appliances, recreation and fitness equipment, and office products. Manufacturers have responded by designing products that meet consumer needs and wants, such as those sold at Ergonomic.com (www.ergonomic.com).

The technology products teachers and students use in the classroom should promote health, safety, and comfort in the classroom. The very best ergonomically designed products, however, may be beyond the reach of the school budget. For this reason, it is important for teachers to prioritize students' needs and follow them with students' wants.

Healthy use of technology in the classroom involves considering how brief or extended use of technology will affect the physical, mental, and emotional health of students. Taking into consideration how computer use affects the senses is important to ensure that neither short- nor long-term damage is made to the physical senses. Environmental factors, such as facility design and the amount of personal computer space, can either enhance or detract from the overall learning environment. One of the more obvious strains associated with computer use is eye strain. Computer glare, font size, lighting, and other factors can contribute to eye strain and discomfort. The Occupational Safety and Health Administration (OSHA, www.osha.gov/SLTC/etools/computerworkstations) has checklists and quick tips for configuring healthy workstations. Here are OSHA's three monitor placement quick tips:

- Put monitor directly in front of you and at least 20 inches away.

- Place monitor so top line of screen is at or below eye level.

- Place monitor perpendicular to window. (OSHA, n.d., para. 4)

Repetitive stress injury (RSI), also known as repetitive strain injury, is injury that results from repetitive use of muscles, tendons, nerves, or tissues that can result in temporary or permanent injury. Carpal tunnel syndrome (CTS) is one of the better-known types of RSIs, but many others are associated with technology use.

CTS affects the hands, wrists, and arms and may result from incorrect use of keyboards and mice. Using seating, tables, mice and keyboard locations effectively can help prevent strain to the muscles, tendons, nerves, and soft tissues in this region. Prevention is preferred to fixing damage once it is done.

Tendonitis, bursitis, and trigger finger are a few other RSIs that can result from improper use of technology. Severe neck and back pain can also develop from improper seating arrangements and poor sitting posture. OSHA provides a checklist, shown here in Table 4.6, for analyzing existing workstations.

TABLE 4.6 ▪ OSHA evaluation checklist for posture and seating

Working Postures—The workstation is designed or arranged for doing computer tasks so it allows your …		
1. Head and neck to be upright, or in-line with the torso (not bent down/back). If *no*, refer to Monitors, Chairs and Work Surfaces.	YES	NO
2. Head, neck, and trunk to face forward (not twisted). If *no*, refer to Monitors or Chairs.	YES	NO
3. Trunk to be perpendicular to floor (may lean back into backrest but not forward). If *no*, refer to Chairs or Monitors.	YES	NO
4. Shoulders and upper arms to be in-line with the torso, generally about perpendicular to the floor and relaxed (not elevated or stretched forward). If *no*, refer to Chairs.	YES	NO
5. Upper arms and elbows to be close to the body (not extended outward). If *no*, refer to Chairs, Work Surfaces, Keyboards, and Pointers.	YES	NO
6. Forearms, wrists, and hands to be straight and in-line (forearm at about 90 degrees to the upper arm). If *no*, refer to Chairs, Keyboards, Pointers.	YES	NO
7. Wrists and hands to be straight (not bent up/down or sideways toward the little finger). If *no*, refer to Keyboards, or Pointers.	YES	NO
8. Thighs to be parallel to the floor and the lower legs to be perpendicular to floor (thighs may be slightly elevated above knees). If *no*, refer to Chairs or Work Surfaces.	YES	NO
9. Feet rest flat on the floor or are supported by a stable footrest. If *no*, refer to Chairs, Work Surfaces.	YES	NO
Seating—Consider these points when evaluating the chair:		
10. Backrest provides support for your lower back (lumbar area).	YES	NO
11. Seat width and depth accommodate the specific user (seat pan not too big/small).	YES	NO
12. Seat front does not press against the back of your knees and lower legs (seat pan not too long).	YES	NO
13. Seat has cushioning and is rounded with a "waterfall" front (no sharp edge).	YES	NO
14. Armrests, if used, support both forearms while you perform computer tasks and they do not interfere with movement.	YES	NO
"No" answers to any of these questions (10–14) should prompt a review of Chairs.		

Source: www.osha.gov/SLTC/etools/computerworkstations/checklist.html

Figure 4.2 shows how lighting can impact quantity, contrast, and direct and reflected glare. Figure 4.3 illustrates proper workstation user position. Measurements will vary based on individual characteristics such as height.

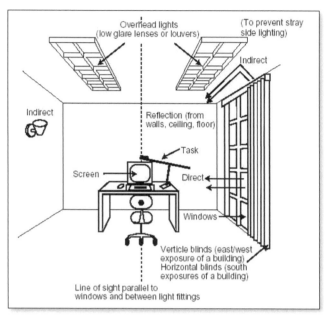

FIGURE 4.2 Workstation lighting (OSHA, 1997, fig. 1).[6]

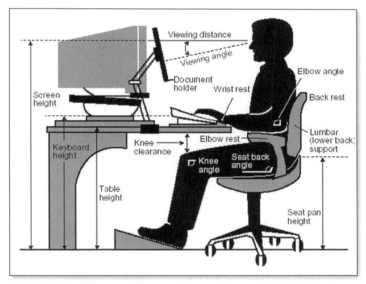

FIGURE 4.3 Proper workstation user position and support (OSHA, 1997, fig. 3).

Table 4.7 is a purchasing guide checklist provided by OSHA to evaluate new monitor and keyboard purchases.

TABLE 4.7 ■ OSHA purchasing guide checklist for monitors and keyboards

Monitor—Consider these points when evaluating the monitor:	✓
1. Make sure the screen is large enough for adequate visibility. Usually a 15- to 20-inch monitor is sufficient. Smaller units will make it difficult to read characters and larger units may require excessive space.	
2. The angle and tilt should be easily adjustable.	
3. Flat panel displays take less room on the desk and may be more suitable for locations with limited space.	
Keyboard/Input Device—Consider these points when evaluating the keyboard or pointing device:	✓
1. Split keyboard designs will allow you to maintain neutral wrist postures.	
2. Keyboards with adjustable feet will accommodate a wider range of keyboard positions and angles. Adjustable feet on the front as well as the back will further aid adjustments. Increased adjustability will facilitate neutral wrist postures.	
3. The cord that plugs into the CPU should be long enough to allow the user to place the keyboard and the CPU in a variety of positions. At least six feet of cord length is desirable.	
4. Consider a keyboard without a 10-key keypad if the task does not require one. If the task does require one occasionally, a keyboard with a separate 10-key keypad may be appropriate. Keyboards without keypads allow the user to place the mouse closer to the keyboard.	
5. Consider the shape and size of the keyboard if a keyboard tray is used. The keyboard should fit comfortably on the tray.	
6. Consider keyboards without built-in wrist rest, because separate wrist rests are usually better.	
7. Keyboards should be detached from the display screen if they are used for a long duration keying task. Laptop keyboards are generally not suitable for prolonged typing tasks.	

Source: www.osha.gov/SLTC/etools/computerworkstations/checklist.html

Other issues that may be less affected by ergonomics but are as important when considering health issues related to technology use are childhood fitness and mental, emotional, and social health.[7]

Childhood Fitness

Poor eating habits and lack of activity negatively impact childhood health and fitness. Trends, as seen in the National Health and Nutrition Examination Survey (NHANES) results in Table 4.8 and Figure 4.4, show a rise in childhood and adolescent overweight; see note in Figure 4.4 that defines overweight.

TABLE 4.8 ■ Prevalence of overweight among children and adolescents for select years and ages

Age (years)	NHANES 1971–74	NHANES 1976–80	NHANES 1988–94	NHANES 1999–2000	NHANES 2001–02	NHANES 2003–04
6–11	4	6.5	11.3	15.1	16.3	18.8
12–19	6.1	5	10.5	14.8	16.7	17.4

Source: National Center for Health Statistics (Centers for Disease Control and Prevention, 2006) (www.cdc.gov/nchs/data/hestat/overweight/overweight_child_03.htm)

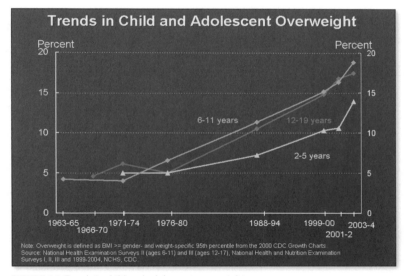

FIGURE 4.4 Trends in child and adolescent overweight

Source: National Center for Health Statistics (Centers for Disease Control and Prevention, 2005) (www.cdc.gov/nchs/data/hestat/overweight/overweight_child_03.htm)

Teachers can help promote healthy practices by encouraging wise technology habits. In the classroom, students can be encouraged to take short breaks if they are using the computer for an extended period of time. Teachers can set timers that remind students to get up and move around the classroom periodically or at least stand up and stretch if movement around the classroom is not practical. Teachers may want to set such reminders for themselves as well.

Another strategy is to help students realize that effective use of technology does not require sitting in front of a computer nonstop. Teachers can help students understand that using information gathered from technology resources can be analyzed, synthesized, and evaluated away from the computer.

If mobile technology is available, and it is reasonable, safe, and practical, students can move to a new venue to work. This is admittedly a small step in helping students see that being tethered to a computer station is not the only way to work.

By collaborating with physical educators, teachers can work out ways to combine the use of technology with fitness training. For example, collaboration may yield safe and practical ideas for how students can watch or listen to instructional materials as they exercise in their physical education classrooms.

Students may also have ideas for ways to promote healthy use of technology. Nintendo (www.nintendo. com) has addressed the need for physical activity with children and adults by introducing Wii Sports (www.nintendo.com/wii), a Nintendo video game that requires physical activity along with skill and technology use. The availability and popularity of "exergames" such as Nintendo Wii, Xbox 360 Kinect, and PlayStation Move could lead to numerous applications for education.

If students were polled about how many hours they spend being physically active, teachers might be surprised to learn that far too many students spend considerably more time sitting than moving (see Table 4.9). With this in mind, it is important that teachers be resourceful and creative when thinking about ways to promote movement and activity with technology at both school and home.

TABLE 4.9 ■ Percentage of high school students participating in physical activity and physical education, by sex, 2007

Type of Activity	Girls	Boys
At least 60 minutes/day of physical activity[a]	25.6%	43.7%
Attended physical education class daily[b]	27.3%	33.2%

[a] Any kind of physical activity that increased heart rate and made them breathe hard some of the time for at least 60 minutes per day on 5 or more of the 7 days preceding the survey.

[b] Attended physical education classes 5 days in an average week when they were in school.

Source: Centers for Disease Control and Prevention (2008) (www.cdc.gov/HealthyYouth/physicalActivity/pdf/facts.pdf)

Here are some strategies to help promote physical activity.

- Encourage short breaks from the computer.

- Encourage students to move away from the computer to analyze, synthesize, and evaluate data when possible.

- When appropriate and safe, allow students to use portable technology in different areas around the classroom.

- Enlist the help of physical educators for ideas of ways to combine technology and physical activity.

- Enlist the help of students for ideas of ways to integrate technology and physical activity in different areas around the classroom.

Promoting healthy use of technology not only includes the physical needs of students, but also their mental, emotional, and social health. Although technology offers so much in the way of improved communication, access to information, and convenience, it can pose a danger to students' mental and emotional health if their virtual worlds begin to replace their real worlds.

Developing relationships and support structures in the real world help students grow into well-developed, balanced, and contributing citizens. Teachers can help students realize the differences between healthy and unhealthy uses of technology.

Although friendships maintained or even initiated through email, chats, blogging, and other channels of communication can be healthy and life-enriching if appropriate safety measures are followed, they also pose potential dangers. As noted earlier in this chapter, some "friends" students meet on the Internet are actually individuals who are misrepresenting themselves in age, gender, locale, or other background qualities. In many cases, it is nearly impossible to know who is really on the other end of the communication line without actually meeting the person "in person." And this, as noted before, poses a danger. Students should never meet "in person" individuals they meet on the Internet.

One of the dangers of placing too much emphasis on Internet friends is that students will not learn face-to-face verbal and nonverbal communication skills and how to engage in real-world friendships and relationships. Learning how to contend with acceptance, rejection, uncomfortable social situations, and the like are all a part of developing into a healthy, well-adjusted adult. When youth are already socially uncomfortable, the Internet serves as a temptation to forgo the real world altogether in favor of the virtual, not allowing them the opportunity to learn important, face-to-face social skills. It is really too soon to know the long-term implications of such replacement, but teachers and parents need to be aware that the tendency exists for some individuals to replace the real world with the virtual.

In Your Experience

Is your computer workstation safe and comfortable? If not, what can you do to improve your computer workstation?

Section T4a Explorations

1. Describe a situation that involves a fictional teacher who plans to use a type of copyrighted material in the classroom. Exchange your situation with a peer and decide if the situation is permissible or what actions need to be taken to make use of the copyrighted material permissible. You may wish to role-play some of the scenarios and have your peers determine whether you are observing fair use or obtaining correct copyright permissions.

2. Review different print and digital materials that you may wish to use in teaching and report on their copyright permissions and/or policies.

3. Create content that conveys your Internet safety policy to students and parents/guardians. Review a peer's content and make recommendations for improvement.

4. Review several blocking software programs and report on the strengths and weaknesses of each. Share your reviews with peers. Determine if your reviews parallel their findings.

5. State your position on blocking software. Argue for the opposite position.

6. Using a drawing software program, sketch out a floor plan for a classroom computer station that represents a safe and healthy environment.

7. Make a list of typical computer-related activities in which you participate. Evaluate each item for how well you are practicing safe and healthy behaviors.

Section T4a Review

In this section you learned how to teach and model ethical behaviors in and outside the classroom as they relate to technology. More specifically, you learned about copyright and fair use, parental permissions, plagiarism, and other behaviors. In addition, you learned some strategies for promoting safe and healthy use of technology. While you cannot anticipate every possible danger, you can establish safe and healthy practices in the classroom that may influence students' lives in and outside the classroom. In the next section you will learn how to enable and empower learners so that every student has the chance to benefit from all that technology offers.

NETS•T4b

Address the Diverse Needs of All Learners by Using Learner-Centered Strategies and Providing Equitable Access to Appropriate Digital Tools and Resources

One of the joys of teaching is having the opportunity to enable and empower students through education. Regardless of background, students can soar when introduced to rich experiences and meaningful interactions. More specifically, teachers can help propel students toward success by using technology-enhanced experiences. In this section you will learn how to apply technology to enable and empower learners with diverse backgrounds, characteristics, and abilities.

Ensuring Accessibility of Technology for All Students

When a teacher engages all learners intellectually, he or she is practicing culturally responsive teaching (Burns, Keyes, & Kusimo, 2005). Having good intentions for practicing culturally responsive teaching and ensuring equitable access for all students is a positive step, but it is not enough. Planning is required to ensure that thoughts translate into action where culturally responsive practices in the classroom are the norm.

Access refers to the right of entry into something; allowing people to enter a building provides them with the right of entry or access to the facility. In the same way, providing access to technology allows entry into the world of technology. Though many young people today have access to a wide assortment of technology, including computers, Internet, and cell phones, many are still on the other side of the digital divide.[8] Lack of resources and opportunities and other circumstances have prevented them from obtaining and using technology regularly. A teacher can help bridge the digital divide by ensuring that all students are permitted access to technology.

Diversity in student backgrounds, characteristics, and abilities should not limit students' right of entry into the world of technology. Although accessibility and diversity in terms of technology are discussed in more detail elsewhere in this book, a few modifications will be discussed here that can allow teachers to ensure accessibility for all.

Students in households with low socioeconomic status (SES) or those from other situations with limited resources may enter the classroom with fewer technology-enriched experiences than other, more resource-privileged students. Although students may lack Internet access at home, they likely have had other experiences with technology, such as television, cell phones, and video players. Keeping with the constructivist approach, it is important to use their prior knowledge and experiences as springboards when introducing educational technology to students.

Students are often very adept at using technology devices such as video remotes. The ability to make connections between digital input devices (remote) and output devices (television screen) is a transferable skill. (See Chapter 3.) Helping students to realize the transferable nature of this and other skills they use daily will ease them into using technology in the classroom. This not only promotes technology skills, but also builds confidence and removes the intimidation factor when students learn new technology.

Students may have limited experiences with educational technology for other reasons besides SES and restricted resources. Cultural differences may play a role in how technology is used in the home. Some households place great emphasis on family connections and the roles individuals play in the collective household, but place a smaller role on technology use. Here again, capitalizing on the strengths and experiences of students who have strong social connections and skills allows them to use these skills in educational experiences, such as cooperative technology group work. By reflecting on the diverse characteristics of their students, teachers can find ways to use students' prior skills and experiences to promote their educational success.

Students with individualized education programs (IEPs) have prescribed plans that are designed with student success in mind. Becoming aware of students' individual needs allows teachers to accommodate and provide technology-enriched experiences for all students.[9] Providing equal access and equal opportunities to all students is not only important for students' educational success, but also helps promote student inclusion. Resource List 4.8 shows a number of online resources teachers may wish to use to help provide technology-enriched experiences for a population with special needs.

RESOURCE LIST 4.8 ■ Resources for assistive technology and Universal Design for Learning

AbleData: www.abledata.com

Sponsored by the National Institute on Disability and Rehabilitation Research (NIDRR), part of the Special Education and Rehabilitative Services (OSERS) of the U.S. Department of Education; contains a large, searchable database of assistive technology and rehabilitation equipment. Visitors can search products from national and international vendors by categories (e.g., communication, computers, education) and can search for companies by state. Also available are a library, a consumer forum, and links to other helpful resources.

AssistiveTech.net: www.assistivetech.net

This is a searchable database of assistive technology products. The site is created and maintained through the partnership of the Georgia Tech Center for Assistive Technology and Environmental Access (CATEA), the National Institute on Disability and Rehabilitation Research, and Rehabilitation Services Administration. In addition to its database, CATEA maintains a number of helpful resources, including an assistive technology (AT) wiki it describes as an online AT encyclopedia. It also features notable events on its "This Day in AT History" calendar.

The Center for Applied Special Technology (CAST): www.cast.org

The Center for Applied Special Technology publishes and makes available a number of helpful guides, books, and resources to promote Universal Design for Learning (UDL), including some available for free online viewing. One such resource, Teaching Every Student in the Digital Age: Universal Design for Learning (Rose & Meyer, 2002) is available at www.cast.org/teachingeverystudent/ideas/tes.

DisabilityInfo.gov: www.disabilityinfo.gov

Describes itself as "Your online connection to the federal government's disability-related information and resources." Especially helpful to educators are its links to Education and Technology. Its Education link leads visitors to grade-specific resources, information on education and the law, assistive technology, and more. Its Technology link provides visitors with information on accessibility, assistive and information technology, the law, and other related content. Similar to ABLEDATA site, visitors can search resources by state.

National Library Service (NLS) for the Blind and Physically Handicapped, the Library of Congress (LOC):
www.loc.gov/nls

Provides an NLS Reference Circular on Assistive Technology Products for Information Access (NLS, LOC, www.loc.gov/nls/reference/circulars/assistive.html). Here teachers will find information on screen readers, speech synthesizers, voice-recognition software, and other assistive technologies. Teachers can visit the Assistive Technology Act Programs link (http://assistivetech. net/webresources/techActProjects.php) to learn more about the Assistive Technology Act of 2004 and the National Assistive Technology Technical Assistance Partnership. Helpful information on device loan and reutilization programs is available.

Vischeck: www.vischeck.com

Vischeck is a tool that simulates colorblind vision and may be used on web pages and image files. Daltonize is a colorblind image correction tool available on the same website.

World Wide Web Consortium: www.w3.org

The Web Accessibility Initiative (WAI), as part of World Wide Web Consortium (W3C), helps coordinate global efforts to ensure accessibility standards so that users of all abilities may use computers effectively. Many web-accessibility evaluators exist that check conformance to these standards. Some evaluators, or validators as they are sometimes called, are more user-friendly than others and provide simpler means for correcting nonconformance problems. An extensive list of providers is available at the W3C website.

In addition to virtual accessibility (such as web accessibility) and assistive technologies, teachers need to be aware of physical accessibility issues as well, such as wheelchair accessibility at computer workstations. Architects and builders are familiar with the principle of universal design for physical accessibility, much like educators use principles of Universal Design for Learning (UDL) in the educational environment. Teachers should consult with designated district personnel to ensure accessibility in the physical environment.

Students with special needs can benefit greatly from well-structured activities that serve as inclusive experiences, such as cooperative learning activities and collaborative ICT-assisted PBL projects.[10] In cooperative learning groups, everyone is responsible for contributing to the success of the group. Cooperative learning is a research-supported strategy (Marzano, Pickering, & Pollock, 2001) that actively engages all learners by assigning roles to small groups of students to achieve a common goal (Johnson & Johnson, 1997). Various cooperative-learning strategies exist that can be used in a variety of lessons. Students with IEPs can be given appropriate roles that help them realize their connection to the group and the importance of their contributions in the technology-enriched learning experience. These strategies also build respect and camaraderie among members of the group. They constitute some degree of success; learning lesson content and building rapport together are colossal achievements. Resource List 4.9 shows some resources associated with cooperative learning.

RESOURCE LIST 4.9 ■ Websites associated with leading educators/researchers in cooperative learning strategies

Center for Research on Learning and Teaching (Cooperative Learning, Best Practices):
www.crlt.umich.edu/publinks/clgt_bestpractices.php

This website provides a list of resources related to cooperative learning.

The Cooperative Learning Institute, University of Minnesota: www.co-operation.org

> Robert T. Johnson and David W. Johnson are well-known for their work with cooperative learning. Links to content and resources on cooperative learning are located on this site.

Successes for All Foundation: www.successforall.net/about/about_bios.htm

> Robert Slavin is chairman and co-director, and Nancy A. Madden is president of the foundation. Here you will find resources on cooperative learning and on other means through which students achieve.

Collaborative ICT-assisted PBL projects using various collaborative digital tools are discussed in Chapters 1, 2, and 3 as appropriate strategies to use with students. As contributing members of society, all students—including those with special needs—should have practice working together with others toward a common goal, making ICT-assisted PBL projects appropriate for all learners.

Here are some ways to help maximize technology access for all students:

- Acknowledge and capitalize on prior knowledge and experiences of students, and use them as springboards when introducing educational technology to students.

- Help students to realize the transferable nature of the skills they use daily, and ease them into using technology in the classroom.

- Capitalize on the strengths and experiences of students who have strong social connections and skills, and allow them to use these skills in educational experiences, such as cooperative technology group work.

- Reflect on the diverse characteristics of your students and use their knowledge and experiences toward their educational success.

- Become aware of students' individual needs, and tailor technology-enriched experiences so that all students can participate and achieve.

- Use assistive technology when appropriate, and ensure web-page accessibility.

- Use cooperative learning groups and collaborative ICT-assisted PBL strategies when the learning situation lends itself to these practices.

When all students are given access to technology and all students are intellectually engaged, their opportunities to succeed in all aspects of the curriculum are increased through technology-enriched experiences. As noted earlier, when students achieve academic or social success, their confidence is likely to increase. This is one instance where the old adage, "success breeds success," rings true. Armed with academic skills and confidence, students are able to achieve anything they wish. This is the power of education: enabling by way of access and empowering through success allows all learners to meet their educational potential.

Enabling and empowering all learners have important and far-reaching implications. Helping all students achieve their educational potential allows them to enter the workforce or post-secondary education better equipped to achieve. This is not only good for individuals, but also for everyone in society. Encouraging all students to discover the joy of making important contributions for the betterment of all (e.g., cooperative group work and PBL-IT work), allows them to draw on these experiences later in life and to make further contributions as citizens. Moreover, as learners mature and have families of their own, they are better equipped to enable and empower their own children in their educational pursuits.

Affirming Diversity in the Technology-Enriched Environment

Teachers have many opportunities to affirm diversity in the classroom. Research shows that teachers trained in culturally responsive teaching can positively impact the classroom environment in many ways and provide a better quality of instruction (Burns, Keyes, & Kusimo, 2006). Using technology, teachers can expand on traditional opportunities so that diversity is celebrated. Some strategies for celebrating diversity, for selecting technology resources that affirm diversity, and for using diversity-affirming resources in the classroom are presented here.

Celebrating diversity involves recognizing the value each student brings to the classroom and how the diverse backgrounds, characteristics, and abilities of all make the classroom a more vibrant community of learners. All classes are heterogeneous if diversity is defined in this sense of the word. Therefore, diversity here refers to differences of all types, such as differences in culture, abilities, and socioeconomic status.

Teachers can use a number of strategies to celebrate diversity using technology. Perhaps the most obvious is to include technology-enriched lessons that allow students to learn about different types of diversity and how individuals with various characteristics have contributed in significant ways to society.

WebQuests are great technology-enriched lessons for this purpose.[11] A WebQuest can be centered around one type of diversity and contributions made by individuals of the diverse group or can focus in a more general sense on various types of diversities. WebQuests can be timed to celebrate groups when the group is nationally recognized. For example, National African-American History Month is celebrated in February. Teachers may choose not to wait for such an occurrence but celebrate different types of diversities throughout the year. Many resources, including those at the Smithsonian Center for Education and Museum Studies (www.smithsonianeducation.org/educators), are available to help teachers and their students celebrate the heritage of diverse groups throughout the year.

Internet scavenger hunts can be designed to help students discover how contributions have been made from diverse groups throughout history for the greater good. In some cases, at certain developmental levels, students can create scavenger hunts to be used by peers.

Role-plays and reenactments based on research collected through the use of technology are other ways to celebrate diversity and contributions from individuals of diverse backgrounds. This is especially helpful when particular ethnic groups are underrepresented or misrepresented in commercially available products.

Another way to create a diversity-affirming product that does not exist is to use puzzles, worksheets, and other teacher-generated tools. In some cases, traditional teaching tools, such as textbooks, and technology-enriched tools, such as digital encyclopedias, provide only cursory coverage of a topic or contributions by diverse groups. Teachers can take over where these tools left off to create ancillary materials, such as e-books and wikis, with other teachers and students.

Student-constructed interactive bulletin boards[12] and learning centers[13] challenge students to use technology-based research findings to show the contributions of diverse people. This is an appropriate way to allow students to interact and learn from peers as they collaborate to construct these instructional materials.

Students in a given class will undoubtedly represent a wide variety of diverse backgrounds. Welcoming presentations by students and their families—both traditional and technology-enhanced—will help build rapport and respect in class as students realize how each family contributes significantly to the fabric of society. Using virtual field trips that help represent the native cultures and geographic regions of students is another way of using diversity-affirming experiences in the classroom.

Teachers can brainstorm with their colleagues virtually or face-to-face to identify and implement ideas. Doing so will surely yield a large list of additional strategies to help prepare diversity-affirming experiences for students.

Here are some strategies for celebrating diversity through the use of technology:

- Use WebQuests and scavenger hunts to help students identify contributions from diverse groups.

- Use role-playing and reenactments associated with historical events of diverse groups.

- Create teacher-generated teaching tools (e.g., worksheets, crossword puzzles) that represent diverse populations.

- Use cooperative group work that allows students to create interactive bulletin boards and learning centers on their research of diverse groups.

- Invite guest speakers (e.g., face-to-face, Internet chats), watch videos, or listen to podcasts to learn more about diverse groups.

- Take real and virtual field trips to culturally diverse places.

- Brainstorm with colleagues, students, and others for additional ideas.

Selecting Technology Resources that Affirm Diversity

Introducing lessons that celebrate diversity is one way of affirming diversity in the classroom. A more subtle method is to select technology resources that affirm diversity. When students use technology resources that include adults and children of diverse backgrounds, students get the message that all people are valuable parts of the larger whole of society.

When selecting software products, teachers should consider subtle forms of inclusion such as names, attributes, and contributions of characters. For example, do the characters represent a wide variety of ethnic and cultural backgrounds? Are people of color and those with disabilities fairly represented? Are the contributions of characters fairly distributed?

If sound is used in the technology product, are various accents represented by narrators and characters? Are various musical compositions used that represent different cultures? Are rural, suburban, and city dwellers present? Are various socioeconomic statuses represented? Are various vocations represented?

It is unlikely that any one product will represent every type of diversity adequately, but by carefully selecting an assortment of technology resources that collectively represent diversity fairly, teachers will send a message that all people and their contributions are important. Resource List 4.10 includes sites for developing a culturally responsive teaching practice.

RESOURCE LIST 4.10 ■ Resources for developing a culturally responsive teaching practice

The Knowledge Loom: http://knowledgeloom.org *(then navigate to Culturally Responsive Teaching)*

Describes culturally responsive education practices and provides links to stories, research, and other resources

Responsive Classroom: www.responsiveclassroom.org

Provides guiding principles, classroom practices, and schoolwide practices. Research and professional development links, downloads, and related information are also provided

InTime (Introducing New Technologies Into the Methods of Education): www.intime.uni.edu/multiculture/curriculum/Culture/Teaching.htm

Describes culturally responsive teaching practices and provides links to teaching practices

The Center for Culturally Responsive Teaching and Learning: www.culturallyresponsive.org

Provides professional development opportunities and materials to enhance culturally responsive teaching and learning

Using Diversity-Affirming Resources in the Classroom

The manner in which teachers use the technology-affirming resources they locate are as important as selecting the resources themselves. Are they allowing equitable amounts of time to resources that represent diversity? For example, if teachers locate some powerful diversity-affirming technology resources but only use these resources for a brief time in the classroom, that, too, sends a message to students. Teachers do not want to give the impression that they are only using such material as an obligation. Students are particularly savvy to what is fair and just and will see through any behavior that is merely perfunctory in nature.

Using various diversity-affirming technology resources with enthusiasm and sincerity is also imperative. Teachers mocking music from a culture different from their own in front of students also sends a poor message. Allowing students to do the same is just as detrimental to a sense of respect. To help teachers become more accustomed to hearing different types of music and accents foreign to their ears, they may wish to spend some personal time listening to recordings and learning about cultures different from their own. Online videos and podcasts that represent a wide assortment of music are plentiful on the Internet and can be used for this purpose.

Designing and Implementing an Equitable Technology Use Plan

This chapter includes a number of strategies for creating diversity-affirming, safe, and healthy technology-enriched experiences in the classroom. To help teachers apply their understandings, they may wish to create a technology plan that will help keep them mindful of important considerations. In devising a plan, they should consider the needs, wants, and comforts of their students. Teachers also need to consider the physical and affective[14] environments, as well as the equity of their technology plan.

Needs, Wants, and Comforts of Students

When considering the needs, wants, and comforts of students, teachers should consider at least the following: What are the actual needs, wants, and comforts of all students? What resources are available to meet these needs, wants, and comforts? For those resources not available, how can needs, wants, and comforts be prioritized to address things of a critical concern first?

To help teachers answer these questions, they may wish to survey their students and their students' parents. The surveys can be anonymous if they think they will yield more honest or fruitful results.[15] In the survey, teachers may wish to ask students what they believe is absolutely critical to their learning in terms of technology. Of course, teachers will have to review the results critically, for what students consider essential, teachers may consider frivolous at best. Their input, however, can help alert teachers to issues not considered and help teachers prioritize needs, wants, and comforts.

Parents/guardians may offer teachers another perspective on what students truly need, needs that teachers might not be aware of. In any case, having input from teachers, students, and parents/guardians will help teachers better prioritize for the effective use of resources. These inputs will help ensure that all students are given access to what they need to maximize learning.

Physical and Affective Environment

Some questions teachers may wish to consider regarding the physical and affective environments include the following: How will they set up the physical environment to best promote the safe and healthy use of technology? What routines will they use to encourage safe and healthy use of technology outside the classroom? How will they create a technology-learning environment that promotes a positive self-concept[16] and maximal learning for all students?

As noted earlier, the physical environment can be used to help promote the safe and healthy use of technology for all students by providing physically accessible, ergonomically sound technology to all students. The affective environment, which includes the atmosphere, appearance, and impression cast by the environment, is equally important. Interior designers, architects, artists, and builders have long realized that the physical and affective environments together help make buildings much more pleasurable to inhabit. Teachers have some influence on the physical and affective environments they create. Again, polling students and parents about the best physical and affective environments in which students learn may lead you to modify seating arrangements, routines, and other such things that can improve learning for all students.

Equitable Access for All Students

All students have the right to equal access to technology and effective technology-enriched experiences. Some of the questions teachers may consider when planning for equitable access for all students include the following: What kinds of diversity-affirming assignments will teachers use with their students so that diversity is welcome and celebrated in the classroom? How will teachers ensure that their assignments are fair and just for all students? What steps will teachers take to make sure all students have equitable access to technology? Are there things teachers can do to promote equitable technology outside the classroom?

Here again, asking for students' honest input through surveys or through other means will help teachers discover whether their good intentions are actually realistic and beneficial. Including parents is another way. Also, self-reflection will help teachers see if they are meeting their goals for providing equal access for all.

Teachers may wish to revisit their plan periodically to make modifications either in questions or responses. Doing so will help them stay current and abreast of changing or emerging situations. They have much to say about the equity that takes place in their classroom. Creating and maintaining a plan is a proactive step toward ensuring technology access for all.

A technology plan does not have to be elaborate, but it does need to be practical and attainable. It should contain information based on the information obtained from polling students and parents/guardians. Teachers should collaborate with colleagues who can help them meet their students' needs, such as special education teachers, county technology coordinators, administrators, counselors, parents, and others. Form 4.1 illustrates a technology plan that teachers may modify for their unique circumstances. You may wish to align parts of your plan to the NETS•T and NETS•S elements.

TECHNOLOGY PLAN

Date _____

Needs/wants of students based on questionnaire:

_____
_____

Ways I can help address these needs/wants, including assistive technology:

_____
_____
_____
_____

People/organizations to contact for assistance, approval, funding:

_____
_____

Progress Made

Date _____

Actions Taken:

_____
_____

Further Action Needed:

_____
_____

FORM 4.1 Sample technology plan.

In Your Experience

What types of classroom experiences, if any, have you had that you consider diversity-affirming? Explain.

Section T4b Explorations

1. Create a background knowledge probe that helps you assess students' prior knowledge and skills. Describe how this probe can help you introduce new technology concepts and skills.

2. Research diverse groups you are not familiar with and create a brochure that highlights achievements and contributions of these groups.

3. Create a timeline that shows the history of contributions of a diverse group. See Chapter 3 for timeline tools.

4. Create a calendar for one or two months that celebrates diversity. See Chapter 3 for calendar tools.

5. Visit one of the websites featured in this section on assistive technologies. Research one assistive technology and create a one-page information sheet that describes the technology and shows how it can be used in the classroom environment. Exchange your information sheet with your peers.

6. Create a podcast that broadcasts an interview with an individual from an under-represented group.

7. Create a teaching tool that represents under-represented groups.

8. Visit www.w3.org/WAI and read about web-page accessibility. Design a simple website and ensure its accessibility.

Section T4b Review

In this section you learned ways to apply technology to enable and empower all learners. You learned specific strategies that address and affirm the diverse characteristics of your students. You also learned some ways to celebrate diversity in the classroom and strategies for selecting diversity-affirming technology resources and the importance of creating a technology plan to help ensure equitable access to technology for all students. Including student and parent input in the development of your plan is consistent with a student-centered, constructivist approach to teaching. Knowing the needs, wants, and desired comforts of your students will help you prioritize what you should provide with the limited resources at your disposal. In the next section, you will learn how creating and maintaining your public persona relates to your teaching practice and personal life.

NETS•T4c

Promote and Model Digital Etiquette and Responsible Social Interactions Related to the Use of Technology and Information

Your public persona involves the image you convey via all of your words and actions and how this image is perceived by the public. A teacher's public persona is critical to establishing his or her credibility in the immediate educational community and profession. While it typically takes time to build credibility and respect, it takes very little to crush it. As you have learned throughout this chapter, a careless word or action in the classroom, online, or in some other venue could destroy your credibility overnight. For the sake of your career and in the best interest of your students, think before you speak, and think before you act. In this section you will learn specific ways to enhance your public persona and how to avoid behaviors that can destroy it.

Netiquette and Other Civil Behaviors

One way to exhibit socially responsible behavior is to use appropriate netiquette online. Netiquette is the use of proper etiquette online or on the Net (as the Internet is sometimes called). The use of profanity, bullying, intimidation of all types, and similar uncivil behaviors shows poor Internet citizenship and poor netiquette and, depending on the behavior, can get people into legal trouble. Even if teachers are using such behaviors within a discussion board, remember that many discussion posts are searchable on major search engines. Students can easily see Internet behavior through simple searches if teachers use their real names or names that students know they use.

In the real world, if people verbally interact in a socially inappropriate way through profanity, curt replies, yelling, or some other unacceptable interaction, they often convey a less-than-pleasant persona. The same applies in written form and in the virtual world. Whether reading a hand-written letter, an email message, or a text message, the written word can have the same effects on its audience.

When writing messages that are transmitted via digital means, all writers should remember that their words having staying power—for good or bad. Chances are that any email ever written is archived somewhere on a network server or backed up in some digital way. The same goes for any discussion forum message posted or social-networking content created. Archiving has its practical purposes; it provides backup services in case a system goes down and data has to be retrieved. On the flip side, messages, good and bad, are out there somewhere indefinitely in cyberspace.

The information that portrays a person in a less-than-favorable light via digital means is sometimes referred to as "digital dirt" (Tahmincioglu, 2008). Digital dirt can come back to haunt job seekers (Zupek, 2009) and hurt other potential professional relationships long after the dirt was kicked up. Even if it did not prevent a job offer, no teacher wants a student to uncover digital dirt. The images teachers portray via digital means are critical to establishing and maintaining their public personas. For this reason, they should choose their words wisely.

The use of profanity on public sites leaves teachers open to criticism by students, parents, and the larger community. Furthermore, it has the potential to diminish a teacher's classroom management ability. For example, it is more difficult for a teacher to reprimand students in class for using vulgar language if students have witnessed the teacher's rants or expressions of hostility posted on a public forum. The same applies to bullying, intimidation, manipulation, dishonesty, and yelling (also known as *flaming* in the virtual world). Any uncivil behavior that is generally unacceptable in the real world is likewise generally unacceptable in the virtual world.

One of the risks of expressing the written word without the use of verbal or nonverbal cues is that words can be easily misinterpreted. For instance, some people naturally use short sentences when they write, but others may interpret these short sentences as curt replies and be offended or put on the defensive. An Internet neophyte may unknowingly post to a discussion forum in all capital letters (all caps) without ever realizing that all caps in the virtual world are meant to be interpreted as yelling. The use of *emoticons*, or symbols that portray emotions, may not be understood by those who do not use them, and those who use instant messaging text may write in shortcuts that are not easily understood by those who do not use instant messaging. Websites such as NetLingo (www.netlingo.com) can help users understand more about text messaging lingo and acronyms, popular terms, smileys, and emoticons. Table 4.10 shows examples of misinterpretations of the written word.

TABLE 4.10 ■ Misinterpretation of the written word

What Was Written	What Is (Mis)Interpreted	What Was Intended to Be Conveyed
Don't send emails to this address.	He doesn't want to hear from me.	My mailbox is getting full, and there's a chance I won't receive your message.
Things are going well. :)	I wonder what she means by :)	:) is an emoticon for a smile. (Look sideways and you'll see two eyes and a smile.)
I CAN'T COME OVER SATURDAY.	Okay. So you can't come over Saturday. You don't have to get mad about it!	I can't come over Saturday.
BB4N, TTUL	What in the world?	Bye-bye for now, talk to you later

When communicating with individuals of another cultural heritage, it is imperative that teachers become familiar with the cultural norms and mores of the other culture. What is acceptable in one culture may be taboo in another. Even within the same culture, generational divides can impact written communication.

It is worth noting that even if words are properly interpreted, careless use of grammar, spelling, and syntax might not give the impression that teachers wish to portray. Poor spellers who repeatedly send off unchecked messages may leave the impression that the writer is illiterate or at best lazy for not proofreading before sending.

Podcasts, Videos, and Virtual Meetings

Using podcasts and videoconferencing to communicate with others on social-networking sites and through other virtual means allows others to see body language or hear the spoken word, but here again, communication stands a risk of misinterpretation since the benefit of full- or real-body cues is not possible. Even still, teachers should try their best to portray on the screen or on a recording the persona they intend. For example, wearing clothing that offends the communicator on the other side of the screen is not the way to make a positive impression and show cultural sensitivity.

Social-networking sites and video-sharing sites allow users to portray themselves to the outside world through the written word, through audio recording, and through video. Teachers who choose to use any of the social-networking sites need to be mindful of the image that they wish to portray. When developing content for these sites, teachers should write so that their most revered viewer—a parent, grandparent, employer, potential employer, colleague, student, or other individual—will look favorably upon what he or she sees.

Blogging and Other Personal Outlets

Blogging and microblogging have become popular ways of communicating. Blogs are essentially Internet journals created and maintained by Internet users for world viewing. Some teachers may argue that what they do and write on their own time is their own business, but this may be challenged in a court of law if what teachers do and write is of a questionable nature. When teachers blog to share personal thoughts and facts with others, there is always the possibility that students, parents, or others in the educational community will access the blog. If teachers share inappropriate information or details about their personal lives, this could diminish or ruin a teacher's credibility and career.

Blogging software is easily accessible, often free, and relatively easy to set up. Some teachers use blogs to keep students, colleagues, and friends abreast of what they are doing, for informational purposes on a topic about which they have a passion, and for educational purposes. Locating blogs is relatively easy through search engines such as Google, which has a separate category for searching blogs. This is a good thing if bloggers want their blogs to be found but not if they would rather not be discovered by a wide audience. Although most blogging software allows users to apply restrictions to allow only certain visitors to view their site, remember that if they accidentally use the controls incorrectly or if the software does not work as they wish, they may be exposing their blog to a wider audience than intended.

Microblogging sites such as Twitter allow users to share, in short messages, their frequent activities. The nature of these short and frequent posts can, in theory, paint a more accurate picture of a person's life and character than a website or blog that is posted to less frequently. Again, this could be a good thing if bloggers wish to share frequent details of their activities, but a negative thing if what they are sharing portrays them negatively.

Chat Groups, Discussion Forums, and Blog Replies

If a teacher is discovered to be participating in chat groups of a questionable nature, the teacher may be dismissed and possibly could lose his or her teaching license, depending on how the discovery is made and shared with the educational community. Keep in mind that some Internet behaviors may be legal but might still jeopardize a teacher's career.

Before using a public virtual forum, such as a discussion forum, be sure to read the user agreements and privacy statements and become knowledgeable about permitted and restricted forum activities. For example, you may be required to select a screen name different from your real name to help preserve anonymity. You will also want to become familiar with consequences for violating forum policies.

The Principle of "Do No Harm"

The medical profession has a code of ethics under which its members practice, just as the teaching profession does. Physicians take a Hippocratic oath to affirm that they will practice ethical behaviors of the medical profession. The concept of *Primum non nocere*, Latin for "First, do no harm," also helps guide the practices of medical professionals. This principle reminds physicians to consider the possible harm their interventions could induce.

Teachers may do well to observe this principle. Remembering to consider any possible harm that may come about from their educational interventions may help them to proceed gingerly, conscientiously, and justly. When blogging, communicating, sharing, and using the Internet, teachers who remember *Primum non nocere* will not only keep their best interests in mind, but also the interests of their students. Conversely, practicing poor netiquette and Internet citizenship, communicating in a bullying manner, or participating in questionable Interact activities has the potential for destroying credibility at the least.

Modeling digital etiquette and responsible social interactions related to technology and information promotes appropriate student behavior and helps preserve teacher integrity. Teaching these principles through modeling promotes responsible digital citizenship. It is fitting to remember the oft-quoted saying, "Actions speak louder than words."

In Your Experience

Have you ever experienced a time when you misinterpreted another person's email message? Have you ever been misinterpreted in the online environment?

Section T4c Explorations

1. Write a brief email message using standard written English. Then rewrite the message using text speak. Share the textese version with several people, and see if they can interpret it correctly.

2. Visit an Internet forum, and see if any posts are written in all caps (known as flaming). If you find any, do you believe the message was intended to be "yelled"?

3. Write a one-page guide to common Internet terms that would be helpful for new or inexperienced Internet users.

4. Write a blog entry that is either informational or educational in nature. Exchange your blog with a classmate's blog. Determine whether the blog portrays your classmate in a positive, negative, or neutral light. Have him or her do the same for you.

5. Visit a social-networking site and view a profile. Note whether the individual is portraying himself or herself as you believe he or she intends.

6. Introduce yourself to viewers in a videotape or podcast that you could use in a social-networking site. Exchange videos with a classmate and ask him or her to note whether you were practicing netiquette and good citizenship.

7. Make a list of all Internet services you use in which you portray your public persona. Review your websites, social-networking profiles, emails, and the like and note if you are pleased with what you reviewed in terms of your public persona.

Section T4c Review

In this section you learned that practicing netiquette and being a good Internet citizen is important in building and maintaining your public persona. You learned that careless words or actions can destroy an otherwise promising career and that your public persona online reflects your public persona in person. In the next section, you will learn how to use your awareness of culturally responsive teaching and good citizenship to communicate and collaborate in the digital environment cross-culturally.

NETS·T4d

Develop and Model Cultural Understanding and Global Awareness by Engaging with Colleagues and Students of Other Cultures Using Digital-Age Communication and Collaboration Tools

In recent years global communication has increased through email, websites, blogs, social networks, collaborative tools, and virtual worlds. These tools allow users to develop relationships with people from different backgrounds, cultural heritages, and geographic regions without leaving their own borders. Where student exchanges were once limited to the real world, now the virtual world provides opportunities for students and teachers to exchange ideas, experiences, and contributions in cyberspace. In this chapter you have already learned much about developing a culturally responsive teaching practice. In this section you will learn specific ways to communicate and collaborate with colleagues and students of various cultures through digital means. Modeling and providing opportunities for your students to participate in these exchanges increases their chances of forming habits of communication and collaboration that can last a lifetime.

Communicating and Collaborating in the Global Environment

Communicating with colleagues and students from different cultures is easier than ever. Many digital-age tools are available, easy-to-use, and often free for educational purposes. These tools vary in nature and include an assortment of features, such as video, audio, graphics, animation, and the printed word, and using them appropriately can bring the world into the classroom.

Communicating Through Exchange of Text

Selecting text as a primary means of communication is an option if resources are limited or if text will serve a given purpose just as well as some other form of communication. A number of options are available for exchanges of text, some of which include email, discussion forums, blogs, websites, email groups, professional societies, and e-pal services. The purpose of communication should guide the choice of tools.

If teachers wish to communicate regularly with colleagues who share a special interest in a given topic, then participating in an email group may be an appropriate means of doing so. Another avenue for fulfilling this purpose is to participate in discussion forums often available on professional society websites. Some professional societies keep members abreast of important information through email groups and wikis.

If, on the other hand, teachers wish to have their students communicate with students in a class from a different geographic region or culture (Lemkuhl, 2002), they may want to enlist the services of a safe, secure, electronic pen-pal web service. Resource List 4.11 lists several available electronic pen-pal websites. Teachers must check on district and school policies regarding permissions and restrictions associated with this form of communication for students and fully investigate any service to make sure it provides safe and secure communication.

RESOURCE LIST 4.11 ▪ Electronic pen-pal services

A Girl's World: Circle of Friends Pen Pal Club: http://members.agirlsworld.com

Creative Connections: www.creativeconnections.org

e-pals Classroom Exchange: www.epals.com

Gaggle.Net: www.gaggle.net

Communication through blogs or microblogs can serve as a means of text communication and can be set up to receive comments from others. Blogs normally have password protection or selective release. Even with selective release, teachers need to check with their district or school administration regarding permissions, restrictions, and policies.

Teachers should help students understand and practice safe Internet communication (see Section T4a). For example, students should use screen names and not their real names and should not reveal any identifying information. Teachers will need to obtain written permission from parents/guardians for this type of communication, as they will with any form of Internet communication in which their students engage. Blogging sites can be located by searching via Google blogs search (http://blogsearch.google.com), BlogCatalog (www.blogcatalog.com), and Blog Toplist (www.blogtoplist.com). Some are listed in Resource List 4.12.

RESOURCE LIST 4.12 ▪ Blogging sites

21classes.com: www.21classes.com

ClassBlogmeister.com: www.classblogmeister.com

Edublogs.org: www.edublogs.org

Gaggle.Net: www.gaggle.net

Using Graphics, Audio, and Video

When graphics, audio, and video are available for communication, options are plentiful. Graphics, including still images and animation, can be used on websites and blogs, can be sent as attachments in email, and can be exchanged in many other ways. Social-networking sites also have advanced capabilities for including podcasts and video, text, and links. Consensus has not been reached on whether social networking is appropriate for classroom use, even though outside the classroom many students spend hours engaged in social networking.

According to a 2007 report by the National School Boards Association (www.nsba.org), teens spend about nine hours a week on social-networking activities, compared with about 10 hours watching television. The report indicates 41% of online tweens and teens were engaged in posting messages at least weekly, and 9% were engaged at least weekly in creating polls, quizzes, or surveys (p. 3). Here are the activities in which the students engaged in order of popularity:

- posting messages

- downloading music

- downloading videos

- uploading music

- updating personal websites or online profiles

- posting photos

- blogging

- creating and sharing virtual objects

- creating new characters

- participating in collaborative projects

- sending suggestions or ideas to websites

- submitting articles to websites

- creating polls, quizzes, or surveys (NSBA, 2007, p. 3)

Although some teachers are using social networking as part of their teaching, educators in general have been slow to accept this form of communication in the classroom. Two state National Education Association (NEA) affiliates, Missouri and Ohio, have issued statements indicating that teachers should not use social-networking sites even for personal use (Davis, 2008).

Users of social-networking sites that are available for public use, such as Facebook (www.facebook. com), can create pages for classroom use, however, some teachers prefer to use social-networking sites designed for education. Others forgo social-networking platforms in favor of wikis, e-pals, and other technology media. Eden Prairie High School in Minnesota, for example, uses Moodle (http://moodle. org), an open source software, for social networking (Davis, 2008). Whichever medium is chosen, here again, district or school permissions and restrictions must be explored and safeguards established.

Learning Management Systems

A learning management system (LMS) is software that facilitates online learning. Typical features associated with LMSs include places to post content, participate in discussion forums, chat, share, collaborate on projects, upload content, download content, link to resources, and submit assignments. Video, audio, graphics, text, and synchronous and asynchronous communication, videoconferences, and other tools are possible in LMSs, making them especially suitable for educational social networking. Selective release allows only permitted users to enter sections or classes, and numerous administrative tools are available for teacher control. Since most files can be easily exchanged, some educators use these systems to communicate and collaborate with colleagues. Some of the LMSs being used for delivering distance education are listed in Resource List 4.13.

RESOURCE LIST 4.13 ■ Learning management systems for distance education

Moodle: http://moodle.org

Blackboard: www.blackboard.com

Edvance360: www.edvance360.com

Pearson eCollege: www.ecollege.com

Virtual Worlds

A virtual world is a simulation of the real world. Visitors and occupants of the virtual world interact, collaborate, and create through avatars or computer-generated characters. Second Life (www.secondlife.com) is a virtual world that allows users to establish virtual worlds, engage in virtual commerce, and carry on many of the same activities that individuals conduct in the real world. For education purposes, some consider Second Life's platform a grid for interactive experiences capable of bringing a new dimension to learning. Harvard University, Texas State University, and Stanford University are among the many institutions that have set up virtual campuses where students meet, attend classes, and create.

Educators and students worldwide are using virtual worlds in creative ways to enhance teaching and learning. Some of the projects that have been created using Second Life (http://secondlife.com) include the following:

- A San Diego State University 3-D version of a WebQuest entitled Meet the Immigrants

- PacificRim Exchange—Virtual Exchange Program is being built by Stan Trevena, the director of technology for Modesto City Schools in Modesto, California

- Language Apartment at Glidden Campus is designed by Dayton Elseth, a student of Bryon Carter at Central Missouri State University, as an interactive language apartment

- Global Kids' Digital Media Initiative is a project that focuses on raising young people's awareness of human rights, respecting differences, and other social and environmental issues

- Roma—Ancient Rome is a simulation of ancient Rome created by Torin Golding

- Second Life in Education (http://sleducation.wikispaces.com) is a wikispace maintained by Jo Kay and Sean Fitzgerald to explore the educational possibilities of Second Life

Collaboration Tools and Projects

All of the communication tools described in this section allow users to collaborate on various projects at some level, but some allow exchange of information, collaboration of projects, and sharing more easily. In addition to the collaborative tools discussed in Chapters 1, 2, and 3 (such as those used for co-authoring written works, brainstorming, sharing graphics, and so forth), some websites and services are geared toward promoting global and cross-cultural collaboration. Resource List 4.14 provides sites for online collaboration.

RESOURCE LIST 4.14 ■ Online collaboration websites

Global SchoolNet: www.globalschoolnet.org

Global SchoolNet is a nonprofit education organization whose "mission is to support 21st century learning and improve academic performance through content driven collaboration. We engage teachers and students in meaningful e-learning projects worldwide to develop science, math, literacy and communication skills, foster teamwork, civic responsibility and collaboration, encourage workforce preparedness and create multi-cultural understanding. We prepare youth for full participation as productive and compassionate citizens in an increasing global economy" (www.globalschoolnet.org, para. 1).

Global Learning and Observations to Benefit the Environment (GLOBE) Program: www.globe.gov

GLOBE is an international environmental science and education program that promotes collaboration among K–12 students and teachers and scientists in global environmental work.

ThinkQuest: www.thinkquest.org

ThinkQuest, from the Oracle Foundation, is "a complete learning environment for primary and secondary schools."

ProjectFoundry: www.projectfoundry.org

Project Foundry is an online LMS (and student portfolio system) that "puts everything under one hood" and "allows innovative educators to scale authentic, integrated, individualized learning."

Wikis

Wikis are collaborative web pages that anyone with access can modify and collaborate. Wikipedia (www.wikipedia.org) is an example of a massive collaborative project in which everyone is granted access to create and modify entries to the online encyclopedia. The encyclopedia contains millions of articles in hundreds of languages with contributions made by a global audience.

Wikipedia is only one of many projects that use wiki software. Wiki communities have sprung up around the globe and represent various fields, such as those in Resource List 4.15.

RESOURCE LIST 4.15 ■ Wiki communities

Scholarpedia: www.scholarpedia.org

Includes articles written by scholars and is subject to peer review

wikiHow: www.wikihow.com

A collaborative how-to manual

Wikiversity: http://en.wikiversity.org

An online learning project

A Million Penguins: http://en.wikipedia.org/wiki/A_Million_Penguins

A collaboratively written novel

Wikijunior: http://en.wikibooks.org/wiki/Wikijunior

A collection of free books written collaboratively for children, in many languages

Some wiki projects are created for specific audiences, such as Wikijunior (http://en.wikibooks.org/wiki/Wikijunior), an open-content textbook collection. Wikijunior is a collaborative project of writers, teachers, students, and young people working together to produce books for a young audience.

Many wikis are only accessible to a select group of collaborators such as an organization where access to a wiki or limited collaboration is desired. Teachers can learn about starting a wiki by visiting the following Wikipedia site: http://en.wikibooks.org/wiki/Starting_and_Running_a_Wiki_Website.

History Project Collaboration

Collaborative history projects represent the collective input and contributions of users from across the globe. The Library of Congress has a "Veterans History Project" (www.loc.gov/vets) and through the help of volunteers collects and preserves the stories of wartime service. Volunteers interview veterans and civilians who supported veterans to document first-hand accounts. The accounts are archived in the American Folklife Center (www.loc.gov/folklife) at the Library of Congress for research and as an inspiration to future generations. With certain grade-specific and other stipulations, students are permitted to help support this project. In addition to oral histories, the project collects narrative histories and histories recorded in video. They also accept original collections of diaries, letters, maps, home movies, and photographs. Visit this project online to find out how educators and students can contribute to this collaborative project.

Another collaborative history project, "This I Believe" (http://thisibelieve.org), is an international project that, as it says on the site, "engages people in writing and describing the core values that guide their daily lives." The website provides guidelines for students and educators to help use the project in teaching and learning, including stipulations for essay submission and curricula for using This I Believe materials in the classroom.

Science Project Collaboration

Collaborative science involves contributors who contribute to data collection, analysis, synthesis, and evaluation. The Center for Innovation in Engineering and Science Education (www.ciese.org) invites participation from the global community on various science and engineering projects. One collaborative project, "Down the Drain: How Much Water Do You Use?" (www.ciese.org/curriculum/drainproj) allows students from around the world to contribute information about how much water they use and share this information with others around the country and the world. Another project, "The Noon Day Project: Measuring the Circumference of the Earth" (www.ciese.org/curriculum/noonday), has students record shadows cast by a meter stick and contribute their findings. From this information, students are able to calculate the circumference of the earth.

Modeling Global Collaboration

TeacherTube (www.teachertube.com) is an online site that allows users to share instructional videos. Videos can be made public or private to share with others. Another site, Teachers Without Borders (www.teacherswithoutborders.org) aims to close the digital divide through teacher training and community teaching and learning centers. Their focus is on the building of teacher leaders. Volunteer opportunities are available for collaboration on course development for their Certificate of Mastery program, where free professional development is created by and for teachers.

Teachers can learn more about using collaborative tools to promote global awareness and understanding through the use of digital tools by visiting some of the websites in Resource List 4.16.

RESOURCE LIST 4.16 ▪ Resources for promoting global awareness and understanding

Global Dimension: www.globaldimension.org.uk

Teacher's Guide to International Collaboration on the Internet:
www.ed.gov/teachers/how/tech/international/guide.html

National Geographic Education (Beta):
http://education.nationalgeographic.com/education/collections/geographyawarenessweek/?ar_a=1

United Nations Cyberschoolbus: www.un.org/cyberschoolbus

In Your Experience

What educational experiences have you encountered in terms of cultural or global awareness? How could collaborative digital tools have enhanced the experiences?

Section T4d Explorations

1. Visit the website of a professional society associated with your field of expertise (see Chapter 5). Identify communication tools, such as email groups or forums, that the society provides for communication with the global community.

2. Search for a blog that pertains to your field of expertise. Review the blog in one or two paragraphs, and report on its usefulness for communicating with the international community.

3. Visit an e-pal website. Review the user policies and user agreements. Do the e-pal policies and agreements comply with local district policies, privacy laws, and ethics?

4. Visit a professional social-networking site. Navigate around the site to become more familiar with its services. Describe whether you would or would not use this website to socialize with others in the global community.

5. Visit the websites of two of the learning management systems (LMSs) mentioned in this section. Review the features associated with each, and describe which one you prefer in terms of social networking.

6. Visit a virtual world website and note any projects that pertain to education. Describe how, if in any way, you might use the virtual world in your classroom to promote global awareness and understanding. Explain your response.

7. Search for and identify a wiki that you may be able to use in your classroom to promote global awareness. If you are unable to locate a wiki for this purpose, describe how you might create a wiki for your classroom.

Section T4d Review

In this section you learned how to use your awareness of culturally responsive teaching and good citizenship to communicate and collaborate in the digital environment cross-culturally. You became familiar with specific tools and resources available in the digital age to use for communication and collaboration, and you learned some ways to use these tools in your teaching practice. In the next chapter, you will learn about professional development and lifelong learning.

Chapter 4 Summary

In this chapter you learned ways to model ethical and legal technology practices. You became familiar with ways to apply technology resources to enable and empower students with diverse backgrounds. You learned ways to use technology resources to celebrate diversity and some strategies for promoting the safe and healthy use of technology. Furthermore, you discovered ways to help provide equitable access to technology for all students and how to use digital-age tools in the global environment for communication and collaboration. Throughout this chapter, you no doubt started to realize the complexities associated with technology use in the classroom. New issues are expected to emerge as new technology is introduced in society and the classroom. In the next chapter, you will learn about some of the obstacles to integrating technology in teaching and some ways for overcoming these obstacles.

Chapter 4 Notes

1   The Software and Information Industry Association (SIIA, www.siia.net/piracy) is a source for statistics on commercial piracy rates and losses.

2   Free software should not be confused with freeware and shareware (often bundled with adware), discussed in more detail in Chapter 3.

3   Visit www.gnu.org/copyleft/fdl.html for more on GNU Free Documentation Licensing and the concept of "copyleft."

4   "Volatile mismatch" is a term used by the Carnegie Council on Adolescent Development (1989) to describe the mismatch between the organization and curriculum of middle grade schools and the young adolescents' intellectual and emotional needs.

5   Computer fraud is the unethical use of a computer to steal information, deceive, or cause harm to others or to their equipment. Examples of computer fraud include email hoaxes, malware, spyware, and phishing. (In phishing scams, scammers impersonate a trustworthy entity in order to steal personal information from unsuspecting victims.)

6   Figures 4.2 and 4.3 are contained in a U.S. government publication (www.osha.gov/Publications/videoDisplay/videoDisplay.html, fig.1 and fig. 3), which is in the public domain and may be reproduced, fully or partially, without permission of the federal government source. Credit is requested but not required.

7   For more information on safe and comfortable computer workstations, visit www.osha.gov/SLTC/etools/computerworkstations.

8   "The digital divide" is a term used to describe the figurative divide between those who have access to technology and those who do not.

9   Chapter 3 presents various types of assistive technologies and web accessibility issues.

10   See Chapter 1 for more on project-based learning-IT/ICT-assisted PBL.

11   See WebQuest.org for more on the WebQuest model.

12 Interactive bulletin boards have a component that allows student engagement. For example, students lifting flaps on the bulletin board to reveal terms is an example of an interactive component.

13 Learning centers are stations set aside in the classroom to engage students in interactive learning. A three-sided board set up with content and activities that students follow and perform individually or in cooperative groups is an example of a learning center.

14 Affect is associated with feelings, appreciation, and sentiments.

15 See Chapter 3 for online polling tools.

16 Self-concept is "the way in which one perceives oneself" (Gale, 2000).

17 As with all websites, teachers should read user agreements very carefully. For example, Second Life's terms of service include age requirements for Second Life, age requirements for use of areas of the service, and age requirements for Adult Only Second Life.

Chapter 4 References

Association for Educational Communications and Technology. (2007, November). Code of Professional Ethics. Retrieved from www.aect.org/About/Ethics.asp

Burns, R., Keyes M., & Kusimo, P. (2006). *It takes a school: Closing achievement gaps through culturally responsive schools.* Charleston, WV: Edvantia.

Carnegie Council on Adolescent Development. (1989). *Turning points: Preparing American youth for the 21st century.* New York, NY: Carnegie Corporation of New York.

Centers for Disease Control and Prevention. (2006). *NCHS Health E-Stat: Prevalence of overweight among children and adolescents: United States, 2003-2004.* Washington, DC: Author. Retrieved from www.cdc.gov/nchs/data/hestat/overweight/overweight_child_03.htm

Centers for Disease Control and Prevention. (2008). Youth Risk Behavior Surveillance—United States, 2007. *Morbidity and Mortality Weekly Report* 2008, 57(No.SS-4): 1–131.

Colvin, B. (2007, December). Another look at plagiarism in the digital age: Is it time to turn in my badge? *Teaching English in the Two-Year College, 35*(2), 149–158.

Creative Commons. (2011, January 17). [Letter to Steve Midgley, Office of Educational Technology, U.S. Department of Education]. Creative Commons comments to Dept of Ed RFI January 17, 2011. Available from www2.ed.gov

Davis, M. (2008, June 9). Finding appropriate educational uses. *Education Week Digital Directions, 2,* 18–19. Retrieved June 18, 2008, from www.edweek.org/dd/articles/2008/06/09/01networks_side.h02.html

Gale Encyclopedia of Psychology (2000). (2nd ed.). Detroit, MI: Gale.

Glod, M. (2007, March 29). McLean students sue anti-cheating service: Plaintiffs say company's database of term papers, essays violates copyright laws. *The Washington Post*, p. B5. Retrieved from www.washingtonpost.com

Howard, R. (2007). Understanding "Internet plagiarism." *Computers and Composition, 24*(1), 3–15.

Johnson, R., & Johnson, D. (1997). *Cooperative learning and conflict resolution.* Retrieved September 25, 2011, from http://education.jhu.edu/newhorizons/strategies/topics/Cooperative%20Learning/cooperative_conflict.html

Kaste, M. (2009, October 27). *Is your Facebook profile as private as you think?* Retrieved October 30, 2009, from www.npr.org/templates/story/story.php?storyId=114187478

Lemkuhl, M. (2002). Pen-pal letters: The cross-curricular experience. *The Reading Teacher, 55*(8), 720–722.

Marzano, R., Pickering, D., & Pollock, J. (2001). *Classroom instruction that works: Research-based strategies for increasing student achievement.* Alexandria, VA: Association for Supervision & Curriculum Development.

Mason, K. (2008, April). Cyberbullying: A preliminary assessment for school personnel. *Psychology in the Schools, 45*(4), 323–348.

Myers, J., Frieden, T., Bherwani, K., & Henning, K. (2008). Ethics in public health research: Privacy and public health at risk: Public health confidentiality in the digital age. *American Journal of Public Health, 98*(5), 793–801.

National Public Radio. (n.d.). *Timeline: Privacy and the law.* Retrieved October 30, 2009, from www.npr.org/templates/story/story.php?storyId=114250943

National School Boards Assocation. (2007). Creating and connecting: Research and guidelines on online social—and educational—networking. Alexandria: VA. Retrieved from socialnetworking.procon.org/sourcefiles/CreateandConnect.pdf

Occupational Safety and Health Administration. (n.d.). [Web page]. Computer workstations: Workstation components: Monitors. Washington, DC: U.S. Department of Labor. Retrieved from www.osha.gov/SLTC/etools/computerworkstations/components_monitors.html

Occupational Safety and Health Administration. (1997). [Web page]. Working safely with video display terminals. Washington, DC: U.S. Department of Labor. Retrieved from www.osha.gov/Publications/videoDisplay/videoDisplay.html

Quenqua, D. (2009, October 23). Guardians of their smiles. *The New York Times,* p. ST1. Retrieved from www.nytimes.com

Rife, M. (2007). The fair use doctrine: History, application, and implications for (new media) writing teachers. *Computers and Composition, 24*(2), 154–178.

Shariff, S., & Johnny, L. (2007). Cyber-libel and cyber-bullying: Can schools protect student reputations and free-expression in virtual environments? *Education & Law Journal, 16*(3), 307–342.

Tahmincioglu, E. (2008, September 29). Cleaning up your digital dirt: Remember, prospective employers could be checking you out online. Retrieved October 30, 2009, from www.msnbc.msn.com/id/26904049

Tartakoff, J. (2009, March 25). Facebook hires ACLU privacy lawyer. *The Washington Post.* Retrieved from www.washingtonpost.com

U.S. Copyright Office. (2006a, July). *Copyright basics* (Circular 1). Retrieved June 18, 2008, from www.copyright.gov/circs/circ01.pdf

U.S. Copyright Office. (2006b, July). *Copyright: Fair use* (FL-102). Retrieved June 18, 2008, from www.copyright.gov/fls/fl102.html

Warnick, B. (2007, Fall). Surveillance cameras in schools: An ethical analysis. *Harvard Educational Review, 77*(3), 317–343.

Zupek, R. (2009, October 12). *"Digital dirt" can haunt your job search.* Retrieved October 30, 2009, from www.cnn.com/2009/LIVING/worklife/10/12/cb.digital.trail.job.search

nets•t5

Engage in Professional Growth and Leadership

STANDARD IN BRIEF

Teachers continuously improve their professional practice, model lifelong learning, and exhibit leadership in their school and professional community by promoting and demonstrating the effective use of digital tools and resources.

PERFORMANCE INDICATORS

Teachers:

a. participate in local and global learning communities to explore creative applications of technology to improve student learning

b. exhibit leadership by demonstrating a vision of technology infusion, participating in shared decision making and community building, and developing the leadership and technology skills of others

c. evaluate and reflect on current research and professional practice on a regular basis to make effective use of existing and emerging digital tools and resources in support of student learning

d. contribute to the effectiveness, vitality, and self-renewal of the teaching profession and of their school and community

GROWING AS A PROFESSIONAL IN THE DIGITAL AGE

Teachers routinely engage in promoting growth and development in their students. One of the greatest advantages of teaching is that the growth you stimulate will also be your own; each time you teach is an opportunity for you to learn. At times you grow in your understanding of a concept as you interact with students. Together, you and your students help construct meaning as you connect prior knowledge with new. Each member of the learning community brings a unique set of experiences to every teaching-learning encounter, and each contributes to the learning environment. In such a fertile environment, it is inevitable that all participants will grow.

At other times, you grow in appreciation as you learn to value and respect ideas, people, and cultures different from your own. On some occasions you even develop skills that you never considered but that your students have used successfully for years. As you reflect on the interactions of any given day, you will probably realize that you have grown in your understanding of yourself and your teaching practice even if the day was less than stellar. The opportunity to develop continuously as a professional and individual is one of the perks of teaching.

As a teacher you naturally engage in professional development and lifelong learning in the classroom. Deliberately seeking professional growth opportunities outside the classroom, however, helps stimulate additional growth. There are numerous ways to do this in the digital age. Aligning yourself with professional societies is one way to inform, inspire, and motivate. Continuing your education in a formal setting is another. In addition, informal opportunities for growth abound, as do collaborative exchanges with teacher colleagues and others in the larger learning community.

You've likely heard the old adage, "Work smarter, not harder." The goal of this chapter is to help you apply this sage advice to your own professional growth, development, and practice through the effective use of technology. In this chapter you will be provided with resources for professional development, suggestions for reflection practices, tools for productivity, and strategies for communicating through technology. You will see how technology has the power to help make your job as a teacher more efficient, more enjoyable, and more creative. Most important, you will learn ways to help improve your teaching effectiveness to help enhance student learning.

LEARNER OUTCOMES

The reading and assignments presented in Chapter 5 should help you:

- Identify and use digital-age technology resources as part of the global community to enhance student learning

- Identify leadership skills that promote technology integration

- Describe how technology plays an important role in professional development and lifelong learning

- Recognize that technology practices can complement teacher evaluation and reflection

- Use technology tools effectively to improve productivity

- Identify ways to give back to the education profession and larger learning community

NETS•T5a

Participate in Local and Global Learning Communities to Explore Creative Applications of Technology to Improve Student Learning

Learning does not—or at least should not—stop when you receive your degree or teaching license. It is a continuous journey of discovery and renewal that happens over time and sometimes, delightfully, in spurts. Barth (2000) describes the at-risk teacher or principal as one "who leaves school at the end of the day or year with little possibility of continuing learning about the important work they do" (p. 68). Learning is not confined to an institution, limited by circumstances, or restricted to geographic boundaries; rather, opportunities for growth, development, and learning are ever present and unlimited. In this section you will learn how to participate in the global community to enhance student learning.

Learning with Others through the Use of Technology

In the digital age, learning is virtually at teachers' fingertips. With a click of a key, the world and all its wonders enter teachers' private, public, and professional worlds, and rapid exchanges of experiences, knowledge, and skills are possible.

As a teacher, this exchange is critical for professional development and growth, and it provides opportunities to give back to the professional and larger learning community. Digital-age resources are abundant for making this exchange possible and include tools such as blogs, email groups, social bookmarking sites, podcasts, social networks, and more. When exchanges of ideas, research, and contributions are made through these tools, teachers have a greater repertoire of teaching tools from which to choose to enhance student learning.

Professional learning communities (PLCs) were described earlier in this book as a collective body of learners and contributors with a common shared vision. Teachers, students, parents, staff, community members, experts, and all stakeholders make up these communities. In this section, contributions from various members of PLCs will be explored to help enhance the work of teachers in increasing student learning. In some cases the learning community shares in face-to-face encounters, and in others in virtual learning communities (VLCs).

Learning through Professional Societies

Professional societies, organizations, or associations exist for virtually every profession and specialization.[1] The American Medical Association (AMA) is a well-known professional society that represents a wide variety of medical practitioners with varying specialties. Many of these specialists belong to a professional society associated with their specialty as well as to the larger, more encompassing AMA. Most professions have one main organizational body that represents the profession and numerous other organizations that represent subspecialties.

A similar organizational structure exists within the education community. Unlike the medical community, however, the education profession does not claim a single association that represents the entire education community. The National Education Association (www.nea.org) and the American Federation of Teachers (www.aft.org) are America's two largest professional employee organizations. Although separate, they have now formed a partnership, NEAFT (www.nea.org/home/11204.htm), to work together on behalf of their members and those they serve. These organizations do not appeal to all educators, however. Some educators decline membership in either organization.

Some of the professional international and national societies that are geared toward specialty areas are listed in Resource List 5.1.

RESOURCE LIST 5.1 ■ Education societies that focus on specific subjects

Reading

International Reading Association: www.reading.org

Technology

International Society for Technology in Education: www.iste.org

Social Studies

National Council for Social Studies: www.socialstudies.org

Early Childhood

National Association for the Education of Young Children: www.naeyc.org

Science

National Science Teachers Association: www.nsta.org

English

National Council of Teachers of English: www.ncte.org

Math

National Council of Teachers of Mathematics: www.nctm.org

Foreign Languages

American Council on the Teaching of Foreign Languages: www.actfl.org

Family and Consumer Sciences

American Association of Family & Consumer Sciences: www.aafcs.org

Special Education

National Association of Special Education Teachers: www.naset.org

Professional societies provide a venue for members to network, collaborate, learn, and express concerns through face-to-face interactions and through electronic means. They also help unite teachers from local and global locations. Membership in professional societies benefits teachers in a number of ways and provides numerous opportunities for shared learning.

Members are usually privy to the leading research, development, and practices in their field. The research and development reported by these professional societies is typically peer reviewed or juried. This type of review helps weed out insignificant or unreliable research and lends credence to what is published. In addition, members usually receive a publication as a part of their membership fees. This might be a printed newsletter or journal, or they may receive electronic access to an exclusive, members-only website. Some societies have special interest groups (SIGs) that members can join. SIGs provide an outlet for like-minded teachers to share their strengths and requests for additional training and education. SIGs may also sponsor webinars, provide publishing opportunities, and arrange face-to-face and virtual communication and collaboration opportunities.

Other benefits of membership include opportunities to attend conferences and less formal gatherings to discuss cutting-edge research, development, and best practices in the field. Not only do these gatherings provide a venue for exchange, but they bring together diverse members from various locales who share common, professional interests.

Furthermore, professional societies often serve as clearinghouses[2] for information related to their fields that members and nonmembers may use for educational purposes. The information is, therefore, made available to the public and represents the field to the outside world. Added bonuses are professional discounts for services and items within and outside the organization that some professional societies offer to their members.

Many professional societies can help teachers become better prepared to use technology to enhance their teaching. For example, ISTE (www.iste.org) provides a wealth of resources for members, such as webinars, discussion groups, and article archives, as well as limited resources for nonmembers. NCTE and NCTM also publish materials for integrating technology (Erbas, Ledford, Polly, & Orrill, 2004; NCTM, 2007).

As noted, professional societies usually provide dissemination of knowledge and communication through printed and electronic means. Printed journals and newsletters and their electronic counterparts (e-journals and e-newsletters) are often available to society members and sometimes to the general public. These publications, usually linked to professional society websites, may be peer reviewed or reviewed by an editor or editorial board. Members, and normally nonmembers, can submit articles, ideas, and comments, based on submission guidelines. Again, this is an excellent way of growing with a wide community of learners in the exchange of ideas, research, and concerns.

Some professional societies provide communication to their members through technology tools, such as online chats, discussion boards, podcasts, videoconferences, and webinars. These tools are excellent ways for teachers to share with peers outside their immediate geographic region.

Online chats allow participants to exchange ideas and experiences synchronously through text-based messages. Text-based chats delivered in real time in this manner are often referred to as instant messaging (IMing). If interactive whiteboards are available with the chat tool, learning and growth can occur as teachers "think out loud" and other teachers comment on ideas presented on the whiteboard in drawings, formulas, diagrams, or other graphics. This type of communication allows teachers to exchange ideas in rapid succession, similar to a face-to-face chat. Teachers, for example, may chat on the success or failure of various arrangements of computer stations and use the whiteboard to demonstrate these arrangements.

Some chat tools allow participants to attach documents for other participants to see and on which to comment. Teachers may wish to use online chats to share documents that they are currently using to help integrate technology, such as technology lesson plans, and receive feedback from each other. If chat rooms are not available on a professional society's website, teachers can use one of many available chat tools to converse with others they have met previously at a professional society meeting. Resource List 5.2 lists a few available chat tools/software with varying functionalities.

RESOURCE LIST 5.2 ▪ Online chat tools

Google Talk: www.google.com/talk

iChat: www.apple.com/macosx/apps/all.html#ichat

AOL Instant Messenger: http://dashboard.aim.com/aim

Windows Live Messenger: http://explore.live.com/windows-live-messenger

Yahoo! Messenger: http://messenger.yahoo.com

Skype: www.skype.com

Discussion boards allow teachers to share information and engage in community learning asynchronously. Most discussion boards have separately arranged topics for easy use. Participants can post a message related to a topic or respond to another poster's message within the topic. Engaging in a discussion forum is an efficient way of conversing and learning with others who share a common interest. For example, a topic entitled "Ways to Use MP3s with Students," can help practicing teachers share successes and the challenges of using this technology in the classroom.

Many discussion forums allow participants to attach documents and add links to help enhance the conversation. Subscribing to an email group devoted to a special interest or cause within a professional society is another way to stay abreast of developments in education and technology integration. As members of such a group, users receive emails from other members and have the ability to post messages as well. This is a convenient way of receiving pertinent information delivered via email. Resource List 5.3 shows websites and descriptions from the sites themselves; the URLs can be used to locate teacher email groups outside professional societies. Email can also be used in other ways to support peer collaboration. For example, teachers can build relationships with peers whom they've met at a face-to-face professional conference by frequently communicating across the miles. Teachers can also create their own email groups and use them in ways similar to email lists.

Resource List 5.3 shows URLs that can be used to locate or subscribe to teacher email lists and groups. Email can be used in many ways to support peer collaboration, such as helping teachers build relationships with peers whom they met at a face-to-face professional conference by frequently communicating across the miles. Teachers can also create their own email groups and use them in similar ways.

RESOURCE LIST 5.3 ▪ Websites to help locate or subscribe to teacher email lists and groups

Google Groups: http://groups.google.com

Teachers can locate groups by category or search for groups using search terms.

Teachers.Net: http://teachers.net/mailrings

"Once you're subscribed to the [teacher] mailring, you'll receive further instruction for posting and immediately receive email from your teacher colleagues around the world!"

Videoconferences are often offered by professional societies that allow long-distance opportunities for peer communication and learning. Videoconferences are typically designed around a special topic, such as strategies for reaching learners, and are open to a limited audience. Two-way communication is usually used so that participants can comment and ask questions. Depending on how the videoconference is set up, participants "attend" conferences or meetings using their personal computers (e.g., through webinars), through satellite technology at a specified geographic location (such as at a school district central office), or by some other means. Textbook publishers, education institutions, and industries also sponsor videoconferences.

Podcasts are sometimes offered by professional societies as audio recordings on topics of interest related to teaching and learning. Podcasts typically offer one-way communication in that the listener is not able to communicate with the presenter; the presentation is not normally a live performance but a recorded one. Podcasts are sometimes accompanied by discussion forums, however, so that listeners can respond to the content presented.

Clearly, professional societies promote teacher-to-teacher learning through the many services and opportunities they provide. As digital technology advances, teachers should have increasing opportunities to learn from each other through professional societies.

Formal Schooling Using Technology

Another way to engage in local and global community learning is through formal schooling. Formal schooling is any deliberate medium for educating students. Formal schooling can be obtained from institutions of higher learning, through nonprofit associations, or through other professional development offerings. Traditional courses, teacher workshops, videoconferences, and distance-learning opportunities are some of the ways formal schooling is delivered.

Nearly all teachers will have to document engagement in professional development in order to renew their teaching licenses, and formal schooling is often used for this purpose.

Depending on licensure renewal requirements, teachers may be required to earn college credits in order to renew their teaching licenses. In some cases, graduate courses or a master's degree is required to teach or retain teaching positions. These requirements are mandated by licensing bodies—typically state departments of education charged with issuing teaching licenses or certificates—to ensure the professional development of their teachers. This is commendable; it is in everyone's best interest for teachers to stay abreast of new research and best practices in their fields.

Formal schooling opportunities are plentiful. Nearly every institution of higher learning provides courses suitable for teachers. Teachers should contact their state's licensing body to find out what qualifies as professional development in their state. Equipped with this information, they can then contact potential education providers to see what they have to offer. Each licensing body is different, so they should check before working toward renewal credit.

More and more distance-learning courses are being offered as a way of staying professionally current. Most traditional learning institutions have at least some distance-learning opportunities or courses as adjuncts to their face-to-face offerings. For many teachers, distance learning is an ideal way to continue professional development while teaching and juggling other responsibilities. Some teachers use distance learning to complete entire advanced degrees.

Distance learning, also known as distance education, provides a convenient way for many practicing teachers to continue learning and allows them to meet continuing education and recertification requirements from a variety of alternatives.

Advantages to distance learning include:

- Access to education from a large variety of providers, including many traditional, accredited institutions

- Freedom to learn according to the learner's own schedule and not from a limited, local schedule

- Opportunities to "meet" and collaborate with other professionals and students from diverse backgrounds related to culture, place, and like interests

- Costs often comparable to traditional, face-to-face instruction. Many free distance-learning opportunities exist from notable institutions and governmental agencies

For a quick tour of online professional development opportunities, teachers can visit the TeAchnology website (www.teach-nology.com) and search the site for "professional development."

Teachers should check with their state certification office before enrolling in any distance or face-to-face professional development courses to make sure credits will apply toward certificate renewal.

In the summer, scores of special projects—often funded in part by government grants and many on technology subjects—are organized specifically for the professional growth of teachers. Teacher participants may receive a stipend and free or reduced tuition. They frequently receive university credit as well. To learn more about professional development activities, teachers can contact their school superintendent's office, which can direct them to the grade-level or subject specialists responsible for promoting professional development opportunities in their school district. They can also use Internet search engines to locate summer project offerings.

Informal Opportunities

Informal opportunities are similar to formal schooling in that they provide opportunities for professional growth. They differ, however, in their set intent. Formal schooling is typically organized around particular goals and objectives, while informal opportunities can be quite a bit looser but just as personally meaningful. For example, social studies teachers may volunteer to serve as summer interns at a state history museum, cataloging artifacts. They will likely learn about history and at the same time make valuable contributions in return.

Family and consumer-science teachers may have a chance to work as aides to fashion designers and use cutting-edge design software in the process, enhancing their technology experience, which they may then bring back to the classroom. In both instances, professional development is the end result, but the means to the end is not clearly defined. Instead, the "learning program" emerges on a day-to-day basis, contingent on the needs and desires of the mentor and apprentice.

Depending on state licensing regulations, some teachers may be able to use documentation of these experiences for license renewal purposes. Even without such an incentive, teachers would be wise to consider these opportunities for career enrichment. Resource List 5.4 lists some professional development opportunities for teachers.

RESOURCE LIST 5.4 ■ Professional development opportunities

Appalachian Regional Commission with the Department of Energy: www.orau.gov/arc2003

NASA: http://education.nasa.gov/divisions/eleandsec/overview

National Archives: www.archives.gov/education

National Gallery of Art: www.nga.gov/education/internsumm.shtm

National Oceanic and Atmospheric Administration (NOAA): www.careers.noaa.gov/special_programs.html

Department of Labor: Bureau of Labor Statistics: www.bls.gov/jobs

U.S. Department of Education: www2.ed.gov/programs/teacherfellowship

As noted earlier, distance education can help teachers stay abreast of cutting-edge, effective, and novel teaching practices and help promote teacher-to-teacher learning. With advances in technology have come a greater assortment of tools available for informal distance-education opportunities. Tools such as social-bookmarking sites, blogs, wikis, podcasts, and videos allow teachers to read, listen to, and view a wide assortment of content from a vast array of writers and posters, giving teachers opportunities to read, reflect, and make connections on any number of topics both personal and professional.

Social-bookmarking sites, such as Digg (http://digg.com); Technorati (http://technorati.com); and Delicious (http://delicious.com) use digital tools that permit users to create web-page bookmarks remotely and virtually store and share these bookmarks with other site users.

One advantage to using social bookmarks is the convenience of having remote access to bookmarks when away from home or work. Furthermore, the social-networking feature that permits sharing bookmarks helps users locate helpful and relevant websites that they might otherwise have overlooked. The feature that allows user-defined "tags" or categories to be created can further help users locate important information; these tags can help connect ideas and interests in ways that one user alone may not identify.

Teacher-to-Teacher Learning

Professional development activities are not only found in classrooms via formal schooling, and through informal opportunities; they also are found every day in schools throughout the nation and world. In a culture of collegiality, teachers talk about practice, share knowledge of their craft, observe one another, and root for one another (Barth, 2006). These interactions can be high-tech (such as social networking in the virtual world), but they do not have to be (face-to-face meetings also work).

Teacher-to-teacher collaboration can often get lost among the day-to-day operations of teaching students. Time is one of the greatest hindrances to teacher collaboration. Even the most efficient teacher has little time to devote specifically to daily collaboration and learning. However, strides are being made. Some districts are encouraging teacher collaboration as a means for professional development by providing substitute teachers to free up time for teachers to connect with each other. This is an excellent way of allowing teachers to capitalize on growth opportunities with other teaching professionals.

Limited in-service professional development time—usually immediately before and after the opening and closing of school—is often available to teachers to participate in school-district professional development opportunities. Typical district-provided opportunities include make-and-take workshops, where teachers make useful classroom materials to take back to their classrooms; technology training (e.g., how to use a new gradebook software); and presentations on new research and applications by consultants, seasoned teachers, and other experts. Unfortunately, the times set aside for these opportunities conflict with other important year-beginning and -ending duties, such as long-term planning and final grade reporting.

Teacher-to-teacher learning can take many forms. Grant writing may be a collaborative effort of several interested faculty, administrators, and community members to bring about a change to the school environment. For example, several teachers may see a need for an after-school program to reteach reading skills to elementary students. Collectively they may investigate the problem, decide on a solution, seek out grant opportunities, and write grants to help fund the initiative.

Other ways teachers may learn and grow together is to engage in school- or district-wide research. College and university faculty are often eager to assist teachers with their action research.

Other opportunities for teacher-to-teacher learning may emerge at meetings designated specifically for sharing successful techniques and challenging tasks. Together teachers can help solve problems and make informed decisions that will benefit all affected parties. As an example, teachers may note the general lack of skill retention by students following summer recess. Together teachers may come up with a plan to help improve retention by organizing a once-a-week summer school program that provides fun, skill-oriented sessions for students.

Formal collaboration between PK–12 teachers, higher-education faculty, and community stakeholders can be enhanced through professional development school (PDS) partnerships whose efforts can result in educational improvement at all levels. The possibilities for teacher-to-teacher learning and collaboration are virtually limitless.

Social Networking for Growth and Learning

Teacher collaboration and communication is a critical component of professional development. While teacher-to-teacher learning among teachers in a school or school district is essential, learning with peers outside teachers' own geographic boundaries also holds great potential for professional development. Technology can help facilitate learning within and outside their immediate circle of peers.

Digital-age tools allow teachers to open their public and professional lives to the world.[3] A teacher-created web page is a relatively simple way of not only keeping students and parents informed of class events and expectations, but also of promoting teacher-to-teacher learning and peer review.

Teachers' web pages can be virtual representations of their teaching practices for others to explore. For instance, they can upload rubrics that they created and that they use in their teaching practice for peer review. Teachers can also visit other teachers' websites and explore what they have shared. This reciprocal exchange is just one of many examples for using technology for teacher-to-teacher learning in the virtual world. By engaging in such activities, teachers not only can foster their own growth, but also may help contribute to the larger education community by sharing their experiences and expertise with others.

Teacher Advancement Program (TAP) (www2.ed.gov/programs/transitionteach/resourcestq.html) is a free professional development resource that addresses questions common to many teachers. The content of this website is developed by former K–12 teachers who are now teaching online in higher education. This website is an example of teachers helping teachers through their web-page presence.

Blogs are types of online journals that allow bloggers to post content related to a particular topic and receive feedback from readers. Some teachers create blogs as an extension of their teaching practices and include links, attachments, podcasts, videos, and other items that relate to their expertise and experience. Blogs are updated according to the schedule of the blogger; sometimes blog entries are posted many times a day and sometimes every few days. By using an RSS feed reader, teachers can easily follow a number of different blogs and have a central access point where they can read various bloggers' entries in one place.[4]

Locating and following blogs that pertain to a given teaching field can help teachers stay abreast of cutting-edge ideas allowing them to engage in dialogue with others who share a common interest. By reading and participating in blogs through comments, teachers may find effective, creative means for improving learning. Resource List 5.5 contains website addresses for various blog directories.

RESOURCE LIST 5.5 ■ Blog-directory websites

Blog Catalog: www.blogcatalog.com

Blogging Fusion: www.bloggingfusion.com

Bloghub: www.bloghub.com

Teacher-created videos and podcasts can be easily posted on the Internet for other teachers and the general public to access, view, and use. At TeacherTube (www.teachertube.com), teachers from all over the world contribute videos that other teachers can access to help improve student learning. For example, if teachers need better ways to present plate tectonics to their science students, they can search the videos to see what is available. They may find a video that they are permitted to use in their class, or they may find a video representing an effective teaching strategy.

The Education Podcast Network website (http://epnweb.org) represents an effort to bring together a wide range of podcasts for teachers in one place. Here teachers might locate podcasts that students can listen to in a computer learning station, or they may find a podcast that helps them better understand a confusing concept that they are expected to teach. Resource List 5.6 names a few of the many podcast directories that teachers may wish to explore and resources for creating and using podcasts in education.

RESOURCE LIST 5.6 ■ Podcast directories and podcasting resources

Podcast Directories

Digital Podcast: www.digitalpodcast.com

Find Podcasts: www.findpodcasts.com

Podcast Alley: www.podcastalley.com

Podseek: www.podseek.net

The Education Podcast Network (EPN): http://epnweb.org

Library of Congress Podcasts: www.loc.gov/podcasts

Podcasting Resources

Audacity: http://audacity.sourceforge.net

PoducateMe: http://poducateme.com

wikiHow: How to Use Podcasting: www.wikihow.com/Use-Podcasting

Wikiversity, Podcasting: http://en.wikiversity.org/wiki/Podcasting

Connecting with peers across a school, a district, or the world is made easier through a number of digital-age social-networking sites and allows teachers to network with professionals from near and far. Sharing successes and challenges with practicing teachers exposes both new and seasoned teachers to ideas and strategies for improving student learning. A few social networks for teachers are listed in Resource List 5.7.

RESOURCE LIST 5.7 ■ Social-networking sites for teachers

Collaborative Teacher Network: www.uic.edu/orgs/ctn

Moodle: Community: http://moodle.org/community

Ning in Education: http://education.ning.com

Partners in Learning Network: http://us.partnersinlearningnetwork.com/Pages

Reading Teachers Network: www.readingteachernetwork.com

Participating in education wikis also serves to inform teaching practices. These tools further provide teachers with ideas and glimpses of how other teachers worldwide are teaching students in the 21st century. Resource List 5.8 lists a few wiki directories that teachers may wish to explore to locate appropriate wikis.

RESOURCE LIST 5.8 ■ Wiki directories and resources

Everything Wiki: http://wiki.wetpaint.com/page/Wiki+Directory

Wiki Spot: http://wikispot.org/Wiki_Directory

Wikipedia: List of Wikis: http://en.wikipedia.org/wiki/List_of_wikis

Virtual worlds and simulations are increasingly popular ways for teachers to connect and learn from each other. Two of the virtual worlds that educators are using are Active Worlds (www.activeworlds.com/edu/awedu.asp) and Second Life (www.secondlife.com). Massachusetts Institute of Technology's (MIT's) Education Arcade (www.educationarcade.org/projects) highlights simulation projects with educational merit, and the Creative Learning Exchange (www.clexchange.org) allows teachers to share resources for systems thinking and modeling. In coming years, virtual worlds and simulations may play a greater role in teacher-to-teacher learning, communication, and collaboration.

The Teacher's Guide to International Collaboration on the Internet (www.ed.gov/teachers) can provide teachers with additional ideas and resources. As a matter of efficiency, teachers may wish to use aggregators to bring regularly read and visited blogs, podcasts, and so forth together. Teachers may wish to explore the use of services provided by Google's Reader (www.google.com/reader) service; Bloglines (www.bloglines.com); and Netvibes (www.netvibes.com) to keep up with various resources.

Learning from Experts

As noted in earlier chapters, experts and content-area specialists are among those in a professional learning community. Tapping into the resources available to PLCs has potential for both teachers and students. Teachers themselves may serve as experts and help other teachers. At Teacher2Teacher (http://mathforum.org/t2t/), teachers and parents can ask a panel of teaching professionals questions about teaching math. Edutopia's Ask An Expert: Get Online and Get Advice Page (www.edutopia.org/node/1312) connects novice and experienced teachers.

In some cases, experts are professionals in specific fields such as science, math, or health. *Scientific American* features a web page, Ask the Expert (www.scientificamerican.com/section.cfm?id=ask-the-experts), that addresses science-related questions. The Minnesota Orchestra's site has an Inside the Classics' Ask an Expert (http://insidetheclassics.myminnesotaorchestra.org/category/ask-an-expert/) feature that allows readers to ask music-related questions. Other resources address topics of a general nature. Teachers may wish to visit the Educator's Reference Desk (www.eduref.org), which lists archived responses to questions as well as many other resources.

Experts exist in the local community as well as the global one. Parents working in different sectors of society may be willing to offer their expertise to teachers and the school community. Stay-at-home and telecommuting parents have expertise in areas that they may be willing to offer. Teachers may find that others in the professional development community may also be willing to lend their expertise. Experts may just be waiting to be asked.

In Your Experience

Where do you see yourself five years from now? Ten years? How do you anticipate professional development being a part of your five- and ten-year plans?

Section T5a Explorations

1. Visit a professional society website associated with your field. What kinds of learning opportunities are available for you?

2. Locate, explore, and describe one distance-education opportunity that can help you enhance your teaching practice.

3. Locate, explore, and describe one informal learning opportunity that can help you enhance your teaching practice.

4. Create a web page that you could use as an extension of your teaching practice.

5. Create a blog that can be used as an extension of your teaching practice. Exchange your blog with a peer for review.

6. Locate a wiki that can be used to help you increase your teaching effectiveness and improve student learning. Describe how you can use this resource in your teaching practice.

7. Explore a virtual world or simulation and describe its implications for education and teacher-to-teacher learning.

Section T5a Review

In this section you learned about technology resources that can help enhance your professional development and teaching practice. A wide array of digital-age tools is available to help you learn and communicate with others in the local and global learning communities. Exploring these tools and participating in learning through professional societies, formal schooling, informal opportunities, teacher-to-teacher learning, social networking, virtual worlds, and simulations can help improve your own 21st-century skills. In the next section you will learn how teachers are called to lead in the classroom and beyond and impact education and all professions by virtue of their position.

NETS·T5b

Exhibit Leadership by Demonstrating a Vision of Technology Infusion, Participating in Shared Decision Making and Community Building, and Developing the Leadership and Technology Skills of Others

Teachers are natural leaders in their classrooms, but they are also leaders in their schools, communities, and profession. Although some leaders may be born, many are made by hard work, determination, and community support. In this section, you will learn strategies for acquiring leadership skills to impact your students, community, and the education profession in positive ways.

Teacher as Leader

Barth (2001) supports the definition of leadership as "making happen what you believe in" (p. 446) and relates the success of teacher leaders to three factors: having a goal, persisting, and enjoying incremental gains in desirable directions and not needing total fulfillment (what Barth calls "half a loaf," p. 447).

ISTE has addressed Barth's first goal with regard to teacher leadership and technology integration through its work with the NETS and other projects. ISTE's vision for technology integration is a collective one and is shared by the many practicing teachers, administrators, and the stakeholders who helped develop its mission and NETS for Teachers, Students, and Administrators.[5] Creating and believing in this shared goal or vision for technology integration is important in helping to bring to fruition what Barth calls "making it happen."[6, 7]

The second factor described by Barth emphasizes the importance of following through even in the face of obstacles. History remembers doggedly persistent leaders who helped improve the quality of life for countless others, and today's leaders are making their mark on the educational landscape. Wendy Kopp, who started Teach for America (www.teachforamerica.org) in 1990, is one such leader whose vision, now shared by many others, is helping to change the lives of students in underperforming schools across the country. As teachers integrate technology and consider uses for emerging technologies, they will no doubt face obstacles that would otherwise stand in the way of progress if not for teacher persistence.

Being able to enjoy the incremental fruits of one's labor is the third factor Barth notes as characteristic of successful leaders. Reflecting on the successes of each day is a practice that can yield big dividends, as day by day, year by year teachers become aware of steady movement toward their vision for education.[8] A strong network of teachers is important to help cheer and promote the individual and collective goals of teachers.

Teacher leadership provides benefits to the community of learners, including students, the school, teachers, and the principal (Barth, 2001). Many teachers have natural qualities that lend themselves to leadership; if they do not have them, they can acquire them. Having or developing these qualities can help teachers take the lead in shared decision making and community building, favorably affecting not only their students but also society and the education profession.

Phelps (2008) identifies knowledge, skills, and dispositions essential for teacher leaders. Essential knowledge is knowledge of change, school culture, reform recommendations, and servant leadership; essential skills include advocacy, empathy, questioning, vision creating, and collaborating/networking; and essential dispositions are risk-taking and persistence, challenge, service, efficacy, and resiliency.

Teachers can practice leadership by engaging in community efforts, such as student advocacy, by supporting community efforts to improve education. They can engage in collaboration and networking with colleagues locally and globally, and they can demonstrate persistence and resiliency when faced with difficult tasks. Teachers can celebrate their accomplishments and know that they are individually making a difference in the lives of their students and the larger learning community as part of an effort bigger than themselves.

Teachers need to take the initiative to acquire or develop any knowledge and skills they lack to help make their success as leaders more likely. Becoming a teacher leader allows teachers to impact their students, school, and larger education community by participating in important decision making and by making meaningful contributions. Barth's (2002) vision for the school as a community emphasizes the collective care and support of all its members and the ongoing learning that should take place:

> The vision is, first, that the school will be a community, a place full of adults and students who care about, look after, and root for one another and who work together for the good of the whole, in times of need and in times of celebration. Every member of the community holds some responsibility for the welfare of every other and for the welfare of the community as a whole. … As if community were not ambitious enough, the defining, underlying culture of this community is learning. The condition for membership in the community is that one learns, continues to learn, and supports the learning of others. Everyone. A tall order to fill, and one to which few schools aspire and even fewer attain. (p. 11)

As a member of the school and larger learning community, then, it is the responsibility of each teacher to participate in community building by supporting others in the community and by supporting the learning of others. Just as they should follow the lead of experienced teacher mentors, novice teachers will be able to do the same for other members of the learning community.

Many digital tools are available to help support learning. Knowledge can be acquired by using search engines, reading e-books, engaging in distance education, and participating in webinars. Collaborative and networking skills can be honed through the use of social networks, blogs, wikis, and chat tools. Some of these digital tools as they relate to promoting knowledge and skills are shown in Table 5.1.

TABLE 5.1 ▪ Digital tools for promoting knowledge and skills

Knowledge	Skills
▪ Search engines	▪ Social networks
▪ e-books, e-journals, e-content	▪ Blogs
▪ Web pages	▪ Wikis
▪ Electronic databases	▪ Social bookmarks
▪ Distance education	▪ Chat tools
▪ Professional societies	▪ Videoconferencing
▪ Webinars	▪ Mind-mapping tools
▪ Videos	
▪ Podcasts	
▪ Webcasts	
▪ Slidecasts	

Embracing Technology Infusion

At the preservice level, much can be done to prepare teachers to embrace and use technology effectively in their teaching practices. A review of 26 studies, surveys, and reports (Cradler, Freeman, Cradler, & McNabb, 2002) concluded that an effective strategy for promoting technology integration among new teachers is for college faculty to infuse technology into instructional practices as a teaching and learning tool in assignments and activities. The Section Explorations throughout this book infuse technology integration in this way. For example, when readers use technology resources, such as software, and principles of best practice, such as collaboration, to complete Section Explorations, they are practicing technology infusion. When college instructors use technology as part of their teaching practice, they are modeling technology infusion as well (Wepner, Ziomek, & Tao, 2003).

A second strategy includes integrating technology standards with professional development at state, regional, and local levels. Here again, this text promotes the NETS•T as a way to prepare teachers to use technology effectively in their teaching practices. Continued professional development, aligned according to technology standards, supports this action.

A third strategy culled from the 26 studies (Cradler et al., 2002) showed the importance of building teacher confidence and interest in the following ways:

1. being mentored by an experienced teacher who is proficient with technology

2. having sufficient time for collaborative learning and practice with technology

3. participating actively in professional meetings

4. using computers at home (p. 52)

These strategies have been emphasized throughout this book.

Researchers concluded that school leaders (such as principals) should provide resources to teachers for successful technology integration by doing the following:

1. customizing professional development according to teachers' needs

2. providing needed computers and connectivity

3. using technology in their own work and in communication with teachers

4. committing funds to support teacher involvement in decision making (Cradler et al., 2002, p. 53)

As well as ISTE, a number of other professional societies, organizations, services, and communities are committed to promoting technology integration. Some of these are listed in Resource List 5.9.

RESOURCE LIST 5.9 ■ Professional societies, organizations, and communities that promote technology integration

EDUCAUSE: www.educause.edu

Edutopia: www.edutopia.org

International Society for Technology in Education: www.iste.org

Multimedia Educational Resource for Learning and Online Teaching: www.merlot.org

Sloan Consortium: www.sloan-c.org

Thinkfinity: www.thinkfinity.org

ThinkQuest: www.thinkquest.org

Technology leaders are making their marks toward technology infusion. Dave Moursund is one such leader who exemplifies the qualities described above. Moursund founded the International Council for Computers in Education (ICCE) which later merged with the International Association for Computing in Education to become the International Society for Technology in Education (ISTE). In addition to his record of teaching, he has also written many articles and books on educational technology issues, presents workshops and keynote addresses around the world, and shares many of his works online with a worldwide audience. Moursund promotes and uses an abundance of digital-age tools, such as web pages, games, and wikis.[9]

David Warlick is a technology leader. He has worked as a middle school teacher and has held administrator positions at the local and state levels. He is the author of several books; gives presentations on educational technology; is the owner and principal consultant of the Landmark Project (http://landmark-project.com); and has created numerous helpful computer tools, such as Citation Machine (http://citationmachine.net) and Rubric Builder (http://landmark-project.com/rubric_builder/index.php).[10]

Curtis Bonk is a teacher leader whose work in e-learning has helped educators grow and provide quality online and blended learning environments to students.[11] Brenda Dyck, a teacher and writer, is a leader in technology integration.[12] Helen Barrett, a retired educator and current researcher and writer, has made important contributions in the areas of electronic portfolios and digital storytelling.[13] Tony Vincent is a leader who is helping teachers use technology to engage learners.[14] These are just a few of the many teacher leaders at different levels of instruction who contribute to the advancement of technology integration and infusion.

In Your Experience

Reflect on the list of characteristics for effective teacher leaders. Can you identify any teacher leaders in your school experience who exhibit these qualities and may be willing to serve as your mentor?

Section T5b Explorations

1. Create a checklist that includes various teacher-leader qualities based on the content of this section.

   ■ Rate yourself on a scale of 1–4, with 1 being "Inadequately Prepared" and 4 being "Very Prepared."

   ■ Based on your checklist, write a brief plan for how you can improve on any qualities that you rated as below 4.

2. Research a past or current leader who has impacted education. Note this leader's qualities that were included by Barth or Phelps or by both of them.

3. Consider one area in your teacher preparation or development where you can practice shared decision making.

4. Identify one area in your community that would benefit from your involvement and advocacy. For instance, does a local youth organization need assistance in writing or revising its vision or mission statement? How might you be able to contribute?

5. Reflect on ways that you have acquired expertise in a professional or personal skill.

   ■ Consider how you may be ready to serve as a mentor to others.

   ■ Summarize your qualifications and how you can serve in a one-page report.

6. Consider one of your past or current accomplishments.

   ■ How did you respond to this accomplishment? Did you celebrate your achievement, or did you fret over not accomplishing more?

   ■ How does your reaction relate to Barth's third factor of successful leaders (see p. 259)?

7. Consider one accomplishment of another learner in your learning community. How did you react to his or her accomplishment?

   ■ Did you support and celebrate your peer's accomplishment?

   ■ If not, what could you have done to "root" for your peer?

8. What digital tools can you use to strengthen your knowledge and skills? Create a list and exchange the list with a peer.

9. Visit the website of a professional society, organization, association, or community that promotes technology infusion. Summarize resources available that serve to promote teacher leadership.

Section T5b Review

In this section you learned about knowledge, skills, and dispositions essential for teacher leaders and the importance of supporting the learning community. You became familiar with some of the digital tools available for promoting knowledge and skills. You also learned about strategies for infusing technology effectively into the curriculum. In the next section you will learn how reflection on research and practice can help enhance student learning.

NETS·T5c

Evaluate and Reflect on Current Research and Professional Practice on a Regular Basis to Make Effective Use of Existing and Emerging Digital Tools and Resources in Support of Student Learning

Teachers across the country and world execute the same teaching tasks day after day. So what makes the difference between truly effective teachers and those who fall short of their potential? One marked difference is reflection. Teachers who reflect on their teaching practices examine their actions and the actions of all those affected. They observe, interpret, and assess those actions. Based on their discoveries, they construct improvement plans for themselves. This continuous cycle of reflection helps ensure ongoing development and an evolution of their teaching practices. In this section we will consider strategies to help you develop frequent, effective reflection practices.

Practicing Reflection

Collaboration with colleagues and reflection can help teachers cope with challenges inherent in teaching and learning (Dearman & Alber, 2005). "In short, teachers need to think about their practice; they need time to think about their thinking; and they need to talk to one another. Collaboration and reflection are natural partners" (Holbein & Reigner, 2007, p. 41).

Reflective teachers naturally make informed decisions because they have already spent energy and time examining the teaching-learning experience. Informed decisions are enlightened and typically better justified than uninformed ones. Reflective practice benefits everyone in the education community (Wagner, 2006).

Teachers may appreciate the sentiment of reflection but wonder how it can realistically be applied to their busy teaching practices. Although some perceive reflection as annoying or busywork (see Mills, 2008), reflection can benefit teachers (Gimbel, 2008) and improve instruction (Boyd & Boyd, 2005). It can be "built in" to what teachers already do.

Reflection in Lesson Planning

One task teachers already do every teaching day is create and use lesson plans. Reflecting at the end of each lesson can help teachers plan for improvement for the next time they teach; they can identify weak components, changes they wish to implement, and areas they need to reteach to their students. Research suggests (O'Donnell & Taylor, 2007) that using reflection in lesson planning can result in professional development. To help facilitate reflection, teachers may wish to include a section for reflection at the end of each lesson. Typical questions might read as follow:

- What were the planned successes of this lesson?

- What were the unplanned successes of this lesson?

- What was not accomplished?

- How might I improve on this lesson?

- What kinds of digital technology could be used to enhance this lesson or improve its effectiveness?

- What collaboration techniques and tools could I use next time to improve my teaching effectiveness?

- Would any assistive technologies have helped improve this lesson for all learners?

The last three questions are important with regard to technology integration, digital-age collaboration, and assistive technology. Asking such questions reminds teachers to infuse available technology tools and strategies into lessons and nudges them to reflect on their day-to-day teaching practices.

Reflective Journaling

Another practice teachers can use to reflect on their teaching is to engage in the process of journaling. Journaling includes mindful, purposeful, and intentional reflection and recording of reflections on the teaching-learning experience. Reflections can be recorded in many different formats, such as in a hardbound book dedicated to journaling, on a computer, in a mobile technology, in a blog, or in a podcast or video, and so forth. Teachers may record their reflections extensively or simply outline their reflections.[15] Either way, they should be sure to include observations, interpretations, and plans for improvement in their written reflections. Reflection 5.1 provides an example of what a fourth grade teacher's reflective journal entry might include. Here the teacher looks back on her experience, evaluates its implications, and makes informed decisions about future experiences.

```
Date: November 5, 2011       Period/Subject: 4th/Social Studies

Student Teacher:

Students were engaged in the discussion of how socioeconomic status
involves more than just family income. They liked the exercise
that followed the discussion, but they were reluctant to reveal any
personal information concerning family income, education, etc. Next
time I am going to present students with case studies of fictitious
families to remove unnecessary stress and to increase the comfort
level of students. Coming from an upper-middle-class family, I
didn't think about how students might be embarrassed to describe
their own SES. I need to be more sensitive to SES diversity, as well
as to other types of diversity in the classroom.
```

REFLECTION 5.1 Reflective journal entry.

Teachers may choose to record their spoken reflections on a tape recorder or a computer recorder. Many computers have built-in microphones and are capable of voice recording.

Teachers may wish to engage in interactive journaling with a teaching colleague or mentor. Dialogue journaling involves an exchange of reflections between teachers and can be helpful to both parties (Stegman, 2007). The first teacher writes his or her reflection and then passes the reflection to the second teacher. The second teacher reads the reflection, makes comments, and returns it to the first teacher. The second teacher may also write his or her own reflections that will be read by the first teacher. This continuous dialogue helps teachers share perspectives and construct meaning from the learning-teaching experience. Dialogue journaling can be especially effective in a team-teaching situation.

Reflection 5.2 depicts entries that might be taken from a dialogue journal between a student teacher and his or her cooperating teacher.[16] In this example, the veteran teacher is helping the student teacher grapple with sensitivity issues in the classroom and how this can affect the curriculum.

Date: November 5, 2011   Period/Subject: 4th/Social Studies

Student Teacher:

Students were engaged in the discussion of how socioeconomic status involves more than just family income. They liked the exercise that followed the discussion, but they were reluctant to reveal any personal information concerning family income, education, etc. Next time I am going to present students with case studies of fictitious families to remove unnecessary stress and to increase the comfort level of students. Coming from an upper-middle-class family, I didn't think about how students might be embarrassed to describe their own SES. I need to be more sensitive to SES diversity, as well as to other types of diversity in the classroom.

Veteran Teacher:

I don't believe students were embarrassed as much as they were peer-aware. Even if every child came from an affluent family, there would still be some children who "had" and some children who "had more." Do you see my point? You might want to teach a lesson such as this in a way that students aren't asked to "share" out loud. Instead, students could reflect on their own situations and write individual reports on their reflections. I commend you for your sensitivity.

Student Teacher:

Thanks for your input. I have an activity planned for our next unit that also involves sensitivity of another kind. In your experience, how do you think this group of children would react to an activity for locating life expectancies across the globe? Do you believe their maturity and developmental levels are advanced enough for them to "handle" infant mortality and death issues?

REFLECTION 5.2 Excerpt from a dialogue journal showing entries from a student teacher and his or her cooperating teacher.

Digital dialogue journaling can be recorded using email (Meyers, 2006) and web-based discussion boards. Peer journaling and communication through electronic means is often referred to as computer mediated discussion, or CMD, and has shown to be useful to teachers (Maher & Jacob, 2006; Qian & Tao, 2005; Ruan & Beach, 2005).

Although chat rooms allow for dialogue, they may not be as effective as discussion boards for dialogue journaling. The synchronous nature of chat rooms does not allow ample time for reflection before responding; discussion boards, as asynchronous tools, have the built-in advantage of permitting time to ponder.

In some cases, three or more teachers may wish to participate in dialogue journaling. An electronic discussion board with threaded discussion capabilities is especially useful for these interchanges. Figure 5.1 illustrates the use of threaded discussions in dialogue journaling.

Dialogue Journal for 2nd Placement

Topic	Date	Poster
Assertive	August 29, 2011, 11:17 a.m.	Student 1
	August 29, 2011, 2:31 p.m.	Teacher 1
	August 29, 2011, 4:51 p.m.	Teacher 2
Recess	August 30, 2011, 9:15 p.m.	Student 2
	September 1, 2011, 9:12 a.m.	Teacher 1
	September 1, 2011, 3:39 p.m.	Student 1
	September 1, 2011, 8:59 p.m.	Teacher 2
	September 1, 2011, 11:15 p.m.	Student 3
Grading	September 1, 2011, 9:06 a.m.	Student 3
	September 1, 2011, 8:35 p.m.	Teacher 3

FIGURE 5.1 Threaded dialogue journal involving three student teachers and their cooperating teachers.

Blogs and Wikis

A blog can be a convenient tool to record reflections, and blogs are being used by some (West, Wright, Gabbitas, & Graham, 2006) in the reflective process. Blogs can be used for journaling experiences, sharing with colleagues, and inviting peer comments. Here again, teachers must never use identifying information that would reveal personal information about their students. See Chapter 4 for additional precautions related to blogs, confidentiality, privacy, safety, and exhibiting a public persona.

Many teachers regularly reflect on their teaching practices through blogs and share their successes and areas needing improvement with other teachers. Being open to peer critique and suggestions can help teachers become more effective practitioners. An added benefit of journaling in this manner is that teachers will be forced to write their reflections carefully and purposefully, knowing that others will read what they wrote on the virtual page. Because of the nature of blogging, teachers may wish to selectively share or password protect so that only members of their intended audience are able to access, read, and respond to their reflections.

Wikis can be used to share reflections and invite peer input. McKenzie Wark, a professor of media and cultural studies, used a wiki to invite critiques from colleagues and wiki readers on his monograph. Scholars such as Wark entertain the idea of using Web 2.0 tools as a way of advancing scholarship and communicating big ideas rather than relying on printed books (Young, 2006).

Peer- and Self-Reflections

Peer reflection is another way for teachers to reflect on their teaching practices. Having other teachers examine and comment on teaching practices and materials allows teachers to learn more about how others perceive them and their actions. Equipped with these discoveries, teachers may be better able to create a plan for improving the teaching-learning experience than through self-reflection alone.

In some districts, mentor teachers are formally paired with novice teachers. If such formal structures are not available, beginning teachers may wish to identify their own mentors whom they trust and respect and who will provide them with constructive feedback. Experienced teachers can also benefit from peer reflection with other experienced teachers (and novices) and should seek out colleagues who are willing to share their experiences openly and honestly.

Peer critiques can be an effective means of helping each other learn if the critiques are conducted in a humane way rather than as a hunt for errors (Dossin, 2003). Furthermore, peer observation can be useful for both observer and observee (Kohut, Burnap, & Yon, 2007). Investigations into improving the peer-review process (Bernstein, 2008; Yon, Burnap, & Kohut, 2002; Kumrow & Dahlen, 2002) may help make this important practice even more beneficial.

A number of digital tools can help enhance the self- and peer-reflection process. Digital cameras and recorders can help capture peer observations; mobile technologies can be used to regularly exchange observations (e.g., via text messages); email messages can be sent to communicate concerns and praises to peers; and collaborative tools (e.g., brainstorming tools) can be used to share ideas for improving teaching practices.

Professional Portfolios

Creating and maintaining a professional portfolio is another way for teachers to enrich their teaching practices. Constructing a professional portfolio is by its nature a reflective process. The act of gathering and documenting materials naturally causes teachers to pause and evaluate their teaching practices. A portfolio is also a valuable tool for demonstrating to others that teachers are reflective practitioners.

Professional portfolios can be arranged in many different ways and used for different purposes. Some portfolios are designed around professional standards for teaching (Hackmann & Alsbury 2005). Others are arranged chronologically to demonstrate growth, development, or learning over time (Niguidula, 2005). Portfolios help in program assessment and individual assessment (Tuttle, 2007) and are sometimes used for career purposes to demonstrate readiness to enter a profession or position (Mobley, 2007; Ceperly, 2007). Regardless of their organization, professional portfolios should consist of tangible ways to demonstrate professional growth and development.

Because teachers want to convey a professional look, technology is useful in creating professional portfolios. Bound portfolios can look beautifully finished with the help of word-processing software. Labels, cover pages, and tables can all be computer generated. CDs, DVDS, or other electronically stored portfolios can be included in protective pockets. VHS videotapes, although bulkier than digitally recorded and stored videos, can be included to demonstrate teaching strengths.

Some teachers choose to create digital portfolios (Lambert, DePaepe, Lambert, & Anderson, 2007). These can be designed using various tools, including those in Resource List 5.10.

RESOURCE LIST 5.10 ■ Tools for creating digital portfolios

Software-presentation programs

> **Microsoft PowerPoint:** http://office.microsoft.com/powerpoint
>
> **Open Office Impress:** www.openoffice.org/product/impress.html

Web-based programs

> **NVU:** http://net2.com/nvu

In addition to the tools listed in Resource List 5.10, various teacher websites offer access to web-page templates.[17]

Digital portfolios have the advantage of compactness. It is much easier and less expensive to provide digital copies of professional portfolios on CDs or DVDs to prospective employers or school administrators than to reproduce multiple hard copies. If teachers have access to a reasonably priced or free web space, a web-based professional portfolio is a convenient way to store a portfolio and enable others to view professional development from afar. For confidentiality and privacy purposes, teachers should check into making their web-based portfolios password protected.

Tomorrow's e-portfolios may serve as even more powerful representations of student work and reflection, as Web 2.0 tools are used to allow greater collaboration and social learning (Zhang, Olfman, Ractham, 2007). Table 5.2 compares various types of digital portfolios. Note that one or more of the arrangements can be combined.

TABLE 5.2 ■ Various arrangements of digital portfolios

Primary Arrangement	Description
Standards-based	Documents are arranged to demonstrate competency in the standards used (e.g., ISTE NETS for Teachers or INTASC—Interstate New Teacher Assessment and Support Consortium).
Chronological	Documents are arranged to show growth and development over time.
Marketing	Documents are arranged to "market" or show strengths in particular areas (for example, a marketing portfolio may be used to secure a teaching position and may contain documents geared toward the job description).

Productivity Tools and Technology in the Reflection Process

Teachers lead busy lives. In the course of one day, they carry out large numbers of teaching tasks, such as preparing, implementing, and evaluating lessons; grading papers; communicating with parents; ordering supplies; calculating figures (grades, lunch money, fundraising); organizing, decorating, and arranging classrooms; performing lunch and other duties; sponsoring clubs and teams; and guiding young, impressionable students to reach their utmost potential. These tasks can be daunting, especially to novice teachers. Seasoned teachers, however, still struggle to meet all the demands inherent in teaching. As noted earlier, professional development and reflection are invaluable in helping teachers carry out their responsibilities effectively. Fortunately, specific technologies are available to help streamline many of these important teacher tasks.

Many digital-age productivity tools—tools that can help increase efficiency and effectiveness—are available to teachers. Some of these tools are software applications, and others are hardware devices. These digital tools serve many useful purposes for teachers by allowing them to streamline teacher tasks and reflect on their teaching practices.

In simple terms, *informatics* is the science of information, and it is being used in various fields, such as the legal profession (Hinson, 2005); the health profession (Delaney, 2008); and the sciences (i.e., bioinformatics) (Chu & Sun, 2007). One element of informatics is interpreting information. Figure 5.2 shows patient data in a health information system. Much in the same way health practitioners can use these data to improve patient care and use collective data to improve the health care system, teachers can use data and information from students to improve individual students' learning and the education system.

Teachers can borrow from these fields by learning to study the information and data they obtain in their day-to-day teaching practices. Many of the productivity tools and technology discussed below yield data that can be used to identify patterns, strengths, weaknesses, extrapolations, and other data in relation to teaching and learning.

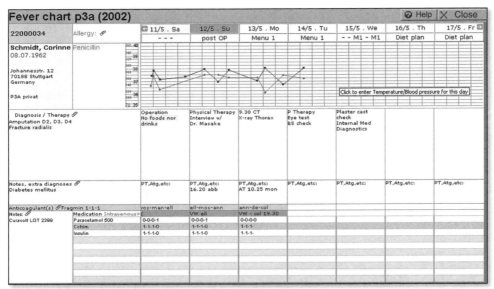

FIGURE 5.2 Patient data in a health information system using Care2x.

Source: http://en.wikipedia.org/wiki; licensed under the GNU Free Documentation License and the Creative Commons Attribution-ShareAlike 3.0 License (accessed 11/17/09).

Spreadsheets

As noted in an earlier chapter, spreadsheets are digital documents primarily used to calculate. Microsoft Excel (http://office.microsoft.com/en-us/excel/) and Open Office Calc (www.openoffice.org/product/calc.html) are examples of spreadsheet software applications. Most spreadsheet applications have the ability to graph and sort data and to create reports. For the reflective teacher, these types of documents provide visible representations of actual experiences. For example, teachers may suspect that a change in school policy has resulted in improved learning in their students. Using grades as one indicator of learning, teachers can run an overall class report, individual student reports, and assignment reports to examine any changes in patterns that correlate with changes in policy. Teachers can reflect on data collected and, when appropriate, share data with peers and administrators to help enhance student learning. (See Chapter 4.)

Word Processing and Desktop Publishing

Some word-processed and desktop-published documents lend themselves more to reflective practices than others. For example, reflecting on a teacher-completed KWL chart can help teachers determine the actual learning that took place, both expected and unexpected. (See Chapters 1 and 2.) From this data teachers can decide how best to approach the next unit or the same unit the next time they teach it. Table 5.3 shows a teacher-completed KWL chart created using a word-processing application.

TABLE 5.3 ■ Teacher-completed KWL chart created using a word-processing application

K: What do you know?	W: What do you want to know?	L: What did you learn?
■ That technology changes ■ The basic difference between hardware and software ■ Most of the different types of input devices ■ Different types of storage devices including flash drives and zips	■ More information on emerging storage devices ■ How memory works on a chip ■ How to use assistive technologies in the classroom ■ How to decide what kind of technology to request from the school system ■ How to get a driver for an older-model disk drive ■ More about emerging technologies *August 2, 2011*	■ That ISTE NETS help provide direction, checkpoints, and a destination for teacher candidates ■ The standards and performance indicators for NETS for Teachers ■ How I can use NETS for Teachers to better prepare me to use technology in my classroom ■ The difference between memory and storage ■ How a basic computer works ■ A description and examples of assistive technologies ■ A description and examples of emerging technologies ■ Basic troubleshooting techniques ■ How a KWL diagram can help me in self-assessment and self-improvement *August 23, 2011*

Another word-processing tool that can be used in the reflection process is the readability statistic function that is featured in some word-processing applications. For example, reflecting on readability statistics for teacher-created teaching materials distributed to students allows teachers to determine what level is best for each student, according to his or her reading level. Without these statistics teachers may be apt to overlook connections related to assignment difficulty and student success.

Reflection of a graphic organizer used as a presentation tool or as a summary of what students have learned may be more revealing than reflection based on a nonvisual representation of connections. Similarly, reflecting on correction- and tracking-tool results may help teachers identify patterns of students' writing errors that may otherwise go unnoticed.

Teachers may wish to reflect on a brochure they create that features a brief statement of their teaching philosophy and practice. Doing so will help them compare their beliefs to their actual practices and may help them identify discrepancies that might otherwise go undetected.

Databases

In addition to streamlining record-keeping tasks in a compact manner, databases support teacher reflection. For example, creating reports based on recorded data can reveal subtleties and nuances previously undetected. More specifically, creating and reflecting on a report containing comments on student qualitative assignments may reveal a pattern of decreased performance. In the day-to-day, busy practice of teaching, it is all too common for such things to go unnoticed, allowing students to slip through the proverbial cracks.

Reflecting on student records may help teachers plan more effective cooperative groups based on various criteria. For example, teachers may want to construct groups based on the results of an interest inventory whose answers are recorded in a database. Database software can easily help teachers generate a report based on interests or other categories that they can reflect on as they make informed decisions about their teaching practices.

Multimedia and Presentation Software

Like many of the productivity tools described earlier, multimedia and presentation software can be used in reflection. Teachers can use photographs and video clips of students engaged in the learning process (such as while working in cooperative groups), scanned images of student work, student narration, and other digital-storytelling features to create a class story that chronicles the year-long learning process. Digital stories, like printed ones, can reveal subtle nuances, patterns, and other disclosures that might not be obvious. Furthermore, being able to review videos can help improve reflection so that teachers do not have to rely on memory alone (Welsch & Devlin, 2006). Teachers may note, for example, how reserved one student is when working in particular cooperative groups. Or teachers may notice their habit of calling on the same students in a video featuring their teaching performance. From memory alone, teachers may not have realized these occurrences. See Chapter 3 for information on obtaining permissions to photograph and videotape students.

Digital-Imaging Technology

Teacher reflection can be enhanced using digital-imaging technology. Photographs of students, student work, events, and the teaching environment are a few such ways to document the learning that takes place in the classroom.

Showing changes over time in students and in processes are other ways to document learning. For example, teachers may photograph students performing a certain skill at an early stage of development. By taking incremental photographs over time, they can note growth or development in that skill in what might be called incremental photography. Reflecting on the changes in students can help teachers tailor their teaching to better meet their students' developmental needs.

If teachers do not have access to digital cameras, they can still create digital images by using a scanner. Photographs can easily be scanned and converted into digital images.

Digital videos can capture similar images of growth and development. They have the advantage, however, of including movement and sound, which may be invaluable in some instances, such as the performing arts (e.g., music) or gross motor skills (e.g., tennis). A digital video, for example, of a student learning to use fine motor skills or speaking is more valuable than a still photograph. Here again, be sure to obtain any necessary permission before photographing, videotaping, or recording students.

Mobile Technologies

Mobile technologies, such as personal digital assistants, handheld computers, portable media players, electronic book readers, tablets, and smartphones, have their place in teacher reflection. Many different types of mobile technologies allow teachers to retain and access important information text, sound, and images quickly. Data, content, and images can be reflected upon in these technologies in some of the same ways described earlier: using presentation software, spreadsheets, databases, and word-processing software. The difference is that mobile technologies offer compact and portable access to this content.

The Internet and Reflection

All of the software applications described earlier are available as web-based applications.[18] When using web-based applications, teachers must comply with district policies, ethics, and laws with regard to privacy, safety, and other human issues. (See Chapter 4.) Web-based applications can be used in some of the same ways described earlier for the computer-based productivity software products, but teachers should remember that in most cases, the data will be stored externally, which requires a high level of vigilance on the part of teachers.

Additional ways to use the Internet for reflection may not be as obvious. For example, teachers can follow trends related to teaching, learning, and the education system by using an aggregator (such as an RSS feed reader) and reflect on what is "fed" into their readers based on teacher-selected qualifiers. When various sources feed similarly related articles, podcasts, videos, and other resources into one web-based place, teachers may be able to reflect on the collective content and make connections hitherto unnoticed.

Teachers can also use a tool such as Google Trends (www.google.com/trends) that allows users to search for trends related to search-engine words or terms. They can even compare two or more words or terms to see how they compare in terms of search volume and news-reference volume. Data can be generated and reported in graph form, and links to relevant websites can be provided. The data can also be graphed according to regions, cities, dates, and languages. Reflecting on this data may give teachers ideas for emerging trends in education that can help them teach their students more effectively.

Using combined data from different sources, also known as *mashups,* can help teachers reflect on unapparent connections. For example, a mashup including geographic data, health statistics, and graduation rates may provide teachers with food for thought that leads them to identify relationships for further exploration.

In Your Experience

Do you consider yourself a naturally reflective person? What are some steps you could take to improve your reflectivity?

Section T5c Explorations

1. Create a lesson plan template with a component that allows for reflection using word-processing or other appropriate software.

2. Create a reflective journal entry related to teaching or learning, noting your successes and what you can do to improve your performance. If you are willing, share your journal with a peer and allow your peer to respond to your entry.

3. Read several blog posts from a teacher-written blog. What examples of reflection, if at all, did you note?

4. Create a digital portfolio that demonstrates your role as a reflective practitioner.

5. Create a web page that you can use to demonstrate reflective practice. What components of your web page demonstrate reflection?

6. Create a rubric that you can use to critique your own web page with regard to reflection. Critique your page and note areas for improvement.

7. Use your rubric to critique a peer's web page, noting how the page demonstrates reflective practice. Offer suggestions for improvement.

8. Create a gradebook spreadsheet with faux data on fictional students. Reflect on and use these data to inform your teaching practice. For example, analyze student performance and identify any patterns that need pursuing, such as marked decline in performance.

9. Create a database with faux data on fictional students. Reflect on and use these data to inform your teaching practice. For example, consider cooperative group placement based on data.

10. Reflect on your growth as a professional. Create a presentation or digital story that chronicles your professional growth.

11. Ask a peer to videotape you presenting a concept that you might teach in the future.

    ▪ Reflect on the video and note any of your actions that surprised you.

    ▪ Record your reflections using word-processing software and note how this practice may help you be a more reflective practitioner.

12. If you use mobile technology, reflect on how you can use this technology in the reflection process, making note of any special features available on the technology you use. If you do not have access to mobile technology, visit manufacturer websites and report on one of the technologies in terms of how it can help in the reflection process.

13. Develop a list of ways to use a portable media player in the reflection process. Exchange your list with your peers and create a collective list.

14. Visit Google Trends (at www.google.com/trends) and compare two education-relevant topics. How can the data you obtain be used in reflection? (Note: You may use an alternative trend finder if you wish, such as those that track trends in blogs, current events, etc.)

Section T5c Review

In this section you learned about some of today's methods and tools for using technology in your teaching practice to enhance reflection. Some of the technology tools available include spreadsheets, word-processing software, desktop-publishing software, databases, presentation software, digital-imaging technology, mobile technologies, web-based applications, and websites.

By examining your professional practices, you are better able to make informed decisions to support student learning. Introducing even a few technology-enhanced reflective practices into your daily routine may noticeably improve your teaching performance and students' learning. In the next section you will learn more about giving back to the community to help build the education profession and improve learning.

NETS·T5d

Contribute to the Effectiveness, Vitality, and Self-Renewal of the Teaching Profession and of Their School and Community

Teaching is a service profession. Along with nurses, police officers, doctors, social workers, firefighters, and all other professionals who give of themselves for the greater good, teachers are part of a philanthropic effort to give back to the profession and society. Each teacher has unique qualities, talents, and abilities to use in the service of others. In this section you will learn ways to contribute to the greater good by giving back to your school, community, profession, and society.

Service for the Common Good

Sir Isaac Newton, regarded as one of the greatest scientists who ever lived, once wrote, "If I have seen further it is by standing on the shoulders of giants." No doubt Newton was a very bright and talented man, yet he recognized that it was to others that he owed his insights and accomplishments. Teachers would do well to recognize how they, too, can see further—and deeper and wider—because of those who went before them. When they look back after growing into giants themselves, they should realize that others, too, will see further and deeper and wider because of their work and contributions. In this continuous cycle of giving and receiving, members of a community and profession grow individually and collectively.

Learning to Give

One way teachers can give back to the community is to promote and model philanthropy. Learning to Give (www.learningtogive.org) is part of an effort to educate K–12 students to give of their time, talents, and treasures for the greater good. As stated on its website's "about us" page (www.learningtogive.org/about, para. 1):

> Learning to Give:
>
> ■ *Educates* youth about philanthropy, the civil society sector, and the importance of giving their time, talent and treasure for the common good (knowledge);
>
> ■ *Develops* philanthropic behavior and experience (skills); and,
>
> ■ *Empowers* youth to take voluntary citizen action for the common good in their classrooms, their lives and their communities (behavior).

Learning to Give outlines standards of philanthropy for grades K–12 and offers resources to teachers, parents, students, youth workers, faith groups, and independent schools to help meet these standards and to support service learning. Some of the resources available to teachers include lesson plans, professional development opportunities, and activities (e.g., online games).

Four strands undergird the Learning to Give project: definitions of philanthropy (Strand I); philanthropy and civil society (Strand II); philanthropy and the individual (Strand III); and volunteering and service (Strand IV).[19]

Under each strand fall standards and benchmarks with accompanying lessons to help students reach benchmarks. The grade-level standards are aligned with state standards, and teachers can use the searchable database provided on the Learning to Give website to see how the Learning to Give standards meet state and international standards.

According to Learning to Give, *philanthropy* is defined as "the giving and sharing of time, talent, or treasure intended for the common good" (http://learningtogive.org/philthemes/all_phil.asp). Teachers often engage in philanthropy, but they may not recognize their good deeds as such. For example, when teachers stay after school to tutor children, engage in service projects, help the uninitiated with computer skills, or donate to a nonprofit organization that helps people in their community, they are practicing philanthropy.

Although the strands, standards, and benchmarks delineated by Learning to Give are intended for the K–12 audience, teachers can benefit from them as a framework for practicing personal and professional philanthropy, as well as for teaching philanthropy to their students.

Practicing philanthropy in their schools and communities allows teachers to model good citizenship and positive actions for their students and others. Regardless of the way teachers give of their time, talents, and treasures—whether through collaboration, monetary support, membership, research, publications, volunteerism, or through some other means—they are helping to advance the education profession.

By being model citizens, participating in civic duties, and carrying out their teaching practices with dignity and professionalism, teachers are building up the profession and presenting a positive impression to those inside and outside education. Teachers may think that doing these things is just doing their jobs—and they are right—but the effects of taking opposite actions can have profoundly negative effects on the profession. When those in and outside education read about a teacher who committed a felonious and heinous crime or one who has a reputation for being irresponsible and unethical, the teaching profession is soiled. However, when teachers do their jobs well and act as model citizens, they further the profession by upholding the respect from those in and outside education.

Being active in their school and local learning community shows others that teachers care about more than a paycheck. It demonstrates that they are willing to act in philanthropic ways to advance their community and the learning of students. Their actions speak volumes about their personal and teaching philosophies, perhaps more than their written statements of teaching philosophy.

There are enough needs to go around to give all teachers ample opportunities to give back to their school, community, and profession. Many colleges and universities have service-learning projects with which students and faculty can get involved. Service learning is a way of providing service to others and learning at the same time. Different models of service learning exist (Jones, Stein, & Kiser, 2008), each having its own framework and purpose. Preservice teachers and others can benefit from engaging in service-learning projects (Kirtman, 2008; Krensky & Steffen, 2008; Handa et al., 2008; Karayan & Gathercoal, 2005). A number of organizations exist to promote service learning, some of which are included in Resource List 5.11.

RESOURCE LIST 5.11 ■ Organizations that promote service learning

National Youth Leadership Council: www.nylc.org

Charity Guide: http://volunteerguide.org

National Service-Learning Clearinghouse: www.servicelearning.org

International Service Learning: www.islonline.org

National Service-Learning Partnership: www.service-learningpartnership.org

National Service-Learning Clearinghouse: www.servicelearning.org

Learn and Serve America: www.learnandserve.gov

The International Partnership for Service-Learning and Leadership: www.ipsl.org

Campus Compact: www.compact.org

iLeap: The Center for Critical Service: www.ileap.org

Project Adventure: www.pa.org

Global Volunteers: www.globalvolunteers.org

Innovations in Civic Participation: www.icicp.org

Epic Change: www.epicchange.org

Learning in Deed: www.learningindeed.org

American Association of Community Colleges: Horizons Service Learning Project:
www.aacc.nche.edu/Resources/aaccprograms/horizons

Community-Campus Partnerships for Health: http://depts.washington.edu/ccph/servicelearningres.html

Volunteer Match: www.volunteermatch.org

Amizade: www.amizade.org

Resource List 5.12 names some service-learning projects.

RESOURCE LIST 5.12 ■ Service-learning projects

African Library Project: www.africanlibraryproject.org

Roots and Shoots: www.rootsandshoots.org

The National Archives: *(see the link Establishing a School Archives)*
www.archives.gov/about/history/building-an-archives

Teachers can check with their local United Way to identify organizations that can use their services. Local schools will likely have many needs for which prospective and practicing teachers can lend a hand, such as assisting with after-school programs or helping to write grants for project funding. Professional societies offer many opportunities to serve. Professional societies are often in need of volunteers to help organize conferences, edit newsletters, and give presentations at workshops.

In addition to serving the local school and community, teachers can serve the extended and global learning community by contributing to the work of organizations such as Teachers Without Borders (www.teacherswithoutborders.org), the Peace Corps (www.peacecorps.gov) and AmeriCorps Vista (www.americorps.gov). Many thousands of opportunities to serve globally as a volunteer or in a paid position with a nonprofit organization can be found at the Idealist website (www.idealist.org). In some cases teachers can work from home and make contributions from afar, and in other cases face-to-face contributions are needed.

The many technology skills teachers have acquired can be used in the service of others. For example, teachers can create documents, analyze data, write reports, and develop plans for nonprofit groups in need of assistance. Resource List 5.13 provides some ideas for practicing philanthropy at various levels.

RESOURCE LIST 5.13 ■ Ways to practice philanthropy

Organize a school or community beautification project

Keep America Beautiful: www.kab.org

Participate in a community house-building project

Habitat for Humanity: www.habitat.org

Help those with special needs

Special Olympics: www.specialolympics.org

Volunteer as a literacy tutor

ProLiteracy Worldwide: www.proliteracy.org

Donate to a worthy cause

United Way International: http://worldwide.unitedway.org

Serve as a mentor

Big Brothers Big Sisters: www.bbbs.org

Engage in civic leadership

USA.gov (local governments): www.usa.gov/Agencies/Local.shtml

Write grants for a school project

TeachersCount: www.teacherscount.org

Teachers should consider ways that they can use their technology skills to be of service. For example, if teachers organize a school or community beautification project, they can create a database to help organize names and contact information of volunteers, they can use a spreadsheet to record and graph time donated by volunteers, and they can show progress being made on the project by creating a website containing digital images at various stages of progress.

A number of organizations exist to help individuals practice philanthropy, some offering resources that teachers might be able to use when teaching philanthropy or practicing philanthropy themselves. Resource List 5.14 shows just a few of the many organizations devoted to practicing good deeds and philanthropy to improve society. By reflecting on local needs (such as those of their school and community), the needs of the profession, and the needs of the global community, teachers will likely find numerous ways to contribute their time, talents, and treasures for the common good.

RESOURCE LIST 5.14 ■ Websites that promote kindness and good deeds

Youth Frontiers: www.youthfrontiers.org

Youth Frontiers (YF) helps build positive school communities and provides a number of resources for parents, teachers, and students.

"Over the last two decades, Cavanaugh built an organization on the idea of fostering safe, positive school communities where students and educators can thrive emotionally, socially, and, therefore, academically. Says Cavanaugh, 'We are not succeeding as a society if our children receive an A in Math ... and an F in life.' " (www.youthfrontiers.org/about.shtml, para. 3)

The Random Acts of Kindness Foundation: www.randomactsofkindness.org

RAK was formed to help spread kindness throughout the world and provides free educational and community ideas, guidance, and other resources (classroom and community resources such as lesson plans, website space, and a teacher's guide). RAK is dedicated to the following:

"Inspiring people to practice kindness and pass it on to others." (www.randomactsofkindness.org, para. 1)

HelpOthers.org: www.helpothers.org

This organization is committed to promoting kind acts that can spread throughout society. Its members use smile cards as tangible evidence of the spread of good throughout the world. The website's welcome note reads,

"HelpOthers.org—Kindness is contagious. Welcome to a portal dedicated to small acts of kindness."

Many ways to make a difference require small efforts to yield big benefits to those helped. For example, when using technology, teachers can make a few adjustments in their habits to help improve the lives of others. Resource List 5.15 shows a few ways to use websites to spread goodness.

RESOURCE LIST 5.15 ■ Websites that benefit others

GoodSearch: www.goodsearch.com

By using GoodSearch to search the Internet, you can make donations to one of the organizations listed. You may also add eligible organizations to the list, and you and others can help donate through searching.

FreeRice: www.freerice.com

You can help your students' vocabulary improve and help feed the world by introducing this website into your curriculum. For each correctly answered vocabulary question, 10 grains of rice are donated to the United Nations World Food Program.

Adopt-A-Classroom: www.adoptaclassroom.org

Adopt-A-Classroom partners teachers with donors so teachers can have funds to purchase critical resources and materials for their classrooms.

In Your Experience

Have you ever practiced philanthropy as defined by Learning to Give? Who or what benefited from your philanthropy?

Section T5d Explorations

1. Visit the Learning to Give website (http://learningtogive.org).

   - Identify one strand, standard, benchmark, and lesson plan that you could use in your teaching practice.

   - How could you model the exemplified actions to your students?

2. Investigate service-learning opportunities.

   - Do any of these opportunities appeal to you in a personal or professional way?

   - Are you able to contribute your time, talents, or treasures to any of the service-learning projects?

3. Refer to Resource List 5.13, Ways to practice philanthropy. Create a list of ways to use technology for each "way to give" that is listed.

4. Visit a professional society website. Locate opportunities to serve that are included on the site. If you cannot locate this information, contact the society and ask what opportunities are available.

5. Visit the website of one of the organizations mentioned in this section. Are there any philanthropic opportunities that appeal to you and to which you can contribute your time, talents, or treasures?

6. Interview someone who practices philanthropy; see the definition given by Learning to Give (p. 279). Ask the interviewee questions about his or her philanthropy, how he or she benefits from practicing philanthropy, and who or what benefits from these philanthropic actions.

7. Reflect on your own past or current philanthropic efforts. Create a plan for increasing or maintaining your philanthropic efforts.

8. Use presentation or multimedia software to chronicle your story of participation in philanthropy. If you have not participated in philanthropy, chronicle ways in which you have benefited from other people's philanthropic efforts.

Section T5d Review

You have much to give to help advance the profession, your school, and your local and global communities. Developing a habit of philanthropy now or reflecting on more useful ways to serve others can help you become the giant of an educator that you aspire to become, one who helps new and upcoming teachers to see beyond what can be imagined today.

Chapter 5 Summary

In this chapter you learned how technology can help you be more efficient, resourceful, and creative in your teaching practice. You learned the role and potential of technology in professional development, the qualities of an effective teacher leader, and some ways that technology practices can complement teacher evaluation and reflection. Finally, you learned how to give back to the local and global community and the profession. The next chapter offers concluding remarks about the direction of technology integration and emerging technologies with regard to education.

Chapter 5 Notes

1 See the Introduction for more about the mission of professional societies.

2 Clearinghouses are repositories for material and information.

3 See Chapters 1, 2, and 3 for information about digital tools that enhance communication and collaboration. See Chapter 4 for a discussion of the risks, laws, ethics, and safety issues involved with developing a public persona using digital-age tools.

4 RSS, or Really Simple Syndication, refers to the aggregation of content (e.g., blogs, podcasts) into one central location using software known as an RSS reader. Google Reader (available at www.google.com) is an example of an RSS reader. RSS readers recognize the XML format of content and feed the content into a user interface where viewers can view updated content.

5 See Introduction and the appendix for more details on the NETS.

6 To review a study on the qualities of effective educational technology leaders, see Langlie's *Educational Technology Leaders: Competencies for a Conceptual Age* (2008).

7 See *Teachers as Technology Leaders: A Guide to ISTE Technology Facilitation and Technology Leadership Accreditation* by Twomey, Shamburg, and Zieger (2006) for more on technology leadership.

8 See the next section, Section T5c, for practical applications for teacher reflection.

9 To learn more about Dave Moursund and his work, see www.uoregon.edu/~moursund/dave.

10 To read more about David Warlick's work, see http://davidwarlick.com/wordpress/?page_id=2.

11 See Curtis Bonk's web page at http://mypage.iu.edu/~cjbonk/ for more information about his contributions and work.

12 See Brenda Dyck's blog at www.educationworld.com/a_tech/columnists/dyck/dyck039.shtml.

13 See http://electronicportfolios.com for more on Helen Barrett and her work.

14 See Tony Vincent's resource for educational technology, Learning Hand, at http://learninginhand.com and read posts by him at http://tonyvincent.net/TonyVincent.net/Tony_Vincent__Teaching,_Learning,_Technology,_Consulting,_Workshops.html

15 To protect students' identities in the event the journal is misplaced, read, listened to, or viewed by an unintended audience, teachers must not include identifying information, such as student names or other qualifiers that would link information with particular students.

16 For more information on the use of dialogue journaling, refer to *Dialogue Journal Bibliography: Published Works about Dialogue Journal Research* by Peyton and Staton (2000).

17 See Chapter 3 for more on digital-age tools.

18 See Chapter 3 for more on web-based applications.

19 More details on the four Learning to Give strands:

> **Strand I,** in addition to exploring the definition of philanthropy, addresses the roles of government, business and philanthropy; names and types of organizations within the civil society sector; operational characteristics of nonprofit organizations; the role of foundations; and the role of family in philanthropy. Teachers who reflect on their own actions and how their actions impact their families, schools, the community, and society are exhibiting the sentiment associated with this strand.

> **Strand II** highlights the relationship between self and society including the nature of citizenship, diverse cultures, economics, geography, government, history, and civic engagement. Teachers who vote, participate in community recycling, and donate to worthy causes are nurturing the relationships between self and society.

> **Strand III** addresses reasons for individual philanthropy and careers in the nonprofit sector. When teachers become involved in programs such as Teach for America and Teachers Without Borders, they are exemplifying the intent of this strand.

> **Strand IV** explores the concept of needs assessment, service and learning, providing service, raising private resources, and integrating the service experience into learning. Participating in a community fund-raising project and providing a professional service pro bono puts into practice the concept of Strand IV. (www.learningtogive.org)

Chapter 5 References

Barth, R. (2000). Building a community of learners. *Principal, 79*(4), 68–69.

Barth, R. (2001). Teacher leader. *Phi Delta Kappan, 82*(6), 443–449.

Barth, R. (2002). The culture builder. *Educational Leadership, 59*(8), 6–11.

Barth, R. (2006). Improving relationships within the schoolhouse. *Educational Leadership, 63*(6), 8–13.

Bernstein, D. (2008). Peer review and evaluation on the intellectual work of teaching. *Change, 40*(2), 48–51.

Boyd, J., & Boyd, S. (2005). Reflect and improve: Instructional development through a teaching journal. *College Teaching, 53*(3), 110–114.

Ceperly, A. (2007). Adaptation of the career portfolio at the University of California, San Diego: A case study. *New Directions for Student Services, 119*, 65–72.

Chu, Y., & Sun, C. (2007). Problem-based approach for bioinformatics. *International Journal of Instructional Media, 34*(4), 441–447.

Cradler, J., Freeman, M., Cradler, R., & McNabb, M. (2002). Research implications for preparing teachers to use technology. *Learning & Leading with Technology, 30*(1), 50–54.

Dearman, C., & Alber, S. (2005, April). The changing face of education: Teachers cope with challenges through collaboration and reflective study. *The Reading Teacher, 58*(7), 634–640.

Delaney, C. (2008). Facilitating cultural competence and computer literacy in RN-to-BSN students. *Journal of Nursing Education, 47*(5), 240.

Dossin, M. (2003). Among friends: Effective peer critiquing. *The Clearing House, 76*(4), 206–207.

Erbas, A., Ledford, S., Polly, D., & Orrill, C. (2004, February). Engaging students through technology. *Mathematics Teaching in the Middle School, 9*(6), 300–305.

Gimbel, P. (2008, January). Helping new teachers reflect. *Principal Leadership, 8*(5), 6–8.

Hackman, D., & Alsbury, T. (2005). Standards-based leadership preparation program improvement through the use of portfolio assessments. *Educational Considerations, 32*(2), 36–45.

Handa, V., Tippins, D., Thomson, N., Bilbao, P., Morano, L., Hallar, B., & Miller, K. (2008). A dialogue of life: Integrating service learning in a community-immersion model of preservice science-teacher preparation. *Journal of College Science Teaching, 37*(6), 14–20.

Hinson, C. (2005). Legal informatics: Opportunities for information science. *Journal of Education for Library and Information Science, 46*(2), 134–153.

Holbein, M., & Reigner, R. (2007). Collaboration, reflection, and research in teaching reading: A teacher education perspective. *Journal of Reading Education, 32*(3), 40–42.

Jones, A., Stein, J., & Kiser, P. (2008). Making the transition to collaborative service-learning. *Planning for Higher Education, 36*(4), 17–22.

Karayan, S., & Gathercoal, K. (2005). Assessing service-learning in teacher education. *Teacher Education Quarterly, 32*(3), 79–92. Retrieved August 2, 2008, from www.teqjournal.org/backvols/2005/32_3/14karayan&gathercoal.pdf

Kirtman, L. (2008). Pre-service teachers and mathematics: The impact of service-learning on teacher preparation. *School Science and Mathematics, 108*(3), 94–102.

Kohut, G., Burnap, C., & Yon, M. (2007). Peer observation of teaching: Perceptions of the observer and the observed. *College Teaching, 55*(1), 19–25.

Krensky, B., & Steffen, S. (2008). Arts-based service-learning: A state of the field. *Art Education, 61*(4), 13–18.

Kumrow, D., & Dahlen, B. (2002). Is peer review an effective approach for evaluating teachers? *The Clearing House, 75*(5), 238–241.

Lambert, C., DePaepe, J., Lambert, L., & Anderson, D. (2007). e-Portfolios in action. *Kappa Delta Pi Record, 43*(2), 76–81.

Langlie, N. (2008). *Educational technology leaders: Competencies for a conceptual age* [Doctoral dissertation]. Minneapolis, MN: Capella University.

Maher, M., & Jacob, E. (2006). Peer computer conferencing to support teachers' reflection during action research. *Journal of Technology and Teacher Education, 14*(1), 127–150.

Meyers, E. (2006). Using electronic journals to facilitate reflective thinking regarding instructional practices during early field experiences. *Education, 126*(4), 756–762.

Mills, R. (2008). It's just a nuisance: Improving college student reflective journal writing. *College Student Journal, 42*(2), 684–690.

Mobley, R. (2007). Adaptation of a career portfolio at Georgia Tech: A case study. *New Directions for Student Services, 119,* 73–81.

National Council of Teachers of Mathematics (NCTM). (2007). 21st-century literacies. *National Council of Teachers of Mathematics: An NCTM Policy Research Brief.*

Niguidula, D. (2005). Documenting learning with digital portfolios. *Educational Leadership, 63*(3), 44–47.

O'Donnell, B., & Taylor, A. (2007). A lesson plan as professional development? You've got to be kidding! *Teaching Children Mathematics, 13*(5), 272–278.

Peyton, J. K., & Staton, J. (2000-12-00). *Dialogue journal bibliography: Published works about dialogue journal research.* Washington DC: NCLE. Retrieved from http://eric.ed.gov/ERICWebPortal/detail?accno=ED451731

Phelps, P. (2008). Helping teachers become leaders. *The Clearing House, 81*(3), 119–122.

Qian, G., & Tao, L. (2005). In-service teachers and computer mediated discussions: Ranges and purposes of reflection. *Reading Horizons, 46*(2), 115–142.

Ruan, J., & Beach, S. (2005). Using online peer dialog journaling to promote reflection in elementary preservice teachers. *Action in Teacher Education, 27*(3), 64–75.

Stegman, S. (2007). An exploration of reflective dialog between student teachers in music and their cooperating teachers. *Journal of Research in Music Education, 55*(1), 65–82.

Tuttle, H. (2007). Digital-age assessment. *Technology & Learning, 27*(7), 22–24.

Twomey, C., Shamburg, C., & Zieger, L. (2006). *Teachers as technology leaders: A guide to ISTE technology facilitation and technology leadership accreditation.* Eugene, OR: ISTE.

Wagner, K. (2006). Benefits of reflective practice. *Leadership, 36*(2), 30–32.

Welsch, R., & Devlin, P. (2006). Developing preservice teachers' reflection: Examining the use of video. *Action in Teacher Education, 28*(4), 53–61.

Wepner, S., Ziomek, N., & Tao, L. (2003). Three teacher educators' perspectives about the shifting responsibilities of infusing technology into the curriculum. *Action in Teacher Education, 24*(4), 53–63.

West, R., Wright, G., Gabbitas, B., & Graham, C. (2006). Reflections from the introduction of blogs and RSS feeds into a preservice instructional technology course. *Tech Trends, 50*(4), 54–60.

Yon, M., Burnap, C., & Kohut, G. (2002). Evidence of effective teaching: Perceptions of peer reviewers. *College Teaching, 50*(3), 104–110.

Young, J. (2006, July 28). Book 2.0: Scholars turn monographs into digital conversations. *The Chronicle of Higher Education, 52*(47), A20–24.

Zhang, S., Olfman, L., & Ractham, P. (2007). Designing ePortfolio 2.0: Integrating and coordinating Web 2.0 services with ePortfolio systems for enhancing users' learning. *Journal of Information Systems Education, 18*(2), 203–214.

Concluding Remarks:
Facing the Challenge of Integrating Technology in the Classroom

Throughout this book you have learned how to integrate technology into the curriculum. You were provided with research to inform your teaching practice, you were introduced to digital-age tools to help you integrate technology, and you were made aware of strategies to help you use technology effectively. Being prepared to use technology in your teaching practice is critical if all of your students are going to benefit from engaging, meaningful lessons that integrate technology. However, even with the best preparation, you will likely face obstacles in carrying out best practices. Some of these obstacles are presented here, along with ways to face these challenges.

The reading and assignments presented in this chapter should help you to identify and overcome obstacles associated with integrating technology into the curriculum and to anticipate the use of emerging technologies in education and the ways that the classroom environment will change.

Recognizing and Facing the Challenges

All professions present challenges, and teaching is no different. Teachers face challenges of various types. Challenges range from the day-to-day frustrations associated with too little time to accomplish professional goals to the broader frustrations associated with education in general. Facing these challenges with knowledge, wisdom, persistence, patience, and determination can help teachers successfully overcome obstacles. Beginning teachers would be wise to glean as much wisdom, knowledge, and experience as they can from their teacher-preparation programs and from mentors, supervisors, colleagues, and former teachers whom they respect.

More specific to this text are the challenges teachers face for integrating technology into their teaching practices. While technology has increased in schools, technology integration has not mirrored this increase. The percent of Internet access in schools in the United States rose from 35% in 1994 to around 100% in 2005, and the number of instructional computers with Internet access rose from 8% in 1995 to 97% in 2005. Moreover, the percent of instructional rooms with Internet access rose from around 3% in 1994 to about 94% in 2005 (Wells & Lewis, 2006). Clearly, most schools have computers and Internet access available, yet with this widespread availability, only 43.3% of prekindergarten–12th grade students used the Internet in school in 2003 (Wells & Lewis, 2006).

Even well-educated, capable teachers face challenges. In a study of 30 teachers who were highly educated and skilled in technology and who were innovative and adept at overcoming obstacles, researchers found that these teachers did not consistently integrate technology as a teaching and learning tool (Bauer & Kenton, 2005). Two key impediments included students not having enough time at computers and teachers needing extra planning time for technology lessons. Outdated hardware, lack of appropriate software, technical difficulties, and student skills were additional concerns.

According to Ditzhazy and Poolsup (2002), both external and internal barriers can impact the integration of technology. External barriers can include lack of access to computers or software, insufficient time to plan instruction, lack of technical support, and lack of administrative support. Internal barriers can include fear of computers or feelings of insecurity around computers. Ditzhazy and Poolsup contend that teacher skills and knowledge are critical to success and that a series of workshops can help teachers learn to use computer technology in a nonthreatening environment.

To help overcome obstacles to technology integration, Bauer and Kenton (2005) suggest the need for a school-based, tech-savvy member of the administrative team—such as a technology coordinator—who has time to devote to computer technology. Furthermore, their study supports the use of teacher workshops and other special offerings as important resources for teachers. They see the role of colleges of education as essential in preparing teachers to effectively integrate technology, but they question current teacher preparation based on the results of their study.

Various teacher-preparation programs, such as one at the University of Dayton in Ohio (Rowley, Dysard, & Arnold, 2005), have modified their programs to address the need for effective teacher preparation to help bridge the gap between technology access and technology use, but more is needed.

Access to technology, use of technology, and capacity to use technology was reported by the Editorial Projects in Education (EPE) Research Center (2007) in *Technology Counts 2007: A Digital Decade*. According to the report:

- in the United States, an average of 49.5% of students were reported to have computers in the classroom (Y2005) with an average of 3.8 students per instructional computer (Y2006).

- 48 states' standards for students were reported to include technology, but only 4 states were reported to test students on technology (Y2006–07).

- 45 states' teacher standards were reported to include technology, but only 19 states were reported to have a requirement for an initial teacher license that includes technology coursework or a test, and 9 states were reported as requiring technology training or testing for recertification or participation in technology-related professional development (Y2006–07).

The report assigned a grade to each state and the District of Columbia based on access, use, and capacity and graded only one with an A. (It assigned two A minuses.) The report assigned a C plus to the United States.

The refreshed 2008 ISTE NETS•T standards show promise for helping the situation. These standards emphasize integration of technology in a manner that, if infused into teacher-preparation programs and workshops, may help teachers overcome some of the barriers reported by experienced and new teachers. But as noted earlier, administrative support in terms of funding, time allocations, and other resources also play a prominent role in successful integration.

So what can new teachers do to help ensure their successful tech integration once they have their own classrooms? There are no easy answers, but some guidelines may help novice teachers overcome common obstacles to integrating technology:

- Beginning teachers should take their teacher preparation seriously and apply themselves as those who will potentially impact thousands of lives in a lifetime career of teaching. Using this book or a similar resource as part of their teacher preparation, with an emphasis on the refreshed ISTE NETS•T, is one step toward achieving this goal.

- Beginning teachers should align themselves with competent, motivated mentors who are willing to share their knowledge, skills, and experience.

- Beginning teachers should decide to be effective in the classroom and decide what they may be lacking (e.g., skills, confidence). They need to commit to addressing their shortfalls in order to integrate technology successfully into their teaching practices.

- Once beginning teachers have their own classrooms, they should practice what they learned from their preparation—reflection, planning, professional development—so that they will not be counted among the ineffective. There is much they can do to stay abreast of emerging technologies and new strategies, some of which have been described in this book. They will also learn through other avenues, such as professional practice, workshops, graduate school, or other means.

Anticipating the Future of Techology in Education

Generally speaking, technology emerges as a result of demand; a need (or want) arises, and the technology industry responds to that need by developing new or modifying current technology. In order to anticipate what emerging technologies might arise, it is important to consider our greatest needs in education.

Many developments in technology have already been produced in response to this call. Computer simulations have been developed that help students think critically, assistive technologies have been created to help students with special needs learn more effectively, and improved software has been developed to help educators track and report student progress. Anticipating emerging technologies, then, hinges largely on the needs of students and educators.

Providing equal access to quality education for all students is obviously high on the list of needs in education. One of the greatest obstacles to successfully providing equal access is funding. Schools simply do not have all the resources they need to guarantee the latest and greatest technology for all students. This has forced educators to think outside the box and to make the most of what they do have to spend on technology in creative ways.

In the late 20th century, some schools addressed the funding issue by using alternative technologies that provided some functionalities at a fraction of the cost of what were then more expensive technologies. For example, some teachers were provided with word-processing technology that allowed students to word process and edit writing without having to expend more funds for a fully functioning computer system. The technology had limited features, such as spell check and a calculator, but the technology could be connected to a computer so that word-processed work could be printed and saved to a computer. NEO 2 (www.neo-direct.com) technology is one example that served this purpose and is still being used today, although as a more advanced tool. This and similar technologies arose as a result of the need for reasonably priced, useful tools that could provide some of the functions of a full computer system at a smaller cost.

Personal digital assistant (PDA) technology is another relatively cost-effective way that technology has been brought to students. Sometimes used in conjunction with keyboards, these tools allow students to perform school-related tasks, such as taking notes, recording assignments, checking school emails, calculating formulas, scheduling appointments, taking photographs, and much more, depending on the model of PDA. In many cases, PDA software is capable of interacting with computers so that content can be downloaded to a computer system. This is a creative way of using an existing technology as an educational tool that was originally designed for the personal user in need of a portable, personal computing device.

As technology has advanced, desktop and laptop computers have become more affordable and, therefore, within the price range of school systems and individual students. Some schools have created portable computer labs equipped with laptops and wireless services. The portable computer lab is sometimes used on a rotating basis to give all students an opportunity to use technology. Technology will continue to emerge in a response to a need or want, and education will likely be impacted as a result.[1]

The desire for greater access to technology is not unique to education. In the past and today, many technology users worldwide sought increased access to computer code; this prompted development of the Free Software Foundation (www.fsf.org) and the Open Source Initiative (www.opensource.org). Open source code, used for operating systems and web browsing (such as the Linux operating system and the Firefox (www.mozilla.org) web browser discussed earlier in this book), help allow those with limited resources to access and use technology. These movements are gaining momentum and will likely take a larger role in the educational community in the future.

The increase in quality freeware and shareware also increases accessibility to software applications for all. For nearly every commercial product, there now exists a freeware or shareware alternative. In the past, some of these applications were inferior to commercial products, but this, too, is changing. Although certain safeguards should be taken when using freeware and shareware (see Chapter 3), these resources can sometimes be used as effective teaching tools.

A call for greater assistive technologies in the workforce and in education has led to advances in technology. Improvements in assistive technologies allow greater numbers and varieties of users to have full access to all that technology offers. Assistive technologies have been instrumental in helping students with special needs flourish in technology, but they are also helping students without identified special needs to succeed. For example, text-to-speech communication aids, developed primarily to help students with speech loss and other communication disorders, can also assist beginning readers without any identifiable disorder. Similarly, touch screens are helpful for those unable to operate a mouse, but they are also ideal for use with young children using software applications. Handheld spell-checkers, sold as assistive technologies, can serve all populations. Greater access to assistive technologies can mean greater learning for all students.

Many other technologies have emerged as a result of a recognized need. For this reason, it is essential that teachers recognize that demand is positively correlated with supply. Knowing this empowers teachers to raise a collective voice in the name of serving students better. When teachers raise awareness of educational concerns and student needs, industry listens and responds accordingly. To learn more about the future of technology in education, teachers can visit the Center for Educational Technologies' NASA-sponsored Classroom of the Future website (www.cet.edu/?cat=cotf). Additional institutions, organizations, groups, studies, and programs examine emerging technologies in education, although some focus more on PK–12 education and others on higher education. Examples include ISTE's Innovative Learning Technologies Special Interest Group (SIGILT) (www.iste.org/connect/special-interest-groups/sig-directory/sigilt) and the EDUCAUSE Learning Initiative (ELI) (www.educause.edu/ELI/LearningTechnologies/EmergingTechnologiesandPractic/5673).

Changes in Learning Environments

We have discussed how learning environments are changing in profound ways. Distance education, once more common in higher education and industry, is becoming more prevalent in secondary schools and even in some elementary schools (Zandberg & Lewis, 2008). The use of various software applications is allowing different types and levels of learners to grow and develop in the same classroom without compromising any single student's learning experience. Portable and mobile devices, such as word processors, lightweight laptop computers, PDAs, MP3 players, e-book readers, tablets, smartphones, and GPSs create learning environments that can be transported virtually anywhere that these technologies are permitted.[2]

The physical environment is no longer restricted to a particular school building or district. Through distance education, children may be able to choose a school from anywhere in the country or world based on reputation, offerings, or other factors. Parents can tailor a child's curriculum based on the child's needs and interests. This might involve more than one distance education provider, rather than limiting learning to one "school." School can take place at home or in a building where education service providers congregate students under one roof. Unlimited possibilities and combinations of experiences exist.

Widespread distance education for elementary and secondary children would change the way children build friendships and view the world. Friendship and respect for others outside their immediate culture could increase cooperation among individuals of diverse cultures. This cooperation could lead to a greater sharing in knowledge and understanding, not only in technology, but in all areas of learning and learning theory.

Distance education, also sometimes known as e-learning, is not only growing in use, but also in substance. Just like the web, which has evolved through generations (e.g., Web 2.0 and Web 3.0), advanced e-learning is now being described as "e-learning 2.0."

E-learning 2.0 involves greater creativity from learners and is less about prescribed learning experiences and more about experiences of shared growth and discovery. Wikis, podcasts, and blogs are tools that can be part of an e-learning 2.0 environment (Downes, 2005). While it is impossible to predict tomorrow's distance education, it is likely that it will continue to be an important part of the educational landscape.

Student Learning Revisited

Universal learning principles are supposed to be just that—universal. Although educators around the globe have done an admirable job of unveiling numerous principles of learning, research is usually conducted within one's own culture and location. Having greater access to students in distance education programs allows researchers to conduct their work without these restrictions. Doing so may speed discoveries that might otherwise be confounded by cultural or geographic limitations. In this way, distance education not only connects students and teachers from different cultures and geographic locations, but also encourages greater researcher-to-student and researcher-to-researcher connections. This idea mirrors the hope of the open source community that believes greater access to code yields quicker and better solutions; in the same way, having greater access to student populations may yield quicker and better solutions to educational problems and refinement of theories.

When theories are refined and teaching practices are changed to improve learning, many good things can happen. First and foremost, students may have greater learning success. A corollary is that teachers can capitalize on student success and encourage students to greater heights of learning. In one context, Vygotsky's zone of proximal development (ZPD) can be characterized as "the difference between the child's individual and aided performances" (Kozulin, Gindis, Ageyev, & Miller; 2003). Teachers and peers help students span this distance and, in effect, move toward another, higher zone of development. Vygotsky believed that no upper boundary exists. With this in mind, if students have greater learning success as a result of refined learning theory, then teachers can help raise the upper limits of their students' zones of proximal development.

Professional Practice

Teachers can help chart growth and development in students better when hardware and software make it easier and more convenient to do so. As noted in earlier chapters, a variety of technology tools (e.g., spreadsheets, Gantt charts, databases, online tools) are currently available to help teachers with their assessment and evaluation practices.[3] Rather than relying solely on an intuitive notion that learning is taking place, teachers have greater access to user-friendly, widely available, reasonably priced technology that can easily, quickly, and accurately track short- and long-term data related to learning. These data cannot only be used by teachers and immediate peers, but they can also be used by researchers to better understand learning in specific environments. Improvement in the availability and affordability of technology is only as great as how well these advances lead to improved student success. Having the latest and greatest technology sitting in a classroom unused, underused, or misused does nothing to help foster student success. However, using technology regularly, wisely, and effectively goes a long way toward improving the learning environment and student learning. For this reason, it is imperative that teachers be given every opportunity to learn and use technology in their teaching practices.

Public and private agencies have long recognized the need for improved, expanded, and ongoing training in the use of technology in the classroom. At the same time, resources are spread thinly and may be even scarcer in coming years. Teachers may need to take greater responsibility for their own professional development and training. Chapter 5 presented many ways that teachers can take advantage of professional development through the use of technology such as webinars, collaboration, and video-conferencing. Perhaps mobile technologies will play an even greater role in professional development as they are expected to take in other aspect of our lives.

Improvements in the future may also include a variety of changes in productivity and professional practice, such as improved teacher-generated teaching materials, the use of various online classroom supplements such as e-books, streamlined teaching tasks like better use of teacher-specific databases and spreadsheets, and other related teaching materials. Being open to new ways to improve skills and stay abreast of new and emerging technologies is perhaps the best single thing teachers can do to increase their productivity—besides actually use the technology itself.

Human Issues on the Horizon

A barrage of ethical issues related to technology in education are on the horizon and need to be addressed by all vested in the education of children. Emerging technologies in industry and commerce often find their way into the educational setting. Technology used in business and commerce may benefit the educational community, but it can also have undesired consequences. Making informed decisions with regard to emerging technologies and their impacts on education was stressed in earlier chapters, but the implications of informed decision making is evident here. Biometrics are systems that can help determine the physical characteristics of individuals for security and other reasons. Technology such as biometrics might be used to identify adults and children entering and leaving elementary and secondary school campuses. Scanners, similar to the ones used for airport security, are already used in some schools to increase school safety and security. The use of biometrics in education is another move toward school security. Some would argue, however, that using this technology infringes on personal rights, such as privacy. This is just one of the many issues raised by using biometrics in education, but this example serves to illustrate how an emerging technology can have far-reaching and complex implications in the educational context.

Another issue relates to Internet accessibility. With increased access to the Internet for all comes increased access to information for all. Some schools use Internet-blocking software to limit what students will view in the classroom, but if access is increased so that students have technology available to them day and night, in and outside of school, the question of Internet safety is further raised. Would requiring blocking software on home computers for children under a certain age infringe on personal freedoms? Would such a requirement also block learning of useful information? What kinds of information should be blocked, and would blocking software create a false sense of security because it would likely fail to block all dangerous and questionable material? Furthermore, who would make the decision about what should be blocked? [4]

Even if everyone could agree on the use of blocking software and what should be blocked, that likely would not stop children from using Internet chat rooms and visiting and creating blogs. The information children obtain and share through chat rooms, blogs, and discussion forums can be used by the unscrupulous to bring harm to children. These questions are already being asked among us. Perhaps more difficult questions will continue to be raised as greater access is realized. Because it is virtually impossible to anticipate the specific emerging technologies that will surface in education and because it is equally impossible to predict all questions that will arise in relation to ethical and human issues, teachers must become aware, skilled, knowledgeable, and informed decision makers, capable of making choices in the best interests of the children who count on them.

As beginning teachers enter the workforce, they should be mindful that what they do makes a difference. Not only will they influence the lives of thousands of children in their careers, but they will also influence countless educators and public officials who make decisions for the greater good. What they do now—and in the future—makes a significant difference.

In Your Experience

What technologies are now considered legacy that were once emerging technologies in your lifetime? What factors moved these technologies from emerging to legacy?

Chapter 6 Explorations

1. Consider some of the obstacles to teaching and technology integration that you read about in this chapter. List three obstacles that you believe may interfere with your teaching effectiveness. Next write a brief plan of what you can do now and in the future to help ensure effective teaching and technology integration with regard to each of these obstacles.

2. Interview a teacher who has left the profession. Be sure to ask what the teacher found satisfying about teaching and what the teacher found dissatisfying.

3. Interview a practicing teacher. Be sure to ask what the teacher finds as obstacles to integrating technology and how he or she is working to overcome these obstacles.

4. Identify one emerging technology. Describe the technology in a word-processed document and describe potential implications for education, including usefulness and ethical issues that might arise with its use.

5. Identify five needs of education. Consider what types of technologies might emerge to address these needs. These technologies can be ones you identified on your own or ones you located through research. Write up your findings and exchange your work with your peers.

6. Anticipate what the future of technology in education might look like in terms of a classroom floor plan. Create a futuristic floor plan and exchange your plan with a peer.

7. Research the Open Source Initiative (www.opensource.org) or the Free Software Foundation (www.fsf.org). Write a one-page, word-processed position paper on why the Open Source Initiative or Free Software Foundation should or should not be welcomed and supported by the education community.

8. Research the current status of e-learning and e-learning 2.0. How has e-learning changed since you embarked on your teacher preparation? Write a one-page, word-processed summary of your response and create a timeline to accompany your response.

9. Reflect on your journey through this text. What broad lessons have you learned that you can take with you into your teaching practice? Write these reflections in a two- to three-page word-processed document.

Chapter 6 Summary

In this chapter you learned that a variety of obstacles can stand in the way of teacher effectiveness and technology integration, yet there are actions you can take now to help ensure an effective teaching practice in the future. You also learned how emerging technologies and issues relate to the future of technology in education—most notably, that with each emerging technology introduced into the educational setting comes a concomitant ethical and human issue. This realization brings to full circle the importance of informed decision making and the need to stay abreast of new and emerging technologies.

Your journey through this text has likely brought you to a better understanding of your place in the big picture of technology in education. Equipped with the knowledge and skills you now have, you are more prepared to make your mark in education; your students' successes are your successes.

Chapter 6 Notes

1   To learn more about the One Laptop per Child (OLPC) initiative, which aims to provide the world's poorest children with a laptop and software "designed for collaborative, joyful, self-empowered learning," visit http://laptop.org/en/vision.

2   See *The College of 2020: Students* (Van Der Werf & Sabatier, 2009) for more on trends in distance education, the future of technology in education, and characteristics of 21st-century students of the future.

3   ISTE's Classroom Observation Tool (ICOT) is an online tool available at http://icot.iste.org/icot/ that helps guide classroom observations of a number of key components of technology integration. (See Figures 2.9 and 2.10 in this book for examples of Gantt charts.)

4   See Chapter 4 for a detailed discussion of blocking software.

Chapter 6 References

Bauer, J., & Kenton, J. (2005). Toward technology integration in the schools: Why it isn't happening. *Journal of Technology and Teacher Education, 13*(4), 519–546.

Ditzhazy, H., & Poolsup, S. (2002, Spring). Successful integration of technology into the classroom. *The Delta Kappa Gamma Bulletin, 68*(3), 10–14.

Downes, S. (2005, October). e-learning 2.0. *eLearn Magazine,* (10).

Editorial Projects in Education (EPE) Research Center. (2007, March 29). Technology counts 2007: A digital decade. *Education Week, 26*(30).

Kozulin, A., Gindis, B., Ageyev, V., & Miller, S. (Eds.). (2003). Vygotsky's educational theory in cultural context. In J. Brown, R. Pea, C. Heath, & L. Suchman (Series and General Eds.), *Learning in doing: Social, cognitive and computational perspectives.* Cambridge, UK: Cambridge University Press.

Rowley, J., Dysard, G., & Arnold, J. (2005). Developing a new technology infusion program for preparing tomorrow's teachers. *Journal of Technology and Teacher Education, 13*(1), 105–123.

Van Der Werf, M., & Sabatier, G. (2009, June). *The College of 2020: Students.* A special report for the *Chronicle of Higher Education.* Washington, D.C.: Chronicle Research Services. Available at the Chronicle Store, www. chronicle-store.com

Wells, J., & Lewis, L. (2006). *Internet access in U.S. public schools and classrooms: 1994–2005* (NCES 2007–020). U.S. Department of Education. Washington, DC: National Center for Education Statistics. Retrieved July 14, 2008, from http://nces.ed.gov/pubs2007/2007020.pdf

Zandberg I., & Lewis L. (2008). *Technology-based distance education courses for public elementary and secondary school students: 2002–03 and 2004–05* (NCES 2008-008). Washington, DC: National Center for Education Statistics.

National Educational Technology Standards

NETS for Students (NETS·S)

All K–12 students should be prepared to meet the following standards and performance indicators.

1. **Creativity and Innovation**

   Students demonstrate creative thinking, construct knowledge, and develop innovative products and processes using technology. Students:

   a. apply existing knowledge to generate new ideas, products, or processes

   b. create original works as a means of personal or group expression

   c. use models and simulations to explore complex systems and issues

   d. identify trends and forecast possibilities

2. **Communication and Collaboration**

   Students use digital media and environments to communicate and work collaboratively, including at a distance, to support individual learning and contribute to the learning of others. Students:

   a. interact, collaborate, and publish with peers, experts, or others employing a variety of digital environments and media

   b. communicate information and ideas effectively to multiple audiences using a variety of media and formats

   c. develop cultural understanding and global awareness by engaging with learners of other cultures

   d. contribute to project teams to produce original works or solve problems

3. Research and Information Fluency

Students apply digital tools to gather, evaluate, and use information. Students:

a. plan strategies to guide inquiry

b. locate, organize, analyze, evaluate, synthesize, and ethically use information from a variety of sources and media

c. evaluate and select information sources and digital tools based on the appropriateness to specific tasks

d. process data and report results

4. Critical Thinking, Problem Solving, and Decision Making

Students use critical-thinking skills to plan and conduct research, manage projects, solve problems, and make informed decisions using appropriate digital tools and resources. Students:

a. identify and define authentic problems and significant questions for investigation

b. plan and manage activities to develop a solution or complete a project

c. collect and analyze data to identify solutions and make informed decisions

d. use multiple processes and diverse perspectives to explore alternative solutions

5. Digital Citizenship

Students understand human, cultural, and societal issues related to technology and practice legal and ethical behavior. Students:

a. advocate and practice the safe, legal, and responsible use of information and technology

b. exhibit a positive attitude toward using technology that supports collaboration, learning, and productivity

c. demonstrate personal responsibility for lifelong learning

d. exhibit leadership for digital citizenship

6. Technology Operations and Concepts

Students demonstrate a sound understanding of technology concepts, systems, and operations. Students:

a. understand and use technology systems

b. select and use applications effectively and productively

c. troubleshoot systems and applications

d. transfer current knowledge to the learning of new technologies

NETS for Teachers (NETS•T)

All classroom teachers should be prepared to meet the following standards and performance indicators.

1. **Facilitate and Inspire Student Learning and Creativity**

   Teachers use their knowledge of subject matter, teaching and learning, and technology to facilitate experiences that advance student learning, creativity, and innovation in both face-to-face and virtual environments. Teachers:

   a. promote, support, and model creative and innovative thinking and inventiveness

   b. engage students in exploring real-world issues and solving authentic problems using digital tools and resources

   c. promote student reflection using collaborative tools to reveal and clarify students' conceptual understanding and thinking, planning, and creative processes

   d. model collaborative knowledge construction by engaging in learning with students, colleagues, and others in face-to-face and virtual environments

2. **Design and Develop Digital-Age Learning Experiences and Assessments**

   Teachers design, develop, and evaluate authentic learning experiences and assessments incorporating contemporary tools and resources to maximize content learning in context and to develop the knowledge, skills, and attitudes identified in the NETS•S. Teachers:

   a. design or adapt relevant learning experiences that incorporate digital tools and resources to promote student learning and creativity

   b. develop technology-enriched learning environments that enable all students to pursue their individual curiosities and become active participants in setting their own educational goals, managing their own learning, and assessing their own progress

   c. customize and personalize learning activities to address students' diverse learning styles, working strategies, and abilities using digital tools and resources

   d. provide students with multiple and varied formative and summative assessments aligned with content and technology standards and use resulting data to inform learning and teaching

3. **Model Digital-Age Work and Learning**

   Teachers exhibit knowledge, skills, and work processes representative of an innovative professional in a global and digital society. Teachers:

   a. demonstrate fluency in technology systems and the transfer of current knowledge to new technologies and situations

   b. collaborate with students, peers, parents, and community members using digital tools and resources to support student success and innovation

   c. communicate relevant information and ideas effectively to students, parents, and peers using a variety of digital-age media and formats

   d.   model and facilitate effective use of current and emerging digital tools to locate, analyze, evaluate, and use information resources to support research and learning

4.   Promote and Model Digital Citizenship and Responsibility

Teachers understand local and global societal issues and responsibilities in an evolving digital culture and exhibit legal and ethical behavior in their professional practices. Teachers:

   a.   advocate, model, and teach safe, legal, and ethical use of digital information and technology, including respect for copyright, intellectual property, and the appropriate documentation of sources

   b.   address the diverse needs of all learners by using learner-centered strategies and providing equitable access to appropriate digital tools and resources

   c.   promote and model digital etiquette and responsible social interactions related to the use of technology and information

   d.   develop and model cultural understanding and global awareness by engaging with colleagues and students of other cultures using digital-age communication and collaboration tools

5.   Engage in Professional Growth and Leadership

Teachers continuously improve their professional practice, model lifelong learning, and exhibit leadership in their school and professional community by promoting and demonstrating the effective use of digital tools and resources. Teachers:

   a.   participate in local and global learning communities to explore creative applications of technology to improve student learning

   b.   exhibit leadership by demonstrating a vision of technology infusion, participating in shared decision making and community building, and developing the leadership and technology skills of others

   c.   evaluate and reflect on current research and professional practice on a regular basis to make effective use of existing and emerging digital tools and resources in support of student learning

   d.   contribute to the effectiveness, vitality, and self-renewal of the teaching profession and of their school and community

NETS for Administrators (NETS·A)

All school administrators should be prepared to meet the following standards and performance indicators.

1. Visionary Leadership

Educational Administrators inspire and lead development and implementation of a shared vision for comprehensive integration of technology to promote excellence and support transformation throughout the organization. Educational Administrators:

    a. inspire and facilitate among all stakeholders a shared vision of purposeful change that maximizes use of digital-age resources to meet and exceed learning goals, support effective instructional practice, and maximize performance of district and school leaders

    b. engage in an ongoing process to develop, implement, and communicate technology-infused strategic plans aligned with a shared vision

    c. advocate on local, state, and national levels for policies, programs, and funding to support implementation of a technology-infused vision and strategic plan

2. Digital-Age Learning Culture

Educational Administrators create, promote, and sustain a dynamic, digital-age learning culture that provides a rigorous, relevant, and engaging education for all students. Educational Administrators:

    a. ensure instructional innovation focused on continuous improvement of digital-age learning

    b. model and promote the frequent and effective use of technology for learning

    c. provide learner-centered environments equipped with technology and learning resources to meet the individual, diverse needs of all learners

    d. ensure effective practice in the study of technology and its infusion across the curriculum

    e. promote and participate in local, national, and global learning communities that stimulate innovation, creativity, and digital-age collaboration

3. Excellence in Professional Practice

Educational Administrators promote an environment of professional learning and innovation that empowers educators to enhance student learning through the infusion of contemporary technologies and digital resources. Educational Administrators:

    a. allocate time, resources, and access to ensure ongoing professional growth in technology fluency and integration

    b. facilitate and participate in learning communities that stimulate, nurture, and support administrators, faculty, and staff in the study and use of technology

    c. promote and model effective communication and collaboration among stakeholders using digital-age tools

    d. stay abreast of educational research and emerging trends regarding effective use of technology and encourage evaluation of new technologies for their potential to improve student learning

4. Systemic Improvement

Educational Administrators provide digital-age leadership and management to continuously improve the organization through the effective use of information and technology resources. Educational Administrators:

    a. lead purposeful change to maximize the achievement of learning goals through the appropriate use of technology and media-rich resources

    b. collaborate to establish metrics, collect and analyze data, interpret results, and share findings to improve staff performance and student learning

    c. recruit and retain highly competent personnel who use technology creatively and proficiently to advance academic and operational goals

    d. establish and leverage strategic partnerships to support systemic improvement

    e. establish and maintain a robust infrastructure for technology including integrated, interoperable technology systems to support management, operations, teaching, and learning

5. Digital Citizenship

Educational Administrators model and facilitate understanding of social, ethical, and legal issues and responsibilities related to an evolving digital culture. Educational Administrators:

    a. ensure equitable access to appropriate digital tools and resources to meet the needs of all learners

    b. promote, model, and establish policies for safe, legal, and ethical use of digital information and technology

    c. promote and model responsible social interactions related to the use of technology and information

    d. model and facilitate the development of a shared cultural understanding and involvement in global issues through the use of contemporary communication and collaboration tools

NETS for Coaches (NETS·C)

All technology coaches should be prepared to meet the following standards and performance indicators.

1. Visionary Leadership

Technology Coaches inspire and participate in the development and implementation of a shared vision for the comprehensive integration of technology to promote excellence and support transformational change throughout the instructional environment. Technology Coaches:

   a. contribute to the development, communication, and implementation of a shared vision for the comprehensive use of technology to support a digital-age education for all students

   b. contribute to the planning, development, communication, implementation, and evaluation of technology-infused strategic plans at the district and school levels

   c. advocate for policies, procedures, programs, and funding strategies to support implementation of the shared vision represented in the school and district technology plans and guidelines

   d. implement strategies for initiating and sustaining technology innovations and manage the change process in schools and classrooms

2. Teaching, Learning, and Assessments

Technology Coaches assist teachers in using technology effectively for assessing student learning, differentiating instruction, and providing rigorous, relevant, and engaging learning experiences for all students. Technology Coaches:

   a. Coach teachers in and model design and implementation of technology-enhanced learning experiences addressing content standards and student technology standards

   b. Coach teachers in and model design and implementation of technology-enhanced learning experiences using a variety of research-based, learner-centered instructional strategies and assessment tools to address the diverse needs and interests of all students

   c. Coach teachers in and model engagement of students in local and global interdisciplinary units in which technology helps students assume professional roles, research real-world problems, collaborate with others, and produce products that are meaningful and useful to a wide audience

   d. Coach teachers in and model design and implementation of technology-enhanced learning experiences emphasizing creativity, higher-order thinking skills and processes, and mental habits of mind (e.g., critical thinking, metacognition, and self-regulation)

   e. Coach teachers in and model design and implementation of technology-enhanced learning experiences using differentiation, including adjusting content, process, product, and learning environment based upon student readiness levels, learning styles, interests, and personal goals

   f. Coach teachers in and model incorporation of research-based best practices in instructional design when planning technology-enhanced learning experiences

g. Coach teachers in and model effective use of technology tools and resources to continuously assess student learning and technology literacy by applying a rich variety of formative and summative assessments aligned with content and student technology standards

h. Coach teachers in and model effective use of technology tools and resources to systematically collect and analyze student achievement data, interpret results, and communicate findings to improve instructional practice and maximize student learning

3. Digital-Age Learning Environments

Technology coaches create and support effective digital-age learning environments to maximize the learning of all students. Technology Coaches:

a. Model effective classroom management and collaborative learning strategies to maximize teacher and student use of digital tools and resources and access to technology-rich learning environments

b. Maintain and manage a variety of digital tools and resources for teacher and student use in technology-rich learning environments

c. Coach teachers in and model use of online and blended learning, digital content, and collaborative learning networks to support and extend student learning as well as expand opportunities and choices for online professional development for teachers and administrators

d. Select, evaluate, and facilitate the use of adaptive and assistive technologies to support student learning

e. Troubleshoot basic software, hardware, and connectivity problems common in digital learning environments

f. Collaborate with teachers and administrators to select and evaluate digital tools and resources that enhance teaching and learning and are compatible with the school technology infrastructure

g. Use digital communication and collaboration tools to communicate locally and globally with students, parents, peers, and the larger community

4. Professional Development and Program Evaluation

Technology coaches conduct needs assessments, develop technology-related professional learning programs, and evaluate the impact on instructional practice and student learning. Technology Coaches:

a. Conduct needs assessments to inform the content and delivery of technology-related professional learning programs that result in a positive impact on student learning

b. Design, develop, and implement technology-rich professional learning programs that model principles of adult learning and promote digital-age best practices in teaching, learning, and assessment

c. Evaluate results of professional learning programs to determine their effectiveness on deepening teacher content knowledge, improving teacher pedagogical skills, and/or increasing student learning

5. Digital Citizenship

Technology coaches model and promote digital citizenship. Technology Coaches:

a. Model and promote strategies for achieving equitable access to digital tools and resources and technology-related best practices for all students and teachers

b. Model and facilitate safe, healthy, legal, and ethical uses of digital information and technologies

c. Model and promote diversity, cultural understanding, and global awareness by using digital-age communication and collaboration tools to interact locally and globally with students, peers, parents, and the larger community

6. Content Knowledge and Professional Growth

Technology coaches demonstrate professional knowledge, skills, and dispositions in content, pedagogical, and technological areas, as well as adult learning and leadership, and are continuously deepening their knowledge and expertise. Technology Coaches:

a. Engage in continual learning to deepen content and pedagogical knowledge in technology integration and current and emerging technologies necessary to effectively implement the NETS•S and NETS•T

b. Engage in continuous learning to deepen professional knowledge, skills, and dispositions in organizational change and leadership, project management, and adult learning to improve professional practice

c. Regularly evaluate and reflect on their professional practice and dispositions to improve and strengthen their ability to effectively model and facilitate technology-enhanced learning experiences

Index

Page references followed by f indicate figures.
Page references followed by n indicate notes.
Page references followed by t indicate tables.

A

AbleData, 220
"About Us" links, 184, 185
accessibility of technology. *See also* assistive
     technologies
    diversity and, 219–223
    hardware/software issues, 92–93
    importance of, 291
    less-expensive alternatives, 291–292
    operating systems, 111
    planning for, 225–227, 227f
    websites, 90–91, 91f, 111, 295
AccessIT, 109
accreditation, 7, 9, 120
accuracy in websites, 90, 186
action research, 68, 70, 71, 71f
administrators, NETS for, 303–304
Airasian, P. W, 121
Alliance for Technology Access (ATA), 109
Anderson, L. W., 16, 35
animation tools, 38
anonymous feedback, 124
application software, 151–154, 189n. *See also* specific
    software
Armstrong, T., 18–19, 112
art, original, 201
assessment
    conditions for, 123–124
    evaluation compared to, 121–122
    importance of, 137, 294
    improving learning through, 130–134
    methods, 122–123
    participants, 124
    purpose of, 124
    results of, 134–137, 135f

standards and, 119–121, 137–138
    tools, 124–130
assistive technologies (AT), 111, 158, 220–221, 292
AssistiveTech.net, 220
AT (assistive technologies), 111, 158, 220–221, 292
ATA (Alliance for Technology Access), 109
at-risk students, 113–114
augmented reality game, 37
authoring tools, 38–39, 169
authors' work. *See* copyright

B

backward design, 82, 120–123, 125
Barrett, Helen, 262, 285n
Barth, R., 247, 259–260
basic skills, 19, 20, 25
Bauer, J., 290
Belch, H. E., 174
best practices for research, 67–70, 68f
blind-reviewed research, 66
blocking software, 207–208, 295
blogs
    about, 231
    collaborating with, 167
    communicating with, 173
    identifying world issues with, 32
    modeling constructivist learning with, 52
    reflecting on, 43–44, 269
    sites, 235
    in virtual world, 54–55
Bloom, B. S., 15, 81
Bonk, Curtis, 262, 285n
Boss, S., 30–31, 164
brain development, 17
brain games, 181
brainstorming, 165, 224
Brown, J., 123, 124–125
bulletin boards, 72